Keningale Cook

The Fathers of Jesus

A Study of the Lineage of the Christian Doctrine and Traditions. Vol. 2

Keningale Cook

The Fathers of Jesus
A Study of the Lineage of the Christian Doctrine and Traditions. Vol. 2

ISBN/EAN: 9783337025755

Printed in Europe, USA, Canada, Australia, Japan

Cover: Foto ©Lupo / pixelio.de

More available books at **www.hansebooks.com**

THE FATHERS OF JESUS

*A STUDY OF THE LINEAGE OF THE CHRISTIAN
DOCTRINE AND TRADITIONS*

BY

KENINGALE COOK, M.A., LL.D.

IN TWO VOLUMES
VOL. II.

LONDON
KEGAN PAUL, TRENCH & CO., 1, PATERNOSTER SQUARE
1886

CONTENTS OF VOL. II.

		PAGE
The Brotherhood of the Essenes	...	1
Did Jesus know Greek?	... ...	63
The Tradition of the Elders	... ...	107
A Contemporary of Jesus	...	230
The Sacred and the Profane	... ...	340
The Genius of Parable	... ...	366

THE FATHERS OF JESUS.

THE BROTHERHOOD OF THE ESSENES.

A CLOUD of mystery has been allowed to overhang the Essenes, owing to certain obstinate prejudices which the breadth of modern research is now only beginning to overcome. The chief of these prejudices have been two : that the Jewish nation has been miraculously separated from the rest of humanity ; and that the Christian religion, whether in its primitive simplicity or in its doctrinal projections, is different in kind from general religion.

The Hebrew, it is true, has preserved a marked type almost as unchangeably as the Ethiopian or the leopard ; but our ideas of the exclusiveness of the race are drawn less from ethnology than from traditions which have reached us of the separatist pride and ambition of the Jew, which exclusiveness, however, we may discover to have been more ardently entertained than effectively realized.

The fulminations from the Jewish centre against alien tribes and forbidden marriages imply that the bulk of the people were as fraternal with other tribes with whom they came in contact as near neighbours usually are. We are prone to look on the Jews as a compact race occupying Palestine, but because the land was nominally parcelled out among the tribes, it by no means followed that they monopolized or even occupied it. Joshua's assignment of the territory of the Philistines, the Tyrians, the Sidonians, and the Moabites, remained, so far as we know, an ideal one. Apart from its extension into this land of fancy, no country was ever more overrun than the narrow home of the Jews. They were forced into the most intimate and long-continued relations with Egyptians, Assyrians, Babylonians, Medes, Persians, Greeks, Romans. The reason why Ezra was able to impose such harsh anti-Gentile rules upon his people was that it was so small a remnant upon which he could exercise his theocratic zeal.

Galilee became populous and Gentile; Samaria had her own traditions; the struggling orthodoxy of Judea sent up a cry against the language and influence of Greece, only after Greek thought had made a mark too deep to be erased. Before this reaction, "the terms in which Greek is spoken of verge on the transcendental. This also is the only language which it seems to have been incumbent to teach even to girls." * "When Hellenic scepticism in its most seductive form had, during the Syrian troubles, begun to seek its victims even in the midst of the 'Sacred Vineyard,' and threatened to undermine all patriotism and all independence, a curse was pronounced upon Hellenism." †

If, instead of listening to the plaintive cry of patriotic bigots at Jerusalem, we look to the broad fact of Jewish history, we shall see that the enforced contact of the race with one great nation after another was a great source of its peculiar culture and of its literary and poetic power, for, in addition to the varied influence of those leading nations, oppression and trial are themselves a cause of enhanced power to those strong enough to endure.

Like the Jewish race, Christianity itself owes a debt to the influences from without which it was able to combine and make its own.

The revelation to which doctrinal Christianity has affiliated

---

* Deutsch, "Literary Remains," p. 141. † *Ibid.*, p. 22.

itself was in its primitive form a republication, with a new glow and heightened spirit, of truths known for ages to the wise. They were transformed into a new gospel in the crucible of the heart of an inspired Rabbi, to whom truth new or old made but one eternal fact, who strove not to abolish but to make full. Truth in its virgin and unadulterated essence being too simple and strong a draught for average humanity, soon after the departure of that large angelic soul, the page of the music that he had made was put aside, and discord began. Sects spread widely, with leaders who wanted to take a little of the prestige of the Nazarene, and to build up a great deal of their own. Old myths, long misunderstood, were mingled with the apotheosising reverence paid to the vanished teacher, and a chaos of conflicting dogmas ensued. Finally, one metaphysical monstrosity got the upper hand, and was made hard and solid by political prelates, who saw in such dogmatic fixity a means of power. Christianity, indeed, became different from any other religion under the sun, because, having combined old symbols, it proclaimed the product unique, all-sufficient, and all exclusive.

It was ecclesiastically politic that the mind of the proselyte should be well impregnated with the notion of the miraculous singularity of the Hebrew race, for it gave to the changeling of the Hebrew cradle the appearance of a providential inheritance, and a claim to continuity. But, after centuries of paralysis of the mind of Christendom under an arbitrary dogmatic system which professed to be final, an awakening came. Historical research found its way outside the narrow field that had been walled in so long, as containing all that was necessary to salvation. Some of the bandages fell from the eyes, and the fetters and manacles of a repressive Church were thrown off from the restless limbs of partially-aroused peoples.

Two hundred and sixty years ago an English divine stumbled upon the description of the Essenes, and was so puzzled thereby as to endeavour to account for their not being mentioned in the Gospels, since they were presumably in existence in Palestine in the time of Jesus.* An ingenious clergyman, writing nearly fifty years later,† attempted to demonstrate that all human literature had its origin in the Jewish Scriptures, and made shift to show that Pythagoras derived the whole of his system from the Essenes. This argument implied ignorance of a literature extending over thousands of years in Egypt and India, an ignorance which the recent additions to our sources of knowledge have rendered almost impossible for ourselves.

The German critics began to work upon the Essenes in the early part of the present century, and have been at the subject ever since, with various conclusions, among them that Jesus was the leader of the order, the Essene-master.

De Quincey represents the scare due to the discovery of the Essenes in its most imaginative and extravagant form: "Suppose the Essenes a distinct body from the primitive Christians of Palestine (*i.e.* those particular Christians who stood under the ban of Jerusalem), and you have a deadlier wound inflicted on Christian faith than the whole army of infidels ever attempted. A parhelion—a secondary sun, a mock sun that should shine for centuries with equal arguments for its own authenticity as existed for the original and authentic sun—would not be more shocking to the sense, and to the auguries of man, than a secondary Christianity, not less spiritual, not less heavenly, pretending to a separate and even hostile origin." The conclusion at which he arrives is that the Essenes were "latent Christians," hidden under a cloud of disguise. "The Church of Rome," he alleges, "has always thrown a backward telescopic glance of question, of doubt, and uneasy suspicion, upon these ridiculous Essenes, and has repeatedly come to the right practical conclusion that they

---

* Thomas Godwyn, "Moses and Aaron." London, 1625.
Theophilus Gale, "The Court of the Gentiles." Oxford, 1671.

were, and must have been, Christians under some mask or other; but the failure of Rome has been in carrying the Ariadne's thread through the whole labyrinth from centre to circumference." De Quincey finds occasion for a well-deserved thrust of irony which pierces sectarianism to the marrow: "Oh, the worlds of hypocrites who cant about the divinity of Scriptural morality, and yet would never see any lustre at all in the most resplendent of Christian jewels, provided the pagan thief had a little disguised their setting!"

De Quincey's conclusion that the Essenes were primitive Christians, hiding for safety from the Jews, compels him to do away with the historic character of the extant accounts of their fraternity, which we shall shortly quote. Such testimony he rejects on the ground, partly of natural mistake on the part of the historians, who did not penetrate the secret of the Essene symbol, partly of a subterfuge of Josephus, who "for his own interest screened from the Romans various ebullitions of Hebrew refractoriness."

We shall do better to judge for ourselves than to accept so sweeping and ill-grounded an argument, and will simply take the accounts of the Essenes, as they stand.

First, we have a description by Philo, a Jew of the highest position and culture living at Alexandria, but having visited Palestine. In his time (about 25 B.C.–A.D. 45) Alexandria was one of the important cities of the world, and possessed a library of hundreds of thousands of volumes. Being so near to Palestine, Alexandria afforded a home to very large colonies of Jews, and Philo may be taken to have had open to him many sources of information respecting occurrences in Palestine.

"Our lawgiver trained into fellowship great numbers of pupils, who bear the name of Essenes (Essaioi), being, I imagine, honoured with the appellation by virtue of their holiness.

"They dwell in many cities of Judæa and in many villages, and in large and populous communities.

"Their order does not depend upon natural descent—for natural descent is not a right expression for what is voluntarily taken up—but proceeds from an earnest pursuit after virtue and yearning after love of mankind.

"Among the Essenes there is, correctly speaking, no one altogether an infant, neither moreover youth with budding beard, nor boy; for the dispositions of such as these are unstable and subject to serious change owing to the immaturity of their age; but they consist of men matured and already verging upon old age, men flooded no longer by afflux of what is corporeal, nor led away by the passions, but in the very harvest time of the genuine and only absolute freedom.

"The test of their freedom is their life. Not one of them can abide to be possessor of anything whatever as his own private property, whether house, or slave, or territory, or cattle, or any other of the things which constitute the apparatus or equipment of wealth. But once for all they lay all down in the midst, and reap their harvest from the common prosperity of all. They dwell, too, in the same fashion, in companies, making for themselves clubs and messes, and consistently do all business for the common weal. But the different members have different occupations, at which, like rivals, they engage with untiring energy, never making cold or heat, or any fluctuations of the weather, a pretence of excuse. They betake themselves to their customary works before the sun rises, and scarcely leave off when he sets, finding in them no less zest than those who show their strength in the gymnastic contests. For they deem the employments which they follow to be exercises more beneficial to life, and pleasanter to soul and to body, and more enduring, than any in the games, since they do not fall into desuetude with the bodily prime. Some among them are husbandmen, those who are well skilled in sowing and agriculture. Others again are herdsmen, managers of all kinds of cattle. Some of them are superintendents of hives of bees. Others are artificers in the crafts, for they neglect nothing in the way of innocent provision, so as never to be subjected to the hard compulsion of constraining needs. From these sources, so widely differing, they each get their wage, and hand it over to the steward regularly elected. He takes it and presently buys necessaries, and furnishes food without stint, and such other things as are absolute necessities of human subsistence. They live together and mess together every day, and find satisfaction in the same things, being lovers of contentment with little, and averse from extravagance as a disease of soul and body. Not only have they a common table, but also raiment in common. For they have ready in store for winter felted wool cloaks, and for summer easy vests without sleeves, and whoever wishes may conveniently take whichever he chooses; for what belongs to one is deemed to belong to all, and what belongs to all to each. Should any one of them, too, fall ill, he is medicined from the common store, and is tended with the attention and concern of all. And in fact their old men, even though they happen to be childless, are accustomed to close their lives in a most prosperous and comfortable old age, as if they not only were possessed of many children, but were blest with good ones; for they are looked upon as objects of provident regard and honour, by such as deem it their duty to care for them, and rather from voluntary inclination than from any tie of nature. Furthermore, seeing with more than ordinary quickness of perception what would be the only or the chief thing likely to break up the community, they deprecate marriage, and at the same time exercise an especial self-mastery.

"Indeed no one of the Essenes marries a wife, because the wife is a selfish creature, immoderately smitten with jealousy, and terrible at shaking to their foundations the natural habits of a man, and bringing him under power by continual beguilements. For, as she practises fair false speeches, and other kinds of hypocrisy, as it were upon the stage, when she has succeeded in alluring eyes and ears, like cheated servants, she brings cajolery to bear upon the sovereign mind.

"Moreover, if there are children, she begins to be puffed up with pride and licence of tongue; and all the things which before she speciously uttered in a disguised manner in irony, she now summons forth with a more daring confidence, and shamelessly forces her way into actions, every one of which is hostile to communion. For the man who is bound under spells of wife or children, being made anxious by the bond of nature, is no longer the same person towards others, but is entirely changed, having become, without being aware of it, a slave instead of a free man.

"As above described, then, is their way of life—a life worth struggling after, and such that not only private persons but even great kings have been smitten with jealousy and wonder at these men, and add to their dignity still more by approbation and honours" (Philo, "Apology for the Jews," Fragm. Euseb.).

There seems no reason to doubt that the passage just quoted is the work of Philo. Eusebius presents it distinctly as a portion read from Philo's book, now lost, the "Apology for the Jews." The tirade against wives is more stinging than the words Philo is accustomed to use towards the sex, and, moreover, he was blessed with an excellent wife. On the other hand, the general style is Philo's, and reference to the external senses as servants to the soul their master may be paralleled again and again in his writings.

The following is from a work of Philo's still extant, and contains a fuller and more interesting account of the Essenes than the last: "There were assuredly in former times persons eminent in virtue above those with whom they had to do: men that took God alone for their leader and guide, and lived according to law, to wit, the right reason of nature, and not only possessed freedom in themselves, but even imbued all that came near them with a spirit of freedom. Nay, in our time, there yet are persons, images, as it were, of them, stamped with a perfect nobility from the archetypal model of men of wisdom; for it does not follow, because the souls of their opponents, through the enslavement of folly and the rest of the vices, have been bereft of freedom, that, therefore, so too is the whole race of man. But if people have failed to advance in huge serried masses and by troops, there is no reason for wonder; for, in the first place, things of exceeding beauty are rare; and, in the next, those men who get out of the way of the main crowd of random folk, and have leisure for the contemplation of the things of nature, vow that, so far as may be in their power, they will restore uprightness to life, for virtue is communicative of good service; but when they fail of this by reason of the monstrous things that flood city by city as if by a deluge, which things the passions of the soul have joined with vice in accumulating, they make their escape, so as not to be borne down by the vehemence of the rush that is like a winter torrent's force.

"But with regard to ourselves, were any of us really zealous for improvement, we ought to trace out the hiding-places of these men, and sit as very suppliants and entreat them to come forward to reclaim and humanize our life that has grown savage and brutal, by announcing, in place of war and slavery and ills unspeakable, peace and bountiful plenty of other blessings to flow around.

"But nowadays it is for money's sake only that we search all retired corners and tear open the rigid and craggy veins of the earth. And much of the level country is opened out in mines, and no small part of the mountainous districts too, where we are searching out gold and silver, copper, and iron, and the other material elements; for empty opinion, setting up cloudy conceit as a god, has gone down to the very depths of the sea in its investigations whether there be stored up anywhere out of sight any beautiful thing which might suit the external senses, and, discovering sundry kinds of precious stones, some adhering to rocks and some to oyster shells, which latter fetch a higher price still, has exalted into honour a cheat of the eyes.

"But for the sake of wisdom, or temperance, or courage, or righteousness, the earth, even in its accessible part, remains untraversed, and the sea unnavigated in the regions shippers sail season by season during the year.

"Yet, after all, what need is there of journeying or seafaring for the tracking and investigation of virtue, whose roots the Maker places not a remote way off, but close at hand, exactly as saith the sage lawgiver of the Jews: 'They are in thy mouth, and in thy heart, and in thy hands' (Deut. xxx. 14), giving mystically to understand, by means of figures, our words, actions, and designs, all of which in very truth stand in need of the art of the cultivator.

* * * * * *

"In respect of what grows out of the ground, neither is the fruit trees, nor are the trees fruit; but with respect to what springs forth in the soul, the whole of its scions are absolutely converted into the nature of fruit; for instance, into prudence, righteousness, courage, temperance.

"Since, then, we have such aid given us towards virtue, must we not blush in asserting the lack of wisdom in the race of mankind, when it were possible, by blowing it up after the way of a smouldering spark in wood, to kindle it into flame? But in very fact, in the matters towards which, as being so closely akin and personal, we ought to make our efforts, we show great unreadiness and persistent indifference, whereby the germs of nobility become gradually destroyed, while, on the contrary, we have an insatiate desire and longing for those things which it were reasonable to dispense with. It is owing to this, that, on the one hand, earth and sea are full of men who are rich and of lofty rank, and indulgent in voluptuousness, whilst, on the other hand, of men of prudence and righteousness and urbanity the number is exceedingly small.

"But for a thing to be small, nay, though it be rare too, is not to be non-existent. A witness of this are both Greece and foreign climes; for in the former country flourished those that have been truly styled the seven sages, albeit others had risen high before, and probably after, their time; the memory, as regards the ancients, not having been obliterated by the length of the ages, nor, in the case of the more modern sages, obscured by the prevalent neglect of contemporaries; and in foreign climes, wherein they are ambassadors of words and works, there are very numerous bodies of virtuous and good men.

"Among the Persians there is the order of the Mages, who deeply investigate the works of nature for the discovery of truth, and in leisure's quiet are initiated into and expound in clearest significance the Divine virtues.

"In India, too, there is the sect of the Gymnosophists, who, in addition to speculative philosophy, diligently cultivate the ethical also, and have made their life an absolute ensample of virtue.

"Palestine, moreover, and Syria are not without their harvest of virtuous excellence, which region is inhabited by no small portion of the very populous nation of the Jews.

"There are counted among them certain ones by name Essenes, in number about four thousand, who derive their name, in my opinion, by an inaccurate trace, from the term in the Greek language for holiness [*Essēn* or *Essaios*, Essene; *Hosios*, holy], inasmuch as they have shown themselves pre-eminently devoted to the service of God;* not in sacrifice of living animals, but rather in determination to make their own minds fit for holy offering.†

"In the first place, they dwell in villages, and avoid cities,

---

* Θεραπευται Θεοῦ—therapeuts of God.

† Cf. "Sacrifice and oblation thou wouldest not, but a body didst thou prepare for me. . . . Lo, I come: in the roll of the book it is written for me, I desired to do thy will, O my God, and thy law in the middle of my heart" (Ps. xxxix. [xl.] 6, Septuagint version).

on account of the wonted licentiousness of the citizen class, being sensible that as from pestilential air there springs bodily disease, so from such associations is contracted an irremediable evil influence upon the soul.

"Some of them work the land, and others follow such handicrafts as are co-operative of peace, and so benefit both themselves and those that come in contact with them. They do not lay up treasures of silver and gold, nor acquire vast sections of land out of a desire for revenues, but provide only as many things as pertain to the necessary uses of life. For, notwithstanding that they alone, out of almost all mankind, are in a state without wealth and without possessions, and that by their studied choice rather than from any lack of prosperity, they yet account themselves the most rich, deeming satisfaction with little and contentedness of mind to be, as in truth they are, a superabundance.

"Of arrows, or javelins, or swords, of helmet, or breastplate, or shield, you would not find a single manufacturer among them, or an armourer or military engineer, or, in short, any one who supplies things belonging to war, or indeed such things of a peaceable character as may be available for evil purposes.

"They do not even dream of commerce or pedlary, or shipowning, as they reject with abhorrence every outlet to greed. As for slaves, there is not so much as a single one amongst them, but all are free and mutually yield kind offices one to another.

"Slave-masters they condemn, not only as unjust, inasmuch as they outrage the very principle of equality, but also as impious, because they subvert the ordinance of nature, which, giving birth to all alike, and like a mother nurturing men as legitimate brethren, formed them so not in name but in actual reality. But this natural relationship, treacherous greed, stimulated by success, has thrown into disorder, producing estrangement instead of family feeling, and enmity instead of friendliness.

"Of philosophy, the dialectical department, as being in nowise necessary for the acquisition of virtue, they abandon to the word-catchers; and the part that treats of the nature of things, as being beyond human nature, they leave to speculative air-gazers, with the exception of that part of it which deals with the subsistence of God and the genesis of all things; but the ethical they right well work out, using for trainers their hereditary laws, which it were inconceivable human soul should devise without a possessing inspiration of God.*

"These they expound at all times, but pre-eminently on the seventh days. For the seventh day is held sacred, and thereon they abstain from other works, and go to sacred places called synagogues, where they sit in ranks according to age, the younger below the elder, and with becoming orderliness, hold themselves with listening ears. Then one takes the books and reads, and another of the most experienced comes forward and expounds such things as are not well known, for most things are philosophically treated among them through symbols, according to the old-fashioned mode of pursuit. They are instructed in reverence, devotion, equity, practical economy, civil polity, the understanding of things which, judged by truth, are good, bad, or indifferent, the choice of things that are meet, and the avoidance of the contrary, for which they follow a threefold standard and canon, love of God, love of virtue, and love of mankind.

"Of their love of God they afford numberless evidences in

---

* A very similar view of logic and physics appears in the following extracts:—
"Socrates, perceiving that natural philosophy had no immediate bearing on our interests, began to enter upon moral speculations, both in his workshop and in the market-place. And he said that the objects of his search were—

"'Whatever good or harm can befall man
In his own house' (Diog. Laert. Socr. vi.).

"Ariston discarded altogether the topic of physics, and of logic, saying that the one was above us, and that the other had nothing to do with us; and that the only branch of philosophy with which we had really any concern was ethics" (Diog. Laert. Ariston, ii.).

their persevering and sustained purity through the whole of life, their avoidance of oaths and falsehood, their firm belief that the Divine Being is the author of all good, and of nought that is evil. Of their love of virtue they give proofs in their contempt for riches, glory, or pleasure, in their self-control and steadfastness; also in their contentment with little, their simplicity, cheerfulness, freedom from arrogance, observance of law, healthy calm, and all similar qualities. Of their love for men they give evidences in their benevolence and equality, and in their community of goods that beggars description, whereanent it will not be out of place to say a few words.

"Firstly, then, no one has a house so far his private property as not contingently to belong to all. For, to the end of their living together in companies, it is thrown open also to their brethren in the cause, when they come from other quarters. Moreover, there is one treasury and expenditure for all; they have a common stock of clothing, and victuals in common by the arrangement of mess-rooms.

"Such a thing as the adoption of a joint roof, a joint diet, or a common table, one could not find in matter-of-fact establishment among any other people. And is it at all likely? for whatever those that work during the day get for wages, they do not retain as their own, but hand over to the common stock, and make of their own service a common benefit to all that wish to use it.

"And those that fall sick are not neglected because they cannot provide, since there are kept in readiness out of the common stock the necessaries for tending them, so that they can expend with all freedom out of an ample abundance.

"To elders is paid respect, and honour and attentive heed, such as parents receive at the hands of their own legitimate children, who succour them in their old age by manual service and numberless attentions with entire ungrudgingness.

"Such athletes of virtue as these are turned out by a philosophy that, without fussing with Greek names, sets forth for exercises praiseworthy actions, as the source whence unenslaveable freedom gains its security.

"Now in proof of what I have adduced, there have from time to time risen up in that country many mighty men, bringing into play different characters and policies; for some exerted themselves to surpass wild beasts in untameable ferocity, and left no acts of cruelty undone, sacrificing their subjects in flocks, and like butchers hewing them limb from limb even while yet alive; and made not an end until the same calamities awaited them from the hand of the justice that overlooks human affairs. Others, again, converting their frenzy and madness into a different kind of wickedness, cultivated an inexpressible bitterness, conversed quietly, and under the mask of a gentle voice betrayed a revengeful temper, fawning like venomous dogs and becoming the causes of irremediable evils, and left behind them throughout the cities, as monuments of their impiety and hatred to humankind, the never-to-be-forgotten miseries of the afflicted. But yet not one either of the horribly cruel-hearted, or of the all-wily and false, could succeed in fathering any guilt upon the said assembly of Essenes, or holy ones. But all succumbed before the noble character of these men, recognized them as being independent and free by nature, and chanted the praises of their common meals and of their fellowship that transcends description, and is a pattern of a life perfect and most blest" (Philo, "Every Virtuous Man is Free," § 10–13).

In the preceding account it will have been observed from a foot-note, that the Essenes are described as "Therapeuts of God"—true devotees. In the following is described—under the name of Therapeuts—an order of recluses, in many ways resembling the Essenes, but more extreme in their mode of life.

"Having discoursed of Essenes, who strove after and wrought out the life of action, and excelled in all, or what is, at least, a more supportable thing to say, in most of its parts,

I will forthwith, and in pursuance of the due sequence of my subject, say what is fitting concerning those who embraced the life of contemplation, making no additions of my own for embellishment, which it is the custom of all poets and prose writers to do, through lack of honest diligence, but clinging simply to Truth herself, of whom I know that even the cleverest narrator is apt to grow weary. Nevertheless one must struggle through, and with earnestness contend; for it is not right that the greatness of the virtue of the men should be made an excuse for neglect, with such as deem that nought that is noble should be doomed to silence.

"The scope of these philosophers is manifested at once by their appellation: for they are called, with true literal sense of the words, men and women *Therapeuts;* * either, forsooth, insomuch as they possess a superior healing art to that current in cities (for that heals bodies only, while this one heals souls too, that are carried nigh death by disorders grievous and hard to cure, brought on by pleasures and lusts, griefs and fears, greeds and follies and wrongs, and the endless multitude of the other passions and vices), or else insomuch as they have learned from nature and the sacred laws to serve the One that Is, who is better than goodness, more absolute than unity, and more the first cause than the Monad. For among those that profess piety whom can one fairly class with these men?

* * * * *

"Those entering on the life of a Therapeut do so, not through the influence of custom, nor from the advice or recommendation of others; but because they are carried away by a heavenly love, just as those who are inspired with the Bacchic or Corybantic frenzy are in ecstatic rapture so long as they behold their desire. And so, by reason of their longing for the immortal and blessed life, they deem that their mortal existence has already come to an end, and

---

* The Greek word has the double signification of acts of worship or service, and healing.

abandon their property to sons or daughters, or other kinsfolk, with willing mind assigning their inheritance to them; and if they have no kinsfolk, then to companions and friends.

* * * * *

"The cares of goods and possessions eat up the years; but to be thrifty with time is good; for, according to the physician Hippocrates, life is short, but art is long. This, it seems to me, is what Homer occultly implies in the Iliad at the beginning of the thirteenth book, by the following words:

> "The Mysians fighting hand to hand,
> And the mare-milking, noble band,
> Milk-fed, and used to frugal fare;
> Most righteous of mankind they are."

"For anxiety concerning subsistence and money-getting engenders injustice by reason of the inequality resulting, while the contrary principle of life leads to justice by means of equality, according to which the wealth of nature has been marked out, surpassing in true fortune, as it does, that based upon empty opinions.

"When, therefore, people abandon possession of their property without being caught by any further bait, they flee without turning round, relinquishing brethren, children, wives, parents, multitudinous relationships, friendly companionships, fatherlands wherein they were born and brought up, notwithstanding that the habitual is an attraction and most potent in allurement.

"They leave home, not for another city, as do those who entreat to be purchased from their owners, that is to say, either unfortunate or worthless slaves, contriving a change of masters, not freedom for themselves (for every city, even the best ordered, is full of indescribable uproars and plagues and disorders, which no one once under the guidance of wisdom would undergo); but they make their sojournings outside of walls in gardens or farms, following after an eremite state, not through an uncivilized and studied misanthropy, but because of the intercourse with persons of dissimilar habitude, which they realize to be profitless and harmful.

"There are many parts of the world in which this class may be found; for both Greece and the barbarian lands must needs have their share in what is good and perfect. They are, however, in greatest abundance in Egypt in every one of the so-called departments, and especially round about Alexandria. The principal persons draw up their colony from all quarters, as to a fatherland of Therapeuts, unto a certain well-regarded spot, which lies on Lake Marea, on a somewhat low hill, very well situated, both with regard to security and the mildness of the air. That security is afforded by the encircling farm buildings and villages, and the mildness of the air by the continual breezes dispensed from the lake that opens out into the sea, and from the open sea that lies not far off. For the breezes from the open sea are light, whilst those from the lake that opens out into the sea are heavy, and the mixture of these produces a settled character of much wholesomeness.

"The houses of these associated people are exceedingly simple, merely affording a shelter in respect of the two things most necessary, to wit, against the heat of the sun, and icy chill of the air. They are not close to each other, like those in cities, for it is irksome and unpleasant for those that have striven for an eremite state to have neighbours always at their heels; nor are they far apart, both on account of the fellowship which the brethren cling to, and also to provide for mutual assistance in case of incursion of robbers.

"In each house there is a shrine, known as the sanctuary and place of solitude, which they use for seclusion and the consummation of the mysteries of the life of holiness, for they bring in thither neither drink nor food, nor anything else whatsoever related to the needs of the body, but only laws and oracles divinely given through prophets, and hymns, and such other things as tend to the increase and perfection of knowledge and religion. Nay rather, they ever keep unforgotten the memory of God, so that even in their dreams no image other than the beauties of the divine virtues and powers is presented to the mind.

"Many accordingly, too, are given to speech in sleep, and deal in dreams with the long-praised apophthegms of the sacred philosophy. Twice each day they are wont to pray, at the dawn and at evening; asking at sunrise that the brightness of the day may be a real brightness, so that their mind may be filled with a full measure of heavenly light; praying at set of sun that the soul being on that account completely relieved of the burden of the external senses and their objects, and settled in its own senate house and council chamber, may follow in the track of truth.

"The intervening space, too, from dawn to evening is with them wholly a discipline. For they read the sacred Scriptures and seek after wisdom by allegorical exposition of the hereditary philosophy, inasmuch as they regard what constitutes the letter of each utterance as the symbol of a nature that is withheld from sight but revealed in the hidden meanings.* They possess, besides, compositions of ancient men, who were the founders of the school, and bequeathed many a memorial of the allegorical manner, of which they avail themselves by way of archetypes, and so closely follow the method of the original school. As it appears, they are not given to contemplation only, but likewise compose songs and hymns to God in all kinds of metres and melody, moulding them of necessity in rhythms of some gravity. Each of the six days they severally spend in abiding by themselves in the chosen places of solitude, and seek after wisdom in study, never going beyond the threshold of the open outer court, nor even

---

* With this description of the system of the Therapeuts may be compared Philo's reference to the symbolic studies of the Essenes, contained in the preceding extract.

remotely contemplating such a thing. But on the seventh day they assemble as to a common public meeting, and sit down in order according to age with becoming mien, keeping their hands close, the right betwixt the breast and the beard, and the left withdrawn and by the flank. Then the eldest and most experienced in the apophthegms comes forward, and with steadfast look and steadfast voice, with consideration and purpose, delivers a discourse; not making a display of a power of arguments like the orators, or like the sophists of the present day, but searching through and expounding the precise meaning latent in the thoughts, which is of a kind not to sit at the tips of the ears, but to penetrate through the sense of hearing unto the soul, and with steadiness tarry there. The rest, all in quietness, hearken to what he commends to them, manifesting their feelings merely by an approving gesture of the eye or head. This common sanctuary, into which they congregate every seventh day, is an enclosure made in two parts, the one distinguished as the men's apartment, the other as the women's. For in truth the women are in the habit of joining in the audience, holding as they do the self-same zeal and the same principle of life. The partition between the rooms, as far as to three or four cubits from the ground floor upwards, is built up like a breastwork. But as for the upper part, as far as the roof, it is void, this arrangement being for two reasons; both for the preservation of the becoming modesty of the feminine nature; and secondly, that they may conveniently be able to catch the words by being seated within earshot, with nothing to intercept the voice of the speaker.

"Self-mastery they lay down to be as it were the first foundation of the soul, and build on this the other virtues. Not one of them would take food or drink before sundown, inasmuch as they judge the pursuit of wisdom to be the work worthy of light, whilst the darkness befits the corporeal needs, on which account they apportion the day to the one, and a brief portion of the night to the other. Some of them even have so disproportioned a yearning for knowledge implanted in them, that for three days they make food a mere matter of memory. Nay, some are so rejoiced and so revel in the banquet of wisdom, when she richly and ungrudgingly leads out the chorus of her conceptions, that they hold out even for double that time, and will scarcely, after six days, taste even necessary food, being wont, as folks say of the genus of cicadas, to be nourished on air, their singing, I suppose, making up for their lack in other respects.

"The seventh day they regard as all holy and a high festival, and deem it worthy of special prerogative, and thereon, after the due care of the soul, they anoint their bodies too, giving them, much after the manner of cattle, a respite from the constraint of labour.

"They use for food nothing costly, but a frugal bread with salt for a relish, which the delicate livers do further season with hyssop; their drink is running water. The mistresses which nature has set in the ground of human-kind—hunger and thirst to wit—they charm away, conferring nothing upon them in the way of flattery, but veritable things of use, without which life cannot be sustained. Wherefore they eat so as not to be hungry, and drink so as not to be thirsty, but revolt from repletion as an enemy and traitor to soul and body.

"There are, as we know, two kinds of covering, the one clothing, the other a house; with regard to their houses it has already been said that they are without adornment and simply built, being constructed with a view to the necessary only. And in like manner their clothing is most economical, designed for a defence against both frost and heat, being a thick cloak of some shaggy felt for winter, and a sleeveless vest or fine linen garment for summer. For, in fine, they practise modesty without pride, regarding deception as pride's foundation, whilst freedom from pride owes its origin to truth, each, as it were, acting as a fountain-head. For from deception there flows the multiform species of evils, whilst from truth flows rich abundance of good things both human and divine.

"I purpose moreover describing their common assemblages, and their cheerier pastimes at banquets, by setting in contrast the banquets of other people. For some, when they have greedily gorged themselves with undiluted liquor, as if it was not wine they were drinking, but something of deranging and maddening potency, or the most formidable thing in existence for driving a man out of his natural reason, strike out wildly, and rage about like untamed dogs. . . . Others, amongst such as seem to belong to the more moderate kind of drinkfellows, imbibe the wine raw like a mandrake potion, loll and push forward their left elbow and crane their neck sideways, possessed as it were by the demons of the cups, and then sink into deep sleep, without either sight or hearing of anything, and as if they had but one single sense, taste, the most slavish of all. Others, too, I know, who, when they have become filled to the throat with liquor, before they are completely baptized in it, make preparation beforehand by voluntary contributions and pledges for the booze of the succeeding day, conceiving that a great part of the merriment of the moment lies in the foretaste of the drunkenness of the morrow. In this way they pass their lives, for ever without house or home, the foes of their parents, their wives, their children, the foes, too, of their country, and the enemies of themselves. For a tipsy, sottish life is a snare to every one.

"Perhaps some might be inclined to approve the arrangement of banquets that now is everywhere the fashion, owing to longings after Italian extravagance and luxury, which both Greeks and foreigners have emulated, and so adapt their preparations rather for show than for entertainment. For they use triple couches, and couch coverings adorned with tortoiseshell and ivory, and the costliest material, the greater number being inlaid with precious stones; fleecy cushions of sea purple, with gold and silver embroidery, and others dipped in bright dyes of all the colours of the rainbow, to allure the sight, and an array of drinking goblets arranged according to their particular kinds. . . . They have slave servitors, too, well-shaped and of exceeding beauty, as if they were present, not more for the sake of service than of delighting the eyes of the spectators by their appearance. . . . When they are completely nauseated, with their bellies filled up to the very gorge, but their desires still unsated, they grow tired of foods, and turning their heads round on every side, they cast about with their eyes and nostrils, gloating on the fleshiness and quantity of the viands, and sniffing up the fatty steam and odour as it exhales. Thereafter, when they have become glutted with both sights and scents, they stimulate appetite by lavish belaudments on the score of costliness of the provision made and of their host.

"But why should I enlarge upon these things, which are already esteemed by the generality of more moderate persons as giving the rein to lusts, the diminution of which were profitable? For surely any one would pray for hunger and thirst the most lamentable, rather than for the limitless superfluity of foods and drinks at such sumptuous feasts as these.

"Since the entertainments of the widest celebrity are full of such trifling folly. . . . I will set in contrast the entertainments of those who have consecrated their private life and themselves to knowledge and contemplation of the affairs of nature, in accordance with the most sacred guidance of the prophet Moses.

"In the first place, these people muster every seven weeks, and they venerate not merely the simple period of seven days, but also its square. . . . Therefore when they assemble together, clad in white and of joyful countenance, keeping the highest solemnity, at a signal from one of the ephemereuts (ministers of the day)—the name they give to those engaged in such services—before they sit at table, they stand one after the other in a row in order, and stretching up their eyes and hands toward heaven—the first, because they have learned to turn their gaze upon what is worth looking on; the second, because they are unsoiled by lucre, and defile themselves on no pretext with aught connected with money-getting—they pray that the festivity may be made well-pleasing to God, and may pass off in harmony with intelligence.

"After these prayers, the elders arrange themselves at table, following the order of their entrance. They do not regard any as elders merely on account of length of years and antiquity; nay more, they even regard such as youths, if it be late in life that they have shown love for the principles of the school; but those whom they style elders are they that beginning from their earliest age have spent their youth and bloom in the contemplative sphere of philosophy, which assuredly is its most beautiful and divine portion.

"The women, too, join in the feast, the greater number of whom, though of some advancement in years, are actually virgins in chastity, being so not from necessity like some of the priestesses among the Greeks, who owe it rather to strict ward than to the resolution of their own will; but, by reason of their pursuit of and yearning after wisdom, to which they are earnest to make their life conform, they have disregarded the body's pleasures, reaching after no mortal but an immortal offspring, which can be produced of itself by that soul alone that is God-loving, the Father having sown in it rays of the light, Intelligence, whereby it will be able to perceive the principles of wisdom.

"Their arrangement at table is that the men sit apart at the right, the women apart at the left. In case any one should by any chance imagine that cushions, even though not of a costly character, yet at any rate of some amount of softness, are prepared for people who are of good birth and bred in civilization and practisers of philosophy, I may say that they use mattresses of the commonest material, the papyrus of the country, of which they make piles upon the ground, projecting a little where the elbows rest in order to be leant upon. The Spartan rigour of life they somewhat relax, but always and everywhere cultivate a free-spirited liberal contentment with frugality, hating with all their might the alluring potions of pleasure. They are not served by slaves, for they look upon the possession of servitors or bondmen to be absolutely contrary to nature. For she gave birth to all in a state of freedom, but the injustice and covetousness of some men who emulously desire the arch-evil, inequality, have straitened men and vested the stronger with power over the weaker.

"In this sacred banquet, above all there are, as I said, no bondmen, but freemen serve, performing the offices of service, not under compulsion, not in subjection to orders, but with willing purpose, forestalling by speed and readiness any signal. For they are not any chance freemen that are ordained for these attendances, but the youths most distinguished by merit amongst the whole body, all possible care being taken in selection; and they act as is befitting civilized and well-born persons hasting forwards to the fulness of virtue; and just as legitimate sons with affectionate rivalry attend upon the wants of their fathers and mothers, so do they deem their common parents to be more closely related to them than those connected by blood, inasmuch as with those that are rightly principled there is no nearer bond of kinship than virtuous nobility. They come in to perform their service ungirdled, and with the frock flowing loose, so as not to introduce into this banquet of theirs any semblance whatever to the servile manner. Some persons, I know, will laugh when they hear this; but they that laugh will be people who do things meet for weeping and lamentation. Wine is not brought in on those days, but water of the clearest, cold for the generality, but hot for the delicate livers among the seniors. The table, too, is pure of aught that has blood, and thereon is bread for food, with the addition of salt, to which now and then a seasoning of hyssop is added as a relish on account of the fastidious. For just as the priests are guided by the right and true Logos to sacrifice offerings without wine, so are these people to make such of their lives. For wine is the stimulant of folly, and costly rich fare is the provocative of lust, the most insatiate nursling of the brood.

"The beginning of the banquet is as I have said. Now, after the fellow-feasters have got to table in the order described, and those acting as attendants are standing in their proper place ready for ministry, is there verily no carouse, some one might ask? [There is a gap in the text here which probably was originally filled by a description of the friends partaking of their frugal supper.] [(Suggested reading) Then, as there grows a silence,] nay even more than before, so that no one ventures even to utter a syllable or to breathe hard, some one makes investigation into something of what exists in the sacred literature, or solves some question put by another, taking no thought whatever for display. For, he is not reaching out after laudation for cleverness in words, but desirous only to see some point with greater precision, and when he has thus seen it himself, not to grudge it to others who, though they be not equally sharpsighted with himself, have at all events a corresponding desire to learn. And he adopts indeed a somewhat slow method of instruction, persevering and lingering over it with repetitions, in order to impress the thoughts strongly upon their souls. For, if the interpretation be made by one who glibly and as it were at a breath strings his sentences together, the minds of such hearers as cannot closely follow get behindhand, and fail to catch hold of the words as they are spoken. The listeners, on the other hand, plant themselves uprightly and turn towards him, and remain in one and the same posture to give ear, indicating their attention and apprehension by a nod or a look, and their praise of the speaker by the beaming of the countenance and a gentle bearing round, but any doubt or perplexity by a slighter movement of the head and by the forefinger of the right hand. No less attention, too, than that shown by those at table is paid by the youths in attendance.

"The explanations of the sacred Scriptures are made by giving the deep meanings which lie in allegories. For the whole range of laws seems to these men to be like a living creature which has for body the express commandments, but for soul the invisible meaning which is stored up in the verbal forms, in which significance the rational soul begins distinctly to contemplate that which is properly akin to itself, and beholds, as it were through a mirror of the mere terms, the extraordinary beauties of thought that are introduced; and as it unfolds and reveals the symbols, it brings the naked inner sense into light, for such as are able by the aid of slight indications to behold the invisible through the agency of the visible.

"When the president seems to have adequately discoursed, and to have arrived at a position accordant with his purpose, and the attention of one has been reached by the argumentation and of others by the lecture itself, there proceeds applause from all, as from people rejoicing in concert at what has been brought to view.

"And then one rises up and sings a hymn made in honour of God, either a new one which he has himself composed, or some ancient hymn of the poets of old time. For they have left behind them many measures and melodies, whether of trimeter verse, of processional psalms, or of hymns for libations and the altar, also set pieces and choric songs, well measured out in diversified strains.

"After him others also rise in their rank in befitting order, whilst all else listen in perfect quiet, save when it is proper for them to sing the burden or refrain; for then they all, both men and women, raise their voices. And when each singer has concluded, the young men bring in the table just before mentioned, whereon is the all-hallowed food, namely, leavened bread, together with its additional condiment of prepared salt, with which hyssop is mingled, out of reverence for the holy table votively set up in the hallowed antechamber of the shrine. For upon this there are loaves and prepared salt without spices: the loaves too are unleavened, and the salt is without mixture. For it were fitting that such things as are simplest and most clearly pure should be allotted to the most excellent class of the priests, as an award for their public ministration, whilst others should emulate their likeness, but abstain from the loaves, in order that the most excellent may possess a privilege.

"Now, after the supper they hold the sacred festival of the nocturnal vigil. And this night-long celebration is conducted as follows:—They all stand up in a mass, and about the middle of the entertainment there are at first formed two choruses, the one of men, the other of women. A conductor and coryphæus is chosen for each one, a person selected alike for dignity and tunefulness. Then they sing hymns addressed to the Deity, composed in many measures and melodies, at one time elevating their voices in unison, at another gesticulating and dancing to tune with antiphonal successions of sweet sound, and inspirationally produce, at one time marches, at another uninterrupted periods of song, composing for themselves the strains of the turnings and returnings of the dance where necessary. Then, when each chorus of the men and women has feasted separately by itself, drinking, like as those in the Bacchic orgies drink unmixed wine, the draught of the love of God, they join together and form one chorus out of both, in imitation of that which in old time was established by the Red Sea to commemorate the wondrous works that were done there. . . . Both men and women being moved by rapture became one chorus, and sang hymns of grateful praise to the Saviour God, Moses the prophet acting as coryphæus for the men, and Miriam the prophetess for the women. This especially is the model followed by the chorus of the Therapeuts, male and female; and the high notes of the women answering with re-echoing and antiphonal melodies to the deep tones of the men, produce a most harmonious and thoroughly musical symphony and concert. All-beauteous the ideas, all-beauteous the expressions, and reverend the choral worshippers. The aim, too, of the ideas, the expressions and the worshippers, is religion. Under the intoxicating spell, then, of this beautiful drunkenness, until early morn, without heaviness of head or drowsiness of eye, nay with more perfect wakefulness than when they came to the banquet, both as to their eyes and their whole body, they stand looking towards the dawn, and when they behold the sun uprising, they stretch forth their hands toward heaven, and pray for the happy day and for truth and clear sight of the understanding. And after the prayers they all retire into their own sanctuaries, again to lead their wonted life of philosophy, and to till the soil.

"So far, then, extend my remarks on the subject of the Therapeuts, who have clung to the contemplation of nature, and have lived in it and the soul alone, being citizens of heaven as well as of the world, and unfeignedly united with the Father and the Creator of all, by their virtue, which procured for them love, and added the most appropriate prerogative of nobility which transcends all gifts of fortune, and is the first comer to the very summit of blessedness" (Philo, Vit. Contempl.)

The description of the Essenes that follows is from the pen of Josephus, a Jew born in Jerusalem A.D. 37. He opposed the determination of his countrymen to revolt against Rome, and was present during the siege of Jerusalem. Afterwards he lived principally at Rome. He wrote his "History of the Jewish War" in Syro-Chaldaic, for the use of his countrymen, and afterwards translated it into Greek, for the benefit of the

Western Jews and the Romans, with the cultured amongst whom Greek was the fashionable language. About A.D. 93 he brought out his "Antiquities of the Jews."

"There are three sects of philosophers among the Jews. Those of the first are styled Pharisees, of the second Sadducees, and of the third, and these really seem to follow a holy discipline, are called Essenes. They are Jews by birth, but show fraternal regard one to the other more than the rest. These individuals reject the sensual pleasures as vice, while self-control and non-subjection to the passions they regard as virtue. There is also a disdain of marriage amongst them; but they receive the children of others whilst still tender for learning, and regard them as their own kin, and impress them with their own morals. Marriage and the succession consequent thereon, they do not altogether repudiate; but they shun the wanton ways of women, and are persuaded that not one of them preserves her fidelity to one man.

"They are contemners of riches, and have a marvellous system of holding things in common, and there is not to be found among them one surpassing the rest in possessions. For the rule is for those that enter their sect to make their substance public property for the order. So that, amongst them all, there is not to be seen either the abjectness of poverty or the elevation of wealth, but the possessions of each are thrown into a common fund, and form one property for all like brothers.

"They regard oil as a defilement, and if one gets smeared against his will, his body is straightway washed clean of it. To be dry-skinned they hold to be comely, also to be entirely dressed in white. The stewards of their common property are elected by general vote, and none is distinguishable from the general body in respect of such offices.

"There is no one city appertaining to them, but in each there are many of them dwelling; and to such of their persuasion as arrive from any other place, whatever they have is thrown open as freely as if it were their own; and they go to visit those whom they have never seen before, as if they were most intimate. For this reason, too, they take their journeys away from home without making any special provision whatever, save that they carry arms on account of robbers. In every city of the order a steward is appointed for the special behalf of strangers, to dispense clothing and necessaries. Their bodily dress and fashion is like unto children brought up in fear. They change neither garments nor sandals before they are first altogether in rags or worn threadbare by time. They neither buy nor sell anything amongst themselves, but each one gives of his own things to any one that is in need, and receives correspondingly what is useful from the others. But even without any consideration being given, they get whatever they may want made over to them freely.

"With respect to the Divine Power they are peculiarly reverential, for before the rising of the sun they utter not a word upon worldly matters, but address some of the prayers of their forefathers to it, as if supplicating it to rise. Thereafter they are dismissed by their superintendents to the handicrafts in which each is skilled, and work uninterruptedly until the fifth hour. Then they again gather into one place, girt with linen aprons, and so wash the body with streams of cold water. After this purification they flock to a separate building, where none of those outside the faith has permission to enter; and they themselves go clean to the refectory as into some sacred precinct. And when, with quietness, they have taken their seats, the baker puts loaves before them in order, while the cook sets by each a single dish consisting of one kind of food. The priest prefaces the meal by prayer, and it is unlawful for any one to taste before the prayer. After the meal is ended, there is an invocation again; and so both at beginning and ending they render honour to God as the prime giver of the food. Thereupon they lay aside the garments as if they were sacred, and again partake themselves to their tasks until evening. On their return they sup together, when any strangers who may happen to be among them, equally sit at table along with them. Never does clamour desecrate the house, nor tumult, but each allows to the other his part in the talking in turn; and the silence of those that are within, appears to those that are without as some awful mystery. The reason for this is their continual sobriety, and the fact that their meat and drink are portioned out to them to the extent only of satisfying appetite.

"Whilst in other matters there is nothing which they do without the appointment of their superintendents, there are yet these two things in which they have unfettered spontaneous power—succour and compassion. For of their own accord they are allowed to help the deserving, whensoever they are in need, and to furnish food to the destitute; but to make gifts to their own kindred is not allowed them without the sanction of the stewards.

"They are just masters of anger, curbers of passion, champions of fidelity, ministers of peace. Everything that is said by them is of more force than an oath, while they shun swearing, regarding it as worse than perjury; for, say they, he that is not trusted without the name of God is already condemned.

"They give extraordinary study to the compositions of the ancients, selecting especially such parts as concern the benefit of soul and body. Hence their investigation of protective roots and of the peculiar properties of stones for the cure of sufferings.

"To one that aims at entering their sect admission is not immediate, but he remains a whole year outside it and is subjected to their rule of life, being invested with an axe, the girdle aforesaid, and a white garment. Provided that over this space of time he has given proof of his perseverance, he approaches nearer to their course of life and partakes in the holier waters of cleansing, but he is not yet admitted to their community of life. Following the proof of his strength of control, his moral conduct is tested for two years more; and when he has made clear his worthiness, he is thus adjudged to be of their number. But before he touches the common meal, he pledges to them in oaths to make one shudder; first, that he will reverence the Divine Being; and secondly, that he will abide in justice unto men, and will injure no one, either of his own accord or by command, but will always detest the iniquitous and strive on the side of the righteous; that he will ever show fidelity to all, and most of all to those that are in power, for to no one comes rule without the Deity; and that, if he should become a ruler himself, he will never carry insolence into his authority, or outshine those placed under him by dress or any superior adornment; that he will always love truth and press forward to convict those that tell lies; that he will keep his hands from peculation, and his soul pure of unholy gain; that he will neither conceal anything from the brethren of his order, nor babble to others of any of their secrets, even though in presence of force and at the hazard of his life. In addition to all this, they take oath not to communicate the doctrines to any one in any other way than as imparted to themselves; to abstain from robbery, and to keep close with equal care the books of their sect and the names of the angels. Such are the oaths by which they secure those that join them.

"Such as are caught in heinous sins they cast out of their order, and the excommunicated one often perishes by a most pitiable fate. For, as he is bound by the oaths and usages, he cannot partake of the food of outsiders, but, eating herbs and wasting bodily by famine, he perishes. Wherefore, indeed, they take many back from compassion when at the last gasp, deeming the torture unto death sufficient for their sins.

"In their judgments they are most exact and righteous;

and for sentence assemble in numbers of not less than a hundred. That which is once decreed by them is unalterable. Their greatest reverence, after the Deity, is for the name of the lawgiver; and if any one blasphemes against this he is punished with death. To submit to the elders and to the majority, they hold as seemly; for instance, in a sanhedrin of ten, no one would speak against the wish of the nine. They are careful not to spit in public or to the right hand, and not to touch work on the seventh day, with the most strictness of all the Jews. For they not only prepare their food one day before, so as not even to kindle a fire on that day, but they dare not even move a vessel from one place to another, or go aside for nature's calls. But on other days they dig a pit a foot deep with the spud (for such is the nature of the little axe that is given by them to novices), and covering themselves round with their garment, so as not to insult the rays of the god, they set themselves over the pit, and then rake back into it the dug-up earth; and this they do, choosing the most sequestered places. And, although the voiding of corporeal offscourings is natural, it is customary with them to bathe after it, as if they were defiled.

"They are divided, according to the time of taking up the discipline, into four sections; and the juniors are so inferior to the seniors that the latter must bathe themselves if they happen to be touched by the former, as if contaminated by an alien.

"They live to a great age, so that the generality reach beyond a hundred years, by reason of the simplicity of their diet, as it appears to me, and of their orderliness. They are despisers of dangers; they vanquish griefs by highmindedness, and regard death, if it come with honour, as better than deathlessness.

"The war against the Romans proved in every way their spirit. For, though racked and wrenched, burned and broken, and forced to go through all engines of torture, to make them either blaspheme the lawgiver or eat something of things unwonted, they held out so as to be subject to neither, nor even to fawn once on their tormentors, or shed a tear. But smiling amid their pains, and bantering those that inflicted the torture, they yielded up their souls with alacrity, as if about to get them back again.

"For this opinion holds strongly among them, that though bodies are perishable and their material substance not permanent, yet souls for ever endure untouched by death and proceeding from the finest ether, are involved with the bodies as it were prisons, drawn down by some physical spell. But when they are set free from their bonds according to the flesh, they then have joy and are borne aloft as if released from a long slavery.

"In the case of the good souls, they declare, in harmony with the children of the Greeks, that a way of life beyond the Primeval Water is allotted, and a place oppressed neither by rains nor snows nor burning heats, but one which the mild breeze breathing over from the ocean refreshes ever. But to bad souls they assign a dark and wintry den, full of never-ending punishments.

"It seems to me to be according to the same notion that the Greeks assigned to their manly ones, whom they call Heroes and Demigods, the Islands of the Blessed, but to the souls of the wicked the place of the impious in Hades, where also their myths tell of several undergoing punishment, Sisyphuses, and Tantaluses, and Ixions, and Tityuses; first, because they hold that souls are eternal, and secondly, for encouragement of virtue and discouragement of vice: on the ground that good men are made better in their lives by the hope of reward after their death, whilst the wild desires of the bad are checked by their fearful expectation that, even though they should escape notice in this life, after the dissolution they must suffer deathless punishment. Such is the theology of the Essenes concerning the soul, and they let down an irresistible bait to such as have once tasted of their wisdom.

"There are also some among them who profess foreknowledge of the future, being brought up from youth in the study of sacred books, and divers purifications, and prophetic utterances, and it is seldom that they miss the mark in their predictions.

"There is also another order of Essenes, which agrees with the others as regards way of living, customs and laws, but differs in doctrine respecting marriage. For they think that those who do not marry cut off the principal part of life, to wit, the succession, especially because, if all were to hold the same view, the whole race would soon be extinguished.

"They test their wives for a three years' space, and then, after they have given evidence by three purifications that they are fit to bear children, they marry them. They have no connubial intercourse with their wives when with child, showing that they do not marry for gratification, but for the sake of offspring. The women wear garments when they take the bath, as the men wear the apron. Such are the habits of this order" (Josephus, De B. J., ii. 8, 2–13).

The greater part of this description is found also in Origen's *Philosophumena*, in a paraphrased form. It may be that the later writer translated from the Hebraic text of Josephus. There are, however, important deviations, as may be seen by the following, which comes immediately after the reference in Josephus to the division of the Essenes into four classes.

"Others of them carry their discipline beyond what is right, so far as not even to carry a coin, saying that they ought not either to bear, to see, or to make an image. Wherefore not one of them enters a town, in order that he may not enter through a gate on which there are statues, for they think it unlawful to pass under an image. Others, again, when they hear any one discoursing of God and his laws, if he be uncircumcised, one stands in watch for such a person when somewhere alone, and threatens to slay him without he consents to circumcision; and if he should not wish to be persuaded, he does not shrink from cutting his throat. From such occurrences they were given their name, being called Zealots, and by some Sicarii.

"Others of them call no one master but God, even at the cost of punishment and imprisonment. So deteriorated have those that come afterwards become, as regards the discipline, that those that abide in the ancient ways do not even touch them, and, if they touch them, they have an ablution forthwith, as if they touched a foreigner.

"The majority of them are long lived, so as to attain even more than a hundred years. They say that this is owing to the fact of their supreme religiousness, and that through the condemnation of the excessive supply of food they are self-controlled and incapable of anger. They rejoice in the disdain of death, provided they shall die with a good conscience, and if any one visit such as these with punishments, to make one blaspheme the law, or eat an idol offering, he will not grieve, but endure to die and to bear tortures, so as not to transgress his conscience.

"The doctrine of the *anastasis* holds strongly among them, for they confess that the flesh will be upraised and will be deathless in the same manner as the soul is deathless already, which, as it is, is sundered and reposes until judgment in a place of sweet breezes and shine, to which place the Greeks from hearsay gave the name of Islands of the Blessed."

This account presents a view of men extreme to fanaticism as belonging to the Essenes, ascribing to their peaceful order the uncompromising and extravagant Zealot. One of the disciples of Jesus, it will be remembered, bore this title of Zealot, which at that time denoted a man zealous for the theocratic ideal of government and opposed to Roman domination, while the troubles that came after developed the ruthless character which gave to the body the title of Men of the Dagger.

A further divergence from Josephus is in the account of the Essene faith as to the *anastasis*. According to the earlier writer, they believed in an escape of the soul from the body and its joyous uprise at death. In the account of the later writer the dogma of the resurrection of the flesh has crept in.

Further accounts of Josephus relating to the Essenes, or to members of the order, are as follows:—

"At this time (146 B.C.) there were three sects among the Jews, differing in their opinions about human affairs. One was called the sect of the Pharisees, another that of the Sadducees, and the third that of the Essenes. The Pharisees affirm that some things only, and not all, are the work of Fate, and that some are in our own power, whether they should come about or whether they should not. The family of the Essenes maintains that Fate is mistress of all things, and that nothing befalls man contrary to its decrees" (Antiq., XIII., v. § 9).

"There have been three philosophies among the Jews ever since the ancient time of the fathers, one of the Essenes, another of the Sadducees, and a third which the so-called Pharisees followed.

"The doctrine of the Essenes delights in leaving all things to God. They immortalize the soul, and hold that the approach to virtue must be battled for with all our might. Although they send offerings to the Temple, yet they perform no sacrifices on account of the different rules of purity which they observe; hence, being excluded from the common sanctuary, they perform sacred rites of their own. In other respects, they are, in their way of life, the best of men, and employ themselves wholly in the labour of agriculture. Their uprightness is to be admired above all others that pretend to the practice of virtue; such uprightness, which is by no means to be found among the Greeks and foreigners, is not of recent date, but has existed among them from times of old, and is shown by their anxiety not to disturb the community of goods, and that the rich should not enjoy more of household necessaries than one who is possessed of nothing. The men who so act are more than four thousand in number. They never marry wives, nor make it their custom to own slaves, for they believe that the latter course begets injustice, and the former yields opportunities for discord. Living by themselves, they avail themselves of services one towards another. They choose good men, who are also priests, to be the stewards of their incomes and of the produce of their fields, as well as to procure the corn and food. They live all in the same manner, and are especially like those whom the Dacians call Polistæ" (Antiq. XVIII. i. §§ 2, 5).

"The Essenes (Essaioi), as we call them, were also exempted from this necessity [of taking the oath of allegiance to Herod]. This sect pursues the same manner of life as among the Greeks has been instituted by Pythagoras. I discourse more fully about them elsewhere. The reason, however, why Herod held the Essenes in such honour, and thought more highly of them than in respect of moral nature, is worthy of record. The account seems not out of the historic sort, for it shows the opinion held about the Essenes.

"There was a certain Essene named Menahem, who was celebrated not only for the uprightness of his conduct, but also for that foreknowledge of the future which proceeds from God. When he once saw Herod, as a boy going to school, he addressed him by the name of King of the Jews. Herod thought that either Menahem did not know him, or that he was jesting, and informed the seer that he was merely a private person. But Menahem smiled on him in a friendly way, clapped him on the back with his hand, and said, 'Thou wilt nevertheless be king, and wilt begin thy reign happily, for God has found thee worthy of it; and remember the blows that Menahem has given thee, as being the symbol of the change of thy fortune. For this assurance will be salutary to thee in case thou shouldst love justice and piety towards God, and equity towards thy citizens. However, I know that thou wilt not be such a one, for I perceive it all. Thou wilt indeed, excel more than any one in happiness, and wilt obtain an eternal reputation, but thou wilt forget piety and justice. This will not be concealed from the Divinity, for he will visit thee with his wrath for it towards the end of thy life.' Herod paid scant attention to these things at the time, for he cherished no hope of them. But as he soon afterwards advanced to kingship and good fortune, in the height of his power he ordered Menahem to come to him, and asked him how long he would reign. Menahem said not a word. Seeing that he was silent, Herod asked again whether he would reign ten years. Whereupon he replied, 'Ay, twenty, nay, thirty years,' but fixed no limit. Herod, however, was content with this, gave Menahem his hand and dismissed him, and from that time continued to honour all the Essenes. I decided to relate this to my readers (though to some it may appear incredible), and to speak openly of the things that concern us, because many of the Essenes through matters of such a nature are highly esteemed for their virtuous conduct and knowledge of divine things," (Antiq., XV. x., §§ 4, 5).

"In this place I cannot omit a memorable story of one Judas, by sect an Essene, a man famous for divination, and one that was never charged, in the way of his profession, either with a falsity or a mistake. It was his chance to be passing by as Antigonus went through the Temple, and he exclaimed upon the sight of him to some of his disciples, ' 'Tis time for me to leave the world, since truth itself is dead. My prediction is false, I perceive, and I have foretold a lie, for that very Antigonus, who was to have been slain this day, is still living. The fatal place where he was to have been killed is Straton's Tower, which is no less than six hundred stadia from hence, and we are at the present in the fourth hour of the day.' After these reflections upon the presage, the old man, with a sadness in his countenance that betrayed the anxiety of his heart, sank into a musing, thoughtful, long and sorrowing silence. By-and-by comes the news of the death of Antigonus, in a subterranean passage, bearing the same name of Straton's Tower with that of Cæsarea, upon the sea coast; and this ambiguity it was that misled the prophet" (De Bell. J., I. iii. § 5. Antiq., XIII. xi. § 5).

One gate at Jerusalem, it may be named, was called according to Josephus (B. J., v. 4, § 2), the Gate of Essenes.

The following, from Josephus, refers to a sect distinct from the Essenes, and seems to rectify the error of Origen, who identifies the Zealots (followers of Judas the Galilean, who headed a revolt, A.D. 6) with the Essenes:—

"A fourth sect was introduced by Judas the Galilean, whose followers follow much the same doctrine generally as the Pharisees. But their love of liberty is uncontrollable, and they accept God as the sole leader and master; they make nothing of exposing themselves to various kinds of death, and to tortures of family and friends, rather than address any man by the name of master. This is a truth so well confirmed by observation, that nothing more need be said of their invincible constancy, which is beyond expression. This animosity was yet further inflamed by the insupportable cruelties of Gessius Phlorus, the governor, which ended at last in a revolt from the Romans." (Antiq., XVII. ii., § 6).

The following reference to the Essenes is by a Roman writer, Pliny the elder, who lived A.D. 23–79, and was a friend of the Emperor who took Jerusalem:—

"On the western shore [of the Dead Sea], but distant from the sea far enough to escape from its noxious breezes, dwelt the Essenes. They are an eremite clan, one marvellous beyond all others in the whole world; without any women, with sexual intercourse entirely given up, without money and the associates of palm-trees. Daily is the throng of those that crowd about them renewed, men resorting to them in numbers, driven through weariness of existence and the surges of ill fortune to their manner of life. Thus it is that through thousands of ages—incredible to relate!—their society, in which no one is born, lives on perennial. So fruitful to them is the irksomeness of life experienced by other men" (Hist. Nat., v. 17).

Epiphanius, who was born in Palestine in the early part of the fourth century, and there adopted a monkish discipline until he was made Bishop of Salamis, refers as follows to the Essenes. It will be observed that he speaks of them sometimes as still existent, at others as having existed, whence it is probable that his accounts are derived from older works. His authority is diminished by carelessness or ignorance as to facts.

"The Essenes continue in their first position, and have not altered at all. According to them, there have been dissensions among the Gorthenes for some slight cause, and in consequence of some controversy which has been held between them, I mean among the Sabuœans, Essenes, and Gorthenes. The controversy is on the following matter. The law commands the Israelites of all places to assemble at Jerusalem for the three festivals, the feasts of the Passover, Pentecost, and Tabernacles. As the Jews in Judea and Samaria were largely dispersed, it is supposed that those of them who made their pilgrimage to Jerusalem went through Samaritan cities, and, as the Samaritans assemble at the same time to celebrate the festival, a conflict arose between them" (Adv. Hær., i. 10).

"Next follow the Ossenes, who were closely connected with the former sect. They too are Jews, hypocrites in their demeanour and peculiar in their notions. They originated, according to the tradition which I received, in the regions of Nabatea, Ituræa, Moabitis, and Areïlitis, in the surrounding neighbourhood of the so-called Dead Sea. . . . The name Ossenes, according to its etymology, signifies the sturdy race.

"A certain person named Elxai (Elchasai) joined them in the time of the Emperor Trajan, after the advent of the Saviour. He was a false prophet and produced a book which of course proceeded from a prophetical impulse, or according to divinely given wisdom. They say that a certain other man named Iexeus was his brother, who also misled people in manner of life and caused them to err in doctrine. A Jew by birth, and professing the Jewish doctrines, he did not live according to the Mosaic law, but introduced quite different things and misled his own sect. He enjoined oaths by salt and water, and earth, and bread, and heaven, and ether, and wind, then by heaven, water, spirits, the holy angels of prayer, oil, salt, and earth. He hates virginity and continence [Epiphanius himself was an ascetic, so his language is probably extreme], and compels marriage. Some fantasies, as if revealed by dream, he commits to his followers. He teaches them to be hypocrites, saying there is no sin were one to chance to pay adoration to idols in time of instant persecution, provided only the worship were not from the conscience, and one confessed merely with the mouth and not from the heart. He joined the sect of Ossenes, of which some remnants are still to be found in the same regions of Nabatea and Peræa towards Moabitis. These people are now called Sempsæans" (Adv. Hær., i. 19). In another place (xxx. 3) he seems to treat Sempsæan, Ossene, and Elchasaite as different names for one persuasion.

No other extant accounts of the Essenes are worth quoting, as they are evidently derived from one or other of those we have given. Solinus, who flourished about the middle of the third century of our era, follows Pliny; and Porphyry, about a generation later, draws from Josephus.

Ginsburg draws from Hebrew literature certain references

to an order following a mystical plan of life, which he appears to identify with that of the Essenes, but, as he does not specify from what treatise his information is drawn, his argument lacks the weight it might otherwise possess.

He affirms that, from the beginning of the novitiate to the achievement of the highest spiritual state, there were eight different stages which marked the gradual growth of holiness. The disciple, after being accepted as a novice and girt with the apron, attained by baptisms to the state of outward or bodily purity. Thence he progressed to a state which enabled him to rise above the physical plane of sex. From this he advanced to the stage of inward or spiritual purity. Again he ascended to a state which postulated the banishment of all anger and malice, and the cultivation of a meek and lowly spirit. This led him to the culminating point of holiness. Thereupon he became the temple of the Holy Spirit, and could prophesy. A step further, and he could perform miraculous cures and raise the dead. Finally, he attained to the position of Elias, the forerunner of the Messiah.

A writer in the *Jewish World* (December 24, 1875) states, with regard to the Essenes, that " the great aim of this sect was to endeavour to bring about a revival of the pretended prophetic power of the Nazirites. The prophets had long ceased to be heard, and they believed that by their mode of life the voice of God would again be uttered through them. Their austerities were great, in the hopes that the Holy Spirit, the Rouach-ha-Kadesch, might descend upon them. One of these Essenes is thus recorded to have expressed himself: 'Step by step, zeal for the Lord and Pharisaic purity lead to Hassidouth (to humility and hatred of sin); thence we arrive at the gift of the Holy Spirit, which will at last bring about the resurrection of the dead by Elias.' For further particulars, cf. Mischna Sota fin. Jerus, Sahat Sabat, i. p. 3; Midrasch Canticum, p. 3, etc. . . . The Essenes moreover pretended to excel in exorcism. They studied medicine in a book called

Sepher-Rephorioth, attributed to Solomon. They frequently made use of verses from the Scriptures, and other formulas, which they recited in a low voice (Le'hisha), and at other times they made use of roots or stones to which they attributed a magic power, and it would appear that they were not ignorant of animal magnetism. The Pharisees regarded them with the utmost contempt, and there is no doubt that the expression 'pious fool' (Hassid Schota) which is applied in the Talmud to those who withdraw themselves from the society of even the most pious persons, is intended for them." There is a certain compatibility of this account with the narratives of Essene life, but it is generally held that no sect described in the Talmud has been certainly identified with that of the Essenes.

It may be noted that certain similes employed by Philo in reference to the Essenes are said to be found also in the Zohar (iii. 152)—that the law is a living organism, whose body is the letter and its soul a deeper meaning, and that, as through a mirror, the intelligent soul sees through the words things occult and extraordinary.

There must surely be a certain metaphoric quality in the Essene references to Elias and Messias as their climax of holiness; and one might also infer that the higher stages which the master of these spiritual powers hoped to reach signified a maturity of spirit, a completion of the state of probation which human life affords. An angelic position would thus be attained, empowering and impelling the holder of it to become himself a missionary to brethren still struggling among the beggarly elements, and still far off from the riches of the Kingdom of God.

We of the West know little of the conquest of nature that might be attained by the will of man devoting all its powers to that end, and so producing the apparently miraculous. With us, miracles are attained by exoteric mechanical triumphs and not by development of the latent powers within man.

Essenes and primitive Christians are rare in humanity; still it is not to be wondered at that believers in a spiritual condition adjoining or forming part of the nature of man, should from time to time realize the importance and comparative superiority of that condition, and strive to attain its powers and privileges, at the expense of the luxuries or even of the homely comforts of a more natural life.

From the death of Jesus until the time when the Trinitarian dogma had become developed sufficiently to attract political notice, heresies appear to have been plentiful. Essenes and followers of Jesus are not to be distinguished from one another, and seem to be equally merged in several religious orders which manifest strong mutual resemblances.

Jerome (Epist. ad August.) refers to a sect to be found in the Jewish synagogues of the East in his time, who were commonly named Nazaræans, and while they wished to be both Jews and Christians, succeeded in being neither. Augustine refers also to the Nazarene heretics as combining the baptism of Christians with the circumcision of Jews. The error here is to term baptism a Christian institution. The baptism of John, as well as that of the Essenes, was a Hebrew rite.

Epiphanius (Adv. Hær., ii. 29) speaks of "Nazoræans, who took their name neither from Christ nor from Jesus, while all Christians were then in like manner called Nazoræans. But for a little time it happened that they were called Jessæans (Iessaioi), before that, at Antioch, the disciples first came to be called Christians." This title, he supposes, is derived from Jesse, the father of David, which is but an innocent speculation on his part.

Epiphanius notices, also, the likeness between Jessæans and Essæans, and though he had before satisfied himself with a derivation of the former name from Jesse, when he returns to the subject it is to point out the strange resemblance between Jessæans and Essæans, or Essenes, as described by Philo.

This is noteworthy enough, but when he tells us that it is of none else but Christians that Philo is speaking, we have either to suppose that there were Christians before Christ, or that there were followers of Jesus undistinguishable from Essenes.

The cradle of the Nazaræan heresy is placed by Epiphanius in Gilead and Bashan, Beræa, Cœle-Syria, Decapolis, and generally in the regions beyond Jordan; while another sect, the Ebionites (Hær., xxx. 15, p. 142), who also appear to have been primitive Christians, he locates in the outskirts of Palestine, the Moabite districts beyond the Jordan.

"The Ebionite heresy," he alleges, "takes its abomination from the Samaritans, from the Jews its name, from Ossæans and Nazoræans and Nasaræans its doctrine, from followers of Cerinthus its form, from those of Carpocrates its mischievousness, while it seeks to possess the appellation of Christians." Eventually the Ebionites appear to have coalesced with the Elchasaites, and to have been separate from the more successful and less Jewish development, the Christian heresy proper.

With regard to the Essenes, whom Epiphanius describes as a Samaritan sect, and the Ossæans, which he describes as a Jewish sect, Bishop Lightfoot very reasonably suggests: "He has evidently got his information from two distinct sources, and does not see that the same persons are intended."

In the Talmud, various orders are mentioned, following a more or less ascetic or ceremonial course, but none seem certainly identifiable with the Essenes. Such are the Chassidim or Assidæans, the Men of Deeds, the Chaber or Associates, the Sons of the Congregation, the Holy Congregation, who devoted the winter to the study of the Scriptures and the summer to work, as some say, or who divided their day into study, prayer, and labour (Midrash Qoheleth, ix. 9). There were also the Vethikin, or pious, who prayed before sunrise, the Primitive Elders, the Morning-bathers, the Banaim, wilderness-dwellers and vegetarians, with one of whom

Josephus spent several years. It has been sought to affiliate the Essenes to a School of the Prophets of which Samuel was the founder. Captain Conder, in his "Judas Maccabæus," regards them as the successors of the Rechabites.

The historic evidences we possess, both Jewish and Roman, seem sufficient to support the conclusion that there were Essenes before the time of Jesus, and also after, when they either became extinct or coalesced with the primitive Christians, who were mostly Jews and Unitarian mystics.

We may ask now, Who were the Essenes? Were they purely Hebraic?—for while they cleave strenuously to certain parts of the Jewish law, they reject or transcend other parts.

The meaning of their name has been the bone of a contention which is not yet satisfactorily settled. We have seen the derivation of the term from the Greek *hosioi*, holy ones, which may be supported by the fact that in the Pazand books of the Zoroastrian religion of the fourth or fifth century of our era, a religion by which, at an earlier date, Judaism was much affected, *ashoa* is the name for the pious or the righteous; in Syriac, *chasyo*.

The oracular breast-plate of the Jewish high priest, which contained the Urim and Thummim, the Egyptian symbols of Light and Truth, is *Choshen*, which Josephus transliterates into Greek as *Essen*, as the Greeks transformed the letter *Cheth* into the rough breathing, and eventually into Eta.

Other Greek derivations are *isos*, associate; *esō*, in reference to esoteric doctrine; *aisa*, fate; *ēthos*, morality.

Besides *Jesse* [ishi], which we have already seen in Epiphanius, have been suggested *Isai*, a Rabbi who migrated to Egypt in the time of Alexander Jannæus; *Essa*, a trans-Jordanic town.

Suggested Hebrew or Aramaic etymologies are *asar*, to bind; *chasid*, pious; *s'cha*, to bathe; *chasin*, strong, which recalls the "sturdy" race of Epiphanius; *chotsen*, a fold, supposed to denote the Essene apron; *ăsā*, to heal; *asyā*, *asaia*, a physician; *gasah*, to do; *chaza*, to see; *chazya*, a seer; *chazzan*, watcher, worshipper; *chasha*, secret, or silent; *chashshaim*, the silent ones, reminding us of our word *hush*. To the last derivation we shall refer again.

These suggested etymologies show the labour taken by scholars to penetrate the secret of the Essenes, while the meanings evolved cover almost all the marked qualities which characterized the order.

Speculative etymologies are to be had for the seeking. It is a wonder none of these laborious investigators thought of trying Egypt: they might have been charmed to find Hesi, the name of the Heifer-goddess; Asi, venerable; Ash, tree of life; Isis, the mystic goddess of nature; or Accadian, Essa, an ear of corn.

The most probable derivation, to be found in the Hebrew, is one chosen by the Rev. C. Taylor ("Sayings of the Jewish Fathers"), one of the few scholars who have worked upon Talmudical subjects in a truly scholarly way. He suggests that the name Essaios, or Essene, probably denotes *secret* or *mystic*, as the Hebrew word *chshai*, *secret* or *silent*, would naturally be transliterated *Essaios*. There is an Egyptian word *Kashai*, secret.

The principal modern writers in England upon the Essenes are Bishop Lightfoot, (in his edition of the Epistle to the Colossians), Professor Westcott, and Dr. Ginsburg. There are a host of Germans, and a number of Hebrews.

Only one of these mentions the fact, which to the ordinary intelligence seems too obvious to be altogether overlooked in the keen hunt after etymologies, that whereas the Essenes are first heard of about a century and a half before our era, there were priests in the then ancient temple of Ephesus who bore the same name.[*] This was probably the case at a much

---

[*] Lightfoot, in a foot-note (the "Colossian Heresy," p. 96), states that he regards it as an "accidental coincidence" that there were priests of the Ephesian Artemis bearing the name of Essene.

earlier date than that at which we first hear of the Jewish order, for the word itself is provably more ancient than the probable date of origin—as opposed to the vague "thousands of years" of tradition—of the Palestinian Essenes.

All the more for the strange neglect of the authorities, we are bound to trace out the Greek word Essēn.

The following is from a poem dating about two centuries and a half before our era: "It was not the lots, but deeds done by hands, that made thee president (essēna, from essēn) of the gods—thy force and might, which thou didst set close by thy throne" (Callimachus, "To Zeus," 66).

The connection may seem so remote between "essene," a president deity, and "the Essenes," a set of mystics in Palestine, as to lead to the suspicion that the resemblance between the words is accidental. It is to be remembered, however, that Callimachus wrote in Egypt, where the king was also the high priest, and that the hymn contains probably an oblique compliment to the monarch of the time, Ptolemy Philadelphus, the poet's patron, who reigned during the former half of the third century before our era.

The signification of president or king, attaching to the early use of the word Essene, favours rather than otherwise the probability of its being the designation of priestly celebrants. The crown was originally the ensign of divinity; the chief priest and king were one. We have the Latin expressions Rex Sacrificulus, Rex Sacrorum, while an official styled Basileus, or king, presided in the Eleusinian Mysteries.

In a fragment ascribed to Callimachus we find the expression "Essene of Myrmidons," where the latter term is considered to mean colonizer. The Myrmidons were fabled to have been originally ants, from a similarity in the names in Greek, and to have had no retreat but dens and cavities of trees, until Æakos, a son of Zeus, besought their metamorphosis to people his devastated kingdom, brought them together, and settled them. A colonizing sovereign of this kind may seem to have more likeness to a queen bee than to a Palestinian mystic, and the resemblance between the words may appear to be merely fortuitous. But at the time when Callimachus was writing his hymns, and long before and after, there was a celebrated temple a few hundred miles to the north, across the sea from Alexandria, where he lived. This was the oracular shrine of Artemis, the great Diana of the Ephesians, a deity of Egyptian origin, and symbolical of the maternity of nature.

Pausanias, a traveller of the middle of the second century of our era, in the latter part of the following passage, speaks of the president of the sanctuary of this very temple :—

"In the region of the Orchomenians, in a shelving part of the mountain, is a temple of Artemis Hymnia. . . . For priestess and priest it is ordained that they shall lead a chaste and pure life, not only so far as relates to sex, but in all other respects, and this for as long as they live. They are, moreover, prohibited from taking baths or food in common with the multitude, and from entering into the house of any private individual.

"The identical discipline I know is followed for a twelvemonth, extending to the festal days, by those who succeed to the presidency of the altar of Artemis at Ephesus, and are called by the citizens Essenes. They hold a yearly festival in honour of Artemis Hymnia" (viii. 13. 1).

The expression of Pausanias is peculiar, that it was by the citizens, as if implying that it was by the citizens only, that the presiding priests were called Essenes. There is another name, Megabyzi, regarded as of Persian origin, by which the priests of Artemis were known.

A certain resemblance is now manifest between the ascetic priest-president Essene at Ephesus, and the solemn ascetic Essene of Syria.

The seclusion and bodily fastidiousness of the Ephesian Essene betoken a preparation for unearthly rites ; the Palestinian Essenes took similar precautions of purification, and went more deeply into the supernatural than any other Jewish sect.

These customs recall the observances of the modern Indian adept, which are carried to the degree of refusing to shake hands with persons not in a state of discipline, on the ground of sensitiveness to disturbance arising from an unsanctified animal magnetism.

The Greek word "Essēn" has been the subject of so many unsatisfactory speculations upon its root, that it has been wisely concluded to regard it as of foreign origin. In later Greek (in Origen, for instance) the word is found signifying the queen-bee. A strong probability that the Ephesians were acquainted with this meaning of the word arises from the fact that the priestesses of the same deity Diana, as well as those of Demeter, of Cybele, and of the oracle of Delphi, bore the name of *Melissa*, or bee. This term was also applied to poets, from their culling the beauties of nature, and in the symbolism of the Neo-platonists to any pure chaste being, and also to the moon. The nimbus behind the head of the Ephesian Artemis represents the moon.

How such a term as that of queen-bee came to be applied to the priests of Diana it may be difficult to determine. But the queen-bee is an example of fertility, and so might be an emblem of the goddess whose statues represent her as many-breasted. On the sides or robe, moreover, of the image of Artemis are sculptured bees and flowers.* Metaphors rise in the mind as readily now as they did to the

* The statue of the goddess in the Room of the Doves of the Museo Capitolino at Rome, visited whilst this essay was in progress, shows on its sides, not groups of bees, but single bees of large size, and of the form of a queen. On a like figure, however, in the Museo Torlonia, the reliefs show the rounder form of ordinary working bees. And the same is the case with the larger effigy in the Palazzo dei Conservatori, a noble form of ripe womanhood, bearing in addition to the symbols of Nature's exuberance, winged female forms full of life and motion, and suggestive of something beyond terrestrial Nature. These figures are in fine bas-relief just below the neck of the goddess, while the bees are on her sides. Great was Diana of the Ephesians.

ancient priests, and with the symbol of the queen-bee we may associate many of the notions we have seen attaching to the word Essene, that of a president over lesser beings or companions of the same class, a leader of colonies, a personage of a mysterious seclusion.

It may be that the word Essene derives its roots from a source antecedent to the time when it became used to denote a queen-bee. Diana herself is Isis of Egypt (*aset*). Isa means woman, or the female principle. Essa, a rare Greek word, and regarded as of foreign extraction, means woman also. So does Isshah (Gen. ii. 23). Mylitta, again, is the Assyrian and Sidonian Venus, the universal mother Isis, the child-bearing virgin, under another name.

History tells us that there were celibate priests in Ephesus, and celibate priests in Palestine at the same period, each bearing the same title of Essene: it may be that the fact is a mere coincidence, but the closer the coincidence, the more improbable it becomes that it is a mere coincidence.

A necessary step, however, is to trace the connection between Asia Minor and Palestine, not in the first century of our era, when it is made sufficiently manifest by wandering apostles, but in the third and second centuries before.

The conquests of Alexander the Great carved new roads through the old world. Seleucus, one of his captains, received Babylonia as his province, and made himself master of Media and Syria, founding Greek cities and colonies in different parts of his empire, and sowing luxurious Asia with life. Four principal ones of these cities were called the sister cities, Antioch, his capital Seleucia, near Babylon, Laodicea, and Apamea. The southern provinces of the Syrian empire were Phœnicia and Palestine. After the victory of Issos, or Ipsos, 301 B.C., Selucus obtained dominion over the greater part of Asia Minor, and twenty years later acquired the remaining portion.

Between his death (280 B.C.) and the accession to the

throne of his great-great-grandson's brother, Antiochus the Great, about fifty-five years elapsed. During this period the provinces beyond the Euphrates were lost, and an alliance was broken and again restored between the Seleucidæ and the Ptolemies, the Macedonian monarchs of Egypt, southern Syria changing hands more than once.

The dynasty was a prosperous one, and even the Jews followed the date of its establishment, 312 B.C., as a chronological landmark for many centuries—the Era of Contracts, or the Era of Kings.

The age, it has been pointed out, "displayed remarkable tendencies to religious fusion everywhere; insomuch that—if, with Josephus, we may trust to the letter in the First Book of Maccabees (xii. 21*)—even the Lacedæmonians put in the claim to be regarded as children of Abraham" (F. W. Newman).

If so strong a tendency to fraternize existed on the one side, we may reasonably suppose that the Jews themselves, on the other, were not exempted from foreign influences. Just as Judaism was largely coloured by Zoroastrian influences due to the Babylonian captivity, so now were the Jews subjected to a Greek power ruling over the Babylonians as well as over the cultivated Ionian states and other provinces of Asia Minor.

The magnificent Temple of Diana, reared in place of a still older one by the contributions of all the Greek cities of Asia Minor, was in great part destroyed by fire on the night of the nativity of Alexander the Great: a fact which possibly gave rise to the Hebrew superstition,—"On the day of the birth of the infant [the Messiah], the Temple of Jerusalem is destroyed" (Talmud, Jer., ch. ii. 4 [3]). The Ephesian Temple, restored by the co-operation of all the Ionian states,

---

* There is a touching simplicity in the form of the statement: "It is found in Scripture respecting the Spartans and Jews, that they are brethren, and that they are of the stock of Abraham."

was for centuries the architectural and artistic triumph of the world.

In this sanctuary, the repository of the arts and sciences, adorned by columns of marble, carved and polished work in cypress, cedar, and vine, frescoes by painters whose names are still household words, sculptures, embroideries, wrought work in silver and gold ; the flower of pagan worship was protected for ages, secure through times of conquest and periods of revolution. This was the principal shrine of a naturalistic cult which derived its religious symbolism primarily from Egypt, and hid truths of nature in forms that, to the uninitiated, seemed idolatrous.

Such an illustrious edifice and establishment could not but have been impressive to the mind of surrounding kings and peoples. Whether the rigorous discipline and mystic doctrines of the priests had any secret influence, or not, upon the minds of the Jews, originating Essenism, Therapeutism and the Kabala, the example at least was not far to seek. And it may be remembered that, notwithstanding their outcry against idolatry, even Christian churches were not too proud to appropriate the jasper columns and sacred adornments of the Temple of Diana at second-hand.

Antiochus the Great lost Cœle-Syria and Palestine to Ptolemy Philopator, and the country of the Jews became the borderland between two great empires, represented by the "king of the north" and "king of the south" of the eleventh chapter of Daniel. Importance and danger alike followed their position of a dividing line between two empires, one result of which was that Antiochus Epiphanes, the son of Antiochus the Great, destroyed Jerusalem, and proposed to himself to extirpate those canny Jews who knew so well how to make the most out of the rival governments. His cruelties led to the Jewish revolt under the Maccabees, under whose rule we first hear of the Palestinian Essenes.

A strong bond was established between Judea and Egypt

by the peopling of Alexandria by Jews under Ptolemy Lagus about 320 B.C. This led to the translation of the Hebrew Scriptures into Greek during the next reign, that of Ptolemy Philadelphus, who has already been referred to as the patron of the poet Callimachus.

There were probably many links formed in a similar way between peoples and peoples of Syria and Asia Minor during the dynasty of the Seleucidæ; a formal connection between the Jews and the west of Asia Minor was instituted by the transfer, as the tradition relates (Joseph. Antiq., XII. 3, § 4), of two thousand families of Jews of Mesopotamia and Babylonia, with all their goods, into Lydia and Phrygia. Ephesus was the capital of Lydia, and direct contact between Ephesians and Jews is thus shown to have been established about two centuries before our era.

When left master of southern Syria, 198 B.C., Antiochus heaped honours upon the Jews and Jerusalem. With such seductive influences at work, importations of thought and customs from one part to another of the dominions of Antiochus might not be unpopular; and at a later and more distinctly national period, when foreign importations met with suspicion and opposition from a patriotically aroused Judaism, the Essene tinge may already have passed unnoticed into the sacred garment of one section of Hebrew religionists.

The Essenes show a singular combination of attraction and repulsion to the law, of which the Pharisees reverenced the most minute letter.

When mortals go as deep into an unearthly condition as was the object of the Essenes, they lose nationality to a large extent. Once started on a purely mystic track, they would support themselves equally well upon Pythagorean, Persian, Lydian, or Hebrew traditions.

Moreover, when we see what a readiness for new heresy there was, in the period immediately succeeding that of which we are treating, in Asia Minor, Greece, Palestine, Alexandria, and Rome, how rapidly some of the Christian Apostles made converts, how many names foreign to its birthplace became very early interwoven with the history of Christianity, we ought not to marvel if Palestine itself were affected by foreign thought a century or two before.

Our subject now divides itself into two heads, the investigation of the differences between Essenism and Pharisaism and of the resemblances between Essenism and the religion of the primitive followers of Jesus.

The Essenes paid adoration to the sun as a symbol of life, and even as possessed of life, as it were a mediate God, conveying to man the blessings of the Supreme Being. So much may be drawn from the account of Josephus, which receives support from the name Sempsæans given to the Essenes by Epiphanius. The probable derivation of this word is the Hebrew *shamash*, the sun. On the Moabite stone the sun appears as the national deity of Moab, under the name Chemosh.

The Essenes reject the sacrificial rites of Judaism, and, in raising the idea of sacrifice to a higher plane, are at one with the Hebrew prophetic school,* and with the teachings of Jesus. They read their sacred books in a symbolic sense, as indeed did certain of the Pharisees, but they add mystic doctrines, communicable only orally and through the portals of a severe and protracted initiation.

The Rabbis clearly demarcate the world that is, and the world to come, the present and the future aeon; the Essenes apparently strive to merge natural in spiritual life, making of work a religious recreation, of every meal a sacrament, of every one of their order a brother.

---

* "I desire kindness, and not sacrifice; and the knowledge of God more than burnt offerings" (Hos. vi. 6).

"Wherewith shall I come before the Lord? . . . Will the Lord be pleased with thousands of rams, with ten thousands of rivers of oil? . . . He hath shewn thee, O man, what is good; and what doth the Lord require of thee, but to do justly, and to love mercy, and to walk humbly with thy God?" (Mic. vi. 6-8).

They are communists, and hold aloof from cities, traffic, slave-owning, ambition, weapons of offence, and oaths. They are all, or a portion of them, ascetic celibates. They are priests by mutual service, and have no hierarchy, or temple-worship. In other respects much of the Essene system seems to have been a kind of Pharisaism, heightened in some respects, exaggerated in others. Attempts have been made to draw a parallel between the Essenes and the Pythagoreans; but while they resemble each other in their aim after purity of life, inviolability of doctrine, and symbolic pursuit, each community is characterized by a markedly distinct tone. The Essenes are as much like the Aryan Mages, who wore white garments, eschewed ornament, practised baptism, were mystic ascetics, and believers in angels. But because they have some points in common, we might just as rightly identify them with Nazirites as with either Pythagoreans or Zoroastrians.

Of resemblance between Essenism and the doctrines and practices of the early followers of Jesus, we may briefly note the more obvious examples.

The cheerful confidence in God, the love of peace, the unselfish life, the communism, the simplicity, the acceptance for order's sake of the law of the land and its administrators, combined with contempt for worldly dignities and disdain of personal aggrandisement, the love of one another, the tenderness towards children, to the weak, the sick, the aged, and the distressed, the regard of death as a culmination, not as a calamity, the belief in angels, the love of purity and solitude as enabling the powers of the spirit to recreate and display themselves, the avoidance of oaths, the doctrine that great truths are not welcome and therefore not beneficial to unprepared persons; these are rare attributes, but common to the Essenes and the immediate followers of Jesus.

It has been affirmed that in Essenism there are no traces of the *essential* doctrines of Christianity (by which no doubt is meant the doctrinal extension as opposed to the primitive simplicity), and the Christian sacraments are specially instanced as examples.

It is open to question whether the sacrament of the supper is not a crystallization of an Essene practice. The order remarkably diverged from Judaism in its attitude towards the sacrificial idea. Instead of offering victims they instituted a common table, regarded their refectory as a sanctuary,* and, vowed their lives and minds as a sacrifice. Jesus instituted a supper and a simple ceremonial as a common bond of brotherhood and mutual service. Taking bread as a symbol, he says, "This is my body which is given for you; do this in remembrance of me." If we follow the disciples into the supper-room, made desolate by the vacant place of the Master, how must we suppose they would understand the injunction, "Do this"? Would each one say as he broke the bread, "This is his body which was given for us," or, "This is my body which is given for you"? Is it not possible that the latter would be more truly in the spirit of their training than the former? When Jesus washes the feet of his disciples, a fact which, no doubt, had a symbolical meaning, it is to lead to the injunction, "Ye ought also to wash one another's feet." Again we find, "This is my commandment, that ye love one another as I loved you. Greater love has no one than this, that a man devote his life (soul) for his friends." The spirit of the words is plain: the example of Jesus was one to be followed, not in word but in deed, by those who vowed themselves to adopt his discipline.

The same heightened conception of sacrifice is introduced into the Septuagint version, where it differs from the original Hebrew (Ps. xl. 6): "Sacrifice and oblation thou wouldest not, but *a body hast thou prepared me;* whole burnt offering and

---

* "R. Johanan and R. Elieser both say, So long as the Temple existed, the altar atoned for Israel; now it is man's table which atones for his sins" (Talm. Bab., Berach. 55 a).

sacrifice for sin thou didst not require." The Hebrew text gives here the expression, "Mine ears hast thou pierced." If a bondservant did not choose to go free at the expiration of his period of servitude, the master was required to make a public notification of the fact, and to go through the ceremony of taking an awl and passing it through the servant's ear (through the hole for the ear-ring, it has been suggested), so as to fasten him to the door-post, in sign of his being thenceforth a servant in perpetuity. The symbol is therefore one of voluntary consecration to a perpetual service.

The same spirit fills the apostolic exhortation to the brethren to present their bodies "a living sacrifice," not *perinde ac cadaver*, but living; not sentimental or merely by way of memorial, but real. If this view be the true one, the sacrament of the supper affords the closest resemblance to be found between the doctrine of the Essenes and of the "sons of the prophets," and the teachings of Jesus.

There is a view of fasting to be found in the Talmud, which comes one small step towards the meaning of the symbols of the Supper (Matt. xxvi. 26). It is to be found in a fast-day prayer :—

"Lord of the Universe! Thou knowest that when the Temple existed, the man that sinned brought a sacrifice, and though only the fat and blood thereof were offered, yet he was forgiven. Now that I fast, and my own fat and blood are diminished, let it please thee to accept this sacrifice of my fat and blood, as if offered upon thine altar; and be merciful unto me" (Talmud of Babylon, Berachoth, 17 a).

It was the body and mind and soul, with all their forces, and not merely the fat and blood, that were placed on the altar in the bond of the brotherhood of Jesus.

What deduction do we make from these resemblances— that Jesus was an Essene? By no means. But is there any improbability in his having been brought up and educated among members of the order? While retaining such elements of their manner of life as were spiritual and noble, as much of it was, he would have transcended their straitened discipline and minute ceremonial observances, as naturally as an eagle, placed among brushwood like a blackbird, would escape to the mountains and the sky.

There is a fact unaccounted for, which this theory would explain; that "the prophet, Jesus, from Nazareth," was acknowledged by the Jerusalemite party to possess "literary knowledge," the Rabbi's appanage, while, as they alleged, he had never learned;—that is to say in their schools.

The argument, commonly advanced, that Jesus belonged to the Essenes because he never denounced them, seems to be a weak one. There were doubtless other sects or orders besides Pharisees and Sadducees;— Karaites, Hellenists, Zealots. Jesus says no word against the school of Hillel, who came from Babylon, or against that of the Jews of Alexandria, and yet he must have come in contact with the disciples of the one and pilgrims from the other.

The Essenes constituted a small heresy; a few silent sages, meeting probably with little notice from the powerful, who were content so long as the mystical sheep of the fold were harmless, and kept to their principles of non-interference with earthly authority. The greater part of the life of Jesus himself, for all the blaze that has been thrown upon it, is exceedingly obscure. The political priests of Jerusalem would pass by on the other side any such persons, so long as they did not obtrude themselves upon the domain of the Judaic orthodoxy by stirring up the people.

There are as many differences as resemblances between the Essene tenets and the teachings of Jesus.

Jesus rejected the Sabbath when made a burden, and gave good scriptural authority, Rabbi-fashion, for abrogating it for a good purpose. He scorned to consider himself defiled because his hands had not been washed after a prescribed formal fashion, or because he sat next a person of inferior purity. If fasting was the right course, he taught that one should begin the fast with anointed head as cheerfully as a feast, and without the face being strained into a solemn expression. He respected good motives more than the most slavish obedience to ordinances; he offered his cup freely to all that could make themselves strong enough to drink it.

Jesus was wont to argue, not only in a sublime and generous manner of his own, but also in the subtle manner with which the doctors of the law were conversant. He used the forms of the time, and perhaps would else have been unintelligible, but his own splendid power shines through. He could not long have remained in any sect, and the Essenes, for all their spirituality and fraternity, were a narrow and prejudiced sect, while he manifests the broad unsectarian impress of heaven. The Essenes appear to have possessed thaumaturgic powers; so did Jesus, but he seems to have exercised them reluctantly, for fear lest the crowd should follow him for his marvels rather than for his truths. There seems nothing to make it improbable that Jesus was brought up among Essene priests; there is nothing to make it probable that he remained an Essene, or addicted to any sect whatever.

DID JESUS KNOW GREEK?

IF we suppose the existence of supremely wise persons in the huge planet Jupiter, and that one of them, in the midst of a burst of eloquence, were to be transported instantaneously and unconsciously to earth and placed upon one of our platforms to proceed with his speech, what effect would he be likely to produce upon his new listeners? His mien might be majestic, his gestures might surpass in grace and emphasis those of our own orators; his voice might be of stirring music, his eyes of inspiring fire; he might impress us with an indefinable feeling of awe and admiration; he might even sway us by the influence of his mighty and magnetic presence, but we should be unable to understand a single one of his words. And if we succeeded in mastering his vocabulary, we should in all likelihood find that for a large proportion of his words we had no corresponding ideas. And should we strive, further, to catch the drift of his metaphors and figures of speech (such as we derive in our most ordinary conversation from the host of natural objects and their combinations, either actually or imaginatively present), we should be still more at a loss. His comparisons would be meaningless to us, for lack of any idea on our part of the objects from which they were drawn. We could not possibly reach to any satisfactory appreciation of him, and probably some of us would laugh at the ignorance he, on his part, would show of our conventions, and decry his assumption in addressing us in the guise of a teacher. Was he burdened with some message he was bound to convey to us, he would have to adapt his large and jovial * actions to our terrestrial habits and customs; he would have to laboriously learn the use and meaning of everything by which we are surrounded, and to acquire our language word by word. More than that, he would have to study the modes of thought familiar to us, and how to see things from our points of view; or he would be so terribly original and bizarre that he would shock or startle the weaker minds amongst us, and puzzle our profoundest with sudden and unexpected novelties. And unless he sojourned with us some little while to gain experience of our various needs, of our hopes and fears, our peculiar prejudices and our nobler aspirations, his words would be no more to us than a curiosity: to be seriously addressed we must first be understood. So much for a messenger from another world situated in the same physical plane as ours.

Let us now take up a more difficult hypothesis. We will suppose (in spite of the materialists) that there exists a state of life relative to ours, yet in such a way that its local habitation is not visible to the naked eye, or even by a telescope; a state towards which, in purblind half-awakened fashion, human beings turn with longings; as a dull reader, having a book which he cannot grasp the intention of, while yet he is conscious from time to time of something significant in it, regards it in a way at once sulky, dissatisfied, half-contemptuous, and yet inwardly curious and doubtful. Let us imagine this state to compare with ours as ideal common-sense with bungling misapprehension, as orderly freedom with political semi-chaos. Let us imagine that in this state the province of the individual is so enlarged that his immediate life and surroundings are his own direct outcome, representing the beautiful or terrible truth of himself. This state, which may be called spiritual or ideal, actual or Utopian (if indeed it would

---

* The word "jovial" must be used in the limited sense. It must be difficult to be jovial, in the ordinary sense of the word, at a distance from the sun five times as great as ours.

not be too purgatorial to be called Utopian), we may draw into comparison with that in which we at present dwell, a state muffled (for kindliness to our too sensitive weaknesses) with the veil of the flesh. A state containing many refuges of unrealities, hiding-places of comfort and consolation, coverings of conceit, huge Caliban forms that we hug and fondle. A state or condition with surroundings that insure to us the comparative repose of only a partial responsibility, wherein we are enshrouded from the fierce light that beats about the inner throne of Spirit by wrappages that are not our own ; that is to say, by habits of physical or intellectual inheritance. Outside of our personality we are surrounded by vast elemental coverings from whose dull but kindly thrall we rarely enfranchise ourselves. For we are blind to our native powers, or afraid to know them, lingering by preference in an easier, if more cloudy condition of life.

Let us imagine the sweet and sorrowful prison-house of earth to have become more dull than its wont, its human denizens to have entered into a state too much shrouded from the regions of light for the secret commune known as, or resulting in, inspiration, aspiration, intuition, poetry, revelation, prophecy, to be possible. Let us picture a world assured in worldliness, the generality of individuals wrapped in petty selfishness as in a cloud. What then? Why, the steps of the ladder of light have become a vanishing dream ; the inner ear, that caught the whisper of angels as they passed along, is closed ; for men have the power to close or open as they will, since the citadel of their individuality is their own to keep. This being the state of things, and the people unconsciously deteriorating within it, as is sometimes the case, even with the calmest and most profound ethical teachers among them, high Nature's loving laws must evidently include some new development or fail from inadequacy.

We can imagine only three broad reasons for a human individual being born on earth. We will roughly mark them out, touching as little as possible upon the deeper aspects of birth in a material world. One is pleasure, delight, enjoyment of external activities; which is the main life of nature, and without which human life is unhealthy. Another reason for birth would go further, and include something purgatorial, preparatory, educational. It would comprise the gaining of experience, the growth of strength, the correction of special weaknesses, or the expiation of faults. A third is temporary surrender of a more advanced personal life elsewhere in order to benefit younger brothers here. Sense-life and pleasure; probation and growth; mission and volunteership. There may be interminglings between the classes, and the intermediate one is imperfect without something from both the others; but they are radically distinct; and in their separateness may be represented by animals, men, angels; consciousness, humanity, spirit :—imaginatively only, of course, and by permission of the materialists.

When earth grows dullest, then surely it most requires the brightest teachers.

We are imagining the earth to be very dull, and we have premised that the inward voice man has the power to shut out.

If, then, the greatest archangel from the imagined realms of light were sent on a mission to earth, he could only approach us in two ways.

He could impress such of us as might have any susceptible soul; a poet here and there, or an earnest thinker might feel a strange glow in his heart, and a new power and fire in his upflowing thought. The literature of the day would bear unwonted marks of heightened spirituality, which might enrage the materialists as an outburst of moonshine unamenable to logic, and be voted meaningless and wanton because unprovable, self-condemned as the mere dogmatic assertion of imaginative ecstatics.

The other way of approach to us would be that of our

giant from Jupiter; the angel would have to take lips of flesh and descend to our language by learning our childish speech and our worldly ways. And it would be very difficult for him to reduce his large area of vision, and its exposition in speech, to our customary standards, without assuming one of our hereditary bodies, to do which he would have to take the trouble to be born. Without intellectual training, and the possession of the measure of the habit of our minds, he might indeed communicate as it were by music, might make us conscious of strange and fascinating splendour, might exhale love like perfume, and awe by majestic presence. But if he set in order the grand machinery of the intellect, then indeed, and without losing his more mystic powers, he would be able to speak to us face to face, and in plain speech. We can deaden the heart's voice, we can stifle conscience, we can chill or beat down love, we can be deaf to the inward monitor; but eloquence will win over a mob, and strong reasons appeal to a curmudgeon. The visitor would be able to arrest attention by his commanding speech, to win open-hearted men by his sublime utterances, to hurl words like the sound of an awakening trumpet to those well-nigh buried in the external senses, and to charm or dismay with the example of a fearless and noble life. His presence and influence would come home to us, and he would be an undoubted perplexity and power amongst us, apparently with little effort. A number of quite orthodox and respectable persons, jealous of his influence, made ashamed by his terrible truths, or afraid of his fearlessness, would protest against him as a disturbance; he would become the bane of the officials of autocratic governments, and might be sent to prison. But he would be heard first, and not forgotten afterwards.

A man of a simple habit, but singular splendour, was living on earth near a score centuries ago, born, as was understood, of parents of moderate station, and of pure blood. He had some unusual notions about himself, and even said, not in an arrogant way, but as if he believed he was speaking the truth, that he had come from another plane, and was not staying here for more than a little while, but was going back again. He seemed never to forget, or to lose the presence of that other world, but to have it close to him always, not by any effort of piety, but as a bright and manifest fact.

He entered into no worldly schemes, but when about thirty, or the age when a man was thought to be a man, he left off making ploughs and yokes, the exercise of which craft had in all probability accompanied his studies; and went about the country wherein he was born, as the old national prophets before him, and somewhat more busily than the rabbis of his day. He did more, however, than teaching or expounding, for he found time and strength to cure a number of shattered persons wherever he went, and showed a special gift in the field of healing, and in divers other provinces of which our present men of science have but small knowledge. He seemed to be embodied health and communicative of healthfulness. He made little show or appearance, seeming not to care for grandeur or position, or such greatness as magnates know; and he was a man of few requirements, being content with only one dish at a supper, and ready to go with none. He was ever brimming over with kindliness in his manners, and ready to do anything for any one that needed it. He had a way of speaking out when indignation was called for, and some people are afraid of hearing the truth, and as they are stirred up, get angry. The Rabbis generally were puzzled by him, for he was one of themselves in knowledge, and yet too large for their rules. Whenever they tried to overthrow him in argument, a pursuit in which the learned schools of the time were much accomplished, he had a way of coming off best, and overthrowing them in a manner painful to their pride, and suggestive that they had not studied the Sacred Law in its highest spirit. He showed a knowledge of the dialectical discussions of the time, and of the Scriptures on which they were founded, equal to that of the most reverend and cultivated doctor.

Considering the interest that attaches to him, it is strange that more attention has not been paid to his surroundings and to the probable circumstances of his early life and training. Whether he came from Jupiter or from an unseen world, terrestrial education, we have argued, would be an indispensable preliminary to a useful career. It seems—and it is perhaps indeed not unnatural that it should be so—as if conclusions were formed about him on different rules from those current in respect of ordinary men. And those conclusions, however inadequate their foundations, have been generally regarded as infallible. A modern reaction has led into the other extreme, and one, in whose path many follow, with strange lack of insight alludes to him as being an amiable country youth of but scant culture, and showing unmistakable evidences of provincial narrowness and lack of experience. If he had the narrowness of absorption in a single purpose, we do not on that account undervalue conspicuous genius in music, in art, in poetry, or in philosophy. Furthermore, we find him at least a match, alike in rhetoric, epigram, and acquired knowledge, for the masters amongst a race well trained in learned argument; and, furthermore, he has been able to attract to him, in one way or another, both during his life and afterwards, the widest intellects as well as the largest hearts of the world. Moreover, which is the wider vision, that of two worlds at once, or that of the most cosmopolitan critic of a single sphere?

In his enthusiasm for the great language of culture, Mr. Gladstone is reported to have said, at a dinner party, that it would add to his happiness if he could prove that Jesus spoke Greek. It is unlikely that the Master ordinarily spoke Greek, or that his sayings in the form they are handed down to us are his *ipsissima verba*. He would naturally converse in the best-known language of his locality, which was Chaldee. In this rude Hebraic tongue were no doubt framed the original *logia* of Matthew.

But the question we would discuss is not whether he discoursed in a tongue that was not the vernacular, but whether he knew, sufficiently to read or speak it, a language that was too familiar to be regarded as alien in the country where he dwelt.

Many persons seem averse from considering the question whether Jesus received any scholastic education. Some, perhaps, take it for granted, without proper grounds, that he had no definite intellectual training at all.

Why should he never have been a student, nay, a diligent student; and with fair and full opportunities of learning open to him? He was experienced in the modes of thought of his time; we have expressed an opinion on the somewhat difficult question of the power of the most sublime stranger to use serviceable speech to men without knowing something of the traditional style in which they are wont to be approached. Why should not Jesus have been a student, whether of Hebrew or Hebraic, of Greek, or of Egyptian? There is no apparent impropriety in the idea, and yet when a dozen years ago we first conceived it, and wrote to a learned acquaintance that we were engaged in a research upon the literary or philosophic studies to which Jesus might have had access, he replied, in harmony with what no doubt until recently has been the prevailing opinion, "There seem to be few signs, if any, of Jesus's having been influenced by Greek literature; and the fact that Greek learning was eschewed by his contemporaries adds to the unlikelihood of his having been thus influenced. There seems to be no sort of clue to his history, until he appears on the stage for so short a time."

Was the Master never a disciple? Did the labour and struggle of earth bequeath to him in his natural life no heritage? These questions are such that in every case but this one it would be supererogatory to put them, the answers are so obvious.

Every Jewish Rabbi is described as the son of another Rabbi; the teacher is regarded as the spiritual father of the taught. Diogenes Laertius says of Carneades, "He studied all the books of the Stoics, especially those of Chrysippus ... and used to say, If Chrysippus had not lived, I should never have existed."

"Ben Zoma said, Who is wise? He that learns from every man; For it is said, from all my teachers I gat understanding (Ps. cxix. 99)." (Talmud, Mishna, P. Aboth, iv. 1.)

Every disciple "who receives upon him the yoke of Thorah," or "the yoke of the kingdom of heaven," is, according to the Talmud, freed from "the yoke of royalty and the yoke of worldly care" (P. Aboth, iii. 8). He is, as it were, born again: "Whosoever becomes a proselyte is like a little child just born" (Jalq. Rub., f. 70, 4).* The word regeneration, alike with Jew and Gentile, represents initiation. We can thus understand in what a profound sense the teacher was regarded as the father of the disciple, who was born again by his ministration.† Appuleius, a priest, writer, and great traveller of the second century, calls the day of initiation the *sacred birthday*, and the priest by whom he was initiated he calls his *father*. A manumitted slave counted his birth from the day of his freedom; a king's birthday was the day he came to his throne. Aristotle, "when asked how much

---

* "Except ye become as little children, ye shall in no wise enter the kingdom of heaven. . . . Whoso shall receive one such little child in my name receiveth me" (Matt. xviii. 3, 5).

"Whosoever shall not receive the kingdom of God as a little child, he shall in no wise enter therein" (Mark x. 15).

"That which is born of the flesh is flesh; and that which is born of the spirit is spirit. . . . Ye must be born anew [or, from above]" (John iii. 6.)

† Cf. also—"Of him, who gives natural birth, and him, who gives knowledge of the whole Veda, the giver of sacred knowledge is the more venerable father; since the second, or divine, birth insures life to the twice-born both in this world and hereafter eternally" (Inst. Menu, ii. 146).

educated men were superior to the uneducated, replied, As much as the living are to the dead " (Diog. Laert., v. xi.).

A reference to the baptism of proselytes will illustrate this point more fully: " It was not until he had been baptized that the convert was fully received. According to the Rabbins, baptism was even more essential than circumcision. The ceremony was performed after the healing of the wound caused by the circumcision, in the presence of three persons who had acted as the instructors of the convert, and were regarded as not only witnesses for his baptism, but, with reference to the idea of a new birth therewith connected, as his fathers. Having stripped himself, cut his hair, and pared the nails on his hands and feet, he went into the water up to the arms; the laws were then read to him, and having promised to obey them, he immersed himself wholly " (Alexander, quoting from Maimonides, Hilc. Issur., c. 13, 1, 4, 5).

Elisha addresses Elijah, " My father, my father," and asks of his spiritual parent, " Let a double portion of thy spirit be upon me;" the symbol being derived from the law of inheritance (Deut. xxi. 17) by which the firstborn son had a right to claim a double portion of his father's possessions.

Clement of Alexandria says, " It is a good thing, I reckon, to leave to posterity good children. This is the case with children of our bodies. But words are the progeny of the soul. Hence we call those that have instructed us, *Fathers*." Who in this special sense were the Fathers of Jesus? At whose feet did the boy sit? In what "sacred vineyard" or school? Over what roll of a book did the young man earnestly bend? He learned at his mother's knee, and his books were the Prophets and the Psalms;—such is the ready reply that rises to the lips. Too ready, indeed, it seems in presence of the fact that in his day the language of the Scriptures, with the exception of certain portions of the books of Ezra and Daniel, and a number of writings not included in the canon, was a dead language. The ancient Hebrew had then ceased to be the vernacular, it required a scholar to read it, and was unknown to the masses.

There is only one individual with whom, from the records that have come down to us, it is possible to associate Jesus in the relation of teacher and disciple. And the likelihood of this link is weakened by the existence of a legend which describes this person, a prophet who strove to place religion on a wider because more personal basis, as of about the same age as Jesus himself. An introduction to his principles and practice may, however, throw some light upon the question.

"At what epoch," asks the Talmud, "did the influence of *the merit of ancestors* cease? According to Rabbi Jochanan, at the time of Hezekiah; for it is said (Isai. ix. 6), Of the increase of his government and of peace there shall be no end, to the throne of David, and to his kingdom, to order it and to uphold it with judgment and with right. From henceforth, even for evermore, the zeal of the Eternal of hosts [Jehovah Tsebaoth] will accomplish this" (Talmud, Shabbath, 55 a).

In the spirit of this expansive ideal, Jochanan, the life-long Nazirite known under the name of John the Baptist, proclaims that it is no longer a passport into the kingdom of heaven to rely for merit upon the mere possession of Abraham as a father. The old tree of national preference has ceased to bear fruit, the axe is laid at its roots. Conversion is personal; on this condition, the kingdom of heaven is close at hand for all. Children of Abraham, in a truer sense than the old, may be raised up from the stones of the riverside. From all the country of the Aber-ha-Yerden, as well as from Judea, candidates were flocking to this baptism of repentance. Baptism was not a novelty with the people; it was the hermit's earnest force that drew them.

This John is an historical character, and is described by Josephus as a good man and a preacher, offering to his converts a lustral rite, useful for bodily purity, and symbolic of a spiritual cleansing of the soul :—

"He was a good man and exhorted the Jews to practise virtue and live in righteousness one towards another and piety towards God, and so to engage in baptism : inasmuch as baptism was manifestly acceptable to Him, not if they used it as an excuse for any sins, but for the purity of the body, provided that the soul had been already cleansed by righteousness"* (Ant., XVII. v. 2).

At the hands of this eremite saint, Jesus is recorded to have received the initiatory rite of regeneration.

The different accounts of this baptism are conflicting. All the other candidates had been baptized, and after Jesus had submitted to the ceremony, there is a very hagadistic story of the descent of the Spirit of God upon him. In two Gospels it is stated that this illumination from heaven was visible to Jesus; in the third, a bodily vision, presumably visible to all present, is alleged to have manifested itself; in the fourth, it is the Baptist himself who is conscious of a spiritual presence, of which he had been forewarned, and by which he was instructed to recognize a baptist employing another symbol than water.

Now, these other symbols are worthy of attention, all the more that even in the Revised Version they are obscured by a mistranslation. In one Gospel the words are represented to have been said before the baptism, in another afterwards; but we must allow for the fact that no modern reporter was present.

---

* Josephus seems to be endeavouring here to meet such criticisms as the following upon the baptismal rite :—

"Ah, too easy folk, who deem that sad crimes of blood can be put off by the water of a stream" (Ovid, Fast., ii. 35).

"Once Diogenes saw a man purifying himself by washing, and said to him, Wretched man, do you not know that as you cannot wash away blunders in grammar by purification, you can no more efface the errors of a life by the same means" (Diog. Laert. Diog.).

References to the ancient baptismal ceremony may be found in Judith xii. 7, 8; Berachoth, Hier., f. 6. 3; Philo, Quod D. immut., § 2.

If we analyse closely the saying of John (addressed in *Luke* to a mixed people, including tax-collectors and soldiers; in *Matthew* to a number of Pharisees and Sadducees), we shall see that the symbols which replace the water of the first-named baptism are those of the corn-dresser or winnower.

A blast is produced by the motion of a winnowing fan; against this is flung the grain in its uncleansed state; or by another process it is thrown from a broad basket, the *mystica vannus Iacchi*,* against a strong wind; the pure grain falls upon the threshing floor, the chaff is scattered and blown aside, to be afterwards collected and burned, according to the usage of the period. The physical emblems of this baptism of the grain and destruction of comparatively useless husks, are the blast of air and the fire.

The ordinary translation confuses the metaphors and their interpretation. Let us try and translate as if we were by the side of the Jordan, and the Christian dogma had never existed.

"Whereas I immerse you in water unto repentance, he that is coming after † me is stronger than I, and his sandals I am not sufficient to bear; he will immerse you in a sacred wind and (in) fire: for his winnowing fan is in his hand, and he will thoroughly cleanse his threshing floor, and gather his wheat into the store, but he will burn down the chaff with an unextinguished fire" (Matt. iii. 11).

The whole imagery of the little parable is perfectly clear, and if we had one word more in the English language, the interpretation would be as easy to discover, as no doubt it was in the original.

The Hebrew word *rouach* and the Greek word *pneuma* mean, equally, breath, or wind, and spirit. The old English *gást*, spirit, is thought to be akin to *gust*, a stream of air, but we have no word in common use which represents them both.

---

* Servius (ad Georg., i. 166) explains Virgil's epithet as applied "because the sacred rites of Dionysos had reference to the purification of the soul, and men by his mysteries were purified, just as grain by fans."

† Literally, "behind," and, as being therefore *unseen*, typifying the future.

In such a case, therefore, the expressions must be literally translated from the Greek, and the second meaning must be left to the interpreter, as in the case of any other parable.

The precise terms found in the gospel, *pur* and *pneuma*, are in Plato representative of life: "The parts and members of the mortal animal were naturally connected, and the life corresponded with fire and breath " * (Tim., 77 a).

It is by no means impossible, on the hypothesis that Jesus or his teachers knew Greek, as many other Rabbis knew it, that this very phrase of Plato's was known to him or them. But the terms, though the same, are in different association in the gospel, and the metaphoric setting is purely Hebraic, and is evidently the work of a mind not unaccustomed to parabolic expression.

For the meaning of the second sense of the words, we must look to Hebrew sources. *Fire* might well represent *zeal*, as in the extract quoted above from Isaiah ix., and the following: " My zeal hath cut me off, because my adversaries have forgotten thy words " (Ps. cxix. 139). " The zeal of thine house hath eaten me up " (Ps. lxix. 9).

The *blast* of the winnowing fan may be understood in its other signification of *spirit* (divine activity, pervasive and searching as air), with a poetical sense quite familiar to the Jewish mind :—

> " Create in me a clean heart, O God ;
> And renew a steadfast spirit within me.
> Cast me not away from thy presence ;
> And take not thy *holy spirit* from me.
> Restore unto me the joy of thy salvation ;
> And uphold me with a willing spirit.
> Then will I teach transgressors thy way ;
> And sinners shall return unto thee " (Ps. li. 11).

This passage indeed, from beginning to end, seems fitted to be the hymn of a baptized disciple.

---

* "The breast and lungs, after dismissing the breath (*pneuma*) are again inflated by the entrance of the air " (Tim. 79 c).

The same images of zeal and inspiration, it may be remembered, are reported to have attended the Pentecostal revival: " there came from heaven a sound as of a rushing of a mighty wind . . . there appeared unto them tongues parting asunder, like as of fire."

Clement of Alexandria had not lost hold on the metaphoric meaning, though he substitutes individuals for qualities in his interpretation : " That we may be separated from the chaff, and stored up in the paternal garner. ' For the fan is in the Master's hand, by which the chaff, which ought to go to the fire, is separated from the wheat ' " (Pæd., i. ix.).

In another place (Strom., vii., ch. vi.) he interprets more closely, representing the symbol of fire as meaning " not the all-devouring vulgar fire," which destroys the chaff, " but the fire of wisdom,* which pervades the soul " as by a baptism.

Theodotus (Paris ed. of Clem. Alex., p. 804) reads the symbolism correctly, and interprets the chaff as the clogging husk of material environment : " The grain is separated from the chaff, that is to say, there is a separation from the vesture of matter by means of spirit. As the chaff is separated in being winnowed by the wind, so the spirit has a separative power."

The fire of wisdom and the spiritual life are here understood to be represented by the baptismal emblems of Jesus ; as was purity, following conversion, by the water baptism of John.

The primitive tradition, of which the Gospels are divergent elaborations—retrospective readings, under an enchantment of the mind, of imperfectly recorded events—may have been that John and Jesus had both passed through the Essene discipline, but at different schools ; that the former recognized the latter by his possession of conspicuous spiritual gifts, which a master who knew them both (" he that sent me to baptize

---

* " I will make my words in thy mouth fire " (Jer. v. 15).

" Warm thyself before the fire of the wise, but beware of their embers . . . all their words are as coals of fire " (Pirqe Aboth. ii. 14).

with water") had led him to anticipate he might one day find in a pupil from whom much was expected. Both apparently were started on a proselytizing career with the same gospel, "Convert ye, convert ye; the kingdom of heaven is near."

Withal there is a wide difference between them, for Jesus, like Sakya-muni, abandons asceticism, while John holds to it to the end. Perhaps the former, at an early stage of his career, had taken the limited Nazirite vows, which could be made binding for a specified time only. For Jesus, like John, is represented as having passed a certain time in hermit life in the desert, though the narrative is overlaid with fanciful stories which some have supposed to represent the symbolism of an initiation.

Analyse the scanty records how we will, there is no firmer historic basis than this, upon which we can found a conclusion as to the immediate "fathers" of Jesus.

We can only rely upon internal evidence in respect of the "divine thinking-school" from which were drawn the rudiments which he developed into so splendid a pearl.

To such paradoxes as the saying of Jesus that the least in the kingdom of God was greater than John, there may be yet found a solution in the curious hyperbolisms and *jeux d'esprit* of the Talmudists. Meanwhile we shall be on firmer ground if we endeavour to trace by what channels of language, and through what Hebrew or foreign traditions, thought at this period was passing.

As to the language of Jesus; before concluding that he was acquainted with the Greek philosophy which was making its way in the world in such a permeating stream, it is by no means necessary to suppose that he could express himself in Greek. He might have been able to do so, or he might have been able to write it, or he might have been able to read it only. Josephus could not pronounce Greek well, but wrote it, it is allowed, with singular purity.

In considering the question what literary culture was

likely to reach a carpenter's shop in an obscure village of Galilee, we have to realize the fact that speculation must needs submit to evidence. Jesus, like every one else that has entered this earth, shows a distinct and large indebtedness to the words and thoughts of his predecessors and fathers; the fact is clearly provable by a multiplicity of instances that may be adduced of the correspondence, parallelism, relativeness, or sympathetic connection between their words and thoughts and his.

It remains then only to show how Jesus could have become subject to such influences, or have commanded such culture, and on investigation it will be found that there is no difficulty in the explanation. The matter is simple in itself, and is complicated only by the habitual prejudgment of the many that the career of Jesus, outside the accepted records, which do not profess to be exhaustive histories, is hidden in a vague golden cloud, to pierce which is not only an impossibility, but a profane endeavour.

As Greek was the dominant language of the literature of his time, we may take as a centre of investigation the question, Did Jesus know Greek?

In 1875 the writer asked an opinion upon the question of the knowledge of Greek by Jesus, of a missionary of Oriental birth, who was studying in the library of the British Museum. For a second he pondered, while perhaps his thoughts tended in a practical direction. Then the sublime doctrines which he had been taught enlightened his understanding, and with an air of relief he replied: "He was God; he knew everything: he must have known Greek."

William Blake teaches us with fine suggestiveness :—

> " To see a world in a grain of sand,
> And a heaven in a wild flower,
> Hold Infinity in the palm of your hand,
> And Eternity in an hour."

But even with this pantheistic faith, we ought scarcely

to expect infinite detail to find lodging room in a finite brain. Though Jesus may have said, " My Father and I are one," and in the Egyptian Ritual, the Osiris, the disembodied spirit, was addressed as being one with the Deity of which he was the manifestation, yet such an ideal of essential unity by no means involves identity of infinite and finite faculties. What would the Chaldean Christian have replied to the question, Did Jesus know English? Logically, his reply, if affirmative in the one case, ought to be equally so in the other. We must try to treat the question in a more sober, if less devout, style.

For a period both preceding and subsequent to our era the Jewish people might thus be reckoned :—

An aristocratic but somewhat narrow and bigoted patriotic party at Jerusalem, striving to keep together the semblance of a nation that was in rags and tatters; intensifying an already more than sufficient tendency to exclusiveness, and yet inspired now and again by a more expansive spirit, due to the freedom and culture of the schools.

A mixed multitude in the north, lax and almost cosmopolitan in their habits (here was Galilee of the Gentiles), with whom nationality—perhaps never very strong—had been almost annihilated by repeated invasions ; and where foreign influences conspired against the exclusiveness that Jerusalem strove to maintain.

In Babylon the most famous school of Jewish thought had established itself, and was not to be bound by Jerusalem.

And fourthly, in and about Alexandria were very large and important Jewish colonies, where Egyptian and Greek philosophy flowed over and beyond the Judaic beliefs. Here and elsewhere, scattered over Magna Græcia, transplanted Israelites read their Scriptures in a Greek dress ; and gradually learned to use that language for original composition, as well as for translations of religious books, such as we may find in the collections known as Apocrypha, or mystic writings.

A Hebrew who went to Egypt found it expedient, at the

date, as supposed, of about 130 B.C., to translate into Greek the Hebrew book on Wisdom of his grandfather Jesus ben Sirach, even though he was personally averse from such translations. "For," as he explains, "the same things expressed in Hebrew have not a like force when rendered into another tongue, and not only in the present instance, but the Law and the Prophecies and the rest of the books differ not a little in respect of the things expressed in them."

Greek language and culture overspread the countries traversed by the Macedonian conqueror, with Oriental ideas infusing themselves into the Greek system wherever it penetrated. Pyrrho, one of the philosophers who followed in the train of Alexander, had his mind filled with more doctrines than he could well digest and make fruitful in himself, and, falling into a desolating unbelief and incredulity, established the school whose dogma was the unattainability of truth. Such, fortunately, would not be the lot of all who walked in the roads travelled by the great leaders of armies; when the treasuries of wisdom were unlocked and their stores communicated, there were many eager minds ready to profit thereby. As commerce opened the road between the western bazaars of Hindostan and the traders of Egypt, the scholar passed along it with joy, and the bonds of isolation that cramp the catholicity of thought and knowledge were somewhat loosened. There was a convergence of the remains of the great religious movements of old to the points where they most naturally met; and Judea was unable to be exempt from their influence. The sympathy between the best Oriental, Egyptian, and Hellenic thought, and the spiritual ethics of Jesus and teachings of the Rabbins, is evidenced in hundreds of parallelisms, of form as well as of substance. Prejudice apart, it would have been strange if it had been otherwise, and Palestine had remained untouched by this opening of the old world. The prolific harvest of Egypto-Judaic, Judeo-Babylonian, and Judeo-

Hellenic literature, and the activity of the Jewish schools themselves, evidence the interior ferment; historic records can but show the tracks along which these streams were tending. The disciples were full of doubt, disputation, and intelligence; they were but waiting for the master who should bring them the fire without which intellectual qualities are nothing.

The Greco-Syrians and Greco-Egyptians not only traversed Palestine, as the Babylonians had previously done, but terrible oppression was brought to bear to crush the Jewish bigotry. The obstinate few, persecution doubtless hardened in their proud, patriotic exclusiveness; the reasonable many could not and did not escape a considerable Hellenization.

Deutsch, an undoubted authority, says, In the Talmud "we hear of Coptic, Aramaic, Persian, Median, Latin, but, above all, Greek. The terms in which this last language is spoken of verge on the transcendental. This also is the only language which it seems to have been incumbent to teach even to girls." With the charm of her language—not to name the extent of its vocabulary, and the precision of its grammatical forms—and the poetry of her religion, it is no marvel that Greece wielded a magic wand of influence over those with whom she came in contact. The leading Hebrew Rabbins gave way to her fascination, those that were ever ready to revolt at any foreign indignity, for very fear of being swallowed up imperceptibly by the terrible Gentiles; even the stiff-necked race that proclaimed itself unique, isolated, superior to all, was not insensible to the charm. Says Deutsch again (Deutsch, whose article on the Talmud so interested Englishmen as to lead to repeated editions of the number of the *Quarterly Review* in which it appeared): "As the commonwealth successively came in contact, however much against its will at first, with Greece and Rome, their history, geography, and language came to be added as a matter of instruction to those of Persia and Babylon. . . . When Hellenic scepticism in its most seductive form had, during the Syrian troubles, begun to seek its victims even in the midst of the 'Sacred Vineyard,' and threatened to undermine all patriotism and all independence, a curse was pronounced upon Hellenism.... But, the danger over, the Greek language and culture were restored to their previous high position in both the school and the house." The very denunciations of Greek learning, which in the Talmud mingle with other voices singing its praises, are a sufficient proof that its influence had penetrated far. And the small aristocratic and priestly band of unimpeachable pedigree at Jerusalem, intrenched in the central fortress of Judaism, had no power to prevent that influence from constantly exerting itself upon the mixed bulk of the people. Their jealous words are evidence of their consciousness of the growing cosmopolitanism that was fatal to the old pretensions. The incorporation of foreign thought was gradual and unseen; the forswearing of it spasmodic and local.

It is said in the Talmud, by R. Eleazar (presumably a disciple of the R. Jochanan ben Zakai who is stated to have lived from about 50 to 47 B.C. to A.D. 70 to 73), "Be diligent to learn Thorah wherewith thou mayest make answer to Epicurus [or, "Study Thorah, and also know how to answer Epicurus"]." (P. Aboth, ii. 18).

From this we may deduce that, in the time of Jesus, Greek philosophy was not unknown to the Rabbis. The Epicurean teaching, in the mind of the orthodox Pharisee, must have seemed one step, and that a bad step, beyond Sadduceeism. Both fear of death and fear of the gods were groundless, the soul being resolved into its elements, and the gods not being actively interested in human fate. This view is the polar opposite of the teaching of the Hebrew prophets.

Hebrew commentators have explained the Talmudic injunction to mean that after the student was grounded in Thorah and Talmud, he was to learn Gentile science in order to be able to reason with and refute a latitudinarian brother.

The sayings, "Restrain your sons from meditation" (Berachoth, 28 b) and "Teach not your son Greek science" (Sota, 49 b), are both understood to refer to disciples who have not come to maturity. A very large number of Jews, it is to be remembered, could only read their Thorah in Greek; and Greek thought was probably entering Palestine through Hellenized Jews, if not directly.

Perhaps as striking a memorial as any of the unsettled position of the Hebrew state is that Jesus himself was born under the rule of an Idumean king, lived under a tetrarch, was condemned according to Jewish law, and suffered death in a Roman province, under the government of a Procurator.

In regarding ancient religions from a modern point of view, it is to be borne in mind that, pride and jealousy apart, they do not pretend to a monopoly of orthodoxy. Of all the nations of antiquity, perhaps the Jews were the most tenacious of their traditions, and the most jealous of change. But even they again and again borrowed their ceremonial; and as to their ethical treasures, though they idolized their Scripture even to the letter, yet they had their own familiar methods of making it give sanction and cover, nay, more, an apparent origination, to the widest interpretations and the most unfettered spiritual thought. Amongst other races, however unwilling to break up ceremonial observances, the wise were under no fear or restriction, and communicated such things as they had, to any duly-qualified pilgrim from another land. The seven immortal benefactors or preservers of the universe who form the members of the divine company of heaven, according to the Zoroastrians, are found to represent no persons, and to be named by no proper names, but to be personifications only, or symbols, of the attributes of the one God. So, among the Hellenized races, to add a new God to the Divine Pleroma was to the wise but to enlarge the conception of the supreme qualities of the Eternal. As when an astronomer discovers a new star to swell the list of the heavens, another facet of the infinite lustre was brought to view; another addition to man's faculty of appreciation of the immeasurable was made. A part of Palestine may be considered to have belonged to this school of natural religion.

Such instances as the following tend to show that Rabbis were to be found leaning more to transcendental philosophy than to such dogma as the Western races have developed from misunderstanding of the Oriental imagination.* "'With ten names,' says the Talmud, 'is the Holy Ghost named in Scripture. They are—Parable, Allegory, Enigma, Speech, Sentence, Light, Command, Vision, Prophecy.'" In the same way the Satan of the Talmud, the Seducer, Accuser, and Angel of Death, is understood as a personification of passion, remorse, and death.

Another difference between the present and the past must be borne in mind. Now, the world is open to every one. There are no guarded secrets that may not be mastered by zeal and study—for the truly occult is buried almost out of sight. No writer withholds his most cherished thought from the multitude, which results frequently in the endeavour being made to reach popularity by making a bid to the lowest level of mind. Our means of communication are superb, our power of distributing intelligence unexampled; and the main use of the magnificent faculties of inter-communication is to flash backwards and forwards the prices of stocks and rates of the markets, with the gossip of politics and details of current events viewed chiefly through the eyehole of trade. The daily bread that our newspapers give us is mainly the bread of earth. Almost all can read, but there is no room in the journals, and no eager call from their readers, for a daily word applying to man's spiritual needs and interest, as the ancients held it. The main chance, as now regarded,

---

* Deutsch is responsible for the quotation as it stands ("Lit. Remains," Islam, p. 79), and gives no reference by which to verify it, or correct an obvious error.

is the chance of the nether world, while "divine service," which once meant effort, activity, fervour, difficulty is now chiefly comprised in an easy, periodical attendance at church or chapel, with no strain upon either mind or body.

That the necessary work which results in our sustenance, shelter, and certain civilized advantages, is best done without any intrusion of the mystical part of us, it may be allowed. There is a time for everything, and when we are weighing out coals or speculating in merchandise, our business is to do that well, and not to make a miscalculation from having our brains filled with shining webs. The ideal can well afford to be remote and merely incidental while the bodily needs are being served; it has its own due and lofty place in our economy, and seeks no further; in the highest art work alone, or in that soul only whose religion is a thing of every day, and whose every practical effort is a sign of the joy of awakened life, can the ideal and the real go hand in hand.

It may be said that we accumulate freshly and constantly for our physical needs, but allow the store of the bread of heaven to become thin and dry and eaten out with the worm, because doctrine has lost its vitality. The accumulated religious thought of the world waits but our option; lies ready for our earnestness to turn it over and make it our own; all is easy to us. With the philosophers of old circumstances were very different; the acquirement of knowledge was beset with the gravest difficulties, but they surmounted them for themselves; they perhaps were not many in number, but they had open souls that loved to feed at the founts of inspiration and sacred lore. The few sought strenuously for the esoteric knowledge and eagerly prized it; now every one has it (at least in superficial appearance), but it is not of priceless estimation as of old. We must not forget to reckon our own glorious gains of breadth and freedom and exact science, but the true test of comparison is not in the opportunity but in the use made of it; in the state, and not merely in the position, of the individual man. What was lacking in convenience was made up for by effort; a man would spend half his years in getting hold of a key that would unlock the deepest mysteries of life ; now we are somewhat careless of that deeper spring, and distracted by the multiplicity and importance of the external and superficial :—

> "The world is too much with us ; late and soon,
> Getting and spending, we lay waste our powers ;
> Little we see in Nature that is ours ;
> We have given our hearts away, a sordid boon !"

Some few words of this kind seem to be necessary to enable us to appreciate the difference between the ancient and the modern student. In the time of Jesus knowledge, being more difficult to acquire, was acquired more earnestly, really, vitally. We read widely now of diffuse writings, and outside the field of exact and minute research are but rarely profound students. The oral teaching of old, on the other hand, abbreviated expression and intensified thought, which took the form of the pithy sentences, sayings, epigrams, gnomes, parables, oracles, that have come down to us. The memory, strengthened by exercise, held fast these crystal forms, and gave the mind time to drink their essence to the full. Prominent with us to-day are speculations on the physical origin of man, but they show almost a blank as regards the inner or real man ; the spiritual law that is the essence of his being, past, present, and future, is ignored and misknown.

This apathy in matters in which the ancients found a vivid interest, is strange. How much of it is due to the fact that an unjust doctrinal scheme has established itself with a claim to finality, and for many centuries has shut down the grating, as of a dungeon, upon that heretical effort and curiosity without which there is no life?

Fortunately, the strength of the cruel hand is now relaxed, and the history of its triumphs is in a *diminuendo* scale :—the stake, the prison for the culprit ; social ostracism, and the burning at the hands of the hangman of the offending book; finally, an arrogant, unblushing assumption that the arraigner's motives are wicked; or a feminine appeal to the "fearful man" not to shake the feeble frame of a faith that is with difficulty kept alive.

Perchance, before the centuries of our era come of age, we shall have learned to esteem its founder, and shall have discarded the doctrine to which our pastors are bound to subscribe, and in which English subjects are required "to continue," that "works" done outside the narrow boundaries of a prescribed scheme "have the nature of sin." Perhaps, in the twentieth century, we may be free to begin again at the beginning, and to copy humbly those rarely conscientious and surely excellent folk, "every man" of whom "did that which was right in his own eyes."

These comparisons should rebut modern civilization's shallow arguments in favour of itself, and in depreciation of earlier forms of life. When intercommunication was difficult, Pythagoras, and such as resemble him, are found gathering like bees of the golden honey of many lands. Now we may penetrate into the depths of the ancient mysteries at will, or at least touch their surface, by taking a volume from a shelf close to us; but the prevalent lack of concentration on our part makes those mysteries more remote from us in a true sense than did the continents and seas that barred the eager students of old, or the primitive mechanical knowledge that had failed to provide them with steamboats, newspapers, circulating libraries, penny posts, or telegraphs. Now, with wide knowledge, and power of analysis enlarged, we languidly discuss a sermon, or criticize a new book; then, truths that were felt and held because self-estimable, were passed like a sacred torch from hand to hand, among the reverent and ardent few, kindling beacons of philosophy from which, unknown to ourselves, we still derive illumination.

Were there not determined prejudices in vogue, were

there not an artificial halo surrounding Judea, and a crudely miraculous nimbus made to encircle the head of Jesus (a nimbus of less glory, magnitude, and miracle than his own true light), it would not be necessary so to insist upon the fact that the religious thought of the Jews at the commencement of our era was as largely indebted to foreign influences as to its early sources. The matter proves itself so simple that it needs only that unbiased, unexpurgated history be left to speak for itself. Neither would it be necessary to assert that the teachings of Jesus, although instinct with the inevitable heightening and deepening that he gave to every thought he touched, although indeed almost too original to be borne by his hearers, were not entirely self-originated, but in reasonable part, the heritage of his fathers. Nor, further, would it be necessary to show that in an age of insignificant traffic, as compared with our modern commercial interchange, there was one commodity that so transcended other merchandise that it was sought for from land to land, and borne in the shrine of men's memories over difficult continents and seas,—the priceless freight of wisdom.

It is of outside influences as affecting Jesus that we have first to speak, and some cloudy prejudice has to be fairly met and penetrated. There are many, no doubt, who cannot at once turn their devout gaze from the cradle of a mystical unbegotten child, kept secretly apart for fear of jealous kings, suckled in Egypt, and nurtured by a virgin mother in a prophetically foretold city of Palestine, or from the untriumphant tomb of a more than human man, an ineffable unit of a composite Godhead,—to the critical consideration of a student of laborious learning, a skilled logician and a profound philosopher. Of the quality and character of his life and actions there are many things to say, but here we consider him as a teacher, and have to do with the mundane expression of his thoughts, and with the question how he gained that faculty of expression.

In his time, the Hebrew Scriptures, as has been said, were in a dead language; and Galilee, far from being a sparsely inhabited region of idyl, a sort of poetic lakeland, was the most densely peopled part of Palestine. If we are to believe Josephus, its population extended to millions, and its smallest city or village was of fifteen thousand inhabitants. The province was an object of jealousy, and Galilean a term of reproach, with the southern Jews, whose chief men sought to keep themselves uncontaminated by foreign influence; for it was tenanted by a mixed rather than a Jewish race, and subject to continual intercourse with Greeks, Phœnicians, and others. There were Greek cities on the lake.

Jewish Galilee as a tract was what Palestine was as a country, the least self-contained in the world. Palestine, though severed from other countries by a sea on the west, and bounded in part by desert regions on the east, was isolated in seeming and not in reality. Open on the north and south, it was the highway between Babylon and Egypt. It became thus the meeting ground of opposing nations, and a pathway of commerce; and the sea rather brought foreign influences to its shores than kept them away. Moreover, within its own borders it contained a multitude of tribes that had never been wholly subjugated or banished by the Jew; and it was subject to such a variety of foreign dominion that its physical barriers and hedges could have been of but small account. Galilee, similarly, though apparently the most remote and isolated of provinces, was really the least so. Its division and remoteness was from the province representing national Judaism; its isolation, that it was environed by what was not Jewish. It was bounded on the north by Phœnicia, renowned for its activity and trade, the parent of Semitic languages, prone to letters, and possessed of an immense cosmogonical and theological literature. On the east flows the Jordan, and the districts on the other side were Syrian and Greek. On the south was Samaria, with her own version of the

Pentateuch, her own mount of worship, and her hostility to her rival at Jerusalem. Galilee was not like Jerusalem, fighting the battle of national pride against foreign thought; for the foreigners overpowered the Jews. Cæsarea, a coast town on the borders of Galilee, and twenty-five miles from Nazareth, was the civil and military capital of Palestine, and chiefly inhabited by other races than Jews, though it contained some thousands of the latter. There was a standing dispute to whom the city belonged, and frequent contention arose, owing to the diversity of faiths within its walls. It was built by an Idumæan, Edomite, or half Jew; but filled with statues and temples that were by no means Jehovistic or Jewish. Rather less than a century and three quarters before our era, the temple at Jerusalem bore the name of the Olympian Zeus, and ivy-bearing Bacchic processions replaced Jewish observances. The Samaritan temple in like manner was dedicated to Zeus Xenios. The Maccabees at length restored the national ritual.

Of the time of Antiochus Epiphanes it is related (1 Macc. i. 13) that "certain of the people were so forward that they went to the king; and he gave them licence to do after the ordinances of the Gentiles. And they built a gymnasium in Jerusalem, according to the customs of the Gentiles." Josephus also says of a later date (Antiq., XV. 8. 1): "Herod revolted from the laws of his country, and corrupted the ancient constitution by introducing foreign practices."

The bright side of Pagan life proved attractive to the Hebrew as well as to others. The following passage (2 Macc. iv. 13) evidently marks a reaction in a nationalistic direction, but it is not to be supposed that Greek influences died out because from time to time the tide of them was attempted to be stemmed:—

"Now such was the height of Hellenism, and advance of foreign influence, through the exceeding corruption of Jason, that ungodly man and no high priest, that the priests were no longer zealous for the services of the altar, but despised the temple, neglected the sacrifices, and hurried off to take part in the unlawful choral practice in the palæstra, after the challenge at the quoits. Yea, the honours of their fathers they made of no account, but thought the Greek glories the best." These glories seem at least to have been innocent and healthy, though no doubt, then as now, it was possible for curates to devote themselves too exclusively to lawn tennis or its equivalents.

The rule of Greek sovereigns for more than a century and a half had left its indelible mark—a mark that the succeeding rule of the Maccabees could not put away, and which the Roman rule rather deepened than otherwise. Ptolemais, which owed its name to the first Greek sovereign of the line of the Ptolemies, was but twenty miles from Nazareth. The foreign mark was to be seen in the name of the lovely plain of Esdraelon (the Greek form of Jezreel), which sweep of land extended to within two miles of Nazareth; while the border of Phœnicia was within two hours' walk. Within a mile or two east of the native place of Jesus ran a great trunk road from Damascus southwards, while westward twenty miles was the mystic Mount of Carmel, then Syrian, but always the haunt of prophets, who meditated in its groves that were like "thick tresses of the bride." There were caves there with Greek inscriptions, "cave of the sons of the prophets." Elijah had been there; and Pythagoras, journeying to Egypt, is said to have spent several days upon the mount (Iamblichus, Life of Pythag., iii.). This was a half millennium before the time we are now speaking of; but the character of the place remained, for it now possessed a temple and college, and a few decades after our era commences we find Vespasian consulting the oracle there.

As in Samaria there were great Herodian towns, the capital being given the name of Sebaste, the Greek equivalent of Augustus, so with Galilee. Mount Tabor held a fortified town. Sepphoris, an hour's walk from Nazareth, had a college of doctors, and a Sanhedrin established by the Romans. This and Tiberias (where the Talmud of Jerusalem was afterwards redacted) were the largest cities of Galilee. The "masters of the law" composing such a Sanhedrin were not necessarily all Hebrews. They formed, says Deutsch, "the most mixed assembly in the world. There were not only natives of all the parts of the world-wide Roman Empire among them, but also denizens of Arabia and Judea."

There is no reason to suppose that there were no other towns or villages near to the Galilean lake than those referred to in the Gospels. An important city is described by Josephus and Pliny as situated at the south end of the lake, which, says the latter, was sometimes named from it. This city, Taricheæ, is believed to be the "Tarkaal," visited in the fourteenth century before our era by a travelling official from Egypt, who gave an account of his journeys ("Records of the Past," vol. ii.).

The direct rule of Greek princes had ceased a century and a half before our era commences, but the better educated Romans spoke Greek, and their edicts, though officially published in Latin, were translated into Greek, which was the pre-eminent language of civilization. As the Greek dominion began to wane, whether in Egypt, Judæa, or elsewhere, some two centuries before our era, it might be thought that the language also would have lost ground. It seems rather to have established itself, until it became, not the vernacular of a nation, but the common language of the learned. Without knowing this relation of the Greek language to the Roman power, it would be difficult to see how Palestine, although while under Greek rule it might have been fully impregnated with the Greek influence, should not under Roman rule have lost it. The epigram of Horace (Epist. II. i. 156) will keep the truth in our mind: "Captive Greece took captive her rude conqueror." During the reign of the earlier Ptolemies,

Alexandria, the largest city in the world, and possessed of the largest library, had been the home of scholars, who flocked thither from Athens and the coasts of the Mediterranean. The cruelties of the seventh Ptolemy drove out the scholars in crowds, and they distributed themselves over all the islands and coasts of the Archipelago. Here there were schools at which Roman Emperors were taught. If other evidence were wanting that Greek was not unknown in the large Galilean towns, it would be found in the fact that the Roman standards floated over them. It was an affectation of cultured Romans not only to know Greek but to speak it; and they brought over whole libraries from Greece, with which the Roman poets of the period of which we are treating amply enriched themselves. Julius Cæsar studied at Rhodes in the celebrated Greek school of Molon; Augustus was a master of Greek. Cato, when young, opposed Hellenic influence, and, when old, learned the language. Horace, though his father was in poor circumstances, was sent to the Greek University at Athens to learn philosophy; so also Ovid. Virgil, of course, read Homer. Cicero was a translator from the Greek; so was Catullus. Greeks of talent flocked to Rome, and gave lectures in their own tongue, which had become the natural language of philosophy and letters.

Josephus, the Jerusalemite Jew, who was born soon after the death of Jesus, wrote in the Greek language as well as in Syro-Chaldee. He speaks in his "Life" of Greeks residing at Tiberias in Galilee; among them was one who had written in that language a history of a Galilean war.

The Greek language must have been extending itself rapidly about this time. Josephus says (Bell. Jud., pref.) "I have proposed to myself . . . to translate those books into the Greek tongue, which I formerly composed in the language of our country." To be in the Greek tongue seems to have been a necessity of preservation of a book at this time; there is no relic of his Hebrew works. Of the first book of Maccabees the Hebrew original is lost, the Greek translation remains; so is it also with the Gospel of Matthew.

The law may have had something to do with this transition. Simon ben Gamaliel, probably soon after the middle of the first century, promulgated a statute to the effect that it was not allowable for the Jews to compose books except in the Greek language. This was, in all likelihood, done in obedience to orders, and it is probable that the same influence had been exerted before.

Paul, born according to tradition (Chrys. De Petr. et Paulo, viii., Montf.) in the second year after Jesus, in an important city in Asia Minor, and educated at Jerusalem, is a bilinguist, apparently able, with equal ease, to address an audience in Greek and in Hebraic. In the works attributed to him are three quotations from Greek poets. Gamaliel the elder, his teacher, who, A.D. 30, became president of the Sanhedrin, though a strict Pharisee, was an ardent student of Greek. Finding that in divorce cases difficulties arose owing to the several names by which individuals were called, some Hebrew and some Greek, he ordered that "every other name which describes the person" (Gittin, 34) should be added to each signature. The fact of such an enactment being necessary is a proof of the mixed character of the language of the period.

That Peter was well acquainted with Greek is to be inferred from the account of his delivering a sermon to "men of Cyrene, and strangers of Rome, Jews and proselytes," a mixed congregation much more likely to have been familiar with Greek than with Hebrew.

The common language of these days was, says Deutsch, "an odd mixture of Greek, Aramaic, Latin, Syriac, Hebrew;" a "corrupt Chaldee or Aramaic, mixed with Greek and Latin." "Though gifted with a fine feeling for the distinguishing characters of each of the languages then in common use ('Aramaic lends itself best to elegies, Greek to hymns, Hebrew to prayer, Roman to martial compositions,' as a common saying has it), they yet mixed them all up."

Besides other influences from outside to which Palestine was subject, there was ever the communication open with the scattered ones of their own nation, and there were visits from their foreign brethren. It is difficult adequately to realize what these Jews of the dispersion were. A section only of the captives had returned from Babylon when their own territory had become equally part of the vast empire that extended from Thrace and Egypt to India, and embraced the entire Oriental world. Since that time the Jews of Babylon and of Palestine were always closely linked; they possessed an almost identical tongue. Three centuries before our era Alexander carried the Macedonian rule and the Greek language over the entire region that the Jews inhabited, Babylonia, Media, and Judæa alike. These Jews were under Grecian rule and influence without the break that in Palestine must be allowed for the Maccabæan period. A decree of Gamaliel the elder, issued from the Temple a few years after the death of Jesus, is addressed, "To our brethren the exiles in Babylon, Media, Greece, and all other exiles of Israel, greeting!" (Sanhed. Tosifta, c. ii. Jer. Sanh. 18 a). This exhibition of the idea of banishment has in it something of national ostentation. The absentees were, many of them, exiles in no stricter sense than the Rothschilds and Cohens who live in London and Paris at the present day.

The second area of dispersion was Egypt and the adjacent African regions. Alexander in founding Alexandria peopled a third of it with Jews; and the Ptolemies added to these importations, until the Egyptian Jews were estimated at the commencement of our era at a million in number. These Jews were under purely Greek auspices, and knew no Hebrew. Their Scriptures had been rendered for them into Greek; they read them in a free and liberal way, and books of a broad and cosmopolitan philosophy, written by Hellenized Jews, are numerous and important. The habitable world, says exaggerative Josephus (Ant., XIV. 7. 2), was so full of Jews that there was scarcely a corner of the Roman Empire where they might not be found; and the Talmud (Jer. Meg., iii. 75, cit. Deutsch.) speaks of nearly four hundred synagogues in Jerusalem as belonging to different communities of the Dispersion. There was no interruption to communication between the Jews abroad and the Jews at home, and as Babylon gave its language to the captives, it might fairly be expected, even if there were no other influences tending in the same direction, that no educated Palestinian Jew could be wholly ignorant of Greek, the language of so many thousands of his brethren dwelling in so near a land as Egypt.

We have now fairly combated the prejudice found to be occupying the field of our inquiry, by showing that the country of Jesus was peopled by no mysterious and unique race, separated from the rest of the world, and living a sacred and sequestered life of light in the midst of a pagan darkness; but that its knowledge, like the knowledge of all the world, was to a large extent drawn from other sources than its own inspirations. The mistake which has given rise to the prevalent misconception is perhaps due (apart from its adaptability to minor doctrinal necessities) to the fragmentary early history of the primitive Jewish tribe, as written by itself, having been taken to represent the records of the mixed and divided race of a thousand years later date, both in point of time and experience. Jesus was born, not of Abraham's seed only, but of a people long mingled with the Chaldean, the Egyptian, and the Greek.

We have so far proceeded with our inquiry as connected with a national condition; it must now be entered upon with a more personal reference to its object.

If Jesus was a well-educated son of his time, he knew Greek; if he was able to converse freely with the foreigners that composed the largest element of the towns that lay close around his home, he knew Greek. Was he well-educated? Any argument to the contrary has clearly no basis in fact. The sneering question attributed (John vii. 16) to the southern Jews, "How hath this man literary knowledge, having never learned?" is possibly a depreciatory mode of representing that he came from the north, and was not educated in the schools of Jerusalem. Moreover, it is to be remembered that the Fourth Gospel is not so much a chronicle as a thesis. There is no reason to doubt the story that he entered into the synagogue of Nazareth and stood up to read from the roll of the book; he must then at least have known the language in which it was written, and how to interpret from it to the people in Aramaic, after the usual custom. That he did teach in the synagogues seems to be a historic fact, and such teaching always consisted in taking a portion of the Scripture, and interpreting and commenting upon it. If the narratives we so much prize are credible as we suppose, Jesus constantly taught as a rabbi, and was recognized as a rabbi. This implies the "literary knowledge" of the class. There is no reasonable doubt that Jesus received a thorough scholastic training. Possibly enough he obtained some of it by himself, but so does every deepest student; sufficient for our argument that we may reasonably infer from the history of the time that a solid groundwork of instruction was bestowed upon him in youth. Men of some amount of culture, too, were probably among his disciples, even though they might be only fishing-boat proprietors, and might aid their hired servants by manual labour. For a considerable period schools had been multiplying throughout the country. There were both elementary schools, where a teacher was appointed for every five and twenty children; and superior colleges or academies in the more important towns. Eighty years before our era commences, superior schools were introduced into every large provincial town, and it was ordained that all the "youths from the age of sixteen should visit them" (Kethuboth, Jer.

viii. 11). It is elsewhere said (P. Aboth, v. appendix), "At the age of five, a boy has to study Scripture; at ten, the Mishna; at thirteen, the Precepts; at fifteen, the Talmud." The superior school, therefore, must have been one that succeeded the instruction thus specified. There was one of the colleges where scribes and the bearers of "the traditions of the fathers" received instruction, at Tiberias in Galilee, at a later date, if not at this time. A few quotations from the Talmud will show what importance was given to education at this period: "The world is preserved by the breath of the school-children." "A town in which there is no school must perish." "Teaching of school-children is of such importance that it must not be stopped even for the building of the sanctuary" (Shabb., 119 b). And Josephus says (c. Apion, i. 12), "Our principal care is to educate our children." The most highly esteemed persons were not the priests, whose services had become little more than ceremonial, but the "Masters of the Law," the "Sages," the "Disciples of the Sages." "Let thy house be a meeting-house for the wise, and sit in the dust of their feet; and drink their words with thirstiness" (Pirqe Aboth).

There is no presumption against Jesus and several of his disciples having studied at the higher schools, from the fact of their being fishermen or carpenters. Rabbi Gamaliel, who dates about 40 B.C., declares, "Learning, no matter of what kind, if unaccompanied by a trade, ends in nothing and leads to sin" (P. Aboth, ii. 2). Another Talmudic saying is this (Nedarim, 49 b): "Labour honours the labourer." There was also another pregnant maxim, "He who does not teach his son a trade, teaches him to steal" (Kiddushin). Rabbi Ismael, the great astronomer of about 100 A.D., was a needle-maker; rabbi after rabbi is described as "the tanner," "the shoemaker," "the weaver," "the carpenter." True teachers indeed these may have been, workers the more sincere in that they were men who gloried in the fact that they could teach independently of payment, and were proud of adding to their names the trade that was their means of livelihood.

What possible chance, then, with education compulsory, is there that Jesus remained uneducated, or that the carpenter's shop was not also the "house of learning"? Josephus plumes himself on having made such progress in his studies that when he was fourteen he was sometimes consulted by the priests and elders on points of law. What likelihood is there that the studious boy who is said to have been found engaged in discussion with the Temple doctors, should not have sought in every way and by every channel to add to his education between the years of fifteen and thirty, so as to qualify himself for the work he felt to be his own?

There being such a mixture of races in the borders of Galilee, in that region one might freely learn anything without even heresy being so much as noticed at Jerusalem. Whether dedicated to Syrian or Jewish Deity, what better resort for one whose vision pierced through external forms, and through the merely adventitious seized upon the real and true, than the meditative solitudes of Carmel, whose groves an old prophet had described (Micah vii. 14) as a refuge for hermit priests? "Tend thy people with thy rod, the flock of thine heritage, which dwell solitarily, in the wood in the midst of Carmel; let them feed in Bashan and Gilead, as in the days of old." Where in the world could an eager soul be placed that it could not find something or some one wherefrom to learn? Galilee, despised as were its borders by the exclusives of Jerusalem, was not without its fruit of excellence. A century and a half after this time sprang from it the reputed originator of the Kabbala, and author of the Zohar. In Galilee, even if Jesus never travelled afield to the Essene communities near the Asphaltic Sea, or to the Egypto-Hellenic Therapeuts further south, there was no hindrance to the study of Greek, or to the search into the message of the prophet, the lore of the sage, the ethics of the Talmudist, whether foreign or Hebraic.

We do not know that Jesus never travelled beyond the borders of Palestine before he entered upon his work; he may have traversed Egypt, or visited India, like other students; nothing is told us. And in olden times earnest students were wont to travel. Pythagoras journeyed to Egypt to learn; Megasthenes visited India; Chaldean Magi are described as reaching Palestine; and the disciples themselves, or their successors, traversed Grecized Asia, and reached points widely distant east and west.

Philo, the Jew, wrote in Greek, as Alexandrian Jews had written for two hundred years, or since the time of the Septuagint. Both Greeks, and Hellenists like Philo, were constantly to be found in Judea (Acts vi. 1; ix. 29; xi. 20), that is to say, Jews who knew Greek. Philo himself came over to Jerusalem for the Temple requirements—as, indeed, every devout Jew was supposed to do, and as many of the thousands who were scattered over Egypt and had built up a large Hellenistic literature, must often have done. Few men of culture in Palestine could have been wholly ignorant of a language currently spoken within their own borders, and the tongue, both for speech and writing, of so many thousands of their brethren, from whom they were not cut off by any worse barrier than an oft-traversed route of some few days' journey.

Among the relics of Jesus are to be found thoughts not paralleled in any Hebrew work known, but provably related, and that frequently even by phraseological identity, to passages in the works of Philo, who wrote and spoke in Greek. So, too, must have spoken the school from which Philo drew his spiritual sustenance; and the allegoric lore which they possessed could not have been withheld from an inquirer such as Jesus. There is traceable connection also between the words of Jesus as reported, and those of the books called apocryphal, which were either composed in Greek, or early translated into that language. Paul speaks in Hebraic and writes in Greek; James gives his name to an epistle written in Greek full of Hebraisms, which are to be expected in such a case. Peter and John, if they wrote the books that bear their names, wrote them in Greek. The redactors of the Gospels quote from the Greek Septuagint direct rather than translate from the Hebrew original. The inscription on the cross of Jesus was trilingual—in Greek, Latin, and Hebrew (Luke xxiii. 38 [not in the principal MSS.]; John xix. 20): Hebraic as the language of the common people, Latin as the official language of the rulers, Greek as the tongue generally known.

In the temple at Jerusalem itself, the inscriptions on the columns, warning strangers from entering the sacred interior recesses, were in Greek and Latin (Joseph. Bell. Jud., v. 2. 4).

There was discovered in Jerusalem, in 1871, a stone block on which is engraven an inscription in Greek, forbidding strangers to enter beyond a certain barrier in the temple, under a penalty which is very clear from the last word of the inscription, "ΘΑΝΑΤΟΝ"—death.

During the lifetime of Jesus, a young student, to whom we have already referred, was in Jerusalem, acquiring Hebraic learning and continuing his education in Greek from his master Gamaliel, who was acquainted with both languages. The age at which Paul entered upon study at Jerusalem might most reasonably be about fourteen; he would consequently have been a pupil there between the time that Jesus entered the temple precincts as a boy and as a man. The death of Jesus occurred about the year 28 or 29, when Paul would have been what we term "of age;" that in his writings he should never have referred to Jesus as one whom he might have met, is an almost inexplicable thing. But he realized a mystical attractiveness rather than a personal element in the mission of the Master.

To return to the records, there come, we are told, Greeks (or Hellenized Jews) to Philip, a Galilean disciple (John xii.

20 and 59), and beg him, presumably in Greek, to let them see Jesus; was the disciple of greater linguistic attainments than the master? According to the Fourth Gospel there was nothing improbable in Greek knowledge being attributed to Jesus, for the Jews are represented as saying (John vii. 35), " Will he go unto the dispersed among the Greeks, and teach the Greeks?" Jesus himself meets with a Syro-Phœnician woman, in one place described as a Greek, in another place referred to under the Grecized Roman name of Jousta; and no difficulty is on record as to his ability to converse with her.

An instance going to prove that it was not regarded as difficult to get Hebrew rendered into Greek in the streets of Jerusalem is to be found in the extra-canonical Gospel of Nicodemus, where, in an amplification of the gospel story of the entry of Jesus into Jerusalem, we are told, " The sons of the Hebrews held branches in their hands, and shouted; and others spread their clothes under him, saying, ' Save now, highest; blessed is he that cometh in the name of the Lord!' The Jews cry out and say to the runner [an official], 'The sons of the Hebrews shouted in Hebrew; whence, then, hast thou the Greek?' The runner says to them, ' I asked one of the Jews, and said, "What is it they are shouting in Hebrew?" and he interpreted for me.' "

When the Greek language entered Egypt, it rapidly made its way there: it had been the language of the Government in Syria throughout the reign of the Seleucidæ; it would indeed be strange if it had found itself estopped there from its ordinary power of spreading, in spite of temporary opposition.

It is recorded that Jesus on the Cross repeated in Aramaic the words of a psalm, and cried on Elohim ("[h]elei," or " [h]elōī;" the bystanders were so far Greek that they misunderstood him, and mistook the word—not unlike, indeed, in sound—for Elias (Heleias), the Greek form of Elijah.

The Hebrew coinage bore a bilingual inscription for about a century before our era, namely Hebrew and Greek. From the time of Herod the Great, Greek letters alone were used. When therefore Jesus (Matt. xxii. 19, et al.) asked for a coin to be brought to him, the "eikon" on which he looked was no doubt the laureated head of the reigning Roman emperor, and the superscription a legend in Greek. That the question of Jesus, "Whose is this image and superscription?" betokened ignorance and not a design of eliciting the answer for which his rejoinder was, so to speak, in ambush, it would be absurd to suppose.

Some have gone so far as to argue that Jesus most often discoursed in Greek, but that when most deeply moved he fell into Aramaic, as for instance in the occasional fragments now left to us,—Raka, Bar-Iona, Rabbi, Heloï Heloï (otherwise Helei), lema sabachthanei, Boanērges [bene-regesh], Taleitha koum, Ephphatha, Kephas, Baddach ephkid rouchi = "into thy hands I commend my breath (spirit)"; Matt. v. 22, xvi. 17, xxiii. 7, xxvii. 46; Mark iii. 17, v. 41, vii. 34; John i. 42; Ev. Nicod., Cod. A.), also Mamōn (Matt. vi. 24), and Mahar, "of the morrow," ("Gospel according to the Hebrews," Jerome, Comm. in Matt. vi. 11). But only a part of these could belong to emotional utterances, and the distinct traditional assertion that the entire *logia* were noted down in Hebraic, goes against this hypothesis.

Moreover, mistakes are made by the Greek editors of the Gospels, which are most readily explained by the hypothesis of a Hebraic original. For instance, in *Mark* the crucifixion is stated to have taken place at the third hour, in *Matthew* it is implied to have been at the sixth hour; the difference in the Hebraic is very slight, a copyist's or translator's mistake of reading *schelischith* instead of *shischith*, or a Hebrew letter consisting of a stroke with a crook at either end (gimel), instead of a stroke with only one crook (vau). There are Phœnician and Aramaic alphabets, in which the two letters are mutually undistinguishable.

Two of the disciples who sat at the feet of Jesus "when

he was set," and "followed him," as it was customary for his pupils to follow a Rabbi, on his walks, have Greek names, Andreas [Andreios] and Philippos. The others are Hebraic or Syriac, and approximately transliterate: Shimōn, surnamed Kepha; Yakōb, son of Zevadyah; Yochanan; Bar Talmai; Toma [perhaps also called Yehudah]; Mathai, or Mattathiah; Yakōb, the son of Chalphai, Gr. Halphaios [there is a doubt whether "Levi, son of Chalphai," stands for this Yakōb, or for Mathai]; Thaddai, Hodaiah or Yehudah, who, perhaps, came from Lebba or Iebba, near Carmel; Shimōn the Kanenieh or Kanai; and Yehudah Ish K'rioth.

The Greek language was in the air; it enwraps the whole era of Jesus; no single sentence of his can we find recorded in any other language, if we except the minor fragments of Aramaic, which we have just cited; and there are more than twice as many Greek words as these in a single treatise of the Talmud of Jerusalem. In a neo-Hebrew and Chaldean dialect Jesus doubtless spoke most often, but it is reasonable to regard him as not less cultured than his disciples and followers, and not below the standard of his time. His manifest acquaintance with Greek written thought speaks for itself, and is its own argument.

There is a morsel of evidence to be found, that the language of Jesus was not a pure but a mixed Hebraic dialect. In *Boanērges*, "the sons of thunder," *boane* seems to be a dialectic, perhaps a Galilean, form of the Hebrew *bene*, as seen in its singular number in Ben-ammi, Ben-hadad, Benjamin, etc.; while in *Bar-iōna*, "son of Jona, or John," the word *bar*, used only poetically in Hebrew, is the common Aramaic term for "son."

The hatred of Greek culture expressed at intervals by certain of the rabbis is evidence, at least, that it largely pervaded the community. And all, moreover, were not so bigoted; an allegoric comment upon Genesis (Midrash Rabba Gen., xxxvi.) speaks of the fringed garment of the Jews and the philosopher's robe of the Greeks as parts that ought to be united again to make one whole. R. Jochanan, son of Napucha (Talmud Jer. Sota), not only urges the study of Greek as a needful part of a man's education, but recommends it also for women. And another Rabbi, himself a consummate Greek scholar, quoted this opinion (Jer. Sabb., iii. 1 Sota) and had his daughter instructed in the language, as a necessary element of a good female education.

We may be able to compare the utterances of Jesus with the relics of the religious sages of antiquity without prejudice, now that we see there is no antecedent improbability of his having learned the language in which at his epoch the bulk of the world's treasures of thought were to be found. And we may find for ourselves a deeper interest in so doing if we realize what is submitted at the outset of this paper, that the divinest thought conceivable, to reach man on his own plane, must be brought down to his level, and clothed in garb familiar to his mind.

THE TRADITION OF THE ELDERS.

THE rubbish-heaps of past ages are often their only records. Shells, pottery, arrowheads, insignificant in themselves, become pregnant with meaning to the man who can read their story. Egyptian corn, such as famished Israelites went to buy, has been found in pyramids, and discovered to be not very different from the most familiar modern variety of wheat. What would not be given for a dust-heap of Eden which should contain a few well-preserved pips of the fruit that beguiled our reputed first parents? What anxious arboriculture would there not follow? What palates would not water by anticipation with, perhaps, a not entirely antiquarian curiosity and temptation?

The Talmud has been likened to a gigantic rubbish-heap. Even those who have studied it with patriotic sympathy allow that it is "a literary wilderness." Part of it is in Hebrew; part in a corrupt Chaldee or Aramaic, with Persian, Greek, and Latin idioms. This "confusion of tongues" is not to be wondered at, seeing that Palestine was ruled successively by Assyrians, Egyptians, Persians, Greco-Syrians, Romans. Students of the Talmud can "trace a number of its ethical, ceremonial, and doctrinal points in Zoroastrianism, in Christianity, . . . a vast deal of its metaphysics and philosophy in Plato, Aristotle, the Pythagoreans, the Neoplatonists, the Gnostics." These facts explain why the Hebrews, from time to time, have manifested such patriotic fervour and exclusiveness; had they not done so, they must have been lost as a separate race.

If the Talmud were nothing but a rubbish-heap, the importance of the epoch during which it was slowly accumulating would be enough to give it a value. The traditions it incorporates are prior to, contemporary with, and subsequent to, that other body of tradition to which Christendom yet professes to adhere; and, more than this, the authors of both are compatriots, and have a greater family likeness than some persons would be willing to allow.

Perhaps a chief reason, apart from sectarian considerations, why the Talmud has been the object of obloquy, is that it is so varied and universal in its scope. It contains the profoundest speculations, associated, often by a kind of pious literary legerdemain, with the text of the Pentateuch, the Prophetical writings, and the Hagiography. It contains the most trifling precepts, devised one by one to meet difficulties and questions as they arose, and accumulated into a scarcely organized heap, not very unlike the *indigesta moles* of our own case law. For Judaism, lost in its petty enactments, which lay on men's shoulders as a burden too heavy to be borne, and shut in by its prejudices which kept out free light, no sympathy can be expected in the present day. But in the current of Jewish life two streams are ever found side by side, the Law and the Prophets. Practical life, and the ideal life; this world and the world to come, are the poles of Jewish thought. Both are in extreme even to exaggeration, if we compare the national character with the average of other nations, and yet they meet without clash or conflict. This strongly marked characteristic of Hebrew antiquity is nowhere more fully exemplified than in the Talmud and its appendices, where "halacha," or rules by which to go, and "hagada," or ethical sayings and legends, are found side by side throughout.

Containing many points of sympathy with the gospel modes of thought, and of antagonism to the developed Christian doctrines, it is not surprising that the Talmud has been a sort of bugbear to ecclesiastical doctors. It was too big to refute; the only means of escape was to ignore it; and this course was rendered the more easy by the narrowness of the field of culture.

A literary friar of the "Seraphic Brethren," an order which it may be remembered began by discarding learning, assumed Talmud to be a man, and quoted from him—of course at second hand—with the words, "As Rabbi Talmud relates." To match the effect upon the Hebrew mind of such Christian erudition as this, "Father Pentateuch" and "Doctor Testament" would have to be cited as reverend divines.

The literature of Greece has no relation to religion as understood by evangelical Christendom: it is only in such as Pythagoras and Plato, who represent its ideal and mystical side, that it touches the plane of the Gospels, and even in that it comes within the scope of none but the more advanced students of divinity. With the collections in which the Hebrew oral law of many generations is found committed to writing, the case is very different, and their relation to Christian orthodoxy quite unlike that of pagan poets and philosophers. The latter are altogether dissimilar to either Old or New Testament in form, and their spiritual points of contact are only appreciable by a mind somewhat progressed in catholicity. The extra-biblical lore of the Hebrews, on the contrary, is constantly challenging comparison with the Christian traditions on points of external likeness, to such an extent as to injure the exclusiveness which Christian divines have for the most part striven to maintain as their prerogative.

Thus it has happened that there are countless editions of the manifold works of Greek and Roman writers, even down to those that have little to recommend them whether in style or matter; while up to the present time there has been comparatively little done to render the literary collections of the Hebrews accessible to the general reader. It is true that a number of the pagan books are masterpieces of form and exquisite in manner, while the Hebrew relics are for the most part disjointed collections of patchwork and uneven style; it is true also that the Hebrew is a rude and simple language, while the Greek has a large vocabulary and is the fittest vehicle for philosophic thought in the world. But these considerations lose force in the fact that the Hebrew canon has proved itself convertible into sterling English, and has opened out to us a noble store which we should lack much to lose. This fact but adds to the anomaly. We have editions of the Hebrew written law in number almost as the sands of the seashore, printed in Europe in every language of the earth; of the Hebrew oral law, which is for the most part of later compilation, there is not a single complete edition open to any one who is not a student of the Hebrew tongue and the Chaldean dialects.

A few preliminary definitions may be useful. Talmud is Learning, and represents, in contradistinction to the written law, those canons of tradition which, although purporting to originate in the instructions of Moses, are more probably of later growth. They may have begun soon after the time of Ezra, and before they were noted down by individual students, or collected in writing by editors, they were for a long period orally bequeathed from sage to sage. There are two collections called Talmud, one edited in Babylonia, the other redacted at Tiberias. Each consists of Mishna (traditional precept, learning, repetition) — an abstract of legal decisions; and of a Gemara (complementary learning or commentary, says one; final judgment or conclusion, says another), containing discussion and expansion of the precepts. The Babylonian and Palestinian editions have the same Mishna, but the Gemara of the Babylonian collection is quadruple the size of the Gemara of the other, which is known as the Talmud of Jerusalem.

The work of expounding which produced the Talmud was called Midrash, and the term came to be applied specially to legendary amplifications. The earliest example we have of anything of the nature of Midrash is where a peculiarly valiant King of Judah does and says so much that his doings and sayings and peculiarities go beyond the limits of the chronicler's function and have to be recorded in a kind of miscellany. "Abijah waxed mighty and took unto himself fourteen wives, and begat twenty-two sons and sixteen daughters. And the rest of the acts of Abijah, and his ways, and his sayings, are written in the commentary [Midrash; A.V., story] of the prophet Iddo" (2 Chron. xiii. 21). Another such Midrash is referred to (2 Chron. xxiv. 27) as "the Commentary of the Book of the Kings."

The collections known as Talmud, which succeed the Mikra, or written law, and the prophets, became themselves the text for sundry glosses or additional treatises—Tosephta (supplement), Baraitha (external or excluded tradition); there are also books entitled Siphra (a commentary on Leviticus), Siphre (an explanation of Numbers and Deuteronomy), Mekiltha (a Midrash of several treatises of a date anterior to the redaction of the Mishna), Yesirah (book on cosmogony), Zohar (kabala or qabala, mystical doctrine,—the word kabala meaning tradition, but extended to prophetic and poetical writings), Midrash Rabboth, Midrash Pesikta, Midrash Tanchuma, Pirqe R. Eliezer, Aboth Nathan, etc.

The headings of the orders and treatises of the Talmud will show over how wide a range of subjects this mass of tradition extended, religious and secular without distinction.

The Talmud is divided into six orders (seder), each of these contains treatises (masseceth), each treatise sections, and the separate sentences are called mischnaioth. The orders are (I.) Seeds (Zeraim), (II.) Feasts (Moëd), (III.) Women (Nashim), (IV.) Damages (Nesikin), (V.) Sacred Things (Kodashim), (VI.) Purifications (Taharoth).

The treatises are, of the first order, Benedictions (Berachoth), Corner of the Field (Peah), Doubtful (Demai),

Things Heterogeneous (Kilaïm), Seventh Year (Shebiith), Oblations (Terumoth), Tithes (Maaseroth), Second Tithes (Maaser Sheni), Cake of Dough (Challa), Foreskin of Trees (Orla), First Fruits (Biccurim).

Of the second order, Sabbath (Shabbath), Combinations (Erubin), Passovers (Pesaqim), Shekels (Shekalim), Day of Expiation (Yoma), Tabernacles (Succa), Egg of the Festival (Betza, or Yom Tob), New Year (Rosh Ha-shana), Fasting (Thaanith), Roll of Esther (Megilla), Feast of the Second Order (Moëd Katon), Festal Sacrifices (Chagiga).

Of the third order, Rights of Sisters-in-Law (Yebamoth), Marriage Contracts (Kethuboth), Betrothing (Qiddushin), Divorces (Gittin), Vows (Nedarim), Nazireans (Nazir), Suspected Woman (Sota).

Of the fourth order, First Gate (Baba Kama), Middle Gate (Baba Mezia), Last Gate (Baba Bathra), Judges (Sanhedrin), Blows (Maccoth), Oaths (Shebuoth), Evidences (Edayoth), Punishments (Horayoth), Idolatry (Aboda Zara), Sayings of the Fathers (Pirqe Aboth).

Of the fifth order, Sacrifices (Zebachim), Profane things (Cholin), Offerings (Menachoth), First Born (Becoroth), Estimations (Erachin), Substitution (Themura), Trespass (Meila), Extirpation of Souls (Kerithuth), Daily Sacrifice (Tamid), Measures (Middoth), Nests (Kinnim).

Of the sixth order, Vessels (Kelim), Tabernacles (Oholoth), Plagues (Negaim), Red Heifer (Para), Purifications (Taharoth), Baths (Mikvaoth), Woman who has her Rules (Nidda), Polluted (Zabim), Direction (Makshirin), Laved the Same Day (Tebul Yom), The Hands (Yadaim), Stalks of the Fruits (Oketzin).

The Midrash Rabboth contains the following: Bereschith Rabba, Shemoth R., Vajiqra R., Bemidbar R., Debarim R., Schir Ha Shirim R., Midrash Ruth R., Eicha Rabbathi, Qoheleth, Megilla Esther.

As the Septuagint by its subtle variations from the original text really introduces new elements, so the Targums also, which are strictly translations or paraphrases, practically expand into expositions of new doctrines.

"When at the return from the exile all the ancient institutions were restored, it was found that the people no longer understood their own Scriptures in their vernacular, and a translation into Aramaic (out of which sprang the Targums) had to be added 'so that they might understand them.'" "The Hebrew language—the 'language of Kenaan,' or 'Jehudith' of the Bible—became more and more the language of the few, the learned, the *Holy Language*, or still more exactly, 'Language of the Temple.'" "Since a bare translation could not in all cases suffice, it was necessary to add to the translation an explanation, more particularly of the more difficult and obscure passages. Both translation and explanation were designated by the term *Targum*. In the course of time there sprang up a guild, whose special office it was to act as interpreters in both senses (Meturgeman) [English, Dragoman], while formerly the learned alone volunteered their services."

It seems to be necessary to distinguish these volunteers from the paid officials, the "orators," who "at a later period stood by the side of the Chacham, or President of the Academy . . . (himself seated on a raised daïs), and repeated with a loud voice, and enlarged upon what the latter had whispered into their ear in Hebrew; comp. Matt. x. 27, 'What ye hear in the ear, that preach ye upon the housetops.'"

The Sopherim, or "Scribes" in the original sense of the word (which afterwards denoted a public reader of the law), are those who, from the return from the Captivity to the third century B.C., had the duty of preserving the text of the Thorah or Wisdom—that is, the Pentateuch; of explaining the precepts in accordance with the strict tradition of the oral law, of instructing and preaching; and they added to these functions that of creating additional injunctions designed as a hedge to keep sinners at a safe distance from the sacred precepts. This was termed "making a fence around the law." Many of them were members of what was styled the "Great Synagogue." The names of but few of them are remembered, —Ezra, Nehemiah, the supposed founders of the line, and Shimeon the Just, of about 300 B.C.

With a fine sympathy Deutsch wrote, " A mighty change has come over us. We children of this latter age, are, above all things, utilitarian. We do not read the Koran, the Zend Avesta, the Vedas, with the sole view of refuting them. We look upon all literature, religious, legal, and otherwise, whensoever and wheresoever produced, as part and parcel of humanity. We, in a manner, feel a kind of responsibility for it. We seek to understand the phase of culture which begot these items of our inheritance, the spirit that moves upon their face. And while we bury that which is dead in them, we rejoice in that which lives in them. We enrich our stores of knowledge from theirs, we are stirred by their poetry, we are moved to high and holy thoughts when they touch the divine chord in our hearts." There is perhaps more hope and assurance of what will be, than description of what is, in Deutsch's words. Where is the cultured Jew, who, with so much money that he scarcely knows what investment to turn to next, has come forward to help the country in which he has lived at ease, to the appreciation of the literary monuments of his race ? Where is the learned society which has for its objects to bring into modern light the wondrous stories of poetical and mystic truth which lie hid in the Midracha ? Where is the enthusiastic evangelical person anxious to put in a plea for the production of a work "written by Christ's nearest relations"? We do not burn the Talmud, as our forefathers did : we quote from it, partially and unfairly for the most part, and then leave the dust to gather on it,—a mode of suppressing it which is equally, if not more, efficacious.

Is it orthodox to pry into a literature which may cast a new and unexpected light upon primitive Christian doctrines? * May it not act as a disturber, seeing that faith in the well-worn dogmas is but slight, even when undisturbed? † An old divine of the English Church (Bishop Sherlock) once said in a sermon: "The religion of the Gospel is the true original religion of Reason and Nature. . . . The Gospel was a republication of the Law of Nature, and its precepts declarative of that original religion, which was as old as the Creation." A mind set like this old clergyman's might accept the fragments of the Talmudic allegories without injury. To follow so enticing and catholic an illuminating faith, would it not tend to reduce orthodoxy from a proud exclusive creed to a simple natural religion? It would; and one's place would depend upon the altitude attained within that natural religion. For in nature, if one rise high enough, the spiritual comes in sight, and the clear truth shines which makes free of sectarian bondage. Irradiated by the light of a faith as broad as this, the follower of Jesus might fraternize with the disciple of Hillel, and the little child of unperverted aspiration might lead them. For there need be none to hurt, or destroy, or be jealous, in all the holy mountain, for what under different names we call God is one, and real religion as catholic as the waters of the sea.

Having a kind of choice in our selection from Talmudic lore, instead of quoting absurd trifles among obsolete enactments in order to abuse them, we shall follow a good rule, that of choosing first that which we can admire; and we shall find it in the ethical and poetic illustrations of the more emancipated minds rather than in the drier disquisitions of the disputatious and cavilling legists. As there are preachers who are inspired beyond the narrow limits of their

* In one of his political interludes devoted to Homer and Genesis, Mr. Gladstone has put the pertinent question, "If the reviews and facts of the day have in any way shaken the standing ground of a Christian, is it not his first and most obvious duty to make a humble but searching scrutiny of the foundations?"

† The study of Greek was regarded as heretical at our Universities at the beginning of the sixteenth century. "His persuadent egregii sycophantæ hæresim esse, scire græcas litteras" (Erasmus, Antibarb., L. i., T. ix., p. 1699).

creed, so there were rabbis whose eyes looked past the tortuous passages of Judaism to the same kingdom of the golden age for which a brave man may yearn to-day. There is no penalty attached to heresy in the present day, so that we are free to pick what is most desirable to make us wise from the spiritual harvest of the world.

The vagueness of its dates has probably acted to the prejudice of the Talmud in the Western mind, accustomed to a different kind of historical accuracy than that of the East. The composition of the Talmud, says Deutsch, "ranges over about a thousand years." And, in another place, he says, "As to its 'dates,' nothing can be more authentic than the memory of the East. The Talmud has been preserved with absolute authenticity in the memory of doctors and disciples, in the same way as many Brahmin and Parsee priests can repeat, without the variation of a single accent, entire Vedas and other chapters of their sacred books, although without the slightest conception of their contents, and wholly ignorant of their meaning. The same was true of the followers of Zoroaster. At the same time, there is no doubt that much was written down by way of note by scribes, who yet did not venture upon the work of redaction. What alterations there are in the Talmud are owing to censors, who changed passages that were supposed to clash with Christianity, and produced the most singular obscurities." This idea of the infallibility of the memory of the custodians of the traditions would appear to be an exaggerated one. There is no doubt that modifications and misunderstandings have from time to time crept into the orally preserved treasures, not only of Zoroastrians, Brahmins and Buddhists, but also of Hebrews. It would indeed be an anomaly, seeing how texts, preserved in different countries by generations of manuscript copies, come to show deviations in a few centuries, if an oral tradition should insure an absolute and changeless fidelity, word by word, year by year, passing from memory to mouth, mouth to ear, ear to memory.

Dr. Kalisch ("A Sketch of the Talmud"), in reference to the reduction to writing of the oral law, observes: "In former times only the prophets, heads of congregations and colleges were allowed to have copies of the traditional laws, which they called '*Megilloth Setarim*,' 'Secret Scrolls.' They had to study them secretly in order to commit them to memory, that they might then be able to teach them in public orally. But when the Israelites continued to emigrate into distant countries, and were thus prevented from attending the Jewish academies, Rabbi Jehudah considered it much better to break a time-honoured custom and reduce the oral law to writing, so that it might be in every man's hand, and be thus accessible to all, than to expose the whole tradition to the risk of being misunderstood or forgotten."

Though it is mainly from internal evidence that the earliest date of the composition of the Talmud can be fixed; yet it has been argued with some reason that one of the sayings of Jesus is a proof of the existence of the Mishna, in manuscript, and not merely in memory, at the time when he spoke.* "Have ye not read in the law," he asked (Matt. xii. 5), "how that on the Sabbath day the priests in the Temple profane the sabbath, and are guiltless?" No expression of the kind has been found in the Scripture, but the subject is fully discussed in the treatise *Shabbath* of the Mishna.

The dates of actual compilation are partially determined by the dates of the Rabbis under whose care the redaction took place. The language of the Mishna is a late Hebrew; that of the Gemara of the Talmud of Jerusalem is a Chaldean dialect. The arrangement and committal to writing of the Mishna is believed to have been begun by Hillel about 33 B.C., and completed by Rabbi Jehudah about 217 A.D. The date of the redaction of the Gemara, which was done at Tiberias, is fixed at about 390 A.D., and that of the Babylonian Gemara at 365-427 A.D. Other commentaries which do not belong to

* F. R. Conder, in *Frazer's Magazine*, Dec., 1874.

these main collections, have ascribed to them dates both earlier and later than these; Mechilta, about 90 A.D., Midrash Rabboth, about 278 A.D., Pesikta, about 330–411 A.D., Tanchuma, about 440 A.D., Pirke R. Eliezer, about 70 A.D.

As to the comparative antiquity of the Gospels and the Talmud proper, Deutsch observes, "We need not urge the priority of the Talmud to the New Testament, although the former was redacted at a later period. To assume that the Talmud has borrowed from the New Testament would be like assuming that Sanskrit sprang from Latin, or that French was developed from the Norman words found in English."

To read this passage aright, we have to distinguish, on the one hand, between the earlier Mishnaic collections and the later commentaries (for certain Rabbis are believed to have adopted fragments of the sayings of Jesus as current before the doctrinal severance of Christianity from Judaism); and, on the other hand, to allow that the Gospels themselves contain both a portion of the primitive utterances of Jesus, and editorial glosses and misunderstandings of considerably later date.

The first of the sages of the Mishna was Shimeon the Just, who flourished in the fourth century before our era. He is described as "one of the remnants of the Great Synagogue," an expression which is regarded as comprising a succession of teachers receiving from the line of the prophets. Shimeon is said to have handed down the traditions to Antigonus of Soko; Antigonus to Jose ben Joezer, and Jose ben Jochanan of Jerusalem; these to Jehoshua ben Perachia and Matthai the Arbelite; these to Jehudah ben Tabai and Shimeon ben Shatach, these to Shemayah, Abtalion, and other teachers; these to Hillel and Shammai.

Hillel became president at Jerusalem about 30 B.C. He is said to have had eighty disciples, called "the elders of the house of Hillel." Hillel delivered his office to his son Shimeon and to Rabban Jochanan ben Zakai. During this period our present era commences. Shimeon was succeeded by Gamaliel the elder, who became president of the Sanhedrin 30 A.D.; and he by Shimeon the second, who in his turn was succeeded by Gamaliel the second, and he by Shimeon the third. Then followed Rabbi Jehudah, surnamed Ha-nasi, the chief, or Rabbenu ha-Qadosh, the saint, to whom we have referred as the redactor of the Mishna. Rabban Jochanan ben Zakai lived upwards of a hundred years, and founded a school at Jabne, near the coast, almost due west of Jerusalem. He had five noted disciples, R. Liezer ben Hyrqanos, R. Jehoshua ben Chananiah, R. Jose, the priest, R. Shimeon ben Nathaniel, and R. Eleazar ben Arak. The doctors of this line bear the name of Tanaim, and cover the period from 220 B.C. to 220 A.D.; nearly two hundred of them are known by name.

The Pharisees represented the Jewish religious world of the time when our era commences in much the same way as the Established Church represents the English community of to-day. We are apt to judge the Pharisees generally by denunciations which were meant to apply to spurious, degraded, or perverted Pharisaism. The Talmud itself stigmatizes certain classes of Pharisees as unworthy of the name, amongst which we may find a family likeness to the kind of Pharisee pointed at in the Gospels. There were "those who do the will of God from earthly motives; those who make small steps, or say, 'Just wait a while for me, I have just one more good office to perform;' those who knock their heads against walls in avoiding the sight of a woman; Saints in office; those who implore you to mention some more duties which they might perform; they who are pious because they *fear* God." Among the professors of any religion might, no doubt, be found individuals akin to these. On the other hand, "the real and only Pharisee" is the real and only worthy holder of any faith whatever, he "who does the will of his father which is in Heaven *because he loves Him.*"

If Christendom has despised the Talmud, the thousand years of work and thought which it contains have nevertheless not been made void. No serious work perishes without effect, and this was produced under specially stimulating circumstances. A too-assured worldly prosperity is not the most favourable condition for the development of ideal thought, and the nation which suffers, not seldom rises to a higher spiritual level thereby. The Hebrews suffered and were strong —not politically, but individually; prophets and doctors of the law possessing their souls in patience, and holding fast their faith in the fidelity of God.

Owing to their peculiar geographical position, the Hebrews were brought into contact with the mightiest peoples of the old world, a circumstance which could not but subject them to influences, which, however much from time to time they might attempt to shake them off, must have affected them largely. Egypt, Phœnicia, Assyria, Babylon, Chaldea, Media, Persia, Greece, Rome—these are the most gigantic ghosts of the old world, and with all these in the prime of their development, the Hebrew race was brought into close relations.

When, after the terrible education of exile, the people came to a consciousness of having a literature of their own, there arose a passionate ardour which founded colleges and maintained them, in spite of the disasters of the country and the successive changes of its rulers. The people "began to press round these brands plucked from the fire—the scanty records of their faith and history—with fierce and passionate love. . . These same documents, as they were gradually formed into a canon, became the immutable centre of their lives, their actions, their very dreams." Every thought thereafter was associated with its real or fancied prototype in the written law, and the process begot the appendix to the Scripture, consisting of interminable commentaries, which we now possess in the Talmud.

The heroes of the biblical narrative became exalted into poetical ideals, a fact of which we have an instance in the Gospel parable of Dives and Lazarus, where "Abraham's bosom" is the imaginary representation of life in the folds of Heaven, a symbol which surely no one would think of reading in the hard literal sense of the words. "The persons of the Bible—the kings and the patriarchs, the heroes and the prophets, the women and the children, what they did and suffered, their happiness and doom, their words and their lives —became, apart from their presupposed historical reality, a symbol and an allegory."

The exclusiveness of mediæval Christendom could only formally shut the door on alien doctrines, and they crept in unseen from Jewish as well as Pagan sources. "The great storehouse, the Midrash, teems with gems that have been scattered broadcast over not merely the whole Jewish and Mohammedan, but also over the classical and Christian world, together with all those other elements of civilization and refinement which the Shemites never ceased to impart to our Western lands."

To give an instance of this unrecognized indebtedness, those who are interested in the very tenderly told fable in verse, "The Hermit" of Parnell, may find its original in the Talmud, where the angel Elijah, under the semblance of a man, effects apparent injustices, and afterwards explains them by reference to the spiritual plane where each has its motive.

This mode of fabling is common to the Talmud and the Gospels. "The Good Samaritan" belongs to the Hagada just as much as the "story of the sage, who, walking in a market-place crowded with people, suddenly encountered the prophet Elijah, and asked him who, out of that vast multitude, would be saved. Whereupon the prophet first pointed out a weird-looking creature, a turnkey, 'because he was merciful to his prisoners;' and next, two common-looking tradesmen, who came walking through the crowd, pleasantly chatting. The sage instantly rushed towards them, and asked them what were their saving works. But they, much puzzled, replied, 'We are but poor workmen who live by our trade. All that can be said for us is, that we are always of good cheer, and are good-natured. When we meet anybody who seems sad, we join him, and we talk to him, and cheer him, so long that he must forget his grief. And if we know of two people who have quarrelled, we talk to them and persuade them, until we have made them friends again. This is our whole life.'"

"Were not the whole of our general views on the difference between Judaism and Christianity greatly confused," says Deutsch, "people would certainly not be so very much surprised at the striking parallels of dogma and parable, of allegory and proverb, exhibited by the Gospel and the Talmudical writings. The New Testament, written, as Lightfoot has it, 'among Jews, by Jews, for Jews,' cannot but speak the language of the time, both as to form, and, broadly speaking, as to contents. There are many more vital points of contact between the New Testament and the Talmud than divines yet seem fully to realize; for such terms as 'Redemption,' 'Baptism,' 'Grace,' 'Faith,' 'Salvation,' 'Regeneration,' 'Son of Man,' 'Son of God,' 'Kingdom of Heaven,' were not, as we are apt to think, invented by Christianity, but were household words of Talmudical Judaism."

A peculiar irony of fate attends the completion of the redaction in writing of the much-worshipped oral law. Many of the enactments were already obsolete; and Rome had substituted her own penal code for that which generations of Jewish doctors had elaborated with so much care. The minute injunctions regulating temple services and sacrifices had but a mournful historic value when the solemnities had been done away; and as for the laws which had particular reference to Palestine, the bulk of the nation was sojourning in other lands. The enthusiasts among them looked forward to the days of a restoration when their codified tradition would come into force as one glorious and sufficient law. But century after century has gone by, and probably few Jews of the present day would care to go back to Palestine (which a handful of their wealthy families could accomplish with ease by a purchase of the whole country from the Porte) if the condition were that they were to be bound absolutely and for ever by every burden which the enactments of their ancient law would lay upon their shoulders.

The "Halacha" portion of the Talmud is likely to repel the ordinary reader. Its elaborate tilt of argument against argument, its minute commandments, intended as a hedge or fence to keep men from coming near enough to break one of the larger or diviner ordinances, become tedious to any but a student of ancient law. With the "Hagada" it is quite different; the imaginative faculties have free play, and imagination is more than cosmopolitan in its range. The legendary part of the Talmudic books enshrines the dearest dreams of long lines of studious men, sometimes in poetic fancies, sometimes in occult symbols that hid the meaning implied from any person not likely to care for it. This province of Talmudical literature has a more important place than Deutsch claims for it when he says it was "only a 'saying' [saga], a thing without authority, a play of fancy, an allegory, a parable, a tale, that pointed a moral and illustrated a question, that smoothed the billows of fierce debate, roused the slumbering attention, and was generally—to use its own phrase—a 'comfort and a blessing.'"

What mistakes can be made in reading symbolic expressions by the light only of a superficial common sense may be illustrated by the following example. There is a story in the Talmud which runs thus:—

"Four men entered Paradise. One beheld and died. One beheld and lost his senses. One destroyed the young plants. Only one entered in peace and came out in peace." The men were four illustrious Rabbis; and the heaven they entered was a very mysterious one. The four consonants of the Persian word Paradise, P. R. D. S., are initials of words representing respectively, Simple Understanding, Hint, Hagadistic Allegorizing, and Sôd or Secret Science. The first covers the study of literal meaning in Scripture; the second, traditional indications of meaning by means of points and signs which would be unnoticed by the uninitiated; the third, according to Deutsch, "was a peculiar kind of sermon, with all the aids of dialectics and poetry, of parable, gnome, proverb, legend, and the rest, exactly as we find it in the New Testament;" the fourth was "theosophy, metaphysics, angelology, a host of wild and gloomy visions of things beyond earth. Faint echoes of this science, survive in Neoplatonism, in Gnosticism, in the Kabbala, in Hermes Trismegistus." Eventually the word Paradise indicated this last branch of study, mainly or alone. Ben Zoma, according to *Chagiga*, "looked, and became demented" from indulging too freely in the "honey" (Prov. xxv. 16) of metaphysics. The one who looked and perished wore himself out by his preternatural activity. The Rabbi who destroyed the young plants in Paradise was one who turned from the study of the law to Greek literature, philosophy, and destructive speculation, became a searcher among theosophical problems, then an eminent teacher, and finally a renegade and apostate. The Rabbi who went in and out in peace was the one who, after a heroic life, died in the hands of Roman executioners, and according to the legend, with his last breath proclaimed the central confession of the Hebrew creed, "The Lord our God is ONE." "Paradise" thus represents here the ideal side of the study of the law, the law representing to the Hebrew mind all that was highest in mystical philosophy, as well as in doctrinal certainty.

One ancient saying is peculiarly noteworthy as having constituted the keystone of Sadduceeism, owing to that dwarfing process to which it seems to be fated for all noble expressions to be subjected on their way into the popular mind. The saying is ascribed to Antigonus of Soko, of the third century before our era, and runs as follows: "Be not as slaves that minister to the lord with a view to receive recompense; but as slaves that minister to the lord without a view to receive recompense." An artist would understand this saying. The great Neapolitan painter, Morelli, when asked by the present writer the price of a picture that stood nearly finished in his studio, replied that he never looked at his pictures from the point of view of their value until his work upon them was over. Assuredly if a painter at his work were ever brooding over the sum to be received for his picture, instead of over the picture itself, his result would be valueless. But in the cavern of narrow minds the words of the great Scribe were cramped and darkened into the inference that, as the heavenly service is expressly separated from any view of reward, there is therefore no reward for it; in other words, there is no future life.

The Rabbis appear to have associated Sadducecism with Epicureanism: "All the seals of the blessings in the sanctuary used to say, 'from eternity,' but since the Epicureans perversely taught there is but one world, it was directed that men should say 'from eternity to eternity'" (Talm. Berach., ix. 5 [9], Mishna).

Among the multitude of Rabbis whose labours fill ten centuries at least, there were many crabbed minds which have mainly impressed upon us our views of Judaism as a narrow and unlovely creed. But there were also Rabbis of gentle spirit and broad views. Hillel was one of these.

Hillel was a native of Babylon, who settled in Jerusalem when forty years of age. He studied while yet in Babylon, separating himself from a trading brother. He earned a livelihood as a woodcutter, and offered his services gratuitously to poor Rabbis, so that they might allow him to attend their lectures. When in Jerusalem he attended the academy presided over by the renowned teachers Shemaiah and Abtalion, and of his small daily earnings a moiety went to the gatekeeper of the schools. One day in winter, he could not gain the amount he needed, owing to the shortness of the day. He could, consequently, neither buy for himself the necessary food, nor could he pay the gatekeeper's fee at the college. He climbed up and sat at the window to listen to the words of the sages. The snow covered him, but he listened on, until he became benumbed and his senses left him. In the morning it was said, " Why is the house so dark to-day ? " It was the Sabbath. They spied Hillel, brought him in and attended to his wants, saying, " He is worthy that the Sabbath should be profaned for him." When the doctors were informed of his intense longing for truth, they granted him free admission to the studies. He made great proficiency, and advanced to be head and founder of a school. He became president of the academy about 30 B.C., and died when Jesus was about ten years old.

The story of his appointment is intensely Jewish. "The principle that Passover sets aside Sabbath when they clash, had escaped the elders. . . . Hillel, being interrogated, said it followed *a fortiori* from the fact that more than two hundred minor 'Passovers' (= sacrifices) in the year set aside the Sabbath; and he argued his point from every side, but in vain, since 'Thorah without traditional authority is no Thorah.' At length he said, 'It occurs to me that thus I heard from Shemaiah and Abtalion;' and they arose and appointed him 'nasi'" (C. Taylor, "Sayings of the Jewish Fathers").

A harvest of kindly thought clusters around the name of Hillel.

Once, when he was hastening on some duty, his disciples asked him what caused him to hasten, and he replied he had to look after his guest. When they begged him to tell the name of the guest, he said he meant his soul, which was here to-day and there to-morrow. A beautiful conception, and probably suggested by the thoughts of still older masters.

Stories are told of Hillel's temper being tried for a wager by pertinacious questioners, whose most trifling queries he met with mild patience and with wise answers. Possessed of this character, and occupying a high office, he appears to have been the favourite victim of the querulous persons who ask, as a question which they have a right to have answered however perplexively put, "What must I do to be saved?" One of these said to Hillel, "I wish to become a proselyte, provided the Jewish religion can be taught to me in so short a time as I can stand on one foot." Hillel's answer was characteristic, and may remind us of the words of another Master who was much pestered by trivial people: "Whatever is not pleasant unto thee, do not unto thy fellow-man. This is the substance of the law and the prophets; all the rest is but commentary thereon. Go and reflect on it" (Talm. Bab. Shabb., 31 a).

Among his sayings are the following:—

"A name magnified is a name destroyed; he who increases not, diminishes; he who will not learn deserves death; and whosoever converts to his own use the tiara of the law perishes."

"Separate not thyself from the congregation, and trust not in thyself until the day of thy death; and judge not thy friend until thou comest into his place; and . . . say not, 'When I have leisure I will study;' perchance thou mayest not have leisure."

"The boor is not a sin-fearer; nor is the vulgar pious; nor is the shamefast apt to learn, nor the passionate to teach; nor is every one that has much traffic wise. And in a place where there are no men, endeavour to be a man."

"More flesh, more worms; more treasures, more care; more maidservants, more lewdness; more menservants, more robbery; more women, more witchcrafts; more Thorah, more life; more wisdom, more scholars; more righteousness, more peace. He who has gotten a good name, has gotten it for himself. He who has gotten to himself words of Thorah, has gotten to himself the life of the world to come." We may be reminded here of the expression, "Thou hast the words of everlasting life."

The following emanates from a later Rabbi, and like Hillel's words has something of a gospel ring: "They reveal to him the secrets of Thorah; and he is made, as it were, a spring that ceases not, and as a stream that flows on increasing; and he becomes modest, and long-suffering, and forgiving of insult; and it magnifies him and exalts him over all things" (Pereq R. Meir).

The following are isolated passages, gathered to enable an idea to be formed of the variety and beauty of the thoughts enshrined in the Talmud:—

Rabbi Simeon, son of Gamaliel I., said with stern simplicity, "All my days I have grown up amongst the wise, and have not found aught good for a man but silence; not learning but doing is the groundwork; and whoso multiplies words occasions sin."

"Silence is the fence round wisdom."

"What is a profanation of the name of God?" According to R. Jochanan, that sin is committed by "the man who has abased his own character."

"What has become of thy money?—Is there not a saying in Jerusalem, 'The salt was wanting to the money'? Salt is used to preserve meat; without salt the meat rots. Charity is to money even as salt is to meat."

"Ben Azzai used to say, 'Despise not any man, and carp not at anything; for thou wilt find that there is not a man that has not his hour, nor a thing that has not its place.'"

R. Ishmael, son of R. Jochanan, said, "He that learns in order to teach, they grant him the faculty to learn and to teach: he that learns in order to practise, they grant him the faculty to learn, and to teach, and to practise" (P. Aboth, iv. 8).

"He who gives charity in secret is greater than Moses himself."

"After the thief runs the theft; after the beggar poverty."

"He who humiliates himself will be lifted up; he who raises himself will be humiliated. Whosoever runs after greatness, greatness runs away from him; he who runs from greatness, greatness follows him."

"There is a great difference between him who is ashamed before his own self, and him who is only ashamed before others."

"He who walks daily over his estates finds a little coin each time."

A daring saying like "Greater is he who derives his livelihood from work than he who fears God," shows that some at least among the nation were free from the pretences of veneration which follow priestcraft, and is the strongest statement possible of the doctrine that *laborare est orare*. The following, too, is akin to it, in its contempt of ceremonial devoutness as compared with the devotion of duty, "Rather live on your Sabbath as you would on a week-day, than be dependent on others."

"Do not live near a pious fool."

"There are three crowns: of the law, the priesthood, and the kingship; but the crown of a good name is greater than them all."

"Every man in Israel is a priest, every man's house a temple, every man's table an altar, every man's prayer his sacrifice."

"When a man enters upon the path of truth and justice," said R. Ishmael, "God helps him forward, but when he chooses the way of sin, God says, 'I gave thee reason and freewill, go thy way,' even as the trader will wait upon the customer who purchases a good and pleasant article, while to one who desires pitch or sulphur, he says, 'Go, wait upon thyself!'" The same Rabbi's definition of sin is deserving of study. "Sin is an obstruction in the heart, an inability to feel and comprehend all that is noble, true, and great, and to take part in the good."

"To pray loudly is not a necessity of devotion: when we pray we must direct our hearts towards Heaven."

"As God fills the whole universe, so the soul fills the whole body; as God sees and is not seen, so the soul sees and is not seen; as God nourishes the whole universe, so the soul nourishes the whole body; as God is pure, so the soul is pure."

The following is a grand saying, as showing that liberty of the individual which is part of the process of creation: "Everything is in God's hand save the fear of God."

"This world is like a roadside inn, but the world to come is like the real home."

"For the righteous there is no rest, neither in this world nor in the next, for they go, say the Scriptures, from host to host, from striving to striving."

"Who is strong? He who subdues his passion. Who is rich? He who is satisfied with his lot."

"He who sacrifices a whole offering, shall be rewarded for a whole offering; he who offers a burnt-offering, shall have the reward of a burnt-offering; but he who offers humility to God and man, shall be rewarded with a reward as if he had offered all the sacrifices in the world."

In the following we may be reminded of the parable of the Sower:—

"There are four characters in scholars. Quick to hear and quick to forget, his gain is cancelled by his loss: slow to hear and slow to forget, his loss is cancelled by his gain: quick to hear, and slow to forget, is wise: slow to hear and quick to forget, this is an evil lot" (P. Aboth, v. 18. Trans. C. Taylor).*

---

* Cf. "When the superior scholar hears Taò, he diligently practises it. When the middling scholar hears Taò, he one while keeps it, another while loses it. When the inferior scholar hears Taò, he laughs aloud at it" (Lao-tsè, Taò-tĕ Kĭng, ch. 41).

"There are four characters in those who sit under the wise: a sponge; a funnel; a strainer; and a bolt-sieve. A sponge, which sucks up all; a funnel, which lets in here and lets out there; a strainer, which lets out the wine and keeps back the dregs; a bolt sieve, which lets out the pollard, and keeps back the flour" (P. Aboth, v. 21).

The parable of the Rock and the Sand is paralleled in the following:—

"He who has more learning than good works is like a tree with many branches but few roots, which the first wind throws on its face; while he whose works are greater than his knowledge is like a tree with many roots and fewer branches, but which all the winds of heaven cannot uproot" (P. Aboth, iii. 27).

"If thy wife is small, bend down to her and whisper in her ear. He who forsakes the love of his youth, God's altar weeps for him. He who sees his wife die before him, has, as it were, been present at the destruction of the sanctuary itself—around him the world grows dark."

"He who marries for money, his children shall be a curse to him."

"The man is not without the woman, nor the woman without the man, nor both of them (the union of the two) without the Shekinah" (Talm. Jer. Berach., ix. 1; Bereschith R., viii.).

"Rabbi Josè said, I never call my wife 'wife,' but 'home,' for she indeed makes my home."

"Underneath the wings of the seraphim are stretched the arms of the divine mercy, ever ready to receive sinners."

"The best preacher is the heart, the best teacher is time; the best book is the world; the best friend is God."

"When God was about to create man, great clamour arose among the heavenly host. Some said, 'Create, O God, a being who shall praise thee on earth, even as we sing thy glory in Heaven!' Others said, 'O God, create no more!

Man will destroy the glorious harmony which thou hast set on earth, as in Heaven!' Of a sudden, God turned to the contesting host of Heaven, and deep silence fell upon them all. Then before the Throne of Glory there appeared bending the knee the Angel of Mercy, and he prayed, 'O Father, create man! He will be thine own noble image on earth. I will fill his heart with heavenly pity and sympathy towards all creatures; they will praise thee through him.' And there appeared the Angel of Peace, and wept, 'O God, man will disturb thine own peace. Blood will flow; he will invent war, confusion, horror. Thy place will be no longer in the midst of all thy earthly works.' The Angel of Justice cried, 'Thou wilt judge him God! He shall be subject to my law, and peace shall again find a dwelling-place on earth.' The Angel of Truth said, 'Father of Truth, cease! With man thou createst the lie.' Out of the deep silence then was heard the Divine Word, 'You shall go with him—you, mine own seal, Truth. But you shall remain a denizen of Heaven—between Heaven and earth you shall float, an everlasting link between both.'"

"Repent one day before thy death. There was a king who bade all his servants to a great repast, but did not indicate the hour: some went home and put on their best garments and stood at the door of the palace: others said, 'There is ample time, the king will let us know beforehand.' But the king summoned them of a sudden; and those that came in their best garments were well received, but the foolish ones who came in their slovenliness, were turned away in disgrace. Repent to-day, lest to-morrow ye might be summoned."

This truth is represented on a larger scale in the parable called "The Desert Island." The following is one of a similar kind: "A traveller upon his journey passed through the forest upon a dark and gloomy night. He journeyed in dread; he feared the robbers who infested the route he was travelling; he feared that he might slip and fall into some unseen ditch or pitfall on the way; and he feared, too, the wild beasts, which he knew were about him. By chance he discovered a pine torch, and lighted it, and its gleams afforded him great relief. He no longer feared brambles or pitfalls, for he could see his way before him. But the dread of robbers and wild beasts was still upon him, nor left him till the morning's dawn, the coming of the sun. Still he was uncertain of his way, until he emerged from the forest, and reached the cross-roads, when peace returned unto his heart.

"The darkness in which the man walked was the lack of religious knowledge. The torch he discovered typifies God's precepts, which aided him on the way until he obtained the blessed sunlight, compared to God's holy word. Still, while man is in the forest (the world), he is not entirely at peace; his heart is weak, and he may lose the right path; but when he reaches the cross-roads (death), then may we proclaim him truly pious, and exclaim, 'A good name is more fragrant than rich perfume, and the day of death is better than the day of one's birth.'"

"Antoninus, in conversing with R. Judah said to him: 'In the future world, when the soul comes before the Almighty Creator for judgment, may it not find a plea of excuse for worldly wickedness in saying, "Lo, the sin is the body's, I am now free from the body; the sins were not mine?"' R. Judah answered, 'Let me relate to thee a parable. A king had an orchard of fine figs, which he prized most highly. That the fruit might not be stolen or abused, he placed two watchers in the orchard, and that they themselves might not be tempted to partake of the fruit, he chose one of them a blind man, and the other lame. But lo, when they were in the orchard, the lame man said to his companion, "I see very fine figs, they are luscious and tempting; carry me to the tree, that we may both partake of them." So the blind man carried the lame man, and they ate of the figs. When the king entered the orchard, he noticed at once that the finest figs were missing, and he asked the watchers what had become of them. The blind man answered, "I know not. I could not steal them; I am blind, I cannot even see them." And the lame man answered, "Neither could I steal them, I could not approach the tree." But the king was wise, and he answered: "Lo, the blind carried the lame," and he punished them accordingly.'"

All parables are not so simple as these; the myth of Elijah standing on the mountains of Judæa three days before the appearance of the Messiah, proclaiming peace and redemption to all mankind, followed by the legendary vision of the final consummation of all things, is quite unintelligible on the present popular understanding of the terms, and to explain it would require the quotation of a number of illustrative passages.

The "Sepher Yezirah," is regarded by critics as the first philosophical work written in Hebrew. The title itself means Book on Creation, or Cosmogony. The book contains something of the Kabala, which we may view from its Jewish side, instead of through a Greek or Egyptian medium, as we find it in the Gnostic and Hermetic books. Of the "Yezirah," Dr. J. F. von Meyer remarked, in the preface to an edition published in Leipzic in 1830: "This book is for two reasons highly important: in the first place, that the real Kabala, or mystical doctrine of the Jews, which must be carefully distinguished from its excrescences, is in close connection and perfect accord with the Old and New Testaments; and in the second place, that the knowledge of it is of great importance to the philosophical inquirer, and cannot be put aside. Like a cloud permeated by beams of light, which makes one infer that there is more light behind it, so do the contents of this book, enveloped in obscurity, abound in coruscations of thought, reveal to the mind that there is a still more effulgent light lurking somewhere, and thus invite us to a further contemplation and investigation, demonstrating at the same time the danger of a superficial investigation, which is so prevalent in modern times, rejecting that which cannot be understood at first sight."

Dr. Isidor Kalisch, who has brought out a scholarly edition of the work (New York, 1877), speaks thus of its tendency: "It teaches that a first cause, eternal, all-wise, almighty, and holy, is the origin and the centre of the whole universe, from whom gradually all beings emanated. Thought, speech, and action are an inseparable unity in the divine being: God made or created, is metaphorically expressed by the word: writing. . . . God stands in close relation with the Universe, and just so is Tali* connected with the world, that is, an invisible, celestial, or universal axis carries the whole fabric; in the year by the sphere, in man by the heart; and thus is the ruling spirit of God everywhere."

Perhaps it is not fair to a work of such a nature, hiding its meaning in a metaphorical form to which we have not the key, to quote isolated passages. The book if read at all should be studied as a whole. But some very discerning interpretations heve been reached, and an apparently occult form is sometimes more simple than it seems. Letters will be found possessing a certain arithmetical value and relation, while groups of numbers, however reverentially regarded, have no more sacred significance than to act as a sort of *memoria technica* by which to assort into a comprehensive form for contemplation the varied processes of nature, or they may serve as a kind of mental orrery in which to view the motion of the universe.

* The passage is in the original: "Dragon (Tali) is in the world like a king upon his throne, the sphere is in the year like a king in the empire, and the heart is in the human body like a king in war." Upon this Dr. Kalisch comments that it is maintained that "the ancient Jewish astronomers signified by the word Tali, not the constellation Draco, but the line which joins together the two points in which the orbit of the moon intercepts the ecliptic (Dragon's head and tail). Dr. Cassel is of opinion that our author meant here, probably the invisible, celestial, or universal axis that carries the whole Universe."

"According to the idea of the author," says Kalisch, "there emanated from the unity of God three ethereal elements: primitive air from the spirit, from the air primitive water, and from the water primitive fire or ether, out of which came other spheres of existence in the significant and highly important number, seven, from which descended smaller spheres, which again produced others. He endeavours to show how the ideal became, after numerous emanations, more condensed, palpable, and concrete. The whole creation is thus contemplated as a pyramid, terminating in a point at the top, and having a broad basis."

The contradiction to ditheism is marked in the Yezirah. The deity Yah ordains the universe in paths of wisdom by three sepharim or signs of himself—the idea, the word, the writing of the word. To the Creator, as some ancient Rabbis declared, idea, word, and work are one and the same. Chief among the roads of the formation of the universe are those described as "the decade out of nothing," *i.e.* emanatory powers to which no atomic particles or elements of matter are antecedent. The decade consists of infinitudes, which are the beginning and the end, height and depth, the four points of the east, the west, the north and the south, good and also evil. This is evidently a rough conception of the scaffolding of the universe. The writer says, "Keep thy tongue from speaking, and thy mind from pondering on it, and if thy mouth urges thee to speak, and thy heart to think about it, return! As it reads:—And the living creatures ran and returned (Ezech., vi. 14), and upon this was the covenant made." This is explained to mean that "as the living creatures which the prophet saw in his vision were stricken with such an awe, that they could not go any further to see the divine glory, and had to return, so is the decade an eternal secret to us, and we are not permitted to understand it." With regard to evil and good, the book declares that "God has set one over against the other; the good against the evil, and the evil against the good ; the good proceeds from the good, and the evil from the evil ; the good purifies the bad, and the bad the good."

An elucidation of some of the difficult or misunderstood passages of the Gospels by the aid of parallels drawn from the Talmud, and a comparison of some of its "small coins" and mystic legends with the "logia" and parables of the Gospels, will perhaps do more to familiarize the mind with the Talmudic phraseology and its meaning than a selection made on abstract principles.

The compilers of the hagadistic portion of the Gospels, which in the third Gospel is so conspicuous an element, had ample supplies to choose from amongst floating legends.

"An Arab, who understood the voices of animals, hearing a cow bellow, said to its master, "Son of Juda ! . . . it announces that the Messiah has just been born.' 'What is his name ?' 'Menachem.' 'The name of his father ?' 'Hezekiah.' 'Where is he born ?' 'In the royal city, Bethlehem in Judea'" (Talm. Jer. Berachoth, ii. 4).

"Every one who is written down for life eternal will see the consolation of Israel" (Targum, Isai. iv. 3).

"They long for the years of consolation that are to come" (Targum, Jerem. xxxi. 6).

"There was a man in Jerusalem, whose name was Simeon ; and this man was righteous and devout, looking for the consolation of Israel" (Luke ii. 25).

This Simeon has been supposed to be the father of Gamaliel the elder, and son of Hillel.

Josephus had evidently a stray Talmudic legend in his mind when he wrote (Antiq., v. 10. 4), "Samuel, when he had just completed his twelfth year, did prophesy." A similar story is told of Daniel at the same age (Ignat. ad Magn., also Susanna, 45). At the same age, Jesus in the third Gospel is described as discussing with the temple Rabbis.

The relation of John to Jesus as presented in the Gospel is both that of spiritual father to son, and also that of disciple to doctor, or servant to master; even more the latter than the former: for we learn from the Talmud, "Every labour which a servant does for his lord, a disciple also does for his teacher, with the exception of loosening his shoe" (Kethuboth, f. 90. 1). This was the servile ministry, done by servants to their masters on their arrival at home.

"The spirit of God was borne above the waters, like a dove poised upon its wings" (Talmud, Chagiga, 2).

"The spirit of God descending as a dove, and coming upon him" (Matt. iii. 16).

"Those who study diligently in the Talmud see a great light. For God illuminates their eyes, and shows them those things that are written in the law, but not expressly and particularly explained" (Tanchuma, Isai. ix. 1).

The passage here referred to is quoted in the gospel (Matt. iv. 16) in application to the commencement of the ministry of Jesus:—

> "The people which sat in darkness
> Saw a great light,
> And to them which sat in the region and shadow of death,
> To them did light spring up."

The sermons attributed to Jesus are collections of sayings, and ought naturally to show many points of resemblance to the *dicta* of the Talmud.

"He that forgiveth the grievance done to him, him doth God also forgive his sins" (Bab. Rosh Ha-shana, 17 a).

"Do compassion, that people may do it unto thee; give a loan, that they may give a loan unto thee; show grief, that they may show grief for thee; afford burial, that they may afford burial unto thee; do kindnesses, that they may do kindnesses unto thee" (Qoheleth R., viii. 3, and Kethuboth, f. 71, 1).

"Whosoever hath mercy on man, on him also hath God mercy. But he who showeth no mercy to men, neither to him will God show mercy" (Shabbath, f. 151. 2).

"Blessed are the merciful, for they shall obtain mercy" (Matt. v. 7).

"Four kinds will not see the Godhead—the scoffers, the flatterers, the liars, and the slanderers" (Talm. Bab. Sota, 42 a).

"Blessed are the pure in heart, for they shall see God"* (Matt. v. 8).

"Whosoever does not persecute them that persecute him, whosoever takes an offence in silence, he who does good because of love, he who is cheerful under his sufferings,—they are the friends of God" (Talmud, cit.; Deutsch).

"Be thou the cursed, not he who curses. Be of them that are persecuted, not of them that persecute" (*ibid.*).

"Remember that it is better to be persecuted than to persecute" (Talmud, Yoma).

"Those who are afflicted, and do not afflict in return, who suffer everything for the love of God, and bear their burden with a gladsome heart, shall be rewarded according to the promise, 'Those who love the Lord shall be as invincible as the rising sun in his might'" (Shabbath).

"If the persecutor were a just man, and the persecuted an impious one, God would always espouse the cause of the persecuted" (Midrash, Vajiqra R., 27).

"It is pleasing to the righteous to suffer afflictions on account of God, for thus are they freed from this state of exile" (Synopsis Sohar, 92. Cf. 2 Macc. vii. 14, Heb. xi. 35).

"Blessed are they that have been persecuted for righteousness' sake: for theirs is the kingdom of heaven" (Matt. v. 10).

"All food needs to be salted in order to be preserved. Money, too, requires to be salted to be preserved. Wherewith

---

* The expression is a familiar one in the Hebrew scripture: "Let me behold thy face in righteousness: let me be satisfied, when I awake, with thy similitude" (Ps. xvii. 15). "The similitude of Jehovah shall he (Moses) behold" (Numb. xii. 8). "After my skin hath been stripped off, out from my flesh, I shall see God" (Job. xix. 26).

does money required to be salted? With charity" (Talmud, Kethuboth, f. 66).

"Ye are the salt of the earth, but if the salt have lost its savour, wherewith shall it be salted?" (Matt. v. 13).

"Adam was the first light of the world" (Talmud, Jer. Shabb., 2).

"Ye are the light of the world" (Matt. v. 14).

"Simeon, son of Elieser, said, When Israelites do the will of God, then is his name glorified in the world" (Mekiltha, f. 27. 2).

"Even so let your light shine before men, that they may see your good works, and glorify your father which is in heaven" (Matt. v. 16).

"Avoid a small sin, lest it lead thee on to a great sin. Follow out a small precept, for it will draw thee close to a great precept" (Aboth Nathan, ii.).

"Judas the holy said, Be as careful to obey a trifling commandment as a great one" (Aboth, ii. 4).

"Solomon and thousands like him" [who wished to annul a prohibition against multiplying wives by altering one letter in a precept] "shall perish, but not even an ornament of the *yod* shall pass away from the Law" (Talm. Jer. Sanhedr., ii. 6).

"One jot or one tittle shall in no wise pass away from the law. . . . Whosoever shall break one of these least commandments, and shall teach men so, shall be called least in the kingdom of heaven" (Matt. v. 17).

"Whoso shall have called his neighbour a slave, is to be excommunicated; whoso called his neighbour Mamzer had to be beaten with forty stripes; whoso shall have called his neighbour a wretch, descends with him into his life" (Talmud Qiddushin, f. 28. 2).

"R. Chiskias said, Whosoever calleth his neighbour Resho [wicked], is thrust into Gehenna. He who will cause his brother to be ashamed in public, shall have no place in the future life" (Aboth, iii. 13). Cf. with Matt. v. 22.

"The day of atonement does not expiate sins, unless there has been reconciliation" (Talm., Yoma).

"If the offender should offer in sacrifice all the sheep in Arabia, he would not be absolved until he had asked pardon of him whom he had injured" (Talm., Baba Kama, f. 92).

"The transgressions which a man commits against God, the day of atonement expiates; but the transgressions which he commits against his neighbour, it only expiates when he has satisfied that neighbour (Yoma).

"If thou art offering thy gift at the altar, and there rememberest that thy brother hath aught against thee; leave there thy gift before the altar, and go, first be reconciled to thy brother, and then come and offer thy gift" (Matt. v. 23, 24).

"It is said in the proverb, Whilst thou art in the way, accommodate thyself to thine adversary" (Talm., Sanhedrin, f. 95. 1).

"Agree with thine adversary quickly, whiles thou art with him in the way" (Matt. v. 25).

"Says the house of Shammai, A man becomes guilty as much by purpose as by deed" (Talm., Qiddushin, f. 42. 2).

"Says Rabbi Asa: God does not account evil purpose as act" (Talm., Qiddushin, f. 40. 1).

"Intuens vel in (quiconque s'arrête à contempler) minimum digitum feminæ est ac si intuetur in locum pudendum" (Talm., Bab. Shabb., 64. 2; Berachoth, 24. 1).

"Calcaneum mulieris aspiciens est ac si uterum aspiceret, uterum autem aspiciens est ac si cum ea coiret" (Talm., Jer. Challa, f. 58. 3).

"In every act it is especially the thought, the intention, which God looks at and judges" (Yoma, f. 29 a).

"He who looks upon a woman with an evil intention, hath already, so to speak, committed adultery" (Challa).

"Every one that looketh on a woman to lust after her, hath committed adultery with her already in his heart" (Matt. v. 28). Jesus himself is here making what is technically termed a "fence" about the law, which endeavours to "withhold men from transgression" by establishing a precept which must of necessity be contravened before a breach of the law can be committed.

"It is better for me to be put to shame in this world, and not to be put to shame in the world to come: it is better for me to be burned in this world with extinguishable fire than in the world to come with fire that consumes" (Targum, Jer. Gen., xxxviii. 26).

"It is profitable for thee that one of thy members should perish, and not thy whole body go into Gehenna" (Matt. v. 30).

Seneca had caught up the same thought, and probably also from a Hebrew source, though who knows where it originated? for Buddha says, "Slight your body, composed of four perishable elements, and give heed only to your imperishable soul." Seneca's mode of expressing the thought is very forcible: "Cast forth what things soever tear thy heart; for if they cannot be otherwise extracted, the heart itself will have to be plucked out along with them. . . . Vices tear the heart" (Ep. 51).

"The school of Shammai said, A man must not repudiate his wife, unless he find in her actual immodesty" (Bemidbar, R. S. iv., ad Num. v. 30).

"R. Jochanan said, Repudiation is an odious thing."

"R. Eliezer said, When a first wife is put away, the very altar sheds tears" (Talm., Sanh., f. 22. 1; Gittin, fin.).

"Every one that putteth away his wife, saving for the cause of fornication, maketh her an adulteress" (Matt. v. 32).

"Those who suffer wrong and do it not, who hearken to contumely and make no retort, and do that from the love of God, glorying in chastisements, of these the Scripture saith, May they who love him be as the going forth of the sun in his might" (Yoma, f. 23. 1).

"The saying of the Rabbins: If thy comrade call thee an ass, put also a saddle upon thee" (Baba Kama, f. 92. 2).

"Resist not him that is evil: but whosoever smiteth thee on thy right cheek, turn to him the other also" (Matt. v. 39).*

"Let thy nay be nay, let thy yea be yea" (Baba Mezia, f. 49).

"Let your speech be, Yea, yea; Nay, nay; and whatsoever is more than these is of the evil one" (Matt. v. 38).

"Shemuel ha-Qatan said [used to repeat], Rejoice not when thine enemy falleth, and let not thine heart be glad when he stumbleth [Prov. xxiv. 17]" (Pirqe Aboth, iv: 26).

"We, if we are called servants of God, are also called his children" (Talm., cit. Deutsch).

"Love your enemies, . . . that ye may be sons of your Father which is in heaven" (Matt. v. 44).

"Rabbi Jannæus saw a certain man who was giving a drachma to a poor man, and that publicly. And he said unto him, It had been better that thou hadst given nought, than have given and at the same time publicly affected the man with ignominy" (Qoheleth R., xii. 14).

"If God manifests openly the punishments which he is wont sparingly to set for things done in secret, how much more the recompenses, which in greater measure he is wont to hold out" (Mekiltha, f. 12. 2).

"It is as good not to give at all, as to give ostentatiously and in public" (Chagiga, f. 5).

"He who gives charity in secret is greater than Moses himself" (Baba Bathra).

"Said Rabbi Simeon, son of Jochai, If ye seek gold, look ye, take your gold; but know, whosoever takes now is taking his portion of the age which is to come; for there is no recompense for the Law save the age to come" (Schemoth R., 52).

"They have received their reward. . . . Thy father which seeth in secret shall recompense thee" (Matt. vi. 2-6).

---

* Cf. also: "With an angry man let him not in his turn be angry; abused, let him speak mildly" (Inst. Menu., vi. 48).

"Let no one when praying in the synagogue be more prolix than is meet, lest haply it be imputed to him for empty glory" (R. Jona, Lib. Timoris).

"It is better to make a short prayer with reflection than a long prayer without fervour" (Menachoth, 110).

"Use not vain repetitions" (Matt. vi. 7).

The following are portions of Hebrew prayers:—

"Our Father which art in heavens, be gracious unto us. Hallowed be thy name, O Lord our God; and glorified be the remembrance of thee in heaven above and on earth below" (Tephila Lusitan, 115). "Let thy kingdom reign over us now and for ever" (Sepher Ham., 49. 1). "Do thy will in the heavens above, and grant quietude of spirit to them that fear thee below. . . . Hallowed be thou that listenest to prayer. . . . May it please thee, O Eternal our God, to give unto each the food that he needs" (Berachoth, 29. 2). "Give us this day our daily bread" (Yom Tob, 16 a).

"Cause me to cleave to thy commandments, and bring me not into the hands of sin, nor into the hands of iniquity, nor into the hands of temptation, nor into the hands of disgrace. And bow my nature to be subservient to thee. And remove me from evil man and from evil companion. And cause me to cleave to the good nature, and to a good associate in thy world. And give me over, this day and every day, to grace and to favour, and to lovingkindness, in thine eyes, and in the eyes of all that behold me" (Bab. Berachoth, 60 b).

"Remit and forgive unto all them that do me wrong" (Com. in Pirqe Aboth, f. 24). "Forgive us our debts as we forgive our debtors. . . . Whosoever is ready to forgive, his sins also shall be forgiven him" (Mekiltha, f. 28). "Lead us not into the hands of temptation, but deliver us from evil's onslaught" (Sepher Ham., 9. 12).

There are many slightly varying forms:—

"O God, be thy name magnified and sanctified in the world which thou hast made, according to thy good pleasure. Let thy kingdom have dominion therein. Let the Messiah come speedily, that thy name may be glorified" (Kadish).

"Be there magnified and sanctified the Great Name in the world which he has created according to his will, and which he rules as his kingdom, during your life and your days, and the life of the whole house of Israel, speedily and in a near time; and say ye Amen, be the great name praised for ever and evermore" (Talmud, cit. Deutsch).

"Our Father ... Break and remove the adversary from before and from behind us ... for thou art the God that keepest and deliverest us from every evil word, and from the terrors of the night" (Haschivenu).

"Be it pleasing to thee, O Eternal our God, and God of our fathers, to deliver us from shameless ones as well as from shamelessness, from an evil man as well as from an evil chance, from an evil prompting, an evil companion, an evil neighbour, from Satan the destroyer, from a judgment too severe" (Bab. Berachoth, 16. 2).

"Whosoever is quick in forgiving, his sins also shall be forgiven him" (Megilla, f. 25).

"If ye forgive men their trespasses, your heavenly Father will also forgive you" (Matt. vi. 14).

"There is a great difference between him who is ashamed before his own self, and him who is only ashamed before others" (Talm., cit. Deutsch).

"He who captivates public opinion by feigned virtue, by imposture, is a thief. Whoever steals the esteem, the good opinion of his fellow-creatures, it is the same as if he stole the favour of God" (Kinnim, p. 92; Tosephta, Baba Mezia, M.).

"That they may be seen of men" (Matt. vi. 16, etc.).

"King Monobazus [of Adiabene, Assyria, a proselyte to Judaism, about 45 A.D.] at a time of famine expended his own treasures and those of his fathers. His brothers and kinsfolk came and said unto him, Thy fathers alway added somewhat to their fathers' treasures, but thou dost squander all. He answered and said, My fathers sought to amass treasures for earth, but I for heaven" (Baba Bathra, f. 11. 1).

"I will only teach my son the Law, for we live on its fruits in this world, and the capital is reserved for us, for the life to come" (Qiddushin, f. 82).

"Lay not up for yourselves treasures upon earth; . . . lay up for yourselves treasures in heaven" (Matt. vi. 19, 20).

"The good way . . . a good eye . . . a good heart; the evil way . . . an evil eye . . . an evil heart" (P. Aboth, ii. 12).

"The lamp of the body is the eye; if therefore thine eye be single, thy whole body will be full of light. But if thine eye be evil, thy whole body will be full of darkness" (Matt. vi. 22, 23).

"A similitude of a king who appointed two stewards, and set one over his treasures of gold and silver, the other over his provision of straw. The latter brought himself under suspicion. Moreover, afterwards, he became angered because he had not been appointed over the treasury of gold and silver. They said unto him, however: Thou fool, if thou broughtest thyself under suspicion concerning the provision of straw, how shall be entrusted unto thee the treasure of gold and silver?" (Jalqut Simeoni, i. f. 31. 1).

"God never bestows the gift of great things upon men until he has first tried them thoroughly by small things; thereafter, indeed, he moves them on to large things" (Schemoth R., ii.).

"You must not keep faith in small things, in the hope merely of gaining confidence, so as to have greater things entrusted to you" (Philo, Plant. Noah, ii. § 23).

"The Master saith in the Gospel, If ye kept not that which is little, who will give unto you that which is great? For I say unto you that he which is faithful in the least, is faithful also in much" (Clem. Rom., *pseud*. ii. 8).

"He that is faithful in a very small thing is faithful also in a great one, and he that is unjust in a very small thing is unjust also in a great one. If therefore ye did not prove faithful in the unjust mammon, who will commit to your trust the real and true good?" (Luke xvi. 10).

"Ada, son of Ahava, sits to-day in the bosom of Abraham. To-day Rabbi Juda was born in Babylon" (Qiddushin, f. 72. 1).

"There will be a tree planted near the rivers of waters. This is Abraham whom God accepted and planted ... in Paradise" (Midrasch Tillin, 1. f. 3. 1).

"The fire of Gehenna has no power over the sinners of Israel, for Abraham descends and brings them back out of it" (Erubin ii., and Chagiga, fin.).

"The Rabbins say that Paradise and Gehenna are so placed, that from the one people can overlook the other" (Midrash Ecclesiast., vii. 14. f. 103. 2).

"For a good man on his death there was no celebration of funeral rites, but for a bad one. Afterwards through the calm was seen the good man walking in gardens close to fountains, but the bad one putting out his tongue towards the bend of the stream, and striving to reach the water, and yet ever unable"* (Chagiga, f. 77. 4).

"It is better for me to be confounded in this world which is transitory, than to be confounded before the face of the Father of the just in the world to come" (Targum in Gen. xxxviii. 26).

"There is no everlasting damnation according to the Talmud. There is only a temporary punishment even for the worst sinners. 'Generations upon generations' shall last the damnation of idolators, apostates, and traitors. But there is a space of 'only two fingers' breadth between Hell and Heaven'" (E. Deutsch).

The passages just quoted illustrate the hagadistic fable of the Rich Man and the Beggar (Luke xvi. 19), with its simili-

---

* Compare with this the fable of Tantalus.

tudes of Abraham's bosom, of the chasm dividing the opposite regions of Hades, and of the parching tongue, and its plain and straightforward moral. By Pliny (H. N. ii. 26) the opening of the sky was named by the word which in Luke is rendered chasm or gulf. The same word is also found in Hesiod (Theog., 740) applied to "a great gulf in Tartaros." The moral is charmingly summed up by a poet : " Money . . . has no part in immortality, not even if thou wert to take along with thee what are called the Talents of Tantalus " (Menander ap. Stobæum).

"The want of the means of sustenance prevents a man from obtaining instruction, and studying Thorah. Conversely, Thorah fits a man for the discharge of secular duties, and brings worldly prosperity in its train " (C. Taylor) : " No meal, no Thorah ; no Thorah, no meal " (P. Aboth, iii. 26).

" R. Simeon, son of Eleazar, said : Hast thou ever seen any animal or bird having a trade ? And yet it sustains itself without labour. They were, moreover, only created for my service ; but I for the service of my Creator. Is it not, then, right that I should be able to sustain myself without toil ? But I have badly executed my works, and have squandered my living " (Qiddushin, iv. 14).

" Rabbi Nechorai said : I intermit all the trades of the world, and teach my disciples the Law only, of the recompense whereof a man eats in this age, and his horn increases toward that which is to come. Not so are any other trades besides ; whensoever any one falls ill, or grows old, or is kept captive, he cannot do without his toil, and so is consumed away by hunger ; but the study of the Law, even when one is in utter extremity, bids have a good hope, and is a solace both in youth and old age " (Qiddushin, 1 Kings iii. 11).

" In whom this is, there is all : in whom this is not, what is there ? Hath one gotten this, what lacks ? Hath he not gotten this, what hath he gotten " (Nedarim, 41 a).

" Be not solicitous of what is to come, before it evolves

itself: there is enough vexation in its own time" (Sanhedrin, f. 100. 2, Liber Musar.).

"Said Moses, There is enough of vexation in its own time. There is affliction enough in its own time" (Schemoth R., 11).

"Its trouble sufficeth for each hour" (Bab. Berachoth, f. 9 b).

"Be there no torment to thee from the cark of the morrow, for thou knowest not what a day may bring forth. Maybe there is no morrow, and a man is found troubling himself about the world when he has no connection with it" (Yebamoth, f. 63. 2. Ex Ben Syra, c. 44).

"He that has a morsel of bread in his basket, and yet saith, What shall I eat to-morrow? is a man of little faith" (Bab. Sota, 48 b).

"Fret not for your life, what ye shall eat, or drink; nor yet for your body, what ye shall put on. . . . Behold the birds of the heaven, that they sow not, etc. . . . Seek ye first God's kingdom, and his righteousness, and all these things shall be added unto you. Be not therefore anxious for the morrow; for the morrow will be anxious for itself. Sufficient unto the day is its own evil" (Matt. vi. 25-34).

"With the measure with which a man measures, men will measure to him" (Sota, i. 7).

"Whosoever judges his neighbour with good will, will himself find an indulgent judge in heaven" (Bab. Shabbath, 127 b).

"He who suspects the innocent will be punished for his suspicion" (*Ibid.*, 97 a).

"Whoso giveth a judgment upon his fellow, he will be first punished" (Bab. Rosh Ha-shana, 16 b).

"With what judgment ye judge, ye will be judged: and with what measure ye mete, it will be measured unto you" (Matt. vii. 1).

"Judge not thy neighbour, so long as thou art not in his place" (Hillel in Pirqe Aboth, ii. 6).

"With God the measure of punishment is less than full, while the measure of rewards is full and heaped" (Mekiltha, 20. 2).

"A certain man proceeded from upper Galilee to the south, and there was hired by a house-owner, and served for three years. At length, on the day of Release, he said, Give me my pay, that I may support my wife and children. The house-owner answered: I have no money. Said the servant, Give me produce.—I have none.—Give me a piece of land.—I have none.—Give me rams or raiment.—I have none. He took therefore his garments on his back, and sadly went away home. On the following feast-day his master took his pay in his hands, and took in addition three asses, the one laden with food, the second with drink, the third with raiment, and came to his house. After they had eaten and drunk, he gave him his pay, saying, At the time thou didst ask for thy wage, but I said that I had no money, what didst thou think?—That thou hadst perchance applied to buying certain merchandise at a low price, the money which thou hadst wished to give me.—But what thoughtest thou, when I said that I had no cattle?—That perchance thou hadst let them out to others.—What, when I said that I had no farm?—That thou hadst let it out to others.—But when I said that I had no produce?—That it was perhaps not yet tithed.—What, when I said that I had no sheep or clothing?—That haply thou hadst dedicated all thy means to God. Answered the master, And so the matter was, for I had dedicated all my wealth on behalf of my son Hyrcanus, who would give no attention to the Law. When, however, I met some doctors who dwell towards the south, they absolved me of my vow. Now, therefore, since thou didst judge from charity of me, God also will with equity judge thee" (Talmud).

"With what judgment ye judge ye shall be judged" (Matt. vii. 2).

"In the generation which judged their judges, when

any one said to another, Take the splinter out of thine eye, he was answered, Take the beam out of thine own eye" (Talm. Bab., Baba Bathra, 15 b).

"Why beholdest thou the mote that is in thy brother's eye, but considerest not the beam that is in thine own eye?" (Matt. vii. 3).

The following, from the Talmud, is a later version of the proverb than that presented in the Gospel:—

"Who knows how to retrace his steps? says Rabbi Tryphon. Who knows how to profit by remonstrances? Alas, if any one says to any one, Strike the straw out of thine eye, one is answered, Strike the beam out of thine own" (Bab. Erachin, f. 16. 2).

"Cast not your pearls before swine, nor deliver your wisdom to him who knows not the dignity thereof" (Mishar Happeninim, c. 1).

"All sanctities when cast adrift it is not permitted to redeem, for sanctities are not redeemed to be cast unto dogs for food" (Schebuoth, f. 11. 2).

"Give not that which is holy unto the dogs; neither cast your pearls before the swine, lest haply they trample them under their feet, and turn again and rend you" (Matt. vii. 6).*

"The gates of prayer are never shut" (Sota, 49).

"If any one say to thee, 'I have sought and not found,' believe him not; or 'I have not sought and yet have found,' likewise believe him not; but if he saith, 'I have sought and found,' then believe him" (Bab. Megilla, 6 b).

---

* The following may also be compared:—

"Sing not your song before a four-footed thing" (Pythagoras, Frag. Phil. Mullack).

"Like holding up a mirror in an assembly of the blind" (Persian proverb).

"Sacred Learning, having approached a Brahman, said to him: I am thy precious gem; preserve me with care; deliver me not to a scorner; (so preserved, I shall become supremely strong). But communicate me, as to a vigilant depositary of the gem, to that student whom thou shalt know to be pure, to have subdued his passions, to perform the duties of his order" (Inst. Menu, ii. 114).

"Ask, and it shall be given you; seek, and ye shall find" (Matt. vii. 7).

"Let a man be always urbane like Hillel, and not headstrong and passionate like Shammai. There is a story of a certain Gentile who came to Shammai, and said, Make a proselyte of me on these terms, that thou teach me the whole of the Law, whilst I stand on one foot. Shammai drove him away with a measuring-rod which he was holding in his hand. He came to Hillel, who made a proselyte of him, saying, What thou dost thyself detest, do not to another" (Shabbath, f. 31. 1).

"Hillel said, 'Do not unto others that which it would be disagreeable to thee to experience thyself. This is the chief commandment. All the rest is but the commentary upon it'" (Shabbath, 306).

"Whatsoever ye would that men should do unto you, even so do ye also unto them, for this is the law and the prophets" (Matt. vii. 12).

The parable of the wide road of the many, and the narrow of the few travellers on the way of life (Matt. vii. 13), will find illustration in the following:—

"On a certain highway two roads branched off in opposite directions: the one, level and straight in the beginning, soon turned out rugged, and overgrown with thorns and briars; the other proved itself, when first taken, to be narrow and beset with many difficulties, but ultimately led smoothly and without interruption to the desired goal" (Jalqut, Deut.).

"Precept induces precept, and transgression induces transgression [*i.e.* performance of duty is rewarded by increased facility, and *vice versâ*]" (P. Aboth, iv. 5).

The comedy of a matter which Calvinists have treated too seriously may be found refreshing: "R. Chiskia said in the name of R. Jeremiah, who held it himself of R. Simon ben Yochai, 'I can judge that the number of the elect will be very small.' 'Will there be a thousand?' 'My son and I will be of the number.' 'A hundred?' 'My son and I will be of them.' 'Two only?' 'That will be my son and I'" (Talm. Bab., Succa, 45 a).

The same story is told in the Jerusalem Talmud (Berach., ix. 3), where also R. Chiskia asserts that the supernatural power of R. Simon ben Yochai was "such that, if he desired a valley to be filled with pieces of gold, his wish was fulfilled." Whereupon Dr. Moses Schwab comments: "This is one of those exaggerated expressions put by posterity into the mouth of Doctors who were incapable of such vanity." In this, as well as in a more familiar instance, where a natural reverence has developed into deification and idolatry of its object, we may find reason to appreciate the truth of the ancient Persian proverb, "Spiritual teachers do not soar of themselves, but their disciples make them soar." *

"Providence sees all; liberty is granted; the world is judged by goodness, and everything is recompensed according to works" (Pirqe Aboth, iii. 19).

"By their fruits ye shall know them" (Matt. vii. 20).

The oppositions of theory and practice were a favourite subject of discussion among the Rabbis, both before and after our era, as evidenced in the following passages, which are parallel with the parable of Jesus of the buildings founded upon the rock and upon the sand:—

"Learning is not the foundation, but doing" (Aboth, i. 18).

"Rabbi Chananiah said, 'Whosoever works are more than his wisdom, his wisdom is stable; but whosoever wisdom is greater than his works, his wisdom is not stable" (Pirqe Aboth, iii. 14).

"If any one have good works, and has learned much in the Law, he is like unto a man who so builded his house as to put stones below, and upon them afterwards placed tiles. Though there come great floods, and settle thereby, they cannot move them from their place. A man, however, who has not good works, but has given much labour to the Law,

* Roebuck, "Oriental Proverbs," ed. H. H. Wilson.

is like unto him that places tiles below, and upon them raises stones; if the floods should but gradually rise, they straightway overthrow him.

"Furthermore, such a man is like unto a mason who spreads lime on bricks; though rains descend, they cannot stir it: he, however, who has not good works, but is greatly studious of the Law, is like unto lime which is only poured carelessly on the bricks; however little be the rains that descend, it straightway wastes away and comes down" (Aboth Nathan, 24).

"The tradition of Rabbi Chija is, He who learns the Law, so as to do it, not he who learns so as not to do it. He verily who learns and does not, it were better if he had not been created. Said Rabbi Jochanan, He who learns and does not, it were better for him if his afterbirth had been turned back over his face, and he had not gone forth into the air of the world" (Schemoth R., xl.; Tanchuma, f. 272. 2; Vajikra R., xxxv. 4; and Berachoth Jer., i. 5 [2]).

"Said R. Simeon, son of Chelpatha, Whosoever has learned the words of the Law and does them not, his fault is far graver than that of one who clearly has learned nothing. To illustrate the matter by a simile, A certain king brought two gardeners into his garden; one of them planted trees, but afterwards cut them down; the other verily planted not a single tree, but cut nothing down: with which of them is the king angry? is it not with him that planted and cut down?" (Debarim R., vii.).

"When once Rabbi Tarphon and the elders of Lydda were sitting in the upper room of the house Nitsa, this question arose amongst them: Is knowledge greater than action? R. Tarphon said that action was the greater; R. Akiba, however, gave the precedence to learning. And with him all the rest agreed, saying, Learning is to be preferred, for it leads to action" (Qiddushin, f. 40, 2).

"Rabbi Josua, son of Korcha, said, Whosoever has learned

the Law, but does not regulate his life by its prescription, is like unto a man who sows but reaps not. R. Josua said, Whosoever has learned the Law, and gives it over unto forgetfulness, is like to a woman who brings forth a child, but a while afterwards buries it" (Sanhedrin, f. 99. 1).

The following affords an instance of the importance, for the right understanding of an expression in the Gospels, of knowing its relation to Hebrew doctrine:—

When Jesus says to a leper (Matt. viii. 3), "I will; be thou made clean," it would appear to a Western mind as if there were almost a claim to superhuman attributes.

"Do the will of God, says the Talmud (P. Aboth, ii. 4), and God will accomplish thy will. [Another rendering is, "Do his will as if it were thy will, that he may do thy will as if it were his will."] . . . We read in the Talmud (Moëd Katon, 16 b), What signifies this verse (2 Sam. xxiii. 3), 'Thus hath said the God of Israel, thus hath spoken unto me the Rock of Israel: I reign over man,—the just reigns by the fear of God'? This verse signifies that if God reigns over man in general, the just in his turn, by reason of his godliness, may reign over God" ("La Bible, le Talmud, et l'Évangile," by E. Soloweyczyk).

The following are examples of the Talmudic Hagada:—

"God will one day give a banquet to the pious, on the day on which he rewardeth the offspring of Isaac. After eating and drinking, the cup will be offered to Abraham, Isaac, and Jacob" (Bab. Pesach., 119 b).

"The holy and blessed God said to the Israelites, 'Ye shall offer me showbread and sacrifice; but in the world to come I will spread for you a great table, and the Gentiles shall see and be ashamed;' as it is said (Ps. xxiii. 5), 'Thou preparest a table before me opposite my adversaries,' and (Isai. lxv. 13), 'Behold, my servants shall eat, but ye shall be hungry; behold, my servants shall drink, but ye shall be thirsty'" (Bemidbar Rabba, xxi. 245, 1).

"Like as a king who made a feast for his servants, and bade a torch be kindled for them. But, when he got angry with them, he said to his servant, 'Take the torch from them, and make them sit in darkness'" (Bab. Succa, 29 a).

"Many shall come from the east and the west, and shall recline with Abraham, and Isaac, and Jacob, in the kingdom of heaven; but the sons of the kingdom shall be cast forth into the outer darkness" (Matt. viii. 11, 12).

With Matt. viii. 13 and John iv. 25 may be compared the following Talmudic story: "When, once upon a time, the son of R. Gamaliel was ill, they straightway sent two students to R. Chanina, son of Dosa, to make intercession before God for him. Upon seeing them, he went up to the upper room and prayed for him. When he came down he said to them, Go ye, for his fever has abated. They answered, Art thou a prophet? He rejoined, I am neither a prophet nor a son of a prophet; but if I am able to recite my prayers with ready mouth, then I know that I am hearkened to, but if not, I know that they are vain. They, indeed, wrote and noted the hour; and when they came to R. Gamaliel, he said to them, In your ministry ye have done naught either too much or too little, for so went the matter with my son: at that very hour the fever left him, and he asked for water to drink" (Berachoth, f. 34. 2, Bab. Gem., *cf.* Mishna, v. 5 and Jer. Gem.).

There is a curious Talmudic theory about disorders that can be easily healed. "Rabbi Jochanan being ill, Rabbi Chanina went to visit him, and asked him, Findest thou happiness in thy sufferings? No, replied he, not more in my sufferings than in the recompense which they will be able to yield me. Thereupon R. Chanina said to him, Give me thy hand. He gave it to him, and was immediately healed" (Berachoth, 5 b). According to R. Soloweyczyk, the Talmudic belief was that amongst sufferings inflicted by God upon man there were "chastisements of love," only sent by God to those He loves; given to the just, not for chastisement's sake, but to augment thereby their future felicity. These trials take place only so far as the just man accepts them willingly. Otherwise, God withdraws them, and that is why he ceased afflicting R. Jochanan, who did not resign himself to undeserved pains, even at the price of the increase of happiness which would compensate for them.

The Talmudic treatise above quoted continues, "Why was this? Ought not Jochanan rather to have healed himself, seeing that he wrought miracles? Response: That came to pass in accordance with the proverb, The prisoner does not deliver himself from his prison."

It has been disputed whether this is an ancient proverb or one originating in the mocking question (Matt. xxvii. 42) applied to Jesus on the cross: "He saved others; can he not save himself?"

"'For I have no pleasure in the death of him that dieth' (Ezek. xviii. 32). Can one say that he who is dead dies again? No, it refers to the wicked, who during life are called dead" (Talm. Jer. Berach., ii. 3 [2]).

"Leave the dead to bury their own dead" (Matt. viii. 22).

What may be termed the Talmudic method of ornamentation deserves consideration in any study of the Gospels. A text of canonical Scripture is cited to serve some purpose of illustration or support, but employed in so strained a manner or with so remote an allusion that, judged by a modern literary standard, the reference seems merely fanciful or absurd. With the Talmudists this reference without relation was admissible. It was a practice that had grown up, probably insensibly, from the reverence paid to the sacred books, and the fact that no current work or thought could gain respect unless, implicitly or explicitly, it was made to derive its support from the written law. This written law could not fairly be made the ostensible basis of every new thought, so that the connection between new and old was necessarily often no more than a far-fetched and subtle imagination.

Dr. Moses Schwab comments upon an ingenious misapplication, in the Jerusalem Gemara, of a verse from the Psalms: "Here, as is often the case, the exegetist has diverted the usual sense of the verse to meet the exigencies of his thesis." So have eager Christians oftentimes done since, in laying the burden of unintended prophecies, and occult Trinitarian and Messianic allusions upon the same long-suffering text.

Jesus himself did not profess to utter a new law, or to subvert an old one, but to confirm the Thorah that had been revealed before. "Do not believe that I am come to dissolve the law or the prophets: I am not come to dissolve, but to fill out" (Matt. v. 17).* And yet he was not one who put new wine in old bottles. To proclaim that the Sabbath was made for man, did not destroy the Sabbath as a worn-out institution; it only loosened the cords which were crippling it, by finding for it a new sanction,—that it was for man's benefit.

The minor "fences of the Law" stood in every one's way, and it was the delight of what Renan calls "the middle-class Pharisees," the bye-law beadles, to maintain them. It is probably in reference to the unwitting violation of these besetting precepts that Jesus says, "Woe unto you, for ye are as graves which do not show; and the men that walk over them are not aware of them." Contact with a tomb, however involuntary, rendered any one ceremonially impure, and so graves were carefully marked and made conspicuous, sometimes by whitening the exterior with lime.

The Talmud illustrates, even in comparatively trifling matters, the narrative of the Gospels. For instance, "When the study of the Law and the ordained burial of the dead are

* A story is told in the Babylonian Gemara (Shabb. 116), which it has been suggested contains a quotation of these words, "He ['the Pilos(e)fa;' supposed to be a corruption of *philosophos* or *episcopos*] said to them: 'I have looked further on in the book, and it is written in it, I am not come to take away from the Law of Moses, nor to add to the Law of Moses am I come.'"

concurrent, the care of the dead has precedence. For there is a tradition that in the conduct of obsequies the study of the Law should be intermitted" (Megilla, f. 32). The allowance, however, is elsewhere qualified if there are, otherwise, sufficient funeral attendants. This doctrine gives a kind of shrewdness to the excuse a disciple made to Jesus: "Sir, suffer me first to go and bury my father."

According to the Fourth Gospel (iv. 27) the disciples of Jesus marvel at his discoursing with a woman. "R. Jose ben Hanna said, 'Did not the sages teach, Multiply not colloquy with a woman? They have spoken with regard to one's own wife; how much the less with another's!" (Erubin, f. 53. 2). "Jose ben Jochanan of Jerusalem said, Let thy house be opened wide; and let the needy be thy household; and prolong not converse with woman. (His own wife, they meant, much less his neighbour's wife.) Hence the wise have said, Each time that the man prolongs converse with the woman, he causes evil to himself, and desists from words of Thorah, and, in the end, he inherits Gehinnom" (Pirqe Aboth, i. 5, 6).

Woman, according to the current belief, was not saved through the Law, but through childbearing (1 Tim. ii. 15).

The miracles of the Talmud we shall not dwell upon. They seem to be mostly introduced to "point a moral or adorn a tale," rather than as serious fact. Similarly it has been suspected that the greater part of the Gospel miracles are of parabolic origin, and developed by a process of pious expansion from some uncomprehended fragment of metaphoric truth.

The doctors referred to in the following story are contemporary with Jesus, Eliezer Haggadol's death being given as about 73 A.D. :—

"Rabbi Gamaliel was on the sea when a tempest arose and threatened to swamp the vessel. Said he, Can this be come to pass unto me on account of R. Eliezer bar Hyrqanos? [There had been a dispute among the doctors, and Eliezer having refused to submit to the majority had been put under an interdict.] So he stood upon his feet, and prayed: Lord of the universe, it is manifest and known to thee that I have not acted for the sake of mine own honour, nor for the honour of my father's house, but for the honour of thy name, lest differences should be multiplied amongst the interpreters of thy Law. Straightway the tempest ceased" (Baba Mezia, f. 59. 2).

"Two mutes dwelt in the Rabbi's neighbourhood. Each time that the holy doctor proceeded to his school, they followed him, sat before him, and made all sorts of movements of the head and lips (showing what interest they took in the lessons he gave). Rabbi prayed God in their favour, and they recovered speech" (Chagiga, 3 a).

It is difficult to make sure that the Talmudic vein, even when apparently most serious, contains no suspicion of humour. "Originally, demons had permission to be active every day of the week. One day, one of them met Rabbi Chanina bar Dossa, and said to him: If, on high, we had not been commanded to respect R. Chanina bar Dossa and his science, I should have brought thee to harm. The doctor answered, If it be true that I enjoy such favour in the heaven, I command thee to relieve the world of thy presence for ever. The demon besought him to leave him a little place, and the doctor granted him two nights a week" (Pesaqim, 112 b).

The orthodox creed, according to the Talmud, as to the dignity of a Rabbi, is that "a disciple of the wise does not recline at feasts in the society of the people of the earth [In *Pesaqim*, "the first comer"] (Berachoth, f. 43. 2). It is accordingly asked of the disciples of Jesus, "Why does your teacher eat with the tax-officers and sinners?" His reply rises far above small conventionalities, and yet is equally founded upon the accepted law. The Rabbinical maxim was apparently one of the "fences of the law," its foundation in all likelihood being the idea that "every Doctor who addicts himself to the pleasures of the table, who eats willingly with the first comer, compromises his authority, his honour, and that of his family, exposes himself, in a word, to the most prejudicial consequences" (Pesaqim, 49 a).

With the answer made by Jesus (Matt. ix. 12, 13) may be compared the following :—

"Antisthenes was once reproached for being intimate with wicked men, and said, Physicians also live with those that are sick, and yet they do not catch fevers" (Diog. Laert., vi. 4).

"Physicians are not found with those that are in health, but where the sick are wont to be" (Pausanias, ap. Plut. Prov. Lac., p. 230 f).

The quotation on which the reply of Jesus rests is from Hosea vi. 6: "I desire kindness and not sacrifice; and the knowledge of God more than burnt offerings." There is a similar thought in Prov. xxi. 3 :—

> "To do justice and judgment,
> Is more acceptable to the Lord than sacrifice."

Compare also :—

"Far greater is he who yields fruit of compassion, than if he offers all the oblations" (Succa, f. 49, 2).

"Whosoever refuses instruction to his disciples, is essentially lacking in the duty of charity" (Kethuboth, 96 a).

Fasting was a frequent subject of discussion among the Jewish doctors. Rigid and harsh asceticism marks a state transcended by those who can reign over their inclinations and yet be of a genial spirit; as generous and mellow virtue is beyond the agonizing struggle of an unripe nature.

After practising during six years, the terrible Brahmanic, and even more than Brahmanic austerities, the Buddha Sakya Muni began to think, "To be exhausted thus, is not the way to arrive at assured knowledge;" and taking reasonable food, he found that he was not made less spiritual thereby. Perhaps

Jesus similarly emancipated himself from the most rigid Essene or Pharisaic rule. The Talmud contains a broad as well as a narrow view on fasting: "He who studies the Law ought not to impose fasts upon himself, for fasting hinders the work of God" (Thaanith, 11 b).

The reply of Jesus to the aggravators of the law of fasting, is a beautiful piece of imagery. The wise man, the bridegroom, is with his friends, the sons of the bridechamber, the disciples. The words of wisdom are with them; they are continually feasting, because they are fed on wisdom, and it becomes their joy. When they lose their teacher, if they have not then won wisdom for themselves, and so become bridegrooms and worthy of feasting, then indeed may they fast; and in the spiritual they must, for they have no food.

With regard to Jesus styling himself the bridegroom, or possessor of the bride, wisdom, it was not a piece of self-complacency. Far inferior teachers of that day habitually used such expressions in reference to themselves. The eminence of a teacher was then far more evident than now, education being more restricted, and conveyed rather through persons than books. It would probably have seemed as strange for Jesus to shun mention of himself as the teacher of his disciples and the wise man among them, as for a king to have a delicacy on the subject of owning himself a king. This fact has led to much of the later embellishment of the text, and has made many opportunities for the elevation of a doctrinal image.

In the Talmud (Thaanith, ii. 1) the expression of Joel, of "the bridegroom going out of his chamber," is applied to the Nasi, or prince of the Sanhedrin. The Greek term in the Gospel rendered "bridechamber" is also a name for the ancient temples of Demeter, and might well be applied to the circle of a religious order. There are many ancient references to the higher influx, or eternal wisdom, as a feast and gladness, and to its absence as a season of fasting or deprivation. Compare the following Buddhist sayings :—

"Long is the night to him who is awake;
Long is a mile to him who is tired;
Long is life to the foolish who does not know the true law."
(*Dhammapada*).
"He who lives a hundred years, not seeing the immortal place,
A life of one day is better, if a man sees the immortal place.
And he who lives a hundred years, not seeing the highest law,
A life of one day is better, if a man sees the highest law." (*Ibid.*)

The following is from an Oriental poet: "Being seated to run through the region of the spiritual world,—I have had this advantage in books. To be intoxicated by a single glass of wine,—I have experienced this pleasure when I have drunk the liquor of the esoteric doctrines."

With the figure of the raw cloth and the old garment, and of the new wine and the old skin, we may compare the following :—

"The Law . . . forbids a husbandman to plough with an ass and a heifer yoked, lest the weaker animal, being compelled to exert itself to keep up with the superior power of the stronger animal, should become exhausted and sink under the effort. . . . Resembling these instructions is the precept . . . not to knit together substances of heterogeneous character, such as wool and linen. For in their case also, not only does the difference prevent their union, but also the greater strength of the one will rather bring about a sundrance, at the time of using" (Philo, De Creat. Princip., § xi.).

"R. Jose ben Jehudah, of Kaphar ha-Babli, said, He who learns from his juniors, to whom is he like? To one eating sour grapes and drinking wine from a vat. But whoso learns from elders, to whom is he like? To one eating ripe grapes and drinking old wine. Ribbi said, Look not at the flask, but rather at what is in it; for sometimes a new flask is full of old wine, while now and again you may find an old flask in which there is not even new" (P. Aboth, iv. 28).

"The days are few, and the creditor presses, and the herald cries day by day, and the harvesters of the field are few" (Idra R., 2).

"Rabbi Tarphon ["son" of R. Jochanan ben Zakai, who was a "son" of Hillel] said, The day is short, and heavy is the task, the labourers are sluggish and backward; ample is the meed, and the master is preparing for a consummation of the work. . . . It is not for thee to finish the work, nor art thou free to desist therefrom" (Pirqe Aboth, ii. 19).

"May Jehovah, the God of the spirits of all flesh, set a man over the congregation, who may go out before them, and who may go in before them, and who may lead them out and who may bring them in; that the congregation of Jehovah be not as sheep that have no shepherd" (Prayer of Moses, Numb. xxvii. 15).

Jesus "was moved with compassion for them, because they were distressed and scattered, as sheep not having a shepherd. Then saith he unto his disciples, The harvest truly is plenteous, but the labourers are few. Pray ye therefore the master of the harvest, that he send forth labourers into his harvest" (Matt. ix. 36).

It is doubtful whether the apparent exclusion of the Samaritans from the teachings of the school of Jesus, which occurs in Matthew only (x. 5), is to be read as a general injunction, or the order for a special mission.

Among the Hebrews, the extremes of thought were very wide apart, and included the highest and broadest spiritual freedom, and the most narrow bigotry and exclusiveness. If we compare the words of the Rabbis on this very Samaritan question, there will be little doubt as to the side on which Jesus would be found:—

"R. Gamaliel: A Samaritan is considered as an Israelite in every respect" (Berachoth, Jer. vii. 1).

"Said R. Meir, The Samaritans are proselytes of the truth" (Baba Kama, f. 38. 2).

"The bread of a Samaritan is as the flesh of a swine" (Shebiith, viii. 10).

"Eliezer ben Hyrqanos is a plastered cistern, which loseth not a drop; ... Eleazar ben 'Arak is a welling spring" (Pirqe Aboth, ii. 10). The first-named, Eliezer Haggadol, "father" of Simeon the elder, and a contemporary of Jesus, "never spoke a word that he had not heard from his Rab;" the other, also a contemporary, is described as a teacher of original power and inexhaustible fertility of invention. The metaphor by which he is described has been compared with that of "a spring of water welling up unto life æonian" (John iv. 14). "He who increases not, decreases," said Hillel (P. Aboth, i. 14); on which the Rev. C. Taylor, the eminent Hebrew scholar, comments: "He who learns from his teacher and adds not to his words, not having intelligence to go beyond what he has been expressly taught, will *come to an end,* 'his mother will bury him;' or will *bring to an end* and lose what he has learned by rote." Compare "Unto every one that hath shall be given, and he shall have abundance; but from him that hath not, even that which he hath [thinketh he hath, Luke viii. 18)], shall be taken away" (Matt. xiii. 13, and xxv. 29). The best-cemented cistern may dry up.

"Moses said, I have taught you the laws and statutes, as the Eternal prescribed unto me. ... I taught them freely to you, freely also ought ye to teach them" (Nedarim, 37 a).

"Whence is it proved that it is not lawful for any one to take reward on account of demonstration of a sentence of the Law, and the doctrine of the Law which he shall teach? R. Juda answered that Rab said (Deut. iv. 5), 'Behold, I have taught you;' ... as I have taught you freely, so do ye also teach" (Bab. Becoroth, iv. 6, 29 a).

"Freely ye received, freely give" (Matt. x. 8).

"No man is to go on the mountain of the house [the Temple] with staff, shoes, girdle of money, nor with dust on his feet" (Talm. Jer. Berachoth, ix. 5 [8]).

"Get you no gold, nor silver, nor brass, in your girdles; no wallet for travelling, neither two coats, nor shoes, nor staff" (Matt. x. 9, 10).

The instructions given by Jesus to his disciples appear to have as their object to universalize the peculiar sanctity of the Temple Mount.

In this connection, to understand the orders of Jesus, "Salute no man by the way, and into whatsoever house ye shall enter, first say, Peace to this house. And if a son of peace be there, your peace shall rest thereon; but if not, it shall turn to you again" (Luke x. 4-6), it is necessary to know something of the custom attending the giving of the "Peace" (Hebrew, *Salèm*; Arabic, *Salaam*). "Various set compliments usually follow this salaam, which, when people intend to be polite, are very much extended, and occupy considerable time." From this ceremonial a messenger is exempt, and it is as messengers that the disciples were sent out. Probably the official classes, the priest and the Levite who passed by on the other side of the practical wants of suffering men, were punctilious in spending the prescribed number of minutes over each detail of the ceremonial of the salaam, when they met any person of rank.

With regard to the reversion to the giver of the greeting of "Peace," a Moslem never addresses a salutation to one whom he knows to be of another religion; and if he finds he has made such a salutation in error, he revokes it.

"Said R. Jose ben Qisma, Once I was walking by the way, and there met me a man, and he gave me 'Peace,' and I returned him 'Peace,' etc." (Pereq R. Meir, 9).

"As ye enter into the house, salute it. And if the house be worthy, let your peace come upon it; but if it be not worthy, let your peace return to you" (Matt. x. 12).

"Said R. Juda, son of R. Simeon, God said of the Israelites Towards me they are simple as doves, but towards the Gentiles cunning as serpents" (Schir Ha Shirim Rabba, 17 b).

"What! may the righteous employ a ruse? Yes; for God himself employs it (2 Sam. xxii. 27): Thou art pure with the pure, and with the crooked thou dost use crookedness" (Talm.).

"Be ye wise as serpents and simple as doves" (Matt. x. 16). Compare the "prudens simplicitas" of Martial (x. 47).

"A little before the advent of Messiah, the son will provoke the father, the daughter will rise up against her mother, and the daughter-in-law against her mother-in-law, and, in fine, each man will have his household for enemies. That age, you may know, will have the face of a dog, and a son will not fear his sire. In whom, then, may trust be placed? In our heavenly Father" (Sota, ix. 15).

"Rabbi Nehorai says, In that age wherein Messiah comes, the young man will put to shame the face of the old, and the old man will withstand the young, and the daughter stand against her mother, the daughter-in-law against her mother-in-law; and the men of that age will have a dog face; and the son will not revere his father" (Sanhedrin, f. 97. 1).

A very common Hebrew conceit was paronomasy, the changing of a word by a small change of letter, such as, to make an instance, "from friends, to fiends." By such a minute change in 2 Kings xxiii. 13, the Mount of Olives is changed into the Mount of Corruption. Similarly, Sychem into Sychar—the Samaritan "dwelling" into "the place of drunkenness." In the Talmud, idolaters are represented as turning the face of God into the face of a dog (where indeed a literal inversion holds in our own language). These conceits were perhaps in part designed to catch and help the memory, like the cues of the alphabetic psalms.

"Brother will deliver up brother to death, and the father his child; and children will rise up against parents, and cause them to be put to death" (Matt. x. 21). These strange clashes and internecions can only be reduced to a meaning on the esoteric hypothesis. The warring elements are then the corporeal habits and spiritual impulses struggling for the mastery in the nature of man at the time of the great change. The expressions themselves, used in a plain sense, are to be found in the older writings.

"I came to set a man at variance against his father, and the daughter against her mother, and the daughter-in-law against her mother-in-law: and a man's foes shall be they of his own household" [Micah vii. 6] (Matt. x. 35).

Phrases of the Scripture, which had a literal application in a disturbed and unhappy epoch, it was consonant with the method of Talmudic expositors, whose creed had been modified by Zoroastrian influences and Greek philosophy, to adopt with a new and altered sense. The missionary wave of Buddhism, which has had so extended a vibration as to affect still near one-third of the human family, was in its primitive force in the centuries immediately preceding our era. Some of the esoteric paradoxes of the Indian prophet, showing a remarkable correspondence with the transfigured Hebrew phrases, the obscure symbols of variance and shame now before us, are particularly instanced in vol. i. pp. 143–147. We can only surmise that the key is to be found in the attitude of the inner spirit when it realizes itself, and discards the lower elements with which it has been associated.

"It is enough for the servant that he be as his master," said R. Jochanan (Bab. Berachoth, f. 58 b), meaning that, since the Temple was in ruins, the just must bear it with tranquillity if their own houses were the same.

"It is enough for the disciple that he be as his teacher and the bondservant as his master" (Matt. x. 25).

"Whatever is honestly and modestly done in the world, will be revealed and manifested to all men, in that great judgment" (Targum Eccl., xii. 13, 14).

"There is nothing covered that shall not be revealed; and hid, that shall not be known" (Matt. x. 26).

"'The words of wise men are heard in quiet'—these are the preachers—'more than the cry of him that ruleth among fools:'—these are the meturgemanim who stand above the congregation" (Midr. Koh. to Eccl. ix. 17).

'Nahum Ish Gamza whispered it in the ear [said in secret] to R. Akiba, and R. Akiba repeated it also in secret to the son of Azai, but the son of Azai went out and taught it publicly to his disciples" (Bab. Berachoth, f. 22. 1).

"What I tell you in the darkness, speak ye in the light: and what ye hear in the ear, proclaim upon the housetops" (Matt. x. 27).

"When Rabban Jochanan, son of Zakai, was nigh unto death, and his disciples entered to visit him, he began to weep as soon as he saw them. Whereon his disciples said to him, Lamp of Israel, column of the right hand, hammer of might, wherefore weepest thou? He answered, If it were proposed to conduct me into the presence of the king of flesh and blood, who is here to-day and to-morrow in the tomb, his anger against me could not be eternal; were he to bind me, those bonds would only endure for a time; if he were to go further and kill me, this death would only take effect in the present sphere; moreover, I should be able to sway him by words, or corrupt him by gifts. What ought I, then, to do now that they are ready to conduct me into the presence of One who is the King of kings, the Holy One, blessed be he, he who lives and subsists for ever, for ages of ages; and if he be wrath with me, his anger is eternal; and if he binds me, his bonds are eternal; and if he makes me die, this death will be eternal; and I can neither appease him by words nor win him over by money. And not only that, but I have also before me two roads, the one of the garden of Eden, the other of Gehinnom, and I do not know by which I shall be led, and ought I not to weep? They said to him: Give us thy benediction, our master. He answered: May it please God that the fear of heaven be upon you as much as the fear of flesh and blood" (Bab. Berachoth, f. 28 b, and Aboth Nathan, xxiv.).

"Rabbi Simeon said, Whoso makes any one to sin is worse than if he killed him, because whoso slays, slays for this age; and the man has a portion in the age to come, but whoso makes to sin, slays both in this age and in that which is to come" (Bemidbar R., xxi.).

"The Master saith, 'Ye shall be as lambs in the midst of wolves.' But Peter answered him, and saith, 'What then, if the wolves should tear the lambs asunder?' Jesus said to Peter, 'Let not the lambs after they are dead fear the wolves. And do not ye fear them that kill you and can do nought unto you. But fear him who after ye are dead hath authority over soul and body, to cast into gehenna of fire'" (Clem. Rom. *pseud.*, ep. ii. 5).

"Be not afraid of them which kill the body, but are not able to kill the soul; but rather fear what is able to destroy both soul and body in Gehenna" (Matt. x. 28).

"Nothing, however infinitesimal, is brought forth upon earth without the sanction of God" (Talmud, Cholin, 7. 6).

"Number I not the hairs of every creature?" (Pesikta, f. 18. 4).

A quaint legend is to be found in the Midrash (Bereschith R., 79. 6) of two Rabbis who, in a time of national apostasy, hid for years in a cave and lived on dry pulse. Squatting at the mouth of the cave they watched a bird-catcher, and heard, at the same time, a spiritual voice which, when it uttered one word, the bird escaped, when another, the bird was snared. Whereupon they said, "A single bird is not taken without Heaven; how much less, therefore, so many and so many souls of men!" Probably such a story as this was always regarded in the light of an illustrative fable rather than a fact.

"Are not two sparrows sold for one farthing, and not one

of them shall fall on the ground without your Father: why, the very hairs of your head are all numbered" (Matt. x. 29).

"May it please thee, Eternal God, God of our Fathers, so to dispose our hearts that we may offer thee sincere penitence, that we may not be ashamed before our ancestors in the next life" (Talm. Jer. Berach., iv. 2, Gem.).

"Whosoever shall be ashamed of me and of my words, of him shall the Son of man be ashamed, when he cometh in his own glory and [the glory] of the Father, and of the holy angels" (Luke ix. 26). "Whosoever shall deny me before men, him will I also deny before my Father which is in heaven" (Matt. x. 33).

Whoever has not held firm to the standard of the spirit cannot share in its glory.

"Alexander the Great put ten questions to the doctors of the south . . . (amongst others, these): 'What ought man to do in order to live?' 'Make himself die.' 'What ought man to do to die?' 'Let himself live'" (Talmud, Tamid, 32 a).

"A name enlarged is a name destroyed" (Hillel, in P. Aboth, i. 14).

"Whoso loves his soul slays it" (Apophth. Ebr. and Arab., Drusius).

"A glorious death for the bulwark of the laws is a kind of life" (Philo, Leg. ad Cai., § 29).

A few extracts from classical works will illustrate the theme:—

"Who of my wretched soul is murderer?" (Eurip. Herc. Fur. 452).

"Ship (the soul's vehicle) and soul together he saw destroyed" (Anthol., iii. 22. 10).

"As for him whose evil and distraught disposition implants in him a desire for shameful flight,—before him will I set the flying death of the valley" (Dionys. Hal. A., vi. 9).

"As in battle it often happens that the knavish and fearful soldier, who, as soon as he sees the enemy, throws down his shield and flies as fast as he can, on that very account perishes, even sometimes though his body be unhurt, while to him who has maintained his standing, nought of such sort has befallen ; so those that cannot bear the spectre of trouble, fling themselves away, and so lie afflicted and lifeless, but those who faced it, most often go away with mastery" (Cicero, Tusc. Q., ii. 23).

"He that found his soul will lose it, and he that lost his soul . . . will find it" (Matt. x. 39).

"Whosoever shall seek to hug to himself his soul, will lose it; and whosoever will lose it, shall quicken it" (Luke xvii. 33).

"If any one receives the doctors, it is the same as if he received the Shekina" (Schir Ha Schirim R., f. 12. 3 ; and Mekiltha, f. 38. 2).

"He who enters into strife with a man of learning, is the same as if he were doing it against Him who spoke and the world was made" (Jalqut Rubeni, f. 140. 1).

"R. Chasda said, If any one oppose himself to his doctor, it is the same as if he opposed himself to the Shekina" (Tanchuma, f. 68. 2).

"It is not read (Exod. xxxiii. 7), Whosoever sought Moses, but Whosoever sought the Lord. Whence we conclude, whosoever receives the priest, is the same as if he received the Shekina" (Tanchuma, f. 36. 4).

"The people spoke against God and Moses (Num. xxi. 5). If against God, it were sufficient to say that, and there was no need to add Moses. But it may be noted, that he who speaks against a faithful pastor is the same as if he spoke against God himself" (Jalqut Rubeni, f. 144. 3).

"Aaron said to Moses, My Lord (Num. xii. 11). Was Aaron greater than Moses ? if so, why does he call him Lord, and hold him as a master? We learn hence that he who shows honour to his Rabbi, is doing the same as if he showed honour to God himself" (Jalqut Rubeni, f. 136, 1).

"Whoso hears the word from the mouth of a little one in Israel, be it in his eyes as if he heard it from the mouth of a sage ; and verily not from the mouth of a sage, but from the mouth of sages ; and verily not as if from the mouth of sages, but as if from the mouth of the Sanhedrin ; and verily not as if from the mouth of the Sanhedrin, but as if he heard it from the mouth of Moses ; and not as if he heard it from the mouth of Moses, but as if he heard it from the mouth of God" (Bemidbar, xiv.).

"Behold, I send an angel before thee . . . Give heed to him, and hearken unto his voice ; provoke him not ; for he will not pardon your transgressions ; for my name is in him" (Exod. xxiii. 20, 21).

"He saith, It is not written, but I will speak. If ye receive from him, it is exactly as if ye received from me" (Schemoth R., xxxii. ad Exod. xxiii. 21).

"To receive strangers, to exercise hospitality, is more meritorious than to offer one's homages even to God" (Shabbath, 127 a).

"R. Jose, son of Chanina, said in the name of R. Eliezer, son of Jacob, Whosoever exercises hospitality towards the disciple of a sage in his house, and makes him partake of his abundance, the scripture accounts it to him as if he had offered a perpetual sacrifice" (Bab. Berachoth, f. 10 b).

"He that receiveth you receiveth me, and he that receiveth me receiveth him that sent me" (Matt. x. 40).

"Lot and Abraham received as their guests angels, but not in the name of angels (that is, unawares, or not in their quality of angels). But a widow received Elijah in the name of a prophet, and Laban received Jacob in the name of a just man ; and they received a reward from God" (Jewish Proverb, cit. Wetstein). Cf. "He that prophesieth in the name of an idol" (Sanhedr. x. 1).

References to his own name as a formula of salvation do not imply any unusual or superhuman claim on the part of a prophet or Rabbi. A mystical superstition appears to have attached to the virtue of a name.

"R. Alexander recounts that an archon named Alexandros was judging a brigand : Thy name ? asked the judge. Alexandros, replied the accused. At this name the judge had him released. If this man was saved because he had the same name as his judge, much more so would he be saved in the name of the Lord in virtue of the verse : ' Whoever shall call on the name of the Lord shall be delivered '" (Talm. Jer. Berach., ix. 1 Gem.).

"He that receiveth a prophet in the name of a prophet, shall receive a prophet's reward ; and he that recciveth a righteous man in the name of a righteous man shall receive a righteous man's reward" (Matt. x. 41).

"If there are not little ones, there are not disciples ; if there are not disciples, there are not sages ; if there are not sages, there are not elders ; if there are not elders, there are not prophets ; if there are not prophets, there is not God" (Bereschith R., xlii. 4).

"It is not possible with God that a man, although bad, should lose his recompense of good for a single good action done among more evil ones ; nor, on the other hand, that a man who is good should escape chastisement if among many good actions he should be an evil-doer in anything, for it is an absolute certainty that God distributeth everything by balance and measure" (Philo. Fragm. e Par. Joh. Damasc.).

"Whosoever shall give to drink unto one of these little ones a cup of cold water only, in the name of a disciple, verily I say unto you, he shall in no wise lose his reward" (Matt. x. 42).

A prophet like Moses occupied the highest place in the Hebrew ideal ; even Simon, the Maccabee governor and high priest, was only appointed "until there should rise a faithful prophet" (1 Macc. xiv. 41). But in times when "the prophet is a fool, the man that hath the spirit is mad" (Hosea viii. 7), perhaps the balance of opinion inclined to the soberer sage. In the Talmud we find, "The sage is superior to the prophet, for it is written (Ps. xc. 12), The prophet possesses a wise heart.

Prophecy, then, is allied to wisdom, as the less to the greater and the part to the whole " (Baba Bathra, 12 a).

Simple obedience to the commandments is enough by itself to exalt to the highest place: " Two holy arks accompanied Israel in the Desert; that of the Lord and that of the remains of Joseph. The nations of the world were astonished, and said: Is it possible that the ark of a deceased being should be carried along with the ark of the Eternal Being? It is because, answered Israël, the one obeyed the precepts of the other " (Talm. Jer. Berach., ii. 3 (2) Gem.).

In the Gospel we read, "Wherefore went ye out? to see a prophet? Yea, I say unto you, and much more than a prophet. . . . Among them that are born of women there hath not arisen a greater than John the Baptist: yet he that is but little in the kingdom of heaven is greater than he" (Matt. xi. 9, 11).

There may be an undercurrent of meaning here: such as that an ascetic, by the very fact of his bondage to certain strict rules, practically allows that he is not yet above the plane of temptation in respect of the matters covered by his vow. This view may remind us of the Greek ideal presented by Aristippus (Diog. Laert., ii. 68): "When he was once asked what higher degree philosophers have than others, he replied, If all the laws were abolished, we should still live in the same fashion as now."

" R. Jochanan said, All the prophets prophesied only up to the days of Messiah; but the days of the age to come eye hath not seen " (Sanhedr., f. 99 a).

" R. Chija, son of Abba, spoke also of having heard R. Jochanan say, As for all that the prophets contain, they have only prophesied of the days of the Messiah " (Bab. Berachoth, f. 34 b).

"All the prophets and the law prophesied until John. And if ye are willing to receive it [or him], this is Elijah, which is to come " (Matt. xi. 13).

It is difficult to make certain now what these sayings signified. The Essenes, in their culminating point of holiness, are said to have attained to the position of Elijah, the forerunner of the Messiah.

"If the sage reasons with the foolish, whether he do it with anger or with playfulness, he will have no satisfaction from it" (Prov. xxix. 9).

"The proverb: To weep or laugh with a fool is equally to waste one's trouble; he cannot distinguish good from bad" (Talmud, saying of Rab Pappa).

"Whereunto shall I liken this generation? It is like unto children sitting in the market-places, which call unto their fellows and say, We piped unto you, and ye did not dance; we wailed, and ye did not beat the breast" (Matt. xi. 16).

"Whosoever submits himself to the yoke of the divine Law, from him is raised that of social conventions. But whosoever casts off the yoke of the Law, upon him is imposed the yoke of custom" (Pirqe Aboth, iii. 5).

"The teachings of the Law have their whole force only with the man who regards himself as a nothing" (Sota, 21 b).

The expression "the kingdom of heaven," in Talmudic phraseology, signifies, when used in a technical and restricted sense, a devout attitude and the acknowledgment of the unity of deity. "Let a man, when he has cleansed himself, put on the phylacteries, then recite the Shema, and pray. This is the 'complete Kingdom of Heaven'" (Bab. Berachoth, 15 a).

"May it please thee, Eternal God, God of my fathers, to vanquish and take away the yoke of all bad passions that are in our hearts, for thou hast created us to fulfil thy will, it is our duty so to do, it is also thy wish and ours; the ferment that is in the paste turns us from it" (Talm. Jer. Berach., iv. 2 Gem.).

"It is revealed and known before thee, that our will is to do thy will. And who hinders? The leaven that is in the dough, and servitude to the kingdoms. May it be thy will to deliver us from their hand" (Talm. Bab. Berach., 17 a).

The converse picture to these, of the state when "the servitude to the kingdoms" has been done away, and "the yoke of unruly passions" is taken off the neck, we may find in the words: "Come unto me, all ye that are in weary labour and under heavy burdens, and I will give you rest. Take my yoke upon you, and learn of me, . . . for my yoke is easy and my burden light" (Matt. xi. 28–30).

"Ye shall know the truth, and the truth shall make you free" (John viii. 32).

In argument with the other doctors of his time, Jesus for the most part gains a decisive victory. There is one instance, however, where his retort upon his critics, if allowed to be subject to the conditions of the time, would at first sight appear inconclusive. When the disciples of Jesus are reproved for eating grains of corn on the sabbath (Matt. xii. 1–8; Mark ii. 23–28; Luke vi. 1–5), the grievance of his critics is that the plucking and rubbing in the hand of the ear of corn was a kind of manual labour, which was forbidden during sabbath. "Among servile work," says the Talmud, "they reckon, reaping, thrashing, winnowing, cleansing, grinding, braying" (Shabbath, vii. 2).

David's hunger is cited as the excuse for his eating even the sacred bread; but eating is not "servile work" in the strict Hebrew sense. Where, then, is the point of the reply?

The argument is according to the Rabbinic rule of "analogy." The reasoning is as follows, as succinctly summed by Dr. Ginsburg: "When David was hungry, he ate of the priestly bread, and also gave some to those who were with him. Accordingly, one who is hungry may satisfy his hunger with that which is otherwise only allowed to the priests. Now the priests perform all manner of work on the Sabbath without incurring the guilt of transgression; why, then, should one who is hungry not be allowed to do the same?"

A curious instance of the roundabout, literal, and specious arguments of the Talmud is the following, which bears upon the case before us, of needs *versus* ordinances. "It is written in the Law (Lev. xviii. 5), Keep my statutes and my judgments: which if a man do, he shall *live* by them." He must find life therein, explains the Talmud, and not death; if then he dies to avoid transgression of the law, he is responsible for his own death. An Israelite, then, placed by a conquering foe in the alternative either of transgressing a commandment or of losing his life, ought rather to preserve his life, for it is said, "He shall *live* by the Law." By later scholars this very dubious argument is made somewhat more reasonable by the explanation that the preservation of human life is itself a law of God, and that in case of conflict between two laws the more imperious is to be observed.

"The following question was put to Rabbi* by R. Tanchuma of Naue: Is it permitted to extinguish a lamp on the sabbath day when its light is prejudicial to a sick person? The doctor answered: The life of man also is called a lamp ('The spirit of man is the lamp of God' in the body: Prov. xx. 27); now, it is better to extinguish the earthly lamp than to endanger the lamp divine" (Shabbath, 30 a, b).

There is also an ingenious argument to be found in the Talmud, permitting the sabbath to be broken on the occasion of the birth of a child, "for it may be preserved to keep many sabbaths."

The curious Talmudic method of referring all propositions to a real or fanciful analogy or accordance with the written Law for their sole authentic support, was by the thoughtful minds in the broader schools turned to the good advantage of freedom. Here is an instance common both to Jesus and the Talmudists: "The interest of human life prevails over

---

* The Palestinian title of Rabbi, where found by itself, is generally understood to refer to Jehudah "son" of Shimeon III., but sometimes denotes R. Meir. The expressions, Rab, Rabbi, Rabban, represented progressive shades of meaning; but "greater than Rabban is his *name*,"—that is, to need no title at all.

that of the sabbath; for it is written (Exod. xxxi. 14), 'Ye shall keep the sabbath therefore; for it is holy unto you;' that is to say, the sabbath has been given unto man, and not man unto the sabbath" (Yoma, 85 b).

Compare also the following: "R. Simeon, son of Manasia, said, Keep ye the sabbath, because it is sacred to you; the sabbath is delivered to you, and not ye to the sabbath" (Mekiltha in Exod. xxxi. 14).

"No one must give consolation to the sick, or visit those that grieve, on the sabbath, according to the decree of the school of Shammai, but that of Hillel asserts it to be lawful" (Shabbath, f. 12).

It would be tedious to recount the minute provisions and counter-provisions which are to be found in the treatise just cited and others, on sabbath observance.

"Whosoever has the explanation and not the point at issue, is a strong man not armed; whoso has the point at issue and not the explanation is a weak man armed; whoso has both is a strong man armed" (Aboth Nathan, 29).

It will be noticed how full are the utterances of Jesus of the familiar expressions and metaphors of his race and period. Even when he uses these proverbial phrases in a new sense or informs them with a new spirit, he is still in his manner of speech a Rabbi of the Rabbis. The expression last quoted is familiar to us in the figure, "When the strong man armed guardeth his own court, his goods are in peace" (Luke xi. 21).

"It is written (Prov. xviii. 21), 'Death and life are in the power of the tongue;' which Raba explains thus: The word slays man or makes alive, according to the usage that he makes of it, according to whether he consecrates it to evil, or to good" (Erachin, 15, b).

"Rabbi Ela, hearing a child recite this verse (Amos, iv. 13), 'Lo, it is He that formeth the mountains, and createth the wind, and calls man to account for his own word,' said,

What mean these last words? They mean that even the idle words exchanged between a man and his wife in their closest connection, are recalled to them after death, and that they are called to account for them" (Chagiga, 5 b).

In Lytton's "Zanoni" is a somewhat exaggerated expression of a similar doctrine: "The conduct of the individual can affect but a small circle beyond himself; the permanent good or evil that he works to others lies rather in the sentiments he can diffuse. His acts are limited and momentary; his sentiments may pervade the universe, and inspire generations till the day of doom. . . . Our opinions are the angel part of us; our acts, the earthly."

The form in which Jesus promulgates the doctrine of the importance of words, is the following: "Every idle word that men shall speak, they shall give account thereof in the day of judgment, For by thy words thou shalt be justified, and by thy words thou shalt be condemned" (Matt. xii. 36).

"Theosophic speculations... were only to be communicated with the greatest caution, for it is said, 'Honey and milk are under thy tongue' (Cant. iv. 11), 'Things which are sweeter than honey should be under thy tongue' (Chagiga, 13 a), or should not be revealed" ("Sayings of the Jewish Fathers," C. Taylor).

"It was not out of envy that the Master announced in a certain Gospel: My mystery is to me and to the sons of my house [disciples]" (Clem. Alex. Strom. v.).

"Unto you it is given to know the mysteries of the kingdom of heaven, but to them it is not given. . . . Therefore I speak to them in parables" (Matt. xiii. 11, 13).

"The reward of precept is precept, and the reward of transgression is transgression" (P. Aboth, iv. 5).

"R. Jochanan says: The Holy One, blessed be he, only gives wisdom to him that hath wisdom; for it is said (Dan. ii. 21), Who gives wisdom to the wise and knowledge to them that have intelligence" (Bab. Berachoth, 55 a).

"The way of the Holy One, blessed be he, is not like the way of flesh and blood; the way of flesh and blood is that it can only fill a vessel with anything when it is empty, but when it is full, it can put nothing there. But the Holy One, blessed be he, acts not thus, for he fills still more a full vessel, and puts nothing in a vessel that is empty. For it is said (Exod. xv. 26); If in obeying thou obeyest, that is to say, if thou obeyest (once) thou shalt also obey (many times); but if thou obeyest not (now), thou shalt obey no more (for the future). Others explain, If thou obeyest the ancient precept, thou wilt obey also the new, but if thou puttest it out of thy heart, thou wilt no longer be in a state to lend an ear to it" (Bab. Berachoth, 40 a).

"The words of the Law give life or death; life to those who study with the right hand; death to those who learn with the left hand" (Shabbath, 88 b).

These passages throw light on the meaning of the parable of the talents (Matt. xxv. 14), as well as show a large common measure with the following:—

"For whosoever hath, to him shall be given, and he shall have abundance: but whosoever hath not, from him shall be taken away even that which he hath" (Matt. xiii. 12).

"Blessed the ears which have heard!" (Tanchuma, 188, b). "Blessed are ye; blessed are those that bore you; blessed are mine eyes that have seen this" (Chagiga, f. 14). "What was concealed from all the prophets has been revealed unto me" (Targum Hier. in Numb. xxiv. 3, 15, ref. Balaam). "Whence learnest thou that a maid saw in the sea what neither Ezekiel saw nor the rest of the prophets?" (Mekiltha in Exod. xv. 2).

"Blessed are your eyes, for they see; and your ears, for they hear. For verily I say unto you, that many prophets and righteous men desired to see the things which ye see, and saw them not; and to hear the things which ye hear, and heard them not" (Matt. xiii. 16).

"Rabbi Eliezer, son of Rabbi Simeon, surprised and caught some thieves. Rabbi Josua, son of Korcha, sent to him saying, Vinegar, son of wine, how long dost thou deliver up unto slaughter the people of our God? He replied: I am plucking up brambles from the vineyard. To whom the other: Let the Lord of the vineyard come himself, and himself pluck them up" (Baba Mezia, f. 83 b).

With this may be compared the parable (Matt. xiii. 24) of the Wheat and the Darnel.

"Our Rabbis have handed down: For ever let a man sell whatever he hath, and lead in marriage the daughter of a disciple of the sages" (Pesaqim, f. 49, 1, 2).

"He went off and cut open a fish, and a lovely pearl presented itself to him, from which he fed himself for the whole of his life" (Bereschith R., xi. 5).

These compare with the Treasure in the field, and the Pearl of price, which, in the parable, a man sells all that he has to buy (Matt. xii. 44, 45).

There is a proverb in the Talmud with which we have become familiarized through the Gospel: "Physician, heal thine own limp" (Bereschith R., xxiii. 5; and Tanchuma in Gen., p. 61).

"Doubtless ye will say unto me this parable, Physician, heal thyself" (Luke iv. 23).

"There was a stalk of mustard in Sichin from which sprang out three boughs; of which one was broken off, and covered the tent of a potter, and produced three cabs of mustard. R. Simeon ben Chalaphta said, 'A stalk of mustard was in my field, into which I was wont to climb as men are wont to climb into a fig-tree'" (Jer. Peah., vii. 4).

"The kingdom of heaven is like unto a grain of mustard seed, which a man took, and sowed in his field: which indeed is less than all seeds; but when it is grown, it is greater than the herbs, and becometh a tree, so that the birds of the heaven come and lodge in the branches thereof" (Matt. xiii. 31, 32).

The following have a curious parallelism to the miraculous increase of the Loaves and Fishes as narrated in the Gospels. There is also a Pythagorean saying which suggests a symbolic basis to the stories: "Esteem that to be good above all, which, on being communicated to another, will the more be increased to yourself."

"In the time of Simeon the Just, the fire of the altar was wont to burn the whole day, when no more than a couple of firebrands were placed on the altar in the morning; but after his death it so languished that they were compelled to supply logs throughout the whole day.

"In the time of Simeon the Just, a blessing was on the two pentecostal loaves, and on the twelve loaves of the presentation, so that each priest who received a proportionate quantity of oil, did eat enough, and yet there was a remnant over and above" (Yoma, f. 39 a).

It is probable that fables of this kind were so well known in the Jewish schools that they were no more regarded as literal statements of fact than a work of fiction is with us.

The metaphor of a burning log, communicating its flame, and kindling the intellects of others, was, no doubt, quite a familiar expression. "A great scholar profits from association with the meanest, as 'the small wood is used to set on fire the large'" (Thaanith, 7 a; Maccoth, 10 a).

Such narratives would be furnished with verisimility of detail and local colour. In the present instance, the breaking of the bread, after giving praise, is in accordance with Rabbinical usage: "One pronounces the benediction first, and afterwards breaks the bread" (Bab. Berachoth, 39 b). The usual benediction would run, "Blessed be thou, Eternal, our God, King of the universe, who makest bread to come forth from the earth!"

The proverb of the blind leading the blind has become one of our own proverbs. It probably originated in the sheep-farm, in the tendency of the flock blindly to follow its leader:

"When the shepherd bears any ill-will to his flock, he puts out the eyes of the bellwether" (Proverb cited in Talmud, B. Kama, 52 a).

"The heart ponders, the tongue decides, the mouth puts in execution" (Bab. Berachoth, 61 a).

"The things which proceed out of the mouth come forth out of the heart" (Matt. xv. 18).

With the Talmudists injury counted as murder, which fact helps us more clearly to see why it should be classed with comparatively light offences, as "defiling" a man. The humiliation of one's neighbour also came under the category of murder. A quaint conceit from the Talmud may be given as an instance: "A doctor taught in the presence of R. Nachman bar Isaac, He who publicly humiliates his neighbour (literally, makes him turn pale) is as if he shed his blood. Thou hast well said, remarked the Rabbi, for in reality the blood abandons the cheeks to give place to the pallor." Theft included deceit, and even the gaining of affection by counterfeiting it. "It is forbidden to steal the heart of any one whatever, even of a pagan" (Talmud, Cholin, 94 a). Compare also the following: "Rabban Jochanan ben Zakai asked of his disciples, Which is the evil way that men ought with the most care to shun? R. Eliezer said, The evil eye; R. Jehoshua, A bad companion; R. Jose, An evil neighbour; R. Shimeon, A man that borrows and does not pay; R. Lazar, A bad heart. Said the master: I place the last before all the rest, for it includes them all" (P. Aboth, ii. 13).

The first of the following passages assumes that the oral Law emanates from Moses; the second does away with any such literal sense, and presents us with an idealistic paradox :—

"Rabbi Jose ben Dormaskith having gone to present his respects to R. Eleazar [Haggadol, spiritual parent of this Jose, and also of Simeon the elder], who dwelt at Lydda, the latter asked of him, What new at the school to-day? He related to him what had been taught. R. Eleazar went into a passion, and said to him, Thou darest to give me for a new thing an antique tradition! This doctrine of which thou speakest, I had already received from my master R. Jochanan ben Zakai, who himself held it from his, and it remounts up to Moses! And he cursed R. Jose, saying, Be thine eyes closed to the light. And R. Jose became blind. Some time after, the wrath of the doctor being appeased, he said, Let thy sight revive! and his eyes were opened again" (Chagiga, 3 b).

"Scripture, Mishna, and Talmud, and Hagada, and even that which the diligent scholar was destined to point out before his master, were already spoken to Moses from Sinai" (Talm., Jer. Megilla, iv. 1).

The narration of legendary marvels at least supports the view that miracle-working was claimed as one of the higher attributes of the sages. The Talmudists maintain that Jesus learned the lore of magic from Rabbi Josua ben Perachia. This doctor, however, died, it is believed, about 90 B.C. His disciple, R. Shimeon ben Shatach, was the declared opponent of the Sadducees.

Among the powers to which the Jewish doctors laid claim were instantaneous cures of certain disorders and the like. According to Matt. xvi. 1, they ask for something further from Jesus—a still higher voucher—such as the distinct prediction of some event, the due occurrence of which would set a sanction to his claims to be believed. The following passages will illustrate their views on such a matter. The first implies that a sign was the usual warrant of a prophet, while, if that attestation should attend any prophecy which the nation held to be evil or untrue, there was no solution of such a dilemma but to kill the prophet.

"R. Ismael teaches that: The orders of the Pentateuch contain either prohibitions or permissions. The first are of importance (solemn), the latter are not; but the words of the Doctors are always so. We will prove this: We have learnt that the negation of the precept of the phylacteries, which is an opposition to the Law, is not a sin (for it is only necessary to consult the text to know that it exists); but he who would put five sections to it (instead of four), and thus add to the orders of the Doctors, would be condemnable. . . . The decisions of the elders have more value than those of the Prophets; it is written: 'They shall prophesy; but they shall not prophesy for those whom shame doth not quit;' and, 'I shall predict for thee wine and drink.' What difference is there between prophets and sages? The same as between two mandatories that a king should send into one of his provinces with a different character. Of one he says to his subjects, If he does not show you my royal seal, believe him not. Of the other, Give him credence, even though he should not exhibit to you my seal. The first of these mandatories is the prophet, of whom it is said (Deut. xiii. 2), 'If he give you a proof or a miracle;' the second is the council of sages, of whom it is said (*ib.*, xvii. 11) 'Thou shalt do according to the sentence of the law which they shall teach thee.' This, however, is not decided until after a bath-kol [daughter of voice, echo from the Heaven] has been held; before that, if any one wishes to act severely, and to adopt as rules the solemn opinions of Shammaï and Hillel, he merits to have applied to him the verse, 'The fool walketh in darkness' [Eccles. ii. 14]" (Talm. Jer. Berach., i. 7 (4) Gem.).

The passages referred to are as follows: "If there arise in the midst of thee a prophet, or a dreamer of dreams, and he give thee a sign or a wonder, and the sign or the wonder come to pass, whereof he spake unto thee, saying, Let us go after other gods, which thou hast not known, and let us serve them; thou shalt not hearken unto the words of that prophet, or that dreamer of dreams; for Jehovah your God is trying you, to know whether ye love Jehovah your God with all your heart and with all your soul. . . . And that prophet, or that dreamer of dreams, shall be put to death." The second passage cited refers to a contested judgment, and is as follows:

"Thou shalt do according to the tenor of the sentence, which they shall show thee from *that place* [the seat of judgment] which Jehovah shall choose; and thou shalt observe to do according to all that they shall teach thee. . . . And the man that doeth presumptuously, and will not hearken to the priest, . . . or unto the judge, even that man shall die."

"R. Joseph asked R. Joseph ben Rabba, 'Which commandment has your father admonished you to observe more than any other?' He replied, 'The law about the fringes'" (Talm. Shabb., 118 b). "The law respecting the fringes is as important as all the other laws put together" (Ginsburg, from Rashi on Numb. xv. 41). This "heavy burden" of a trivial law is, however, not quite so inane as it seems at first sight, though its symbolism is of a puerile kind. This fringe was made to have a spiritual import, its five knots representing the five books of the Law, which contains 613 precepts, these again being comprised in the numerical value of the term itself (600), plus its 8 threads and 5 knots.

These passages are, perhaps, enough to show that in Judaism there was a dogmatic school of Doctors who aggravated the ancient rules and ordinances, and claimed to set them above the fresher and diviner teachings of the prophets of expansive mind. If we assume that such doctrines held a place in Jerusalem at the time when the constraining influence of Shammai, Hillel's bitter rival, was yet fresh, it is easy to perceive the kind of jealous opposition which Jesus had to face from Doctors and priests representing this kind of Judaism. If he belonged to any school, it was pre-eminently that of "the sons of the prophets."

That such oppositions were in existence may be seen very plainly from the following brief extracts, which show the effect upon a noble mind of these wearisome burdens and "solemn" absurdities:—

"The scribes and the Pharisees sit on Moses' seat. . . . They bind heavy burdens, and lay them on men's shoulders;

but they themselves will not move them with their finger. ... Hypocrites! because ye shut the kingdom of heaven against men" (Matt. xxiii. 2, 4, 13). "Ye have made void the word [law] of God because of your tradition" (Matt. xv. 6).

"The chief priests and the elders of the people came unto him as he was teaching, and said, By what authority doest thou these things? and who gave thee this authority?" (Matt. xxi. 23).

In spite of the grievousness or triviality of the precepts of the scribes, Jesus enjoins upon his disciples, "All things whatsoever they bid you, do and observe." The following is another instance of a Rabbi holding himself free in opinion, but bound to conformity with established doctrine in practice: "R. Simon was one day, during the sacred year, crossing the fields, and he saw some one gathering the young shoots of that year; he said: Is this not forbidden? Are they not young shoots? On the contrary, was the answer; hast thou not allowed it? Yes, replied the Rabbi; but as my con-disciples contest my opinion, you must apply here the following verse: 'Whoso breaketh a hedge, a serpent shall bite him' (Eccles. x. 8)." (Talm. Jer. Berach., 1. 2 [1] Gem.) The hedge here designated is the fence of the law.

"Mistrust neither the Pharisees, nor those who are not Pharisees, but the hypocrites, who conduct themselves externally like good Pharisees and would gather to themselves with the sins of Zimri, the recompense of Phinehas" (Sota, 22 b).

"The leaven of the Pharisees, which is hypocrisy" (Luke xii. 1).

The main differences between the Rabbis were on the question of binding or loosening, aggravating or alleviating the law. Not only were the schools of Hillel and Shammai reputed to have pursued opposite tendencies in this respect, but in a large number of the Talmudic treatises are references to one Doctor or another, as forbidding or permitting, making heavy or making light.

When Jesus gave to Peter the keys of the kingdom of heaven, the emblem of his responsibility as an apostle of the good tidings of the heavenly life, it was after the manner of a Rabbi investing his disciple with the Semicha. "Before the authorization by his master, a doctor ought not to pronounce any decision" (Sanhedrin, 5).

In the simple ceremonial of the investiture of Peter with the stewardship, we may very naturally expect not to find a single expression that would have sounded either new or unfamiliar to the ears of those that were by :—

"Thou art Kephas, and upon this *Kepha* (rock)* I will build, as a house, my congregation.† Even the gates of Sheol ‡ will not get the better of it. Yea, I will give thee the keys of the kingdom of the heavens § : and what thou shalt bind, shall be bound, and what thou shalt loose shall be loosed."

In other words, Peter was constituted suffragan Rabbi,

---

* "When the patriarchs came, that walked piously before him, then spake he, 'Upon these will I lay the foundation of the world.' Therefore are they called rocks" (Midrash Shemoth, 15).

"When the Holiest of all descried Abraham in the far future, he spake, 'I have now found the rock whereupon to build and to lay the foundation of the world (ref. Isai. li. 1).' Therefore is Abraham called the rocky" (Yalqut Shimoni, Bal., 243).

† The word *ekklesia*, usually rendered "church," and here "congregation," would be more literally translated "convocation." This term and the word "synagogue" represent two Hebrew words, the most common of which is *'edah*, which is to be found in many passages of the written Law, as in Num. xiv. 27, where the Septuagint renders by *sunagōgè*. Both words are found together in Prov. v. 14, where *'edah* is translated "assembly," and the other word, "congregation," rendered in the Septuagint by *ekklesia* and *sunagōgè* respectively.

The ordinary *'edah* appears to have been the gathering together of not less than ten men, which was the minimum number constituting a congregation before whom as a sacred function the Law might be publicly read.

‡ The proximity of death; the precise expression "the gates of hades" is to be found in this sense in 3 Macc. v. 51. Or, as the metaphor is of a house on a rock, the symbol may represent merely the gulf of the underworld.

§ Cf. "I will give him the key of the house of David upon his shoulder; and he shall open, and there shall be none that shuts; and he shall shut, and there shall be none that opens" (Isai. xxii. 22, "The word of the valley of Sion").

"The school of Shammai binds it even on the fourth day of the week, but the school of Hillel looses it" (Talmud, Jer. Shabb., i. 7).

and his decisions were to be taken as final among his condisciples.

The "key of the kingdom of the heavens" is a heightened expression of the phrase "the key of knowledge," as employed in the following passage: "Alas for you, masters of the law! for ye took away the key of knowledge: ye entered not in yourselves, and them that were entering in ye hindered" (Luke xi. 52).

The technical sense of the Jewish phrase "great city" was one that contained ten *batlanim*, or men of leisure, to make a congregation. A place containing less than ten such men could therefore only obtain a congregation when enough of its inhabitants could be found disengaged. Such a place was termed a *Kaphar;* and the village of Nahum, where Jesus had a house (Kaphar-Nahum, Capernaum), was apparently subject to this disability. But by an arrangement with Peter and the other disciples, Jesus could always " summon or convoke an '*Edah*." " R. Chalaftha of Kaphar-Chananiah said, Where ten sit and are occupied in words of Thorah, the Shekinah is among them, for it is said, 'God standeth in the *congregation* of the mighty' (Ps. lxxxii. 1)" (Talm. Pirqe Aboth, iii. 9).

It was argued by the Rabbis (Bereschith R., 75–78) that a blessing given on earth was also a blessing in heaven. It was also argued (Bab. Berachoth, 12 b) that a man who had committed a misdeed, and was ashamed of it, was forgiven all his misdeeds, and the question then arose, whether this forgiveness extended to heaven. The argument by which it was established that it did, is drawn from the words of the apparition of Samuel to Saul (1 Sam. xxviii. 19), "To-morrow shalt thou and thy sons be with me," which was interpreted to mean "in the same degree" as Samuel himself in paradise. Human law must have been regarded as the deputy of the law of Heaven, so absolutely that a man acquitted by the Beth-din, or tribunal of three, was esteemed to have been also forgiven by the celestial Beth-din. This was the divine circle of which Deity was the centre, the heavenly compassion being the nearest to that centre, and justice holding the next place.

When Jesus included in the ceremony of Peter's investiture a faculty to bind or loosen in heaven as well as earth, he was neither innovating, nor conferring a unique privilege, according to the ideas of the time. But in another place (Matt. ix. 6) the authority to forgive is expressly limited—"the son of man has power *on earth* to forgive sin." And the claim is recorded to have found its sanction forthwith in a physical result of the exercise of power. This is at least in harmony with Talmudical views:—

"No death without sin, and no pain without some transgression" (Bab. Shabb., 55 a).

"The sick ariseth not from his sickness until his sins be forgiven him" (Bab. Ned., 41 a).

The expressions "bind" and "loose," "forbid" and "allow," are frequently to be met with in the Talmud, and must have been familiar to the school of Jesus. There were Rabbis who had a high sense of the responsibility of decision which they deemed to be part of their office. The following is the prayer made by R. Nechonia ben Hakana when he arrived at the sacred college :—

"May it be thy will, O Lord, my God, and God of my fathers, that I be not irritated against my disciples, nor my disciples against me. That we may not pronounce to be defiled that which is pure, nor make pure the defiled. That we may not bind the loosed, nor loose the bound ; so that I be not shamed for this world (age), and for the world (age) to come" (Talm., J. Berachoth, iv. 2).

The expression "the kingdom of the heavens," as found in many passages of the synoptic Gospels, cannot with certainty be taken to refer to life after death. The "yoke of the kingdom of heavens," the "yoke of the precepts," * and

* "Why does the section 'Hear' precede 'and it shall come to pass'?

other allied expressions refer in the Talmud to the consecration to sacred learning, the assumption of the sacred discipline, the expression of faith, and of adhesion to the commandments. The "mysteries of the kingdom of heaven" were the advanced truths taught in the school, and correspond to the "secret doctrines" or "mysteries" communicated to initiates in the ancient religious celebrations.

There can be little doubt that the terrestrial "kingdom of heavens," when the expression was used in the limited and technical sense, was by Hebrew teachers regarded as the analogue of the celestial. A similar correspondence is manifest in the Talmudic references to the double "Holy of Holies;"* to "the family above and the family below," that is, the angels and the sages; the celestial and the terrestrial Eden, or paradise: "the upper and the lower Adam:" and in the later Apocalyptic dream of the "new Jerusalem." We may be reminded also of Plato's State, the ideal *Politeia*, and the "State within man," which he so beautifully draws into correspondence with it.

"Grant that we may enjoy happiness in Eden: let us have a good heart and find a good companion" (Jer. Berach., iv. 2 Gem.). It is difficult to know what is here meant by "a good companion;" or if it is to be understood in the Zoroastrian sense of the visible personification of the qualities exercised during the period of corporeal life.

"He said, Jesus, remember me when thou comest into [in other MSS., *in*] thy kingdom. And he said unto him,

(Num. xv. 37-41). That one may first take on himself the yoke of the kingdom of heavens, before he take on himself the yoke of the commandments" (Talm. Mishna, Berach., ii. 3 [2]). "Why is it prescribed that the man should wear phylacteries [the "insignia of Religion"], read the Shema, and pray [the Amída]? It is in order that he should entirely accept the divine yoke" (*Ib.*, Jer. Gemara).

Cf. "Put your neck under the yoke, and let your soul accept discipline" (Prayer of Jesus, the son of Sirach, Sir., li.).

* "If one cannot turn his face he must direct his heart towards the Holy of Holies" (Talm. Berachoth, iv. 6 [5]). "Of which Holy of Holies does it speak [in the Mishna]? . . . the earthly Holy of Holies is just under the heavenly Holy of Holies" (Jer. Gem.).

Verily I say unto thee, To-day thou wilt be with me in Paradise" (Luke xxiii. 42, 43).

Where the plain and obvious first meaning of a phrase makes the sense of a passage intelligible, it would seem to be right to accept that as the true one. It was meant for him "that hath ears to hear" to deduce the implied or "sub-audible" (sous-entendu) meaning.

The natural sense of the phrase "heaven's kingdom" is that in which heaven reigns, whatever it may be. In its relation to Hebrew thought, it is the special province of God in the world; the kingdom, whether in a school of devout men or in the heart of an individual, which the Shekinah was thought to overshadow. It is not to be forgotten that the Hebrew ideal of rule was a theocracy. Though these idealists conformed to the temporal law, bitter and cruel as it might have been in times of foreign domination, they rejoiced in believing that they were more really and more truly under the rule of Heaven.

The depositaries of the *logia* of Jesus, in their ignorance of the history of Jewish symbols and of the concise particularity of the Hebrew mind, did not understand that the expression "the kingdom of the heavens" denoted the divine light shining in the world in the school of sacred law, but took it to refer to the hereafter. If a paragraph had been found describing Jesus as "assuming the celestial sovereignty"* it would probably have been taken for a superhuman assumption, and not as the ordinary description of a Rabbi doing the recitation of the Shema.

Historical investigation discloses the existence of a faculty, sacredly reserved to the Rabbi, of pronouncing, in the largest as well as the most trivial and everyday things, what is an obligation (bound), what is optional or unnecessary (loose). With the apposition in the mind of the rock-founded building, as an earthly institution, and of a transcendental Church

* Talm. Jer. Berach., ii. 1, Gemara.

which has triumphed over (not merely withstood) "the gates of hades," and become "the kingdom of the heavens" in a new, non-Hebrew, but very attractive significance, it has been easy and natural to suppose that the binding and loosing has reference to the supernal state as well.

The words "as in heaven, so on earth" convey a simple idea. If the order of the words be reversed—"Whatsoever thou shalt bind on earth shall be bound in heaven"—we need to be careful not to ascribe to the Master a delegation to Peter of a power unattainable by himself or any other human being, that of binding by Talmudic prescriptions the beings who walk free over the asphodel meadows of paradise.

If so new, so stupendous, and so untenable a claim had ever been put forward among Jews by a Jew, it is at least unlikely that it would have been prefaced by a homely play upon words, such as was dear to the Rabbinical mind.

The true meaning is that the Rabbi's office, like the province of established law, was regarded as of divine ordinance, and everything done *ex cathedrâ*, so to speak, was regarded as enjoying without question the divine seal and sanction, as the act of an acknowledged deputy of heaven.

The *malkuth shamayim*, or "kingdom of heavens," in the Hebrew understanding of the words, is the terrestrial school that is possessed of the divine sanction; and the sincere decision of the chief of that school, the disciple of the light, was regarded as endowed with an authority from heaven.

In another place (Matt. xviii. 18) the authority ascribed to Peter, as holder of the symbols of headship, is attributed in the plural immediately after a reference to the *ekklesia* or *'edah*. A simple interpretation is obvious: "What things soever ye [in orderly assembly for the purpose] shall bind on earth will be bound in heaven: and whatsoever things ye shall loose on earth will be loosed in heaven."

The story of a noted Hebrew doctor, who suffered under Hadrian early in the second century, will form a fit commentary upon the words of Jesus—"Whosoever shall lose his life [for my sake and the sake of the good tidings] will find it." "Rabbi Akiba said, 'Thou shalt love the Eternal, thy God, ... with all thy soul' (Deut. vi. 5). That signifies that thou oughtest to manifest thy love towards God even when they wish to take thy soul, that is to say, to take away thy life. ... When they were conducting him to death, it was just at the hour of the recitation of the Shema (the *Audi*, or profession of faith by proclamation of the unity of God: Deut. vi. 4 ss.). Whilst combs with iron teeth were tearing his body, he continued imperturbably to take upon himself the yoke of the kingdom of heaven [that is, he persisted in reciting the Shema]. What, master, at such a moment! cried his disciples. My friends, responded he, all my life I have been anxious about this verse, 'with all thy soul.' I have been asking myself when and how the occasion would be given me to fulfil this. And now that the opportunity is offered me, should I not embrace it? And he recited slowly the sacred formula [Hear, O Israel, the Eternal is our God, the Eternal is one], so that he expired in pronouncing the last word. And a voice was heard from the heaven, which said, Blessed art thou, Akiba, who hast breathed out thy soul in the confession of the oneness of thy God. And the angels of ministry said, in the presence of the Holy One, Blessed be he; such, then, is thy law, and such thy recompense! And God made answer, Their portion is in this life. And once again the celestial voice made itself heard, Blessed art thou, Akiba, who art destined for the life of the world to come!" (Talmud, Bab. Berachoth, 61 b).

The Rabbinical illustrations of so recondite a narrative as that of the Transfiguration, though they may be unsatisfactory to the modern mind, scientific and orthodox alike, at least do not disclose such a clumsiness of imagination as Raphael's great picture on the subject in the Vatican. A conception of original man, which haunts the Talmud, is that of an upper and celestial Adam, of whom the terrestrial race is the material adumbration, through a lapse from the "image of God." "'God made for them coats of skin and clothed them.' In Rabbi Meir's Book of the Law they found it written: 'Garments of light, these were the garments of the first Adam'" (Bereschith R., xx. 29).

Ginsburg, in his work on the Kabbala, quotes from the Sohar (ii. 229 b) a passage akin to this: "The Lord God made coats of skins unto Adam and to his wife, and clothed them; for prior to this they had garments of light—light of that light which was used in the garden of Eden." On this Ginsburg comments: "The garments of skin therefore mean our present body, which was given to our first parents in order to adapt them to the changes which the Fall introduced."

The word "skin," here representing man's "garment of shame," or corporeal body, is the same as that which describes (Exod. xxxiv. 30, 35) the skin of the face of Moses, which sent forth horns of light after his descent from the holy mount, so that he had to cover his face with a veil. As the Septuagint version renders it, "The appearance of the skin of his face was glorified." "The faces of the just in the time to come will be like the sun and moon" (Jalqut Simeoni, p. ii. f. 10. 3). "Rabbi Chanina and Rabbi Josua ben Levi having gone one day to the house of the Roman proconsul of Cesarea, the latter, seized with respect, arose at the sight of them. What! people said, dost thou arise before these Jews? It is, responded he, because they appeared to me as angels" (Talm., Jer. Berachoth, v. 1). Such a shining of the face, in different degrees, is, in another place, attributed to Moses, Joshua, Adam, Phineas, and Eliezer the great.

The same quality was expected to attach to the appearance of the Messiah.

There is a certain common measure in all these accounts; and it is evident that a narrative of the life of one regarded by his followers as a supereminent prophet would not have been complete, in the view of a Talmudist, without a description of his face as translucent and his apparel as diaphanous.

"Rabbi Samuel said, The kingdom roots up mountains" (Baba Bathra, f. 32).

"If ye have faith . . . ye shall say unto this mountain, Remove hence to yonder place; and it shall remove" (Matt. xvii. 20).

According to the Talmud (Pesaqim, f. 111 b), the formula which would expel a single demon was powerless before a family or kind. This compares with the verse of doubtful authenticity rejected by the Revisers, but appearing in the Authorized Version as Matt. xvii. 21, "This kind goeth not out save by prayer and fasting."

"Rab Nachman, son of Rab Hisda, wished to subject the Doctors to a tax. Rab Nachman, son of Isaac, said to him, Thou dost contravene the intention of the scripture, for it is written (Ezra vii. 24), We certify you that, touching any of the priests and Levites, singers, doorkeepers, nethinim, or ministers of this house of God, it shall not be lawful to impose custom, tribute, or toll upon them" (Baba Bathra, viii. a).

"The kings of the earth, from whom do they receive toll or tribute? from their sons, or from strangers? And when he said, From strangers, Jesus said unto him, Therefore the sons are free. But lest we stumble them, . . . take and give unto them for me and thee" (Matt. xvii. 25). This was in reference to the Temple tax.

"He who teaches the divine law to a child is considered by the scripture as if he had given it life" (Sanhedr., 19 b, and 99 b).

"He who refuses sound doctrine to a disciple, all will curse him, even the child unborn" (*Ibid.*, 91 b).

"He who teaches the divine law to a child, deserves to sit in the midst of the celestial court; for it is said (Jer. xv. 19), If I see thee bring back (thy brethren into the good way) I will permit thee to sit before me" (B. Mezia, 85 a).

"At five years old, Scripture; at ten years, Mishna; at thirteen, the Commandments; at fifteen, Thalmud, etc." (Addendum to P. Aboth).

"Whoso shall receive one such little child in my name, receiveth me" (Matt. xviii. 5).

"The evil, as well as the good, is imputed to him who is its first cause" (Shabb., 32 a).

"Woe to the man through whom the occasion of stumbling comes" (Matt. xviii. 7).

"It is written (Lev. xix. 17), Thou oughtest resolutely to rebuke thy brother. Would it be permitted thereby to rebuke him publicly, and so as to put him to shame? By no means, for the Law immediately adds, Thou oughtest not to do it in a sinful manner" (Erachin, 16 b).

The authority of the "congregation" is shown to be superior, in matters of dispute, to that of "one or two more" besides the disputants, as was the latter over the argument of the two disputants by themselves. Three persons constituted a *Beth-din* for the administration of justice in matters secular, while two might discuss and study Thorah by themselves. The Shekinah was believed to be present with those who were exercising secular functions, because judgment was not only secular but sacred. There were many questions under what circumstances the Shekinah was present with men. Some said, "In the chosen house," that is, in the Temple. The Talmud says (P. Aboth, iii. 9), "Whence [is it proved that the Shekinah is among] even two? Because it is said, Then they that feared the Lord spake often one to another. And whence even one? Because it is said, In all places where I record my name I will come unto *thee*, and I will bless thee (Ex. xx. 24)." Jesus is evidently quoting, though not exactly recorded, where he bases his argument as follows—"For where two or three are gathered together in my name, there am I in the midst of them." This, there is no shadow of a doubt, was understood as a reference to the Shekinah.

In detail after detail, the Talmud and the Gospel are mutually illustrative :—

"Whosoever sins against his brother, he must say to him, 'I have sinned against thee.' If he hear, it is well; if not, let him bring others, and let him appease him before them" (Talm. Jer. Yoma, 45 b ; Bab. Yoma, 87 a).

"If thy brother have committed a fault against thee, go, expostulate [argue the matter] with him, between thee and him alone: if he hearken to thee, thou hast gained thy brother. But if he hearken not, take with thee one or two more ; that 'By mouth of two witnesses or three, every word may be established,' and, if he disregard them, tell the congregation : and if he disregard the congregation, let him be to thee like the Gentile and the tax-officer" (Matt. xviii. 15–17). The doctrine here fails to manifest the inexhaustible patience which is a characteristic of Jesus. It is quite in the spirit of the practice of the time: "They pardon a man once that sins against another; secondly they pardon him; thirdly they pardon him ; fourthly they do not pardon him" (Talm. Bab. Yoma, 86 b). We may question whether the editorial arrangement of the Gospel is not defective here. It looks as if originally Jesus might have quoted the Talmudical precepts and afterwards enhanced them by his own elevating ethics. "How often shall my brother sin against me, and I forgive him? until seven times? Jesus saith unto him, I say not unto thee, Until seven times; but, Until seventy times [and] seven' (Matt. xviii. 21–22).

"Ben Azzai proved admirably by texts the religious obligation of marriage. His colleagues objected, Such an one preaches well, and acts the same ; such another acts well, though unskilled in speech. As for thee, Ben Azzai, what thou sayest is gold, but thou dost not practise what thou preachest.' 'How can I? the study of the Law absorbs my whole existence. Moreover, if I do not occupy myself with the propagation of the species, enough others do, and the world is not near coming to an end'" (Yebamoth, 63 b).

"The disciples say unto him, If the cause of the man with the wife is thus [that is, if the Law does not approve 'every cause' as a ground of divorce], it is not advantageous to marry. But he said unto them, All men cannot receive this saying, but they to whom it is given" (Matt. xix. 9).

To understand both Talmud and Gospels we have to familiarize ourselves with the Rabbinical mode of thought. For an example of the subtle way in which a passage may be read in a quite different sense from that accepted by Western students, the following will serve. According to Isai. lvi. 4, 5, "the eunuchs that keep my sabbaths" are to have "an everlasting name," "a memorial better than of sons and of daughters." In a passage of the Zohar it is asserted that these eunuchs "are students of the Law living in chastity up to the Sabbath night in each week." Though this may seem far-fetched, it is to be borne in mind that even the strict rule of the Nazarite might be adopted for a limited period. So that the pre-christian "eunuchs, which made themselves eunuchs for the kingdom of heaven's sake," may not, after all, have been such infatuates as has been supposed, but only persons who had bound themselves by a vow of restraint for a given period.

There is a story in the Talmud (Jer. Berach., vii. 2) of the burdensome sacrifices required of those who had made vows of abstinence. The Doctor Shimeon ben Shatach had made a bargain with his brother-in-law Alexander Jannæus, the Maccabee king, to provide half of the Temple sacrifices required for three hundred votaries. He obtained the king's promised proportion, and then, with more craft than fairness, paid his own share by finding reasons for rendering the remaining sacrifices unnecessary; supporting his conduct on the words, "For wisdom is a defence, and money is a defence" (Eccl. vii. 12). With regard to these vows, Dr. Moses Schwab takes occasion to observe, "The Rabbis did not approve of the *nazireat*, and were very ingenious in rendering null those engagements, which were often inconsiderately and imprudently made."

"Rêsch Lahisch said, in the name of R. Juda the patriarch, It is the breath of the young disciples, it is the pure atmosphere of the school, that makes the world subsist. What! said Rab Pappa, and do we two count for nothing? What, answered the other, is the influence of men subject to sin, in comparison with that of innocence?" (Shabb. 119 b).

"Suffer the little children, and forbid them not, to come unto me; for of such is the kingdom of heaven" (Matt. xix. 14).

Amongst varieties of Pharisees the Talmud specifies (Sota, f. 22. 2) one who says, "What ought I to do, and I will do it?" and another who asks, "What besides ought I to do, and I will do it?"

"R. Chanina said to the angel of death, Bring the book of the Law, and see whether there be anything written in it which I have not kept" (Kethuboth).

"Teacher, what good thing shall I do, that I may have eternal life? . . . All these things have I observed: what lack I yet?" (Matt. xix. 16, 20).

"The Rabbis have learned that when R. Elieser was ill, his disciples came in to visit him. 'Rabbi,' said they to him, 'teach us rules of life by which we can become partakers of the life of the world to come'" (Bab. Berach., 28 b).

"The distressed condition of a teacher deserves more regard than that of a father; for the father brings his son only into the temporal life, but the teacher, who teaches him wisdom, brings him also into the life eternal" (Baba Mezia, ii. 11).

"Lord, to whom shall we go? thou hast [the] words of eternal life" (John vi. 68).

"Man in dream sees only according to the desire of his

heart (or according to the fancies of the day); for it is said (Dan. ii. 29): 'As for thee, O king, thy thoughts have mounted into thy bed.' ... No one has ever seen in dream a palm-tree of gold, or an elephant passing through the needle's eye" (Bab. Berachoth, 55 b).

"The heart of our first ancestors was as large as the largest gate of the temple; that of the later ones like that of the next large; ours is like the eye of a needle" (Talm., cit. Deutsch).

"It is easier for a camel to go through a needle's eye, than for a rich man to enter into the kingdom of God" (Matt. xix. 24).

A passage in which this reference is given at length is to be found in an extra-canonical book: "The other of the rich men said to him, 'Master, what good thing shall I do and live?' He said unto him, 'Man, perform the Law and the prophets.' He answered him, 'I have performed them.' He said unto him, 'Go, sell all that thou dost possess, and divide it to the poor, and come, follow me.' But the rich man began to scratch his head, and it pleased him not. And the lord said unto him, 'How sayest thou, "I have performed the Law and the prophets"? seeing that it is written in the Law, "Thou shalt love thy neighbour as thyself," and behold many of thy brethren, sons of Abraham, are clad with dung, dying for hunger, and thy house is full of much goods, and there goeth out therefrom nothing at all unto them.' And he turned and said to Simon his disciple, sitting by him, 'Simon, son of John, it is easier for a camel to enter through the eye of a needle than a rich man into the kingdom of the heavens'" (Origen, Comm., cit. Gospel acc. to the Hebr.).

If the Needle's Eye was the name of a small gate of the temple, the picture of the unwieldy camel endeavouring to make his way through, affords a forcible illustration. And the suggestion of Dr. Paspati, the authority on modern Greek, that no one acquainted with that language would think that anything but a *cable*—not a camel—was meant, loses weight.

"Rab Joseph, son of Rab Josue ben Levi, fell into a trance. When he returned to himself, his father asked him, 'What didst thou see?' He replied, 'I saw the world turned upside down; the most powerful in the lowest rank, the humblest in the first.' 'It is not the world upside down which thou hast seen, my son, but the elect age'" (Pesaqim, f. 50 a. Baba Bathra, f. 10. 3).

"Many shall be last that are first; and first that are last" (Matt. xix. 30).

"R. Sira said, in the name of R. Aboon, son of R. Chija: There was a certain king who hired labourers. One of them was diligent in doing his work beyond all the rest. When evening was reached, the labourers came to receive their pay: and together with them came he who had especially proved his diligence; and he received exactly as much as the rest. Then verily did they begin to murmur and say, We have toiled the whole day, but he not even for two whole hours, yet none the less has he received full pay. To whom the lord made answer, He in two hours has produced more result than ye in the whole day" (Schir. R., vi. 2; and Qoheleth, v. 11).

The same story is told with more completeness in the following: "Of what does the death of R. Aboon bar R. Chiya make us think (he died young)? Of a king who, having hired many workmen in his service, perceives that one of them shows more ardour in the work than the others. When he sees this, what does the king do? He calls him, and walks up and down with him. In the evening the workmen came to be paid: he gives also a full day's pay to the man he had walked with. When his comrades see this, they complain and say: We have been working hard all the day, and this one who only laboured two hours receives as much salary as we do. It is, answered the king, because he has done more in two hours than you in the entire day" (Talm. Jer. Berach., ii. 8 [7] Gem.).

"'There are persons,' said Rabbi Juda the Saint, 'who attain heaven in a single hour, whilst others only gain it after long years of effort'" (Aboda Zara, 10 b).

The parable of the Labourers in the Vineyard naturally suggests itself as the parallel to the passages just quoted from the Talmud.

"Tradition says, Three walk on the road, the chief in the middle, the greater of the two on the right hand, the lesser on the left" (Yoma, f. 37. 1). There was also a Talmudic legend that God would place Messiah on his right, and Abraham on his left.

"R. Zira relates, This night, R. Jose, son of R. Chanina, appeared to me in a dream, and I asked him, Near whom art thou seated on high? He answered me, Near R. Jochanan" (B. Mezia, 85 b).

"Say that these my two sons may sit, one on thy right hand, and one on thy left hand, in thy kingdom" (Matt. xx. 21).

The sellers of the half-shekels required for the Temple tax, and of doves for the Passover sacrifice, had a snug monopoly in the precincts, and probably made a kind of corner against buyers. Though Jesus drove these clever tradesmen away, they appear to have returned. Soon afterwards, "pence of gold" were asked for doves in Jerusalem, and Rabban Simeon, son of Gamaliel, vowed not to lie down that night until they were sold for pence of silver. This he effected by pronouncing a decree reducing the number to be offered, whereupon the disappointed speculators offered doves that day for two farthings the pair (*vide* Talm. Cherituth, i. 1).

"'Whoso keepeth a fig-tree shall eat its fruit' [Prov. xxvii. 18]. Why are the words of the law compared with a fig-tree? Because as a man finds figs on a fig-tree whenever he touches it, so also in the words of the Law, at whatever time a man may meditate he finds the savour of wisdom" (Erubin, f. 51).

This suggests a possible oblique meaning in the story of the Barren Fig-tree (Matt. xxi. 18), and in certain Talmudic passages that follow; but it cannot be said to be clear what that meaning is. The narrative possibly took its rise from Jer. viii. 7-13, and Isai. v. 4-7. When in Mark (xi. 13) it is added, "It was not the season of figs," the meaning is probably, it was not the time for ripe figs. The fruit of the fig-tree appears early, but does not mature until the second season, hence the Talmudic observation above quoted.

"That fig-tree, if he pluck it at its own time, benefits him and the tree; if not at its own time, injures him and the tree" (Bereschith R., lxii.). To ravage young plants was understood to signify, to fall into heresy or incredulity (*minouth*).

"R. Jose, of Yokereth, had labourers in the fields. As there was a delay in the arrival of their food from the town, they said to the son of R. Jose, 'We are hungry.' They were seated in the shade of a fig-tree. The son of the doctor then said, 'Fig-tree, fig-tree, give thy fruits, that the labourers of my father may have to eat.' And the fig-tree brought forth figs, and they ate thereof" (Thaanith, 24 a).

There was "a common Jewish metaphor by which Rabbis apt at clearing away difficulties were called 'rooters up of mountains'" (E. B. Nicholson, Comm. Matt.).

"If ye have faith and doubt not, . . . if ye shall say unto this mountain, Be thou taken up and cast into the sea, it shall be done" (Matt. xxi. 21).

"R. Eleazar says, If prayers are said only to fulfil a duty, they will not be heard by God" (Jer. Berach., iv. 4).

"All things whatsoever ye shall ask in prayer, believing, ye shall receive" (Matt. xxi. 22).

There are several parables to be found in the Talmud and Midrash, showing certain points of contact with the parable of the Marriage Feast in Matthew (xxii. 1–14) and its variant, the parable of the Guests (Luke xiv. 15–24). Though these parables, as uttered by Jesus, possess entirely original features, it may be remembered that one of them is prefaced by the words, "The kingdom of heaven *was likened*," instead of the more usual phrase, "*is like*." There is not such accuracy manifest, however, in the redaction of the records as to give any real importance to this trifling detail. The following parable is from the Talmud: "The simile of Rabbi Jehudah the chief [Redactor of the Mishna, A.D. 163-193]. To what is this thing like? To a king who made a feast, and called guests, and said unto them, Go ye, wash and make yourselves white, and anoint, and wash your clothing, and prepare yourselves for the banquet. But he fixed not for them the time the banquet was to be. And there were prudent ones after the ninth hour walking by the door of the king's palace; and they kept saying, Surely something lacketh to the palace of the king? The foolish among them cared not, nor were anxious about the king's word. Quoth they, It is our object to assemble at the king's banquet, and is that a banquet wherein there is no bustle, and society of this one with that? And the stonecutter went to his limestone, the builder to his mortar, the blacksmith to his coal, the bathman to his bath. Quoth the king on a sudden, Come ye each to the banquet with speed. They came, the former in their glory, the others in their squalor. The king was rejoiced in the prudent ones, who established the king's word and honoured his palace. And he was wroth with the foolish, who established not the king's word, but treated his palace with contumely. The king said to those who had made themselves ready for the banquet, Come ye and eat the banquet of the king; but those that made not themselves ready for the banquet shall not eat the king's banquet, but go ye and send them away. Quoth the king again, But let the first be set at table and eat and drink, whilst the others are smitten upon their feet and stand and look on and suffer anguish: so it will be in the time that is to come" (Qoheleth R., ix. 8).

The following is evidently the same as the last, but is from a compilation of the eleventh century: " A parable of a king who made an entertainment and invited all, but fixed no time for them. Those who paid heed to the king's word went off and took trouble about themselves, and anointed themselves, furbished their raiment, and made themselves ready for the feast; those, on the other hand, that heeded not the king's word, went off and busied themselves about their own affairs. When, then, the time of the supper drew nigh, the king said, Let all enter promptly. The former enter in their adornment, the latter in their unsightliness. Quoth the king, with regard to those that came and made themselves ready for the supper, Let them eat of my supper; but those that made not themselves ready for the supper, they shall not eat of my supper. Have they gone away and been held excused? Quoth the king, No. The one set shall eat, drink, and be merry; the others shall stand upon their feet, shall get the bastinado, look on, and be put to the rack" (Midrash Mischle, xvi. 11).

Another version of the same is much earlier, being attributed to Rabbi Jochanan ben Zakai, one of the "sons" of Hillel, and is said to be in reference to the hour of death and being ready.

"R. Jochanan, son of Zakai, propounded a parable. A certain king made ready a feast, to which he called his bondmen at a certain time not fixed. Those amongst them that were prudent, properly dressed themselves and sat before the gate of the king's palace, thinking, Is anything lacking to the house of the king? Those, however, of them that were foolish went off to their work, saying, Is there verily a banquet without busy work? Suddenly the king called his servants to the supper; the prudent appear in proper attire, the foolish, however, in sordidness. The king was glad about the prudent ones, but with the foolish he was very wroth, and said, Those who properly attired themselves shall sit, shall eat on, drink and be merry; those who did not properly attire themselves shall stand and see" (Shabbath, f. 153. 1).

Deutsch gives from the Talmud what seems to be a variant from this ("Literary Remains"): "Repent one day before thy death. There was a king who bade all his servants to a great repast, but did not indicate the hour; some went home and put on their best garments, and stood at the door of the palace; other said, There is ample time; the king will let us know beforehand. But the king summoned them of a sudden; and those that came in their best garments were well received; but the foolish ones, who came in their slovenliness, were turned away in disgrace. Repent to-day, lest to-morrow ye might be summoned."

There is yet another parable which seems to belong to this group, though it wanders further from those given by Jesus.

"It is like to a mortal king who distributed to his bondmen royal apparel. Were there any among them more prudent than the rest, they folded them up and stored them away in a clothes chest; the more stupid put them on, and so went on with their work. After some days the king asked back for the apparel belonging to him: the prudent restored it just as it had been up to this time, truly dazzling white; but the stupid just as it was, befouled. The king rejoiced as he beheld the prudent, but he was wroth with the stupid, and sent word concerning the prudent, Let the garments be placed in the treasury, whilst they themselves go home in peace; but let the stupid have the garments given them for washing, whilst they themselves are to be cast into prison" (Shabbath, f. 152. 2).

"Each age has its guide; there are not two for one and the same generation" (Sanhedrin, 8 a).

"Be not ye called Rabbi; for one is your teacher, and all ye are brethren. . . . Neither be ye called guides: for your guide is the one Christ" (Matt. xxiii. 8, 10).

"Flay a carcase in the street, and receive pay; rather than say, I am Cahana [*or* priest], and a great and learned man" (Pesaqim, 113 a; Baba Bathra, 110 a).

"Amongst abuses which cut short human life, we must reckon, said R. Jehudah, that which consists in seeking to raise one's self to great dignities" (Bab. Berachoth, 55 a).

"He that is the greater among you shall be your servitor" (Matt. xxiii. 11).

"Said Rabba [a doctor of Babylon] to the Rabbis [Palestinian doctors]: I beseech you, become not heirs of the two gehennas" (Yoma, f. 72. 2).

"Ye compass sea and land to make one proselyte [it has been asserted that there was 'a custom of making one representative proselyte annually, to typify the salvability of the Gentiles']; and when he is become so, ye make him twofold more a son of gehenna than yourselves" (Matt. xxiii. 15).

A moot point among the Pharisaic Rabbis was the relation of wife to husband in a future state. "Man takes precedence of woman in various ways, though 'The man is not without the woman, nor the woman without the man, nor both of them without the Shekinah' (Bereshith Rabbah, viii.; cf. Jer. Berach. ix. 1; 1 Cor. xi. 11).

"The Thorah in its entirety is for the man; whereas the woman is exempt from those positive precepts which are to be fulfilled at stated times (Qiddushin, i. 7). She is not to learn Thorah—much less to teach (1 Tim. ii. 12)—not being included in such passages as Deut. xi. 19: 'And ye shall teach them your SONS.' How then shall a woman make out her title to salvation? 'She shall be saved through the childbearing' (1 Tim. ii. 15). Her work is to send her children to be taught in the synagogue: to attend to domestic concerns, and leave her husband free to study in the schools:

to keep house for him till he returns (cf. Berachoth, 17 a). Women, slaves, and children are mentioned together in Berachoth, iii. 3; Sheqalim, i. 5. Another remarkable grouping is found in the Jews' Morning Prayer, where the men in three consecutive Benedictions, bless God 'who hath not made me a GENTILE . . . a SLAVE . . . a WOMAN'" ("Sayings of the Jewish Fathers," by C. Taylor).

With these views current, it is no wonder if the future of the soul of woman raised somewhat of a difficulty in the Pharisaic mind. Had she any soul to speak of?—the Rabbis were probably not all quite sure that she had.

Here was a weak point in their system, and the Sadducees were only too glad in this respect to press their adversaries " feeble " with their own " forte." What the Sadducees denied was not that there was a "resurrection," using the word in the Christian sense of physical rehabilitation; they argued nothing for or against a bodily life hereafter. What they denied was the existence of any spiritual part; they were materialists pure and simple. Says Josephus (Ant., xviii. 1, 4): " The doctrine of the Sadducees annihilates the soul along with the physical form." Again (Bell. Jud., ii. 8, 14): " Both the continuance of the soul and the chastisements and compensations through Hades they put away altogether." The existence of the Levirate law, by which a younger brother had to fill his senior's vacant place, enabled them to put their Pharisaic poser in a very compact and ingenious form.

One of the replies to such a question is that " the woman who has married two in this world is restored to the first in the world to come " (Sohar Genes., f. 24, c. 96). But this simple way of cutting the knot probably was not upheld by any general acceptance of the Rabbis. It was left for Jesus to declare that the earthly methods of taking wives were not those to be looked for in the future world.

" The sons of the resurrection of the dead, when they rise, their body will be clean and innocent, obedient to the instinct of the soul; it will not be an adversary nor an evil snare" (Bechai in legem, f. 14. 3).

"In the resurrection they neither marry, nor are given in marriage, but are as angels in heaven" (Matt. xxii. 30).

The conclusion of the reply, reasoning from the scriptural expression "the God of Abraham, etc.," that Abraham was therefore alive, is a fine and characteristic example of Hebrew argument.

"O . . . law-governed life, which the faithful seal of death perfected" (4 Macc. vii. 15).

"The third day I shall be perfected" (Luke xiii. 33).

A case in which the reply of Jesus to a question put to him is inconclusive according to strict logic and consistency, is to be found in the Fourth Gospel only (ix. 1–3). His disciples ask him, in respect of a man blind from birth, "Rabbi, who sinned, this man, or his parents, that he should be born blind?"

The Rabbi's teaching has been understood to be that evils are a direct consequence of sins; as, for example, when (Matt. ix. 5) a clearance from sin is represented as synchronous and identical with a deliverance from a physical infirmity.

But he is represented as replying, "Neither did this man sin, nor his parents: but that the works of God should be made manifest in him." This does not answer the question, and merely attributes the specific effect to the general cause in as vague a manner as if it were said it was due to accident. A Buddhist would have answered at once that the blindness was due to demerit in a previous life; and the disciples in putting the question were evidently familiar with the theory of pre-existence. Physical science would say the sin lay with the parents, not consciously maybe, but as a result of some ancestral inattention to the laws of nature. But as "accident" —a thunderstorm, for instance—might have given the otherwise dormant weakness its momentum, science fails to cover the ethical ground of the question.

It is noteworthy that this narrative should only be found in the Fourth Gospel. If the Rabbis fell into argument upon details of details to an absurd extent, yet they had a most shrewd grip of logic withal; and they must have regarded certain portions of the Fourth Gospel as neither true halacha nor good hagada.

The evidences that the doctrine of pre-existence was held by the early Talmudists are but scanty:—

"R. Liezer ha-Qappar ... used to say, The born are to die; and the dead to revive; and the living to be judged.... Let not thine imagination assure thee that the grave is an asylum; for perforce thou wast framed (Jer. xviii. 6), and perforce thou wast born, and perforce thou livest, and perforce thou diest, and perforce thou art about to give account and reckoning before the King of the kings of kings, the Holy One, blessed is he" (P. Aboth, iv. 31, 32; tr. Ch. Taylor).

Ginsburg speaks of "the reluctance of the soul to enter the world, depicted in the Kabbala, also in the most ancient tract of the Mishna," where he renders, rather more forcibly than the foregoing version, "Against thy will thou becomest an embryo, against thy will thou art born." On another page is a reference to the Rabbinical doctrine of the pre-existence of Adam before the assumption of the garments of flesh.

There is also the well-known passage in the book, written a short time before our era by an Alexandrian Jew, which Luther removed from the canon, the Book of Wisdom: "I was a lad of parts, and obtained a good soul, yea rather as being good I came into an undefiled body" (viii. 19). Other reference to pre-existence may be found in Chagiga, 12 b; Yebamoth, 62; and Aboda Zara, 5.

The Rabbinical name for transmigration was Gilgul Neshameth, the roll, circle, or revolving of souls; which Shakespeare's saying, "Time's whirligig brings strange revenges," obliquely illustrates.

If we may believe Josephus (Bell. Jud., II. vii.), the

doctrines of immortality and transmigration were held by the Pharisees, the resurrection of the body being not the reinstatement of the old, but the birth of a new one.

It is interesting to trace the Jewish growth of these doctrines, which were probably of foreign extraction. A refrain to the stanzas of Psalm xlix. runs—

> "Man being in honour abideth not,
> But is like the beasts that perish."

In the Septuagint (which version has been proved to have been affected by Talmudic adjudications) we find it: "Man, when he was in honour, did not understand, he was brought into correspondence with the mindless cattle, and likened to them."

In Psalm cxix. 67 is found—

> "Before I was afflicted, I went astray;
> But now I observe thy word."

In the Septuagint it runs: "Before I was brought low, I went wrong (lit. out of tune); wherefore I kept thy oracle."

Both these passages were understood as a confession of the Fall in a pre-existent state, which led to man's being brought into a lower form of life.

At the hour of birth in a human body, "an angel touches the mouth of the child, which causes it to forget all that has been."

Tertullian asks (De Animâ, 35), "Was it really in a Pythagorean sense the Jews approached John with the inquiry, Art thou Elias?"

Among Hagadistic legends is this, that before a spirit comes into the world to be born, an angel places upon his head a burning lamp, whereby he is enabled to obtain a vision of the world for which he is bound. As usual, the legend is affiliated to a passage in the Scripture :—

> "As in the days when God watched over me;
> When his lamp shined upon my head,
> And by his light I walked through darkness."
>
> (*Job* xxix. 2, 3.)

It is a charming philosophic fancy that a ghostly being, approaching a terrestrial incarnation, can peer, as into a mirror of sky, or waters lighted by a magic lamp, into the corporeal world. In "clear dream and solemn vision," it must seek for a home in a tabernacle of flesh which is being prepared in nature's laboratory; the attraction of instinct acting as a guide to that environment which shall be most congenial or most salutary.

Metaphors cluster more closely around the "new birth," which is spiritual initiation, and also around that mystic nativity which is on the further side of the "valley of the shadow."

In the Fourth Gospel are to be found a number of symbols of spiritual life, new birth and resurrection, in "living water," and the draught of transcendental blood which conveys life and precedes "anastasis." In the Talmud is a similar metaphoric connection: "Men should mention the heavy rain when praying for the resurrection of the dead" (Berach. Mishn., v. 2). "In the same manner as the resurrection of the dead is to bring everlasting life, it is hoped that the fall of the rain produces everlasting life also" (*Ib.*, Jer. Gem.). "When the dew was spoken of, it was only used as a metaphor representing the resurrection" (*Ib.*, Dr. Moses Schwab, note). The above Gemara attaches this metaphoric connection to the passage in Hosea (vi. 2), already cited in this work in reference to the *anastasis:* "In two days will he make us to live again; in three days he will forgive, and we shall live before him; let us go to find the knowledge of God." This is the rendering from the Talmudic text: the conclusion of the passage in Hosea, which recalls the favourite symbol of the "reviving water," and of the rivers of death, is, "He shall come unto us as the rain, as the latter rain that watereth the earth" (Hos. vi. 3). In the Babylonian Gemara, the reference is equally vague, as if to a traditional symbol, the clear purport of which had become lost: "What is the reason that they make commemoration [as enjoined in the Mishna] of the abundance of rain? Rab Joseph says that that is in some way equivalent to the resurrection of the dead" (33 a).

"The Most Holy said to Elias, Go and release thyself from the vow concerning the dew, for the dead live only on the dew, and I will make the son of Sarphith [1 Kings xvii. 9, 22] arise from the dead. And how is it known that the dead live only on dew? Because it is written (Isai. xxvi. 19), 'Thy dead men shall live, together with my dead body shall they arise. Sing, ye that dwell in dust, for thy dew is like the dew of herbs, and the earth shall cast out the dead'" (Talm. Jer. Berach. Gem., v. 2).

There may possibly have been a similar symbolic significance in the combination of the terms "water," "word," and "souls," in the graces after food: "Whoever drinks water for his thirst says, 'By whose word everything is,' etc. R. Tarphon says, 'Who createst many souls,' etc." (Talm. Mishn. Berach., vi. 8).

The symbol of resurrection found in manhood has been referred to in another section; curiously enough the rain water, which was understood to have the same symbolic signification, is regarded in the Talmud as masculine. "R. Levi says, The waters from on high are considered male, and those from the earth female. This seems to be indicated by the verse (Isai. xlv. 8), 'Let the earth open,' *velut ad virum se aperit mulier;* 'and let them bring forth salvation' *per congressum;* 'and let righteousness spring up together,' by the coming of the rain. 'I, the Lord, have created it' for the good of the earth" (Jer. Berach., ix. 3, Gemara). There is an archaic and poetic simplicity about this, which requires the use of a dead language in an epoch when the nature with which the law of heaven endows man is regarded with shame.

The following passages show a mutual correspondence :—

"A name made great is a name destroyed" (Hillel, in Pirqe Aboth, i. 14).

"He who abases himself, God exalts him; he who exalts himself, God abases him; who seeks honours, honours evade him; who flees from them, they come to find him" (Erubin, 13 b).

"Whosoever shall exalt himself shall be humbled" (Matt. xxiii. 12).

"Put not thyself forward in the presence of the king, and stand not in the place of great men: for better is it that it be said unto thee, Come up hither; than that thou shouldest be put lower in the presence of the prince" (Prov. xxv. 6, 7).

"Withdraw from thy seat two or three seats, and wait until they call to thee, 'Go up;' but go not up, for they will tell thee at last, for all that, to go down, and it is better to hear 'Up, up,' than 'Down, down'" (Vajikra, R. 50).

"When thou art bidden of any man to a marriage feast, recline not in the chief seat; lest haply a more honourable man than thou be bidden of him, and he that bade thee and him shall come and say to thee, Give this man place; and thou shalt begin with shame to take the lowest room. But when thou art bidden, go and recline in the lowest place; that when he that hath bidden thee cometh, he may say to thee, Friend, go up higher: then shalt thou have glory in the presence of all that sit at meat with thee" (Luke xiv. 8–10).

"The altar sanctifies that which is appropriate for it" (Talm. Zebach., ix. 1).

"As the altar and the (temple-) hill sanctify the things appropriate for them, so also do they sanctify the instruments and utensils" (Talm. Bab. Zebach., 86 a).

"Whether is greater, the gift, or the altar that sanctifieth the gift?" (Matt. xxiii. 19).

Oaths are the subject of long strings of minute regulations in the Talmud. There were "judicial oaths" by Jehovah, with or without imprecations; "frivolous oaths," as of a man swearing to a manifest absurdity, the penalty for which was scourging; adjurations, and what may be described as mock oaths. If one says to another "I adjure thee," the oath is valid; the oath was also taken "by heaven, earth, the sun, Jerusalem, the temple, the angels," etc. But, says Ginsburg, citing the Mishna (Shebuoth, iv. 13), "If any one swears by 'heaven, earth, Jerusalem, or any other creature,' the oath is invalid. As this oath could be taken with impunity, it became very common with the Jews, who thought that because it involved nothing, it meant nothing."

In a passage in Matthew (xxiii. 16-22) Jesus stigmatizes these evasions and inconsistencies, and shows a considerable acquaintance with the various Mishnaioth on the subject.

The system of "fencing" the law led to multitudes of petty observances, upon which the metaphor of "straining out the gnat and gulping down the camel" falls with fine satirical effect. Both were equally unclean according to Levitical law.

How burdensome these petty enactments might be made may be seen from the following: "Whoso killeth a louse on the Sabbath, is as much guilty as if he killed a camel on the Sabbath" (Jer. Shabbath, f. 107, c). Similar in the bearing of its satire to the gnat and the camel proverb is, " He omits the years, but counts the months exactly."

The predial tithe, according to the Jewish canon, embraced all produce, as follows (Mishna, Maaseroth, i. 1): "Whatsoever is esculent, though still kept in the field, and derives its growth from the soil, is tithable; or whatsoever may be eaten from the commencement to the completion of its growth, though left in the field to increase in size, is tithable whether small or great; and whatsoever cannot be eaten at the beginning, but can only be eaten at the end of its growth, is not tithable till it is ripe for food." The tithe was therefore exigible upon the kitchen herbs (mint and dill and cummin) as well as upon the harvest of fruit and grain.

The payment of the sacred tithe was one of the chief

qualifications for membership of the Pharisaic body; and probably the assessor thought no more of "judgment, mercy and faith" (Matt. xxiii. 23), than the collectors of the Queen's taxes look for good conduct in us in order to entitle us to the privilege of paying them.

"A disciple of the wise who is not the same within and without, is not a disciple of the wise" (Yoma, i. f. 72. 2).

"Ye outwardly appear righteous unto men, but inwardly ye are full of hypocrisy and iniquity" (Matt. xxiii. 28).

"The Lord himself, being asked by a certain person when his kingdom would come, said, When the two shall be one, and the outside as the inside, and the male with the female, neither male nor female" (Clement of Rome, *pseud.* 2 Ep. xii.).

"When ye shall trample on the garment of shame, and when the two are become one, and the male with the female, neither male nor female" ("Gospel according to the Egyptians," cit. Clem. Alex., Strom., iii. 13).

The robe or raiment of shame, in the last extract, apparently corresponds to the external as opposed to the inner man, of the quotation preceding it, and the Talmudic passage. It is the physical body which enables the soul to hide its naked truth.

"Such an one [a false prophet or heretic] is not to be executed by the tribunal of his native place, nor by the tribunal at Jabne, but by the supreme court of Jerusalem" (Sanhedrin, xi. 3, 4).

"It cannot be that a prophet perish out of Jerusalem" (Luke xiii. 33).

"If the Israelites, saith Alexander, are pious, then the Saviour cometh flying upon clouds; if not, then he cometh trotting slowly upon an ass" (Bab. Sanhedr., 98 a).

"He who sees an ass in a dream ought to hope for salvation; for it is said (Zech. ix. 9), Behold, thy king shall come unto thee just and protecting himself by himself, lowly, and mounted upon an ass" (Bab. Berach., 56 b).

"They shall see the Son of man coming on the clouds of heaven with power and great glory" (Matt. xxiv. 30).

"They brought the ass, and the colt, and put on them their garments: and he sat thereon. . . . And the crowds . . . cried, saying, Hosanna to the son of David. . . . This is the prophet, Jesus, from Nazareth of Galilee" (Matt. xxi. 7-11).

We shall not here quote the passages from the Talmud which correspond to the millenarian chapter of Matthew (xxiv.), as that chapter has not the true ring of the sayings of Jesus; the subject, moreover, would extend to long quotations from Isaiah, Joel, Daniel, the pseudo-Esdras, the Book of Enoch, Baruch, the Sibylline Verses, and other apocalyptic writings. It is enough to say that in the Talmud are to be found calculations, such as those of which students of prophecy are so fond, of the length of time the present world might last; references to the wars, calamities, famines, and tempests that were to precede the days of a Messiah, and to the thousand years' interval before the resuscitation, or palingenesis.

Certainly in one respect the prophecies have been fulfilled—the signs and prodigies have been very seductive even to the elect (Matt. xxiv. 24). No less a Rabbi than the excellent and devoted Akiba, when he saw the Son of the Star,—Barcochebas, who supported himself on the prophecy of Balaam, "There shall come a star out of Jacob," and was the chief of a revolt of some thousands of Jews in the time of Hadrian, exclaimed (Midrash, Eicha Rabbathi, Lam., ii. 2), "It is he, the Messiah." A brother Rabbi, less sanguine, said to him, "Akiba, the grass will grow upon thy grave, and the Messiah will not yet have come."

If the apocalyptic chapter of Matthew represents a real utterance of Jesus, and has not been foisted into the collection by some one of the millenarian school, who may have thought that no gospel was complete without it, we have the curious dilemma before us, of a reputed Messiah prophesying "the birth-pains of the Messiah" (Shabbath, 118 a) as *still to come.*

We may ingeniously accommodate to more modern meanings those well-accepted signs, but with the mass of Talmudic records becoming year by year more accessible, we should do better to pay some heed to the caution of an ardent scholar and divine of the seventeenth century (John Lightfoot, "Horæ Hebr. et Talmudicæ ") : " It is no matter, what we can beat out concerning these manners of speech on the anvil of our own conceit, but what they signified among them [the Jews] in their ordinary sense and speech."

It is a question worth consideration whether the likenesses between the Talmud and the Gospels would not have been even more sharply manifest but for the Hellenization of the original matter. The recent discovery of a fragment of an early Gospel among the El Fayum manuscripts revives the statement of Papias in a new light : " Matthew compiled the oracles in the Hebraic dialect ; and every one interpreted them as he was able." The further the relics passed from the hands of Hebrews to whom their style was familiar, the more likely, then, were they to be misinterpreted, and then expanded accordingly.

In this ancient fragment, which corresponds to a portion of Matt. xxvi., there is an entire omission of a reputed utterance of Jesus to be found in the first and second Gospels : " But after I am risen again, I will go before you into Galilee." In Matthew (xxvi. 33), " Peter answered and said unto him, Though all men shall be offended [stumbled] because of thee, yet will I never be offended [stumbled]." In this ancient papyrus we find the abrupt phrase only— " And if all, not I." It is but a minor instance, but which of the two versions for style and manner is the more like contemporary speech, as uttered by Hillel ?—" If I am not for myself, who is for me ? and being for my own self, what am I ? If not now, when ? [otherwise rendered, If not now, what then?]" (P. Aboth, i. 15.) The Greek, on the other hand, is a smooth, flowing, *literary* language, in which the terse, concentrated phrases of a Hebrew Rabbi might readily "suffer a sea-change, into something rich and strange."

Two marked currents of thought are manifest in the Talmud; one flowing in the channel of the prophets who had striven to convert the crude material symbols of the early cult into spirituality, morals, and the religion of the heart. This found its representatives in the gentle and expansive school of Hillel. At the opposite pole were those who insisted with fierce bigotry upon the letter of the Law, even so far as to ignore its spirit, resisting with a jealous fanaticism the spiritual influences of the broader school as foreign and dangerous.

Both schools contained, at the time our era commences, a number of eminent teachers. How came it, then, that the greatest Rabbi of his nation was condemned to death amongst them? Where were the genial Doctors, the disciples of the wise, the masters of the Law? How were they powerless?

There may perhaps have been but few of such in Jerusalem; and as for the rest, they were probably busy, teaching in their respective schools; and in Palestine, telegraphs, railways, newspapers, and public opinion did not exist.

We will grant that those who were instrumental in the trial and condemnation were officials, not sages; priests, not teachers. It may be that it is to this period that Deutsch's words apply: "The ordinary priests had mostly sunk into mere local functionaries of the temple, while many of the high priests, who in their later days *bought* their sacred office from the ruling foreign power, had forgotten the very elements of that Bible which they had been especially appointed to teach" ("Literary Remains," p. 139).

The Council, as truly constituted, was composed of seventy-one members, representing three classes: priests, elders of the people, and scribes or lawyers, twenty-three forming a quorum. The legal head at this time was Gamaliel the first, and the assumption by the high priest Joseph Kaiaphas of the presidency is regarded by students of Hebrew law as illegal, as well as the assembling of the court at his house, instead of in the appointed hall in the temple enclosure.

But how came it that there was no protest, no expression of feeling, on the part of those who saw a blameless teacher condemned before their eyes? They could not have been all cowed, like the shameful disciples,—silenced sons of thunder, and a rock that now was but shivering sand.

The condemnation was a public act, and must have followed certain prescribed forms, for a whole court is not likely to have concurred in a stultification of its own ordinances.

If, then, the condemnation were a legal one, it would account for the silence of any possible friends of the accused; —they were powerless.

Dr. Ginsburg says that, according to a Rabbinical treatise, though one of late compilation, one who pretended to be a Messiah, or who led the people away from Jewish doctrine, might be tried and condemned the same day, or in the night.

The fact that Jesus was brought to trial as a false prophet, might account for irregularities in the form of the trial, but the verdict was given, not upon inconclusive testimonies of witnesses to a claim to messiahship on the part of the accused, but on the ground of blasphemy, pure and simple.

The crime of blasphemy, in the strict sense, was the utterance aloud of the mystic name of God (Sanhedrin, 55 b). This sacred name, the *Tetragrammaton*, the sound of which is now lost—and it is said to have been a sound rather than a word—was uttered by the high priest in the Holy of Holies once a year, on the day of expiation, and on no other occasion. The unauthorized utterance of this name was blasphemy, the crime of crimes, to be followed by inevitable death.

It is indeed the irony of fate that one who taught to his

disciples the prayer, " Hallowed be thy name," should perish on the ground of a profanation of that name.

The doctrine of attaching mystery to the Divine name probably had its rise in magical formulæ, and in its developed form came into Palestine from without. In the Vedas we are told that "the gods like concealment" (Asiat. Res., viii. 424). The Egyptians would not utter the names of certain deities (Movers, i. 540), and Herodotus considers it impious to communicate their names (ii. 132, 170). A deity whose name was not pronounced was designated *arrētos* [unutterable, without a name, secret, sacred] (Plut. Cæs., ix. ; Macrob., i. 9).

Where, then, is this blasphemy to be found, the fact of the occurrence of which the high priest marks, not in sudden passion, but according to prescribed rule, by rising to his feet in open court and rending his garments? The assembled council must have agreed in the high priest's conclusion, or the solemn formality of rending the robe would have been recognized as an error, whereas it was received with assent ; and, thereafter, there was no difficulty in persuading the mass of the people to cry aloud for the prisoner's death.

A learned writer in *Fraser's Magazine* suggests that Kaiaphas may have mistaken the Aramaic word of assent used by Jesus for the not dissimilar utterance of the Tetragram, or ineffable name. The word Jehovah, IHVH, the late Samuel Sharpe said, in reply to a question of the writer, is akin to the word "To be," hence the answer "I am," AIIIH, may have sounded like the sacred name. Mr. F. R. Conder, the author of the article in *Fraser*, wrote also that there are several Aramaic words which might be rendered by the " I am," such as AYE, EYE, IYE, and YEIA. They all have a certain likeness to what we may imagine to have been the pronunciation of that rarely uttered word which we have conventionalized as Jehovah, or Jahveh ; and it is not to be forgotten that the speech of Peter betrayed him in Jerusalem as a Galilean, and that when Jesus on the cross called upon Elohim [Hēlei, Eli,

Hēli, Elōi, Elei, Helōi, as it is variously spelled in different readings in Greek] the bystanders mistook the word for Elijah [Heb. Ēliyah, Gr. Hēleias].

The Galilean Dialect is "known and spoken of .... in the Talmud as the one which most carelessly confounds its sounds, vowels as well as consonants. 'The Galileans are negligent with respect to their language, and care not for grammatical forms,' is a common saying in the Gemara."

"Thus, also," says Mr. Conder, "is the forgiveness of Jesus to be understood. The people knew not what they did—for he was guiltless of the tremendous accusation, the very idea of which would strike terror to every Jew. With this horror Jesus would fully sympathize, knowing, at the same time, that it had been excited by a false accusation." He made no complaint; he did not assert himself; he possessed the supreme faculty of being able to hide his goodness in his love. The human agony once over, the struggle of a pure man against the sense of disgrace, the disciple of the light could turn his eyes to the world of truth, and leaving the world of those who knew not what they did, commend his spirit to the Father of the house of many mansions.

It may be possible to illustrate the momentous obscurity of this condemnation a little more fully. According to monumental testimony, the Egyptian circumlocution expressive of the name of deity was *Nuk-pu-Nuk*. "I am he who I am," which at once recalls the name, "I am that I am," which Moses heard out of the midst of the burning bush of the Nilotic Acacia.

Now this mysterious name, Dr. H. Benish asserts consists of the past, present, and future tenses of the verb "to be." The authors of the Revised Version moreover add in the margin, "I am because I am," or, "I am who am, or, I will be that I will be." They also, in the passage, "I AM hath sent me unto you," supply in the margin, "Or, I WILL BE," and add the actual Hebrew word, *Ehyeh*. In the next verse occurs the name Jehovah, to which the Revisers append the note "from the same root as Ehyeh." We can therefore almost reproduce in English the equivalents of this stupendous misunderstanding. The reply of Jesus to the high priest according to the second Gospel (Mark xiv. 62), is "I am :" the incommunicable name, the utterance of which is blasphemy, is "I AM." It is as if a prisoner from Yorkshire wishing to say Yea, should be condemned on the ground of having said Yah, or Jah, in London.

No allowance was made in the Hebrew code for inadvertence in the case of blasphemy. "The erring is as the presumptuous, in profanation of the Name" (P. Aboth, iv. 7). It will be remembered how often in *Matthew* the expression, "the kingdom of *heaven*," is found instead of "the kingdom of *God*." This is due to Hebrew carefulness. A similar custom is still common. The writer remembers rehearsing a play, in which the actors invariably made the substitution.

On this hypothesis of error, however, it is strange that the accident should not have been explained. But when a clamour has once been excited, the popular mind is not always in a state to accept detailed explanation, which, even be its facts unimpeachable, is wont to be looked upon with suspicion when it comes after a condemnation.

Joseph of Arimathæa, a member of the Sanhedrin, "had not consented to their counsel and deed," in this matter, says Luke (xxiii. 50, 51). This is all we hear of protest. If he, too, thought blasphemy had been uttered, what more could he do?

Life was so safeguarded by the law (Sanh., vi. 1), that if on the way to execution the criminal remembered that he had something fresh to adduce in his favour, he was led back to the tribunal, and the validity of his statement was examined.

But in the case of one who gave himself out as the Messiah, or who led the people away from the doctrines of their fathers, the rigours of the Law were without any mitigation (Sanh., 36 b ; 67 a).

VOL. II.

A French Rabbi (E. Soloweyczyk, in "La Bible, le Talmud, et l'Évangile," 1875), in all probability never having seen the suggestion that the accusation of blasphemy was founded upon a mistake, negatives the pronunciation of Jesus of the august name, and relates that the Talmud teaches, "It is to commit a blasphemy to explain literally the passage (Exod. xxiv. 10), 'They *saw* the God of Israel.' In fact, explained literally, this verse would suppose God material; now, Jesus in saying that they would *see* the Son of man seated at the right hand of God [lit. of power], would appear to believe in the corporeity of the divine essence, and thus to commit a marked blasphemy."

This explanation is not so likely as the other, for the expression is made up of Ps. cx. 1, and Dan. vii. 13; and Jesus had quoted the first-named passage before, to the gathered Pharisees (Matt. xxii. 43, 44), although without the objectionable reference to sight.

And yet more support can be found in the Talmud for this theory than might be supposed—a support the more striking as resting on evidence quite unrelated to the present question. "The Talmudical sages," says a writer in the *Jewish World* (January, 1876), "were scrupulously, jealously careful for the honour of the Supreme. We find in section Chagiga, chap. 2, that there was a considerable hesitation before the Book of Ezekiel was admitted into the Scriptural canon, on account of the first chapter, which recounts Ezekiel's vision, wherein most strange and supernatural and enigmatical appearances were seen. Well, the many merits of the book won from our sages their consent to its being received as holy; but yet a condition was attached, viz. that the book should be read by no one less than thirty years of age, when it is fair to presume the reader would be safe from falling into the error of regarding the mystical language of the prophet as literal. 'To make assurance doubly sure,' they further decreed not only that the subject of this vision should never be read in public, but should never be taught except to a single disciple at a time, and that disciple a man sufficiently learned and intellectual to understand it by his own unaided efforts." Among what are called *The Emendations of the Scribes* the majority consist of removals from the Scripture text of anthropomorphisms, and expressions considered to be offensive to an ideal conception of Deity.

If the expression "the right hand of power" was not so stated as to afford a pretext for a charge of blasphemy on the ground of materializing the idea of Deity, yet, if the words of the Gospel were ever uttered as recorded, the prediction of the advent of the Son of man might have been taken as a Messianic reference; and probably a Messianic assumption, supported only by the acclamation of a crowd, might be considered sufficient ground for impeachment as a false prophet. The dates of the Midrashim are so uncertain, that it is difficult to found any argument even upon such a passage as the following, which would seem to show that the words of Jesus before the Council constituted a distinct Messianic claim: "It is to come that God will make King Messias to sit on his right and Abraham on his left" (Midrash Thchillim, xviii. 36).

It is indeed a mystery how so blameless and law-respecting a man as Jesus could run counter to the penal code of his country in any but the first of the several ways that have been suggested. That one who had the profoundest knowledge of the sublimities and subtleties alike of the Hebrew sacred Law, should have laid himself open to incur condemnation on three separate grounds, is a problem of improbability that in all likelihood can never now be solved.

The several points to which it has been suggested he exposed himself may be briefly recapitulated: 1. Blasphemy. Ground: supposed utterance of the forbidden name, through a dialectic mispronunciation of a word which closely resembled it. 2. Blasphemy. Ground: anthropomorphic reference to

Deity. 3. Charge of heresy or impiety as a false prophet. Ground : claim, as recorded, to Messianic attributes.

Whether we can explain the mystery of the condemnation or not, the hurried action of the Council at Jerusalem, disturbed at the appearance of a new force not at all likely to swim with the stream of the politics of the day, precipitated events and affected immeasurably the course of the future and of history. Strange as the paradox may seem ; if Jesus had lived, a noble Gospel would have been given to the world,— the radical religion of the individual, quickened by the *élan* of a willing unselfishness ; the gospel of a strenuous career pursued without evasion, or pretence of escape by any royal road from the reign of law ; a gospel brightened by the good news that the burden of religion was light, and that death was no more than a name; but there would have been no Trinitarian Christianity.

The Jewish axiom was, " The Sanhedrin is to save, not to destroy life " (Sanh. 42 b), and yet, by a strange contrariety, the case by which we know that Council best was a judicial murder !

If the Jews murdered their noble fellow-countryman, and he forgave them, the same cannot be said of his followers. Crusaders, "most Christian kings," and hosts of the rank and file of Christianity, took a sanguinary revenge. In the unbiased page of future history there can be but one answer to the question, Which has been the greater breach of the principles of the teaching and practice of Jesus : his hasty condemnation by the Sanhedrin at Jerusalem, or the persistent persecution during the Middle Ages, and, until very recently, by Christians of Jews ?

We cannot afford to throw the first stone, when it can be said openly, and without contradiction, in a newspaper of the period (*Pall Mall Gazette*, June 25, 1885) : " It is unfortunately but too true that there would have been a very profound feeling of relief on the other side [that of the English

Liberal Government], during the fatal period of indecision that preceded the despatch of the relief expedition, if the news had come that Gordon was no more. In the strife of parties the lives of heroes are but as counters, and it is not difficult to imagine a thorough-going partisan exulting over the Crucifixion if it had happened opportunely in our time at a crisis when it could help the Opposition to dish the Government." Though we cannot accept the hypothesis that a British Government would have felt the death of its apostle to be a relief, yet the Government respecting which so scandalous a conjecture was hazarded, by an ironical coincidence, did not live long after the unhappy event took place. The Jewish political party which smoothed its own path by the death of the troublesome prophet, the gentle but dreaded seer, unconsciously and irretrievably smoothed the way to its own annihilation.

A CONTEMPORARY OF JESUS.

Two assertions—very singular when taken together—may be made with regard to Philo.

One is, that, blending as he does Pharisaic, and perhaps something of Essene teachings, with Platonic elements of thought, his words are found to be in such close relation with expressions contained in the Gospels, that to the meaning of certain mystical and little understood passages he affords the best existing key.

The other assertion is, that, notwithstanding the very large amount of reading accomplished by theological students, Philo is very little read indeed.

That Philo is a long-winded Pharisee and a Plato made tedious, is possibly one reason of this neglect.

That even where his insight is true, his mysticism is too refined and subtle for the average mind, and especially for the non-Rabbinical one, is probably another reason.

A third, the influence of which makes itself felt for the most part unconsciously, may perhaps be found in the strange fact that Philo is a contemporary and compatriot of Jesus, and yet does not once specifically allude to a teacher who, to judge from Philo's writings, must have been so much after his own heart.

That this is a strange fact, it will be easy to show. Philo was a man of the broadest sympathies, of a religious and earnest spirit, and very ready to interest himself in the most advanced and unsectarian ideas, as may be seen in his account of the

Essenes and others who aimed after unworldly life. He was also a man of extended culture and commanding position, so that no important event, material or spiritual, that might affect his countrymen, would be likely to escape him. He was, moreover, of humble mind, and ever expressed extreme veneration for such conduct as to our minds would seem to have been pre-eminently exemplified in the life of Jesus of Nazareth. Though he dwelt in Alexandria and wrote in Greek, yet he visited Jerusalem and northern Palestine, and most probably was as well acquainted with the Hebrew vernacular as Jesus with Greek.

In our endeavour to account for Philo's apparent ignorance of the personal career of Jesus, we shall be helped by remembering how very brief in point of time that career was, and how it was mainly connected with persons who had small means of giving immediate and extended publicity to any events however impressive to themselves.

In what light, moreover, would Philo have regarded Jesus? As another great and gentle Rabbi of his race, as perhaps a second Hillel. It is to be remembered that he could not foresee Christianity. Moses had become so idealized by lapse of time, that probably it was held as an impossibility that there ever could arise in the flesh "a prophet like unto Moses."

Josephus refers to Jesus in the briefest way, and even that passage is held to be spurious. To John the Baptist he accords a notice, probably because his death was due to political considerations. Nicolaus of Damascus, advocate of Herod the Great, who reigned till 4 B.C., made no entry in any record which has become history, of the perturbation of "Herod the king . . . and all Jerusalem" at the report of the mages of the new-born Jewish king.

Justus of Tiberias, contemporary and opponent of Josephus (Phot. *Cod. Bibl.*, 33), though he lived on the shore of the Galilean lake, yet in his history says not a word about the fame that spread through all Syria. These silences have led some minds to the conclusion that "Christianity is a faith ideally constructed on imaginary and not really enacted circumstances." But though, doubtless, it would be easier to write the life of the Gospels than to live it, it would be something of a miracle for any one to have produced so rare and noble a presentment of a hero without any ground of fact to work upon.

It is not by shutting our eyes to such facts, however, that we shall be able to redeem the real man from the image of stone in which dogma has imprisoned him, and bring him back to life.

Philo's ignorance of the spiritual legacy of the great teacher is more difficult to account for. But the *memorabilia* of the master, not yet expanded into complete narratives, were in all likelihood in few hands, making their way like sown seed, very slowly and obscurely at first. Two special points will be open to consideration: whether any words of Philo's can be taken to convey his views of the career now familiar to us, of which he might have but dimly heard: and whether the similarity between certain passages in Philo's writings and certain utterances recorded in the Gospels can be accounted for on the hypothesis alone that both drew from the stream of a common tradition of things divine.

If the works of Philo have so peculiar a relation to the Christian records, it becomes important to know exactly when those works were written, and when Philo lived. Jesus is considered to have been born about four or five years before the commencement of the era which takes its name from him, and to have departed about the year thirty of that era. Philo, we know, was born before Jesus, and passed away after him, but that is all that is particularly known. The facts which afford a basis for the calculation of his age must be left to tell their own story. He cites with approbation in his book, "On the Creation of the World" (§ 36), the saying of

Hippocrates: " In the nature of man there are seven seasons, which men call ages. . . . He is an infant . . . a child . . . a boy . . . a youth till the completion of the growth of his whole body, which coincides with the fourth seven-years' period. Then he is a man till he reaches his forty-ninth year, or seven times seven periods. He is a middle-aged man (elder) till he is fifty-six, or eight times seven years old, and after that he is an old man." This reckoning we may reasonably apply to Philo's allusion to his own age, to be found in his account of an embassy of the Jews to the Roman Emperor Caius Caligula, of which he was the head: " I who was accounted to be possessed of superior prudence, both on account of my age, and my general education also, was less sanguine in respect of the matters over which the others were delighted." And in the exordium to the same treatise he affords a further evidence by the phrase, " We, who are aged men, . . . grey-headed," using the identical word which, in the previously quoted passage he had adopted to denote the period of life beginning with the age of fifty-six. We may presume, then, that Philo had reached at least that age, and probably more, at the date of the embassy (A.D. 39–40); he would thus have been born at least as far back as seventeen years before our era, or twelve or thirteen years before the birth of Jesus. It is much more probable, since a man would scarcely refer pointedly to his age and grey hairs until he had fairly overstepped the limit marking the commencement of the period of old age, that he was born at least five years before that time, or twenty-two years before our era. We have evidence, therefore, that he lived through the life of Jesus, the greater part of twenty years before that life began, and at least ten years after it closed.

Philo has been called the "elder brother of Jesus:" the epithet is not strictly a fit one, for few probably would argue that any direct influences proceeded from him towards Jesus. In spite of extreme improbability, it is not absolutely impossible, however, that Jesus should ever have opened a roll of Philo's writings. In any case, Philo was in a greater degree an adapter than an originator, and his voluminous works are a sufficient evidence that there was a school of mystical thought existing among the cultured Jews before the birth of Jesus.

More specific evidence on this point is to be found in references of Philo's own, such as the following, which is *à propos* of a story in the Hebrew scriptures, respecting Abraham, his wife, and the king of Egypt: "I have heard even natural philosophers giving an allegorical interpretation, and not away from the mark, to the matter of this passage, as containing a symbolical sense" (De Abr., xx.). He also refers to a legend of the ancients, upon the appreciation of the divine work of creation, as being "an old and celebrated saying, originally invented by sages, and handed down by memory, as is wont, in succession to those that come after, which did not escape our ears, always hankering after instruction" (De Plant. Noe, xxx.). Again, speaking of a particular passage concerning the king of Egypt and Joseph, Philo says, "I have heard people investigating the matter of this passage after a different underlying idea, and more figuratively" (De Joseph. xxvi.). The following also refers to these teachers of Philo's, and resembles his description of the Essenes, with which, however, it is unconnected. He is speaking of an exposition which he has heard. This was brought forward by "god-illumined men, who look upon the generality of what is contained in the Law as plain symbols of obscure meanings, and forms of expression of the undivulged" (De Spec. Leg., xxxii.).

Josephus also refers to this latent symbolic element in the Law: "Everything is adapted to the nature of the whole, whilst the lawgiver most adroitly suggests some things as in a riddle, and represents other things with solemnity as in an allegory; those, however, who desire to dive into the cause of each of these things will have to use much and deep philosophical speculation " (Pref. to Ant.).

Eusebius thus refers to Philo, his family and his teachers: " I will produce a man who is a Hebrew, as an interpreter for you of the disposition that exists in the Scripture, one who learned from his father the investigation of what pertained to his country's rites, and had been taught the doctrine by Rabbis. Such a man was Philo" (Præp. Ev., vii. 13).

The centre of this exegetical culture might or might not have been in Palestine; but if it were not, the colleges of the home-country could not be entirely ignorant of the studies pursued abroad. Between the Jewish race dwelling in their own land, and their brethren in Egypt and Babylon, there could not but have been an interchange always in process, both of merchandise and of thought. The students of old, as well as the merchants, were wanderers. Now the merchandise travels without the merchant, and a printed book by its numerical extension conveys ideas from one mind to another with greater rapidity, though perhaps with less impressiveness, than the vagrant seeker for truth could command.

Philo in all likelihood visited Palestine on more occasions than the one which he records. Being a man of wealth and position, devotedly attached to his fatherland, it is exceedingly improbable that he would neglect to visit it when he conveniently could, the more especially as the pilgrimage to the temple was deemed one of the duties of a devout Jew. He speaks little about himself in his writings, but when he does mention a journey to Jerusalem, his narrative contains nothing that should lead us to conclude he was referring to that journey as his only one. "There is a city of Syria on the seaboard, Askalon by name. I happened to be therein, at a time when I was on my way to the temple of my people to pray and sacrifice " (Fragm. ex. Euseb.).

Philo's quotations from the Hebrew scriptures are made in Greek, and evidently from a copy of the Septuagint version very little different from the text handed down to us. This version, originally made for the Alexandrian Jews, is held in great favour by him, as so valuable a support to his cherished idea of spreading the knowledge of the Mosaic lore (read, as Philo believed it ought to be, in symbolic sense) among those whose Greek culture empowered them to appreciate it. But Philo, by his frequent etymological interpretations of Hebrew names—however erroneous some may be—shows that he is acquainted to some extent with the language "used by the Chaldeans," and even with the ancient Hebrew.

There is a curious bit of evidence tending to prove that Philo never even heard of Jesus of Nazareth by name. He says, "Moses changes the name of Hosea into that of Jesus, distinguishing by the change the quality of his character. For Hosea is interpreted, Who is this? but Jesus, The Lord's salvation, a name of the most excellent character" (De Mut. Nom., xxi.). This could scarcely have been written so unconsciously, had Philo heard even a vague rumour of a Jesus such as is presented to us by certain narrative portions of the Gospels. It would have been quite congenial with his discursive style to add a word that the name of the ancient leader of the people was being borne by a new prophet, one whose works manifested the most excellent character which his name was interpreted to mean.

Philo's silence as to the facts recorded in the Gospels has a more important bearing upon what are termed the legendary stories attaching to the narrative of the life of Jesus. We may be almost sure that Philo, as a leading Jewish diplomatist, would have heard of such a strange event as Herod's edict for the slaughter of children under two years of age, for fear of a rival foretold to have been born. Such action on the part of a king, on such a motive, would have had a political significance, especially as all Jerusalem was reported to have been simultaneously moved. And the governor who was to spring from Bethlehem would have been watched for afterwards, and perhaps identified with a man who is said to have perplexed Herod's son* so sorely that that sovereign sought to kill him. At all events, Philo, whose nephew married the daughter of king Agrippa,† who was the nephew of Herod Antipas, and grandson of Herod the Great, could scarcely be supposed to have been ignorant of such events.

The question naturally arises, At what period of his career did Philo compose his voluminous works? There is internal evidence that they were not all written while he was young. The account of his embassy to Caligula was apparently written in the reign of Claudius, who succeeded Caligula A.D. 41, and reigned nearly fourteen years. The following passage is touching and suggestive in itself, and will help us to apprehend Philo's character, and at the same time afford evidence that, although a student of philosophy from early manhood, he wrote comparatively late in life.

"There was once a time, when devoting my leisure to philosophy and to contemplation of the universe and the things therein, I reaped the fruit of excellent, desirable, and truly blessed perceptive faculty, being always stimulated by divine oracles and doctrines, whereon I found delight in feeding covetously and insatiately, entertaining no low or grovelling thoughts, nor ever worming my way in pursuit of glory or riches, or the luxuries of the body ; but as one raised up on high, I appeared to be ever borne along in accordance with some inspiration of the soul, and to follow every whither the sun, the moon, and the whole Heaven and universe.

"At that time, then, stooping from above and looking down from the air, and stretching as it were out of a watchtower the eye of my mind, I surveyed the unutterable contemplations of all things upon the earth, and congratulated

---

* Herod Antipas ("Herod the Tetrarch," Matt. xiv. 1) successor as regards Galilee to Herod the Great ("Herod the King," Matt. ii. 1).

† Herod Agrippa I. ("Herod the King," Acts xii.) father of Herod Agrippa II. ("King Agrippa," Acts xxv. 13).

myself mightily, on account of my escape from the evil fates that are in mortal life.

"Nevertheless, the most grievous of evils was lying in wait for me; envy that hates the beautiful, which suddenly falling upon me ceased not from dragging me by force, until it had flung me down into the vast sea of the cares that attach to public business, tossing in which sea I am not able so much as to keep floating.

"But though I groan, I still hold out and resist, retaining in my soul that yearning for instruction which was implanted in it from my earliest coming to manhood; and this constantly takes pity and compassion on me, and rouses and encourages me till my spirits are lighter again.

"Through this yearning for instruction it comes to pass that there are times when I lift up my head, and with the eyes of my soul, which are indeed but dim—for their sharp-sightedness has been overshadowed by the mist of inconsistent kinds of business—survey, perforce at least, the things that circle round, with eager desire for a long draught of life pure and unalloyed by evils.

"If there but befall me from the unforeseen a brief spell of fair weather, and a calm amid the troubles that belong to public business,* I am on wings and afloat upon the wave, all but soaring in the air, and blown forward by the breezes of knowledge, which often seduces me to take flight, and pass all my days with her, escaping as from pitiless masters, and these not only men, but also affairs which pour upon me from one side and another like a torrent.

"But even in these circumstances I ought to give thanks to God that, though I am overwhelmed, I am not swallowed up in the depths. But I open the eyes of the soul, which

---

* There is sympathy here between Philo and Wordsworth:—

"In a season of calm weather,
Though inland far we be,
Our souls have sight of that immortal sea
Which brought us hither."

from despair of any good hope have been deemed to have become already disabled, and I feel the shine of the light of wisdom, since I am not given up unto darkness for the whole of my life" (De Spec. Leg. i.). This is the writing of a man no longer young, finding his strength—

> "In the faith that looks through death,
> In years that bring the philosophic mind."

Deductions from Philo's silence upon events that we may regard as important must not be pressed too far. Philo was writing for Alexandrians, and though to many of his compatriots resident in Egypt events and persons connected with Jerusalem must have been familiar, yet he seems to have preferred to occupy a platform upon which Greek could stand as well as Jew. Therefore he proffers his teachings upon their own merits and reasonableness, rather than as claiming veneration through association with the most reverend names of his own people.

With regard to events connected with Herod, even such as might have political significance, we are bound to bear in mind that Herod's murders, even of his own relatives, were many,* and Philo has recounted none, so that the absence of record of a single edict of slaughter would not be conspicuous or strange, were it not for the fact that the reason alleged for the massacre of the innocents was of such a kind as not to allow itself to be forgotten in the Herodian family.

Philo's works contain a brief reference to Herod the Great, and to Pilate, the lieutenant of Tiberius, but as he has no word concerning Hillel or Shammai, Gamaliel or Kaiaphas, we ought not to be surprised that he does not even mention by name John the Baptist.

Philo, however, gives evidence of having been acquainted

---

* The Greek pun made by the Emperor Augustus may be remembered in this connection. Herod massacred his relatives, and, of course, did not eat pork. It was better, said Augustus, to be the swine than the son of Herod—ὒν ἢ υἱόν (hūn ē huion).

even with details in the history of Judea. He quotes a reference of Agrippa to Pilate as being one of the emperor's lieutenants and the governor of Judea. And a story is told of Pilate which not improbably prevented his daring to exercise the kindly feeling so manifestly shown towards Jesus at the time of his condemnation. He had dedicated some gilt shields in the palace of Herod. The Jews fastened upon this act as an innovation, and subversal of their national customs, and challenged Pilate to produce an authority from Tiberius. Pilate wrote a supplicatory letter to the emperor, but received one in return sharply commanding him to remove the objectionable shields, and to place them in the temple of Augustus at Cæsarea (Leg. ad Caium, § 38). In the case of Jesus the Jews practically coerced Pilate, by threatening to impeach him as an opponent of Cæsar.

There is no external evidence from which a judgment can be formed whether Philo ever saw or heard Jesus, or read a word of the earliest collection of his sayings, now embedded in the First Gospel. We have to turn to internal sources for evidence of sympathy between the contemporaries.

There is a double connection clearly traceable between the writings of Philo and the collected memorials of Jesus. There is the closest sympathy between certain oft-repeated doctrines of Philo, and certain characteristic portions of the work known as the Gospel after John, which are found in that Gospel alone, and exhibit a marked discordance from the other narratives. Furthermore, in the spiritual and ethical, rather than the doctrinal or metaphysical, passages of Philo's writings, there are to be found again and again more than chance coincidences of thought with sayings that seem to belong to the genuine utterances of Jesus. Though Jesus, therefore, may never have known Philo, he must have had some knowledge of the influences that co-operated to form his philosophy; and taking Philo as a fair embodiment of the Judæo-Hellenic school, it will be interesting to make a somewhat minute comparison between his words and those of Jesus in the Gospels.

The further influences possibly due to Philo may also be touched upon in passing; as, for instance, that he may have somewhat affected the editors of one or more of the Gospels, as he has certainly influenced parts of that varied series of writings known as Pauline; while he has to some extent contributed to the growth of what we may style Christian dogma, as distinguished from the teachings of Jesus.

It may be well to glance for a moment at Philo's personal character before touching on the parallelisms between his writings and the Christian Scriptures. A correspondence of such a kind constitutes in itself so noble a tribute to Philo's earnestness that we must take it to have been strangely overlooked, in order to account for the neglect to which he has been subject. The fates of this world are difficult to comprehend. Paul, a theologian who became distinguished after the death of Jesus, has the honour of a popular vogue, and of an anxious scrutiny paid to every word of his writings by the student. Philo, a man equally versed in theology, and in fact the immediate source from which much of the Pauline doctrine is drawn, is known to the student only, and to but very few indeed even of the student class. The quality against which there are evidences of continual struggle on the part of Paul is spiritual pride; Philo, on the contrary, a man of much higher position and of equal earnestness, manifests a very real and sincere humility. One has been taken, and the other left. It is true that one was preacher as well as writer, the other writer only; but all that reaches us now of the preacher's influence, as indeed all that reached any Christian community of any magnitude, if we except what oral traditions there may have been, is through what he wrote.

Philo is, at all events, a solid fact standing in the way of those who are prone to assert that the world was in a state of utter darkness at the time of the advent of Jesus; and if he helped on, even though only as a forerunner and preparer, the lifting up of the torch of divine fire which for a time at least startled and awakened men, it is surely unworthy of our own calm and considerate day to ignore him altogether.

Philo as a man is eminently reasonable in his mode of life; he would check the immoderation of appetite, but on reasonable and spiritual grounds, not in frantic and fanatical asceticism. If he followed the views which permeate his writings, he would have made an excellent primitive Christian. The following, for instance, represents his pattern man:—

"Those only are true pupils of the sacred Word who are genuine men, lovers of temperance and orderliness and modesty, men who have set self-mastery, contentment with little, fortitude, as a kind of foundation for the whole of life, and safe refuges for the soul, wherein it may anchor without danger and with security; for they are superior to riches and pleasure and opinion, and esteem lightly meats and drinks simply as necessaries to ward off the attack of hunger; being most ready to undergo want and thirst, heat and cold, and the most arduous experiences, for the sake of the possession of virtue" (De Somn., i. § 20).

That Philo practised what he preached, and was sterling rather than merely theoretical as to virtue of his own, may be fairly believed from the following story of his wife:—

"When the wife of Philo was asked, in an assemblage of principal women, why she alone of all her sex did not wear any golden ornament, she replied, 'Her husband's virtue is ornament enough for a wife'" (Fragm. ex Anton., Ser. 123).

We have no contemporary biography of Philo, and only a few eulogistic words from Eusebius, but the genuine ring of his own writings cannot be mistaken. No closet philosopher could have written the following:—

"As among physicians that which is called theoretical healing is a long way removed from doing any good to them that are sick—for diseases are cured by drugs and surgery and regimen, not by theories—so in philosophy there is a set of word-traffickers and word-catchers who occupy the same position, with neither the will not the care to cure life which is full of infirmities, men who from early youth to extreme age are not ashamed to wage argumentative battles upon points of opinion and outward expression, as if happiness consisted in an interminable and profitless over-exactitude with regard to nouns and verbs, rather than in the better establishment of character, the true source of what is fitting for man, and in the expulsion of the vices beyond his border, and the admission of virtues to his household " (Cong. Erud. Grat., § 10).

Strangely enough, it is his very anxiety for edification which makes Philo not always reliable as an interpreter. Being a professed expositor of his national scriptures, he must needs find or foist therein all possible religious sentiments that seem to him to make for righteousness.

We may find some evidence of the manner in which Philo would have borne himself toward the followers of Jesus if he had met them, in his attitude to men of a not very unlike fashion, the Essenes, to whom Philo devotes a lengthy narrative ; but a mystery yet hangs over the connection between that mystical Pharisaic offshoot and the early followers of Jesus.

Philo's search for the number of the virtuous, who, though few, are not in his opinion non-existent, leads up to the account of the Essenes, which reads so like a description of apostolic life. It is as containing such men as these that Philo gives a certain qualified praise to his own country: "Palestine and Syria, inhabited by no small section of the most populous nation of the Jews, form a country not barren of what is virtuous and of good report."

Is Philo only a bystander criticising the noble workers engaged upon the redemption of life, carefully preserving a fine philosophic distance between his theories and reality?

It would be unfair to hold such a view. Philo's proper work is to write, and his spirit in his own work is the spirit of the true apostle.

"Every wise man is a ransom for the sinner . . . as a physician setting himself against the infirmities of an invalid . . . and if ever so small a seed of good health should be disclosed, this like a spark of fire is to be cherished with every possible care" (De Sacrif. Ab. et Caini., § 37). Philo is here at one with the spirit in which Jesus lived and worked: "The son of man came not to be ministered unto, but to minister, and to give his life a ransom for many" (Matt. xx. 28).

When there came the necessity for work of a less tranquil kind than that of the literary philosopher, Philo did not flinch. The times were troublous for the Jews then living in Egypt to the number of a million, through the jealousy of the inhabitants and the restless opposition of the Alexandrian mob. And when we read the story how Philo represented his countrymen before the dreaded Roman emperor, who met their appeal rather as an accuser than a judge, and had the ambassadors led with mockery from room to room of his palace, and threatened them because they had not offered sacrifice to him as to God, and brought them into continual expectation of nothing else than death at his hands, we cannot regard Philo as a mere spinner of mystical fancies, but must allow him to have been a true man of earnest mind.

Like the old prophets, he had an inward monitor which kept him alive to the fact that the true kingdom is not of this world, in which rival partisans make war. Like Jesus, Philo had opened his heart and received within him the blessing of peace, which Buddha called Nirvana :—

"The invisible spirit which is wont viewlessly to hold converse with me prompts me. . . . God alone is the most undissembling and genuine peace, but the whole created and corruptible essence is continual war" (De Somn., ii. § 39).

Very naively does Philo relate his spiritual experiences,

reminding us here of that contemporary of his who confusedly told his visions—whether in the body or out of the body he could not tell :—

"My own experience, which I know from having been subject to it numberless times, I am not ashamed to relate. Sometimes when I have desired to come to my customary writing of the philosophic doctrines, and have clearly in my view the composition I have to make, I find my mind sterile and unproductive, and leave off with my work unaccomplished; reproaching my mind for self-conceit, and amazed at the power of the living God, by whom it comes to pass that the womb of the soul is alike opened and closed up. And at other times I have come to my work empty, and have on a sudden become full, conceptions falling upon me like snow, and being sown invisibly from on high, so that under divine possession I have become like a frenzied celebrant, and have altogether lost cognisance of the place, persons present, myself, what was being said, what was being written. There is power of speech forthcoming to express invention, full enjoyment of light, extreme keenness of vision, a most conspicuous activity in affairs, well-nigh as if coming by way of the eyes, and from the clearest demonstration" (De Abrah., § 7).

He also says elsewhere: "My soul is accustomed to be oftentimes divinely possessed, and to prophesy concerning things it knows not" (De Cherub., § 9).

What was the moral result of these visions? When we read the following passage from Philo's writings, we find ourselves in a moral atmosphere not very different from that spiritual and unworldly life which has bequeathed to us the injunction that "they that buy be as though they possessed not, and they that use the world as not using it in extreme:"—

"Does this belong to another, do not covet it: is that thine own, use it as not abusing it. Hast thou great abundance, share it with others. The beauty of riches is not in purses of money, but in the succour of them that have need. Art thou possessed of but little, be not envious of the wealthy. No one would pity a poor man who is envious. Art thou in good repute, art thou held in honour, be not over-boastful; art thou lowly in fortune, then let not thy courage be depressed. Does everything go to thy mind, take thought concerning a change. Dost thou stumble ofttimes, hope for favourable things" (De Josepho, § 24).

The passage just quoted recalls also the style of that "church-reading book," the "Wisdom of Jesus Ben-Sira," which is often quoted by the Talmudists in its original tongue, and was translated from the Hebrew into Greek for the Egyptian Jews, something over two centuries before Philo's birth.

The correspondences between the Christian Gospels and Epistles and Philo's writings are the more instructive as having to do with thoughts rather than words. Verbal similarities might have been produced by the pen of copyists; resemblances of thought go deeper, and show that a certain mental emancipation and peculiar inspiration characterized the age. As is the case with all new breathings of the Spirit, there were few open to receive these expansive influences.

Some close study of Philo is necessary for any one wishful thoroughly to examine and elucidate for himself this connection. There are passages which are plainly to be paralleled by the possession of a thought, which, allowing for differences of style, is manifestly the same thought in both. There are one or two instances where a thought given in parabolic form by Jesus is in simple form in Philo, a fact which greatly aids in the interpretation of the former.

Before proceeding to trace out these threads, we ought to look into the inner purposes of the man himself, as we learn of them from his own revelations. First, as to the position in which he was placed. He was a devout Jew, with a great love for the scriptures of his race. Being a Jew, he was also bound by the common allegiance to those scriptures, as if by an oath, not to alter, add, or remove one jot from the letter of them. A portion of those scriptures consisted of symbolic writing, to which class of composition the Oriental mind was prone, and in the elucidation of which his fine spiritual faculties led him to take delight. It was no heterodoxy to uncover such symbols in places where they lay hid, or even to discover such where they had not been designed. Philo was not the first in the field with such edifying interpretations, which among the appreciative minds of the race had doubtless been orally handed down from generation to generation.

Aristobulus, an Alexandrian Jew, but believed to have been a Galilean by birth, was one of the first of the school of which Philo is so pronounced an adherent. He belongs to the second century before our era, and is believed to have been one of the translators of the Septuagint. Origen cites his commentaries as an example of the allegorizing method, which afforded an excellent means of mediating between the rude legends, alternating with supremely poetic and religious thought, of the Hebrew scripture, and the more philosophic literature of Greece.

It is no doubt the same Aristobulus, a Jewish priest with a Greek name, who is described in the following: "The people in Jerusalem and Judea, and the council, and Judas, to Aristobulus, teacher of Ptolemy the king, and one that came of the stock of the christ priests, and to the Jews in Egypt, greeting and health" (2 Macc. i. 10).

The origin of the allegorizing practice, however, seems traceable to the tradition that Moses received a double law on Mount Sinai, one the written one, the other a spiritual or mystic one, the sense or explanation of the former.

As far as regards the truly inspired portions of the Hebrew scripture, the work of the Talmudic expositor must have been pleasant and stimulating. But to Philo, and to many other

Pharisees, bound to reverence every letter of their law, there was a large part that must have been a stumbling block. They had before them a most heterogeneous object of worship, for in addition to the noble prophetic utterances and splendid spiritual fragments that composed their sacred books, there were numbers of ancient stories and petty narratives, some of which never perhaps contained, or were designed to contain, any metaphoric truth at all, while others in the process of compilation from still more ancient sources had sadly lost their recognizable form and meaning. Philo might not pick and choose amongst the sacred books, he must take them all as one inspired whole. And, impregnated with Greek philosophic thought, whilst loving his own nation's scriptures, and appreciating the sterling and unsurpassed excellence of large portions of them, he wished to be able to offer to those around him, less Hebrew and more Greek than himself, a system which they could not reject forthwith on the ground of its narrowness. To men possessed of certain attributes of culture, more than had appertained to those to whom the most ancient of his national scriptures had appealed, he strove to present a consistent mass of sacred literature suggestive and attractive throughout.

This course was the more easy for Philo as a resident in Egypt, the head-quarters of the culture of the time, when he could point to Moses, the great lawgiver of his own race, as having originally derived his knowledge from the colleges of Egypt, Moses of whom he speaks as one "who had quickly reached philosophy's very height, and had had interpreted to him from the oracles the main and most comprehensive of the principles of nature" (De Mund. Opif., ii.).

Philo accordingly turned the bible of his people into symbol in an accommodating wholesale way, evolving by a subtle imagination the deepest significances from the smallest indications. As his imagination sometimes outruns his spiritual insight, and not infrequently leaves his common sense far in the rear, some of his unfoldments of latent meanings are such as had never been dreamed of before. Though such results as these were the delight of the Talmudists, and constituted their only way of emancipation from the shackles of the verbal infallibility and all-sufficiency of the law, yet to the freer Western mind, notwithstanding the notorious accommodations to modern doctrine of the same sacred text, they must seem little more than curiosities.

It is doubtless in great part owing to Philo's pursuance of this course, which resulted in desperate strainings after occult significations, and absurd exaltations of trivial narratives, that a great part of the present neglect of him is owing. The student cannot accept him as a whole, and so throws him to one side, disgusted with what he cannot but consider pages of mere absurdity. Cultured readers may not be brought to believe very decidedly that Sarah the wife of Abraham conceived a child when she was ninety, but they lose rather than gain respect for the story through Philo's laboured argument that ninety from its inner significance is necessarily a fertile number. Nor does it seem an interesting fact to learn, that the names Shem, Ham, and Japhet signify respectively "what is good, what is bad, and what is indifferent," or that there are seven distinct reasons why "the days of man shall be a hundred and twenty years," such as because "the number a hundred and twenty is a triangular number, and is the fifteenth number consisting of triangles," or because "it consists of a combination of odd and even numbers, being contained by the power of the faculty of the concurring numbers, sixty-four and fifty-six, etc., etc." This is the Platonic theory of number run mad.

But it would not be fair to judge Philo by such wearisome instances as these. The task he undertook is an impossible one; however grandly parabolic and significant may be large portions of the Hebrew scriptures, it were one of the labours of Hercules to prove that every single passage, confusedly transferred as it may have been from memory to memory amongst priests who had missed its meaning, had remained a pure symbolic form at the last.

It is a question that we are not called upon here to decide, whether a large portion of the Hebrew scripture narrative was composed as symbolic fable, or gathered up solely as vestiges of historical fact. It will be safest to take a middle course in the matter: a narrative that was originally history might well be modified in course of time, and adapted to metaphorical needs; moreover, the collection of the Hebrew books by Ezra was made at a time when the Jews had been subject to those Babylonian influences which so transformed their ancient narrow religion; and it is not known how much or how little had been retained or destroyed of the ancient record, or how much or how little is due to the diligent redaction of his scribes. It is because this matter of symbolism is so important as a mode of expression and is so imperfectly appreciated, that it is worth while to endeavour to show that Philo's method is not wholly due to his having been carried away by mere imagination into a shadow-realm of his own fancy's creation. That he carried his allegoric speculations too far may rightly be granted; that he had no basis at all for such a plan of elucidation it would be rash to assert. His position was peculiar; like many a philosophic writer before him, he had to deal with national monuments too revered for him to hope or wish to displace them, and so honoured by the law of his land that any one would incur serious danger who should attempt to abrogate a letter of their record. The unenlightened and indiscriminate reverence of our own day for these same records (which is really no reverence at all, in the true sense of the term), ought to enable us to sympathize with such a position as that of Philo. He dared not disturb the letter of the law on any pretext; the only part of it which was open to question was its meaning. The contemplation of his position may lead us to realize how in ages before him there might have been men similarly placed; they had writings before them whose power over the people lay in their being composed of familiar words and household tales; without disturbing their external form, it was a relief to the spiritual mind to impregnate these stories with deeper meanings than what they bore on the surface, meanings that would be recognized by other minds of the same order, whilst lying hid to such intelligences as could not take in the higher ranges of truth. Some such stories, too, dealing apparently with well-known occurrences, might even in their original form as narrative have been destined for symbol, and so have waited through the ages for those that could read them.

Philo, then, may be imagined to have been in this position; he wished to enlarge the study, amongst alien as well as Jewish races, of his national scriptures, which, read as mere histories, were many of them trifling and insignificant, but which, read as he had been taught and was apt to read them, bore meanings deep enough, he thought, to make them of abiding interest; and even attractive to that Greek philosophic mind with which he was in as close sympathy as he was with the simpler faith that held the scriptures in awe.

Philo was not the first to read the "Sacred Laws" as allegories, and his only blame is that he allegorized inordinately, finding a symbol in everything, however trivial, and however strained and obscure the connection. We may be thankful that the laws of our country do not now compel us to do homage to the letter of any lore, however reverend in its spirit, and that the comparatively recent withdrawal from our system of kindred penalties to the Jewish punishment of stoning for such an offence as criticism gives us liberty to be rational.

The true parable is that which is conceived in its inner spirit and projected outwards into appropriate symbolic detail; the false parable is that which has to have a meaning found for it by its interpreter, a meaning which must be arbitrary, if not at once verifiable by one able to appreciate a real parable. A reason why Philo's secret influence has been so great, while his personal influence and modern repute are so small, doubtless lies in the fact that he is valuable mainly by reason of the luminous fragments which dot his writings, and which the philosophic student can detect, whilst his works as a whole repel the general reader who finds himself led into a maze of obscurity.

Before Philo's time, many among the Pharisees, as the Talmud evidences, were prone to make and interpret allegories, but chief of the Jews who saw in the body of the law only a covering of the deep meanings residing within it, and appreciable by the spiritually-minded, were the Essenes, to whom Philo devotes a special chapter. There are other references to allegorism which may be cited here.

In the Second Book of the Maccabees, as referred to above, we are told of a man named Aristobulus, of the stock of the "Christ-priests," and a teacher of King Ptolemy Philometor. This great Rabbi is cited by Origen in his commentaries on the Pentateuch as affording an example of the allegoric method (*adv. Celsum*, iv., pp. 198, 204). This would take such interpretation back to fully 150 years before the time of Philo This man, some of whose fragments are preserved by Eusebius and Clement of Alexandria, was, like Philo, interested in proving that Greek wisdom was more akin to the teachings of the Hebrew scriptures than the generality supposed.

In that strange and unequal book, known, in the edition of the Apocrypha that accompanies the English Bible, as the "Second Book of Esdras," there is to be found (cap. vi. 9) an example of allegoric rendering of the scripture narrative. The passage in question is the account of the birth of Esau and Jacob (Gen. xxv. 26), and the interpretation is given as follows: "For Esau represents the end of the world, and Jacob is the beginning of it that followeth;" or, as it is translated from an Arabic version (it is not extant in Greek, but is preserved in Latin), " And the end of this world is in Esau, and Jacob is the beginning of the world to come." The older prophets had got halfway to this kind of allegorizing in using names in a typical way—as, for instance, Obadiah, who says, " The House of Jacob shall be a fire, and the House of Joseph a flame, and the House of Esau for stubble, and they shall kindle against them and devour them. . . . And Saviours shall come up on Mount Zion to judge the mountains of Esau, and the kingdom shall be Jehovah's." The passage from Esdras quoted above is quite in accord with Philo's style, although, to the passage in question, the latter gives a different meaning, saying (Quæst. in Gen. iv. 162), " The brothers represent virtue and wickedness, so far as they are the offspring of one mind, and are enemies, in that they are opposed to each other and at war."

Philo is a link in the chain of Oriental parabolizing, the elder extreme of which is to be found in the remains of India and Egypt, of the Buddhists and Pythagoreans, while its later developments faintly show themselves in Origen, Clement of Alexandria, the Gnostics, and the later Kabbalists. The appearance, moreover, of this kind of symbolism from time to time in the higher flights of poetry, and the communications of ecstatics and the oracular Pythiæ subjects, go to prove that parabolic utterances are not mere whims of a period, or fancies of a school, but realities resting upon some native correspondence of exalted thought with expression.

We have spoken of the quasi-symbolic use of proper names by Philo. He treats " Sodom," for instance, as " being in real fact the soul made barren of all good things, and blinded as to its reason," " Egypt " as " the whole of the district connected with the body "—the " corporeal and external," and the " King of Egypt " as " a figurative representation of the mind devoted to the body " (De Abr., xxi.).

Similarly, in a canonical book (Rev. xi. 8), we find the

same proper names made to represent some not clearly particularized form of earthliness;—"the open street of the great city—namely, that which spiritually is called Sodom and Egypt." The author of the "Epistle to the Galatians" employs the same kind of symbol, when, after referring to the story of the children of Sarah and Hagar, he says, parenthetically (iv. 24), "which things have a second meaning," and makes Hagar answer to "the Jerusalem of the day," and Sarah to an ideal free Jerusalem of above.

That Philo should have a real ground for his symbolic interpretations of what appears to be mere narrative in the Hebrew scriptures, seems in some instances well-nigh incredible, however plausible may be his rendering. The true interest of his versions, however, for our present purpose results, not from the fact whether or not they truly lie concealed in an occult original, but from the light which is thrown by them upon the symbol-making and symbol-reading of his day; such inner thoughts of his being often akin to the concealed signification of other parables of his century, helping us to appreciate the drift and unlock the meaning of these hitherto unsolved enigmas.

In Exodus is a story of the Hebrew clan breaking away in the absence of Moses from his rule, and perpetrating an orgy around the golden effigy of a calf: the story may possibly be based upon some historic fact, or may be the expression of some priestly imagination. The story ends in the return of Moses, who gathers around himself the sons of Levi, whereupon there is given through him the oracular utterance (Exodus xxxii. 27):—"Thus saith Jehovah the God of Israel, Put ye every man his sword by his side, and go to and fro from gate to gate throughout the camp, and slay every man his brother, and every man his companion, and every man his neighbour [and every one him that is nearest to him," LXX.]. Let us hear Philo's reading of this truculent command (De Ebr., §§ 15, 16): "Many are cheated by the mere appearances that are close to their hand, whilst their minds do not penetrate to the powers that lie unseen and shadowed over. What! those that have applied themselves to prayers and sacrifices and the whole ceremonial service of the Temple, are —what is most paradoxical—homicides, fratricides, slayers with their own hands of the nearest and dearest bodies. . . . . It is not the case, as is deemed by some, that the priests slay men, rational animals constituted of soul and body, but as many things as are near and dear to the flesh, these they cut off from their characters. . . . We are to slay a 'brother,' not a man, but the body that is brother to the soul; that is, we shall disjoin from that which is virtue-loving and divine the passion-led and the mortal. Again, we shall slay the 'neighbour,' not a man, but a company and band. For this is alike familiar to the soul and its grievous enemy, laying baits and snares for it, in order that through inundation by the objects of sense that overflow it, it may never erect itself toward heaven for to embrace the natures that are noble and godlike. We shall slay also what is 'nearest.' But what is nearest to the mind is thought in the uttering, inserting false doctrines amongst what are reasonable and likely and persuasive, to the destruction of that bravest possession, truth."

This usage of symbolic form to denote facts in the nature, constitution, and character of man, events transacted not upon the worldly stage, but upon the universal platform of the mind, as on a plane or field, is to be found not only among the seers anterior to Philo, the Buddhists, the Pythagoreans and others, but has a large development among the parables of Jesus recorded in the Gospels. Of these, in fact, more are symbolisms representing the working of the constituents of the nature of man, in its growth, its trial, or its great change, than are expressions of any other thought or moral whatsoever.

To turn again for a moment to the puzzling question of whether Philo is right in attributing a second meaning, so profound, to the barbaric passages of the Hebrew scriptures, the fact is noticeable that while he symbolizes to a very large extent the narrative which seems so unsymbolic, with a result often capricious and unsatisfactory, leading us to regard him as a mere special pleader, he yet now and again brings out a strange force and vitality in his interior unfoldments. If now a parallel instance can be found, a scripture in which the narrative is for the most part apparently mere narrative, or even plainly fabulous, and not impossibly trivial, whilst ever and anon is encountered a brief sentence full of deep ethical meaning, it may throw some light upon the plan of the Hebrew writings, and the method that Philo has followed, or rather that he ought to have followed, had he not overshot its limits.

We all know the old-fashioned "stories with a moral," and how the moral was pleasanter with the story than it would have been without it. This ethical part was generally deduced from the story, which was its illustration and amplification, for the whole was meant to appeal to one class of mind. But amongst ancient writings there are many that seem made to suit two classes of minds; one portion appears to be simple fable, meant for any one to listen to, whilst a smaller portion, hidden in the fable, or added to it, seems to be designed to catch the attention of a more thoughtful reader.

In "Buddhaghosa's Parables" as translated from the Burmese, which is a collection of stories evidently written for the vulgar, there are to be found here and there sentences from an earlier work of high ethical value, the "Dhammapada," which is extant in the Pali, or sacred language of the Hindoo Buddhists. Either these interlarding fragments are meant to catch the chance mind among the ignorant common herd that might be stretching towards higher thought, or they are destined to keep alive the interest of students of superior class, who might otherwise deem the work beneath their notice.

It may be interesting also to note in this connection a Druid song, the third line of each stanza of which contains a didactic kind of burden, the remainder being simple descriptive verse, bearing a slight sequence, stanza with stanza, the whole probably designed for committal to memory—

> " In the oak's high-towering grove
> Dwells the liberty I love—
> *Babblers from thy trust remove.*
>
> " Liberty I seek and have,
> Where green birchen branches wave—
> *Keep a secret from a knave.*
>
> " *Snow on hills*, with tree-boughs hoar,
> Loud the winter storm-winds roar,
> *Nature helps us more than lore.*
>
> " *Snow on hills*, and white are all
> The house-roofs ; ravens hoarsely call—
> *From too much sleep the gain is small.*
>
> " *Snow on hills*, for fish the weir ;
> The dells are haunted by the deer—
> *For the dead in vain the tear.*"

Among the Hebrew writers, similarly, there may have been a method of legend writing so as to include here and there something of suggestion or significance, meant only for those that could so read it, and to all but them standing as mere narrative. It would be too much to say that all the stories of the Hebrew patriarchs and others are constructed upon this fashion, and it is reasonable to suppose that some of them are historic chronicle. But the origin of the older books is so obscure, and they seem to have been gathered from sources so various, that it is impossible to pronounce upon their method and meaning, for these may be as different in character as the fountain-heads from which the books spring. But in such a story as the one which Philo has interpreted for us, there is some plausibility in the suggestion that while the greater part of it is matter-of-fact, or fable, a portion draws a moral into a region quite apart from the story, a field only appreciable by minds accustomed to symbol, and able to receive those mystic truths which it is the function of symbol to preserve and convey.

If Philo's attack upon the literal credibility of a precept of murder having been given to the Levites should be insufficient to convince us that what seems merely matter-of-fact may be an outer shell, we may at least find some interest in the very high and poetical degree of ingenuity which marks some of his symbolical unfoldments. We are well aware, for instance, that we live in a world of some trouble and anxiety —"a world of moan," as a dejected poet has called it, and that whether through lapse or imperfection we are by no means constantly in paradise. From what Philo says, it would seem that the educated sceptics of Alexandria were wont to ridicule the accounts of ancient seers who had endeavoured to explain the origin of existence, treating these primitive legends with a superciliousness such as is exhibited by no small number of very similar persons in other great cities to-day. Philo takes a deeper view, and, as if in answer to a question, What do we know of angels and fiery swords keeping a gate that leads from our world to a paradise? he frames his argument. The passage in the Septuagint reads as follows: "The Lord God sent him forth out of the paradise of delight, to till the ground out of which he was taken. And he cast out the Adam, and fixed his dwelling over against the garden of delight; and stationed the cherubim; and the fiery sword that turns itself about, to guard the way of the tree of life." Philo, after citing this, quotes a passage a little different, as follows: "The flaming sword and the cherubim maintain their abode opposite the paradise," which is probably the paraphrase of some rabbinical commentator. He then proceeds with his exposition (De Cherub., vii.): "What it is that is told like an enigma by means of the cherubim and the flaming sword that turns itself, let us now examine. May we not say then that he (Moses) here introduced by covert allusion an intimation of the circumvolution of the entire heaven?" Philo then points to the extreme outermost sweep of the heaven, wherein "the fixed stars celebrate their divine and orderly dance," and to the inner sphere which contains the planetary orbits, with their apparent contrary motions. He takes the flaming sword to be a symbol of the sun, and in another book (Quæst. in Gen. i. 57) he explains the force of the symbol, on the ground that "by its turning and circumvolution it marks out the season of the year, as being the custodian of life, and of everything which serves to the life of all."

There is some dignity in this conception of the guardians and limits of the external world into which man has passed out of his spiritual home. And if one Oriental philosopher discovered such a latent sense in the words of an ancient scripture, there is no very great improbability in the supposition that another equally imaginative Oriental might have had some such conception in his mind when the parable of Creation was put together.

If we are prone to assume that the thought of the ancient Hebrew is too narrow to attract the mind fed on the broad pasture of later centuries, Philo, who had around him Greek and Egyptian culture, is here in a position to reprove us. His Eden is the spiritual world; his region outside Eden is the world we are in, guarded by the shining powers of the firmament, which no mortal man may pass. Is this a small or insignificant thought? There is no question of Gentile or Jew; there is man and the universe. The Adam is no single individual; he is humanity—ourselves. Perhaps some will be inclined to say that this is as much romantic commentary upon Philo as Philo's surprising developments from the Hebrew scripture are romance upon it. Let us examine, then, another passage. If Adam represents ourselves, what have we to do with nakedness, and coats of skin? God

made coats of skin for Adam and for Life, and clothed them.*
"If we look to the inner signification," says Philo, "the coat of skin is a symbolical expression for the natural skin, that is to say, our body. For God, when first of all he made the intellect, called it Adam; thereafter, the outward sense, to which he gave the name of Life. In the third place, he of necessity makes a body also, calling that by a symbolic expression, a coat of skin; for it was fitting that intellect and outward sense should be clothed in a body as in a coat of skin" (Quæst. and Sol. in Gen. i. 53).

It will be interesting here to show that Philo was not alone in taking this view of the meaning of the parable of Genesis; he is quite at one with the Rabbis of Jerusalem. In a Talmudic commentary redacted in the third century of our era (Bereschith R., xx. 29) we find, "'God made for them coats of skin and clothed them.' In Rabbi Meir's book of the law it was found written, 'Garments of light, these were the garments of the first Adam.'" The conception of the Rabbis, drawn from their national scriptures, is of a celestial man, made in the likeness of God, and a terrestrial man ("in whom we all die," as a Christian Rabbi mystically puts it), who has become subject to a fall from his archetype, and is a material adumbration of the angelic Adam, who is of the nature of the Elohim.

Philo's idea of the incarnate Adam is given more at large in the following:—"Being in a manner God's likeness in respect of the sovereign mind within the soul; albeit it was his duty to preserve that divine image free from spot or stain . . . he chose eagerly what was false and base and evil, and contemned what was good and noble and true, for which he was very fairly made to exchange an immortal for a mortal

---

* "Adam called the name of his wife Life (Zoë), because she was the mother of all living. And the Lord God made for Adam and for his wife garments of skin, and clothed them" (Gen. iii. 21, Sept.). Here it is not garments of skins, but of skin, and the word used in the Hebrew is applicable to human skin, and is so employed in the reference to the shining skin of Moses (Exod. xxxiv. 30, 35).

existence . . . and altered his condition to that of a laborious and ill-starred life" (De Nobil., 3).

If man had remained wholly spiritual, say the Rabbis, he might have been of the Elohim. He may regain his state; he may relapse still further. "Man that is in honour, and understandeth not, is like the beasts that perish" (Psa. xlix. 20).

The Elohim are spiritual beings of creative and administrative power, as being at one with the Logos, the Word, or Power of the Thought Divine. We find in the Psalms (lxxxii.)—

> "God standeth in the congregation of El;
> He judgeth among the gods,—
>   How long will ye judge wrongly,
>   And accept the persons of the wicked ? . . .
>   I said, Ye are gods;
>   And all of you sons of the Most High.
>   But ye shall die like men,
>   And fall like one of the princes."

It is on the ground of capacity to receive the Logos, and do his works, and so to be of the Elohim, that Jesus defends himself from an ignorant charge of blasphemy: "Is it not written in your law, *I said, Ye are gods?* If he called them gods, unto whom the Word of God came, and the Scripture cannot be made void; say ye of him whom the Father sanctified and sent into the world, Thou blasphemest, because I said, I am God's son? If I do not the works of my Father, believe me not" (John x. 34–37).

It is as the type of humanity restored to oneness with its divine origin, that Jesus is set in apposition to Adam. Through the spirit of the works which proved his consecration, or chrism, he became the recipient of the Logos, and so restored the position of the celestial Adam, showing as it were the journey homeward to Eden from the region without into which the terrestrial Adam had strayed. "As in the Adam all die, so in the Christ will all be brought to life" (1 Cor. xv. 22). Passages like these will always be misunderstood so long as to die is regarded as signifying the passage away from terrestrial life, rather than the entrance into a state of subjection to birth and death—a condition in which death is possible.

"While the soul of the wise man comes down from on high from the ether into mortal life, and enters into and is sown in the field of the body, verily it is sojourning in a land not its own" (Quæst. in Gen. iii., § 10). "It is not possible for one who makes a body and the mortal stock his dwelling-place, to hold communion with God, but for one whom God redeems to himself from the prison-house" (Leg. Allegor., ii. § 14). Such is Philo's picture of the downward journey. He even describes corporeal life as the soul's tomb: "The human mind, entangled in so great a crowd of external senses, most competent to lead it astray and cheat it by false opinions, nay entombed in the mortal body which may rightly be termed a grave-mound" (De Creat. Princ., 8). The picture of the soul's upward journey we may draw from a more familiar source: "It is sown in corruption, it riseth in incorruption; it is sown in dishonour, it riseth in glory; it is sown in weakness, it riseth in power. It is sown a soulic (psychic) body, it riseth a spiritual body. There is a soulic body, and there is a spiritual body. So also it is written, the first man Adam became an animated soul, the last Adam a spirit making alive. Howbeit the spiritual is not first, but the soulic, afterwards the spiritual. The first man is of earth, earthy; the second man is of heaven" (1 Cor. xv. 42-47). To understand this passage, and its connection with Philo's philosophy, we must bear in mind that the soulic body means the animal-soulic part of man's constitution; the physical vitality, not the spark of spirit. Philo speaks of "the inferior province of the soul, its irrational part, of which even beasts partake" (De Spec. Leg., § 17).

Another case may be instanced where Philo's interpretation of Hebrew scripture possesses a reasonable ground of probability, and at the same time shows a resemblance between Mosaic, or, more strictly, Neo-Mosaic conceptions, for the versions of the Septuagint are a modernization of their originals, and the Platonic idealism :—

"What is the object of saying, 'And God made every green herb of the field before it was upon the earth, and every grass before it had sprung up'? He here enigmatically signifies the incorporeal species, since the expression *before it was* intimates the consummation of every bush and herb, seedlings and trees. But as to what he says, *before it had sprung up upon the earth*, God had made green herb, and grass, and other things; it is plain that the incorporeal species had been created for types, as it were, and in accordance with intellectual nature; and it is these which the things which are upon the earth perceptible to the external senses were to imitate" (Quæst. in Gen. i. 2).

The conception here is of an existence in an ideal or spiritual state prior to a correspondential or approximate existence upon the lower plane of matter. Such a pre-existence of plants is quite congruous with the notion of the pre-existence of the celestial Adam, and Philo is perhaps thinking of the same hidden archetype of life when he speaks as follows of animals :—" The created animal is imperfect as to quantity, and a proof of this is the growth which belongs to each stage of existence; but it is perfect as to quality, for the same quality abides as was stamped upon it by the abiding and never-changing divine Word" (De Prof., § 2).

Upon the following passage, perhaps, it would be hazardous to speak with assurance; but, if Philo's very philosophic interpretation be not the true one, we can only be grateful to him for so suggestive and valuable an invention :—" Moses prays to learn from God himself what God is. . . 'Thou shalt see my back parts,'[*] saith God, 'but my face thou mayest nowise behold.' It is sufficient, indeed, for the wise man to discern

[*] Exod. xxxiii. 23.

the consequences and the things which are after God; but he who wishes to gaze on the sovereign essence will be blinded by the exceeding shine of the rays before beholding it" (De Prof., § 29). This is a fine thought, that we may study Deity's consummated acts, and learn the lessons of experience, but that to pry into his essence is beyond the power of mortal man.

A similar instance of Philo's most engaging interpretations is the following :—

"Urged forward by the desire of learning, Moses was in the habit of investigating the causes by which the processes of natural law in the world are brought to consummation; beholding how many things in creation perish and are produced afresh, are destroyed and yet abide, he marvelled and was amazed, and cried out, saying, 'The bush is burned, and is not consumed'"* (De Prof., § 29).

It was the tendency of the ancient priests to be secretive, and to envelop in obscure signs their repertory of knowledge. Nevertheless, it is not easy to follow Philo in his belief that the diluvian Ark, though it was unstable, and tossed about by the flood, is meant as a similitude of created nature, the human body. The Ark of the Covenant, on the other hand, a vessel all gold, and sacredly preserved in the Holy of Holies, he regards as a symbol of the incorporeal world, the stable divine nature. The comparison of the proportions of the ark of wood with those of the human body is not very conclusive; the principal points being that the relations of length, breadth, and height of the ark—three hundred, fifty, and thirty cubits respectively—correspond with height, chest-width, and rib-depth and width together. The compartments of the ark are food-receptacles and digestive regions; the doors are orifices, the windows senses, and the people in the ark faculties. The roof is that earthly desire which binds down the soul which otherwise would aspire. The whole comparison, of which we

* Exod. iii. 2.

have quoted only the most plausible particulars, is a curious instance of Rabbinical subtlety.

The representation of the mortal frame by an ark, tabernacle, temple, crumbling old house, or stately palace, has been a favourite symbol with seers and poets :—

"We that are in this tabernacle do groan, being burdened" (2 Cor. v. 4).

"As long as I am in this tabernacle . . . the putting off my tabernacle cometh swiftly" (2 Pet. i. 13).

> " Hie away from this old house,—
> Every crumbling brick embrowned with sin and shame !"
> * * * * *
> " Till crash comes down the carcass in a heap !"
> * * * * *
> "All the worry of flapping door and echoing roof ; and then
> All the fancies . . .
> If you but knew how I dwelt down here !" (BROWNING).

> "Wanderers in that happy valley,
>   Through two luminous windows, saw
> Spirits moving musically
>   To a lute's well-tunèd law,
> Round about a throne where, sitting
>   (Porphyrogene !)
> In state his glory well-befitting,
>   The ruler of the realm was seen.
> And all with pearl and ruby glowing
>   Was the fair palace-door !" (EDGAR POE.)

The influence of Philo, or of his school, in their more spiritual illustrations, may be traced through a double channel in the Gospels. Many apparently genuine utterances therein are pervaded by the same cast of thought as Philo's, while the later doctrinal developments of the compilers have evidently originated in the metaphysical hypotheses of his school; this is most markedly the case in the Fourth Gospel. A few instances of parallelism or sympathy of thought between Philo's words and those recorded as having fallen from Jesus may here be noted by way of example. There are, however, certain broad features of likeness between the spiritual philosophy of Philo and the gospel enounced by Jesus, which cannot be fully shown by comparison of isolated passages. Such a likeness is the more remarkable from the fact of the utter dissimilarity of the word and work of each teacher taken as a whole. Philo is a man who sees the imperfection of earthly life, and finds a refuge and consolation in philosophy; Jesus is a spirit all aglow with the world beyond, who presses forward with his good tidings for the irradiation of this. Where Philo surmises, Jesus sees; where Philo is involved, halting and obscure, Jesus is confident, luminous and crystalline. Philo's hopes fluctuate; Jesus seems to have a consciousness of belonging to a higher plane, to be a member of a spiritual sphere. He appears as if gifted with a freedom of access to a true life, of which men in general are inapprehensive. The similarities in doctrine between the two are all the more remarkable on this account.

Philo represents the soul of the wise man as "coming down from above and approaching mortal life, and entering and being sown in the field of the body, where it sojourns as being in a land not its own" (Quæst. in Gen. iii., § 10). He tells us that the Deity looks upon the wicked as "dead to any true life, bearing about themselves their body like a sepulchre, and burying their wretched soul in it" (Quæst. in Gen. i., § 70). "The death of the good is the beginning of another life. For life is two-fold: one in the body, corruptible; the other without body, incorruptible. Therefore a wicked man dies the death, who even while yet breathing among the living has already been buried, by reason of retaining in himself no inner spark of true life, which is perfect virtue" (Quæst. in Gen. i., § 16).

With these passages may be compared the parable of the Buried Talent, and such an expression of the Master's as "Leave the dead to bury their own dead" (Matt. viii. 22). The understanding of the last-named injunction is often reflected by a misreading of what precedes it. The request, "Permit me first to go away and bury my father," does not necessarily imply that the father was lying dead, but possibly betokens a wish to return to the life previously led, until the death of the head of the house should leave the son free to follow the strange master, which he fancied might then perhaps be his inclination,—a piece of temporizing, which the Master meets by the epigram to the effect that the dead, or world-buried folk, may be left to see to the affairs of one another.

It will be interesting to trace the course of the beautiful thought of the presence of God with man, from its early and somewhat materialistic form in the Pentateuch, through the refinement of the later oral teachings, whose spirit is represented in Philo's writings and in the Hagada of the Talmud, and so along to its familiar form in the simple setting of the Gospels.

The following passage is quoted both by Philo and the author of the Epistles to the Corinthians :—

"I will set my Tabernacle among you, and my soul shall not abhor you. And I will walk [walk-about-within, LXX.] among you and will be your God, and ye shall be my people" (Lev. xxvi. 11, 12).

This Tabernacle was the Shekinah, or symbol of the inhabitation with men of the glory of God.

The following are from Philo :—

"In the minds of those that are in a high degree purified, there doth assuredly inwardly walk, without noise, alone and invisibly, the God and governor of the universe; for truly there is a divine oracle extant, vouchsafed to the wise man, wherein it is said, *I will walk about within you, and I will be your God.* But in the minds of those who are still in process of cleansing, while they are not yet wholly washed clean of the life that sullies, and lies under the ignominious weight of the body, there walk the angels, the divine words. . . . Do thou therefore, O my soul, make haste to become the house of God, and his holy temple" (De Somn., i. § 23).

"In the soul of the wise man God is said to inwardly walk. . . . And into the happy soul which holds out as the most sacred cup its own faculty of reason, who can pour the sacred vessels of the joy that accompanies truth, except the cup-bearer of God and banquet-master—the Word ? . . . We look not for the city of the eternal in the regions of the earth, for it is not constructed of wood or of stone, but seek it in the soul which is free from war. . . . Where could be found a more venerable and holy abode for God, amid all existing things, than the mind fond of contemplation, which presses forward to behold all things, and not even in a dream feels a longing for sedition or disturbance?" (De Somn., ii. 38, 39).

"Inasmuch as God makes his way invisibly into the region of the soul, let us set in order that region to the best of our ability, as deemed worthy of the office of the future dwelling-place of God. If we do otherwise, God will move and go off unknown to another house. The mind of the wise man is the house of God" (Fragm. ex Ant. Ser., lxxxii.).

In the Gospels a kindred symbolism is very distinctly formulated :—

"This man said, I am able to destroy the temple of God and to build it within three days" (Matt. xxvi. 61). "Jesus answered and said unto them, Destroy this temple, and in three days I will raise it up. . . . He spake of the temple of his body" (John ii. 19, 21).

"Jesus yielded up his spirit, and the veil of the temple was rent in twain from the top to the bottom" (Matt. xxvii. 51).

"The veil, that is to say, his flesh" (Heb. x. 20).

The expressions "the kingdom of God," "the kingdom of Heaven," when it was found that they conveyed to some minds the impression of the visible foundation of a millennial kingdom on earth, were shown to denote the divine province within and so become almost synonymous with "the temple of God," the spirit's house which Divinity can enter and make divine. "The kingdom of God cometh not by observation; . . . the kingdom of God is within you" (Luke xvii. 20, 21).

In the following, the same symbol is used:—

"Your body is a temple of the Holy Spirit in you, which ye have from God, and ye are not your own. . . . Therefore glorify God in your body" (1 Cor. vi. 19, 20).

"Ye are the temple of the living God; even as God said, I will indwell within them, and will walk about within, and will be their God, and they shall be to me a people" (2 Cor. vi. 16).

"Know ye not that ye are God's temple, and that the Spirit of God dwells in you? If any one destroys the temple of God, him will God destroy; for the temple of God is holy, of which quality ye are" (1 Cor. iii. 16, 17).

Before entering upon the study of the metaphysical correspondences between Philo's doctrines and those of the early Christian school, we may compare a few simple and obvious parallels in ethical and spiritual teaching.

The motive of the following passages is obvious:—

"If thou be bringing thy oblation to the altar, and there call to mind that thy brother have aught against thee, leave there thine oblation before the altar and begone; first become friends with thy brother, and then come and offer thy oblation" (Matt. v. 23, 24).

"The things which proceed out of the mouth come forth out of the heart; and they defile the man: . . . but to eat with unwashen hands defileth not the man." (Matt. xv. 18, 20).

"Ye cleanse the outside of the cup and of the platter, but within they are full of extortion and excess. . . . Cleanse first the inside of the cup and of the platter, that the outside thereof may become clean also. . . . Ye are like unto whited sepulchres, which outwardly appear beautiful, but inwardly are full of dead men's bones, and of all uncleanness. Even so ye also outwardly appear righteous unto men, but inwardly ye are full of hypocrisy and iniquity" (Matt. xxiii. 25-28).

In Philo's writings we find the same insistence upon intrinsic, as opposed to merely ceremonial or external, purification :—

"Hardly doth one that is vile perform sacrifice in reality; nay, though he should bring ten thousand oxen without ceasing every day. For his most indispensable offering, his mind, is mutilated, and it is impious for mutilations to come nigh the altar" (De Plant. Noe. § 39).

"It is a piece of folly for one not to be allowed to enter the shrines without having first washed and made bright his body, whilst, nevertheless, one may attempt to pray and to sacrifice with a mind still soiled and bemuddled. And yet temples are merely made of stones and timbers—soulless matter! and the body, soulless in itself, touches not the soulless without first using ablutions and purificatory cleansings: and shall any one, whilst uncleansed in his own soul, endure to approach God the most pure, and this, too, without any intention of repentance?" (Quod Deus Immut., § 2).

"They scour their bodies by lustrations and purifications, but to wash off from their souls the passions that pollute their life, they neither desire nor have a care. They are earnest to flock to the temples in raiment of white, robed in garments without a stain, but they have no shame at bringing to the very shrine a mind that is all stains" (De Cherub., § 28).

The following passages offer variations on the comparison of the wide and frequented, and the toilsome and lonely roads of life :—

"Wide the gate and spacious the path that leads away to destruction, and many are they that enter therethrough. Narrow the gate and strict the path that leads unto life, and few they be that find it" (Matt. vii. 13, 14).

"There is nothing higher than God, and if any one has been quick to stretch the eye of the soul unto Him, let him pray for abidance and firm standing. For the uphill ways are toilsome and slow, but the downhill career, which is rather like a downward sweep than a descending path, is swift and easy" (De Abrah., § 12).

This [the well-beaten] road they say most nearly corresponds to pleasure. For almost from birth to extreme old age men traverse and walk about upon it. . . . But the paths of prudence and temperance and the other virtues, if not altogether untravelled, are assuredly entirely unworn by feet. For small is the number of those who proceed by these paths, who have sincerely loved wisdom, and formed association with the Beautiful alone, disregarding wholly all things else" (De Agric., § 23).

The following comparison speaks for itself:—

"Be not in dread of those that slay the body, but are not able to slay the soul, be in dread rather of one able to ruin both soul and body in a gehenna" (Matt. x. 28).

"Let us no wise dread the disease that is from without, but wrong doings, for it is through these that the disease comes; we should dread the soul's disease, not the body's" (Fragm. Bodl.).

The accord between the following passages, too, is obvious:—

"Hoard for yourselves not treasures upon the earth, where moth and rust deface, and where thieves undermine and steal. But hoard for yourselves treasures in heaven, where neither doth moth nor rust deface, and where thieves do not undermine or steal" (Matt. vi. 19, 20).

"The great King himself proves to be poor and helpless if he be put in the balance with one single virtue, for his riches are inanimate, buried deep in treasuries or the earth's recesses; but the wealth of virtue is stored up in the dominant part of the soul. And in it claims a share that purest of all essence,

Heaven, as likewise does the parent of the universe, God" (De Carit., § 6.).

"Receive, O initiates, who are purified as to your ears, these things in your own souls as really sacred mysteries, and babble not to any one among the uninitiated, but store them up in your own selves and guard them as a treasury, not one wherein gold and silver, perishable substances, are hoarded up, but the prize and prime of existing possessions, the knowledge of the first cause, the knowledge of virtue, and thirdly, of the fruit of both" (De Cherub., § 14).

The following forms a pair with the well-known saying of Jesus at the table provided by bustling Martha, "one thing [or one dish] alone is needful:"—

"They tell a story that some one of old time, who had fallen madly in love with the beauty of wisdom, as it had been that of a most comely woman, once, when he beheld an unlimited preparation of most costly magnificence, looked towards some of his friends and said, 'See, comrades, how many things I have no need of'" (De Plantat., § 16).

The following passages shed light on each other:—

"Those who give, hunting for praise or honour in requital, and seeking a return for their favours, are really making a bargain veiled under the name of a gift. . . . God forsooth is not a huckster cheapening his wares, but truly generous in all things, pouring forth inexhaustible treasures of goodwill, and desiring no requital" (De Cherub., § 34).

"When thou doest alms, sound not a trumpet before thee, as the hypocrites do in the synagogues and in the streets, that they may have glory of men. Verily I say unto you, they have received their reward" (Matt. vi. 2).

"Eating is a symbol of spiritual food. For the soul is fed by the reception of comely things, and by the doing of righteous deeds" (Legis Allegor., i. § 31).

"My food is to do the will of him that sent me, and to complete his work" (John iv. 34).

"What is the meaning of the expression, 'I pour out my soul before the Lord'? (1 Sam. i. 15), but, I will consecrate it wholly" (De Ebriet. § 37).

"This cup is the new covenant in my blood, which is shed for you" (Luke xxii. 20).

"He washes the dirt off the feet, that is to say, the supports of pleasure" (Legis Allegor., iii. § 48).

"If I washed your feet, ye also ought to wash one another's feet" (John xiii. 14).

"Heaven is eternal day, having no share in night or shadow at all. . . . Heavenly things partake of a wakefulness that knows no sleep, by reason of energies which wander not, and stumble not, and go straight in all things. But earthly things are weighed down by sleep, and if for a little while they start up, they are dragged down again and buried in slumber, by reason of inability to look with the soul upon anything of straight direction, and so stray and stumble" (De Josepho, § 24).

"If any one walk in the day, he stumbleth not, because he sees the light of this world; but if any one walk in the night, he stumbleth, because the light is not in him" (John xi. 9).

"Well, O Saviour, in that thou revealest thine own works to the soul that yearneth for good things, and hast concealed from it none of thy works: for this cause it is strong to flee from evil, and to conceal and overshadow it, and to destroy for ever the passion that is hurtful" (Legis Allegor., iii. § 8).

"I thank thee, Father, Lord of the heaven and the earth, that thou hiddest these things from the wise and prudent, and revealedst them unto babes. Yea, Father, for so it seemed good in thy sight" (Matt. xi. 25).

The following passages it is interesting to place side by side:—

"It is as impossible that the love of the world can coexist with the love of God, as for light and darkness to coexist with one another" (Fragm., John of Damascus).

"Ye cannot serve God and Mammon" (Matt. vi. 24; Luke xvi. 13).

"Be such in regard to thy household as thou dost pray God to be unto thee; for as we hearken, so we shall be hearkened to by God, and as we see, so we shall be seen by him. Let us then yield pity for the piteous, in order that we in turn may receive like for like" (Philonea, Tischendorf).

"Forgive us our debts, as we also have forgiven our debtors" (Matt. vi. 12).

"He that hungers and thirsts after understanding" (Fragm., John of Damascus).

"They that hunger and thirst after righteousness" (Matt. v. 6).

"It is not lawful to speak out the sacred mysteries to the uninitiated. . . . To bestow equal things upon unequal people is an act of the utmost wrong" (Fragm., John of Damascus).

"Cast not your pearls before swine" (Matt. vii. 6).

The passage which we shall next quote from Philo affords a curious parallelism to some hard sayings of Jesus:—

"If thy hand or thy foot causes thee to offend, cut it off and cast it from thee, for it is better for thee to enter into life halt or maimed, than having two hands or two feet to be cast into eternal fire. And if thine eye causes thee to offend, pluck it out and cast it from thee, for it is better for thee to enter life with one eye, than having two eyes to be cast into the gehenna of the fire" (Matt. xviii. 8).

"There are eunuchs, which made themselves eunuchs for the kingdom of heaven's sake" (Matt. xix. 12).

"It would seem to me that men who are not absolutely uninstructed would choose to be mutilated unto blindness rather than to see what is not seemly; and to be made deaf rather than to hearken to noxious words; and to have their tongues cut out rather than babble a word of the undivulgable. They say at least that some of the sages, when tortured on the wheel to make them betray the undivulgable, have bitten out their tongues, and so have contrived a more grievous torture against their torturers, incapacitating them from learning what they wanted to know. Of a truth it is better even to be made a eunuch than to go mad upon monstrous intercourse" (Quod Det. Potiori Insid., § 48).

The following passages also may be read together:—

"Moses affirms [Deut. xviii. 18] that if they be truly pious, they shall not be utterly shut off from consciousness of things that are about to come. But some God-inspired prophet will suddenly appear and give oracles and prophesy, saying indeed nothing of his own (for one truly possessed and spiritually inspired is unable even fully to grasp what he himself is saying), for whatsoever things he is inly taught will flash through him as if from the dictation of some one else. For the prophets are interpreters of God, who makes use of their organs for the manifestation of whatsoever things he wills" (De Monarch., § 9).

"I can of myself do nothing; as I hear, I judge, and my judgment is just, in that I seek not mine own will, but the will of him that sent me" (John v. 30).

"I do nothing of myself, but as the Father taught me, thus I speak; and he that sent me is with me; he hath not left me alone, for I always do the things that are pleasing to him" (John viii. 28, 29).

One series of passages in the Gospels has been a puzzle and stumbling-block to many: "If any one comes to me and hates not his father and mother and wife and children and brethren and sisters, yea, and his own life also, he cannot be my disciple" (Luke xiv. 26). "Think not I came to fling peace upon the earth: I came not to fling peace, but a sword. For I came to set a man at variance against his father, and the daughter against her mother, and the daughter-in-law against her mother-in-law: and a man's foes shall be they of his own household" (Matt. x. 34–36). It is no wonder that the literal Western mind should revolt at such passages. But it is strange that among scholars it should not have been more fully perceived that, granted the undoubted presence in the Gospels of parable, symbol, or allegory, the inference is obvious that the more naturally unlikely the external form of a phrase, the more probably there lurks within it a second meaning which is the one intended to be discerned. In such a case Philo, in strict accordance with his school of traditional lore, meets with no difficulty whatever. His system is simple and uniform.

"Abandon," he says, "the idea that the expression is used about a person, and direct your examination to the soul as if laying it open for dissection" (Cong. Erud. Grat., § 11).

It would appear strange indeed were we to find Philo in such instances awake to deeper meanings than at first sight are apparent, and at the same time to ascribe to Jesus nothing but bare literality. When we allow the fact that the Oriental mind tends to a parabolic style, we shall be ready to grant that if Philo expounds his own parables he may be the means of unlocking the meaning of others that resemble them. The following have an obvious rapport with the words of Jesus :—

"Abraham, when he left behind his country and kindred and his father's house (Gen. xii. 1), that is to say, the body, the outward senses, and the reason, began to have converse with the powers of the living God" (Quod. Det. Potiori Insid., § 44).

"He saith to his father and mother, he hath not seen thee, and recognized not his brothers, and repudiated his sons, (Deut. xxxiii. 9); he relinquishes his father and mother, that is to say, his mind and the material of his body, in order to have as his inheritance the one God" (Legis Allegor., i. § 14).

"His father—that is the mind, and his mother—that is the external sense" (De Prof. § 20).

"The man of slavish disposition . . . who says, 'I have loved my lord' (Exod. xxi. 5), that is to say, the mind which is sovereign within me, 'and my wife,' that is, the cherished external sense, the keeper of the house of passions, 'and the children,' that is to say, the evils which are the offspring thereof" (Quis Rer. Div. Her., § 38).

The parable of the Prodigal Son will receive many illustrations from Philo, if read in this symbolic way.

The "far country" of the parable may now be understood. It is the region into which the spirit strays so as to be most remote from its true centre, most seemingly independent, with bodily faculties apparently all its own to revel in. The body of the parable might be in great part reconstructed from Philo—the foreign country, the becoming slave instead of master, the houseless wandering, the father forestalling the tardiness of the returning one, the going forward to meet him.

"Looking upon his whole life according to the body as a sojourn in a foreign country, when he is able to live in soul alone, then he apprehends that he is abiding in his own country" (Quis Rer. Div. Her., § 16).

"Every soul of a wise man has become possessed of heaven as its fatherland, and of earth as a strange country; and considers the house of wisdom its own home, but the house of the body a lodging-house, in which it proposes to sojourn for a while" (De Agric., § 14).

"In us the mind corresponds to a man, and the faculties of sensation to a woman. . . . The mind if caught by the bait [of the pleasures of the sense] becomes subordinate instead of sovereign, and slave instead of master, and an exile instead of a citizen, and mortal instead of immortal" (De Mund. Opif., § 59).

"Banishing from himself the unrighteous and godless soul, God disperses it far away unto the region of pleasures and appetites and injustices. And this region is most appropriately called the region of the impious, in place of that which is fabled to exist in Hades. For, indeed, the real Hades is the life of one who is in a state of wickedness, a life which is an avenger, and under defilement, and liable to all curses.

> 'When the Most High distributed the nations,
> When he dispersed the sons of Adam' (*Deut.* xxxii. 8),

he drove out all the earthly dispositions, which showed no zeal to see any good thing of heaven, and rendered them verily houseless and outlaws and wanderers. . . . By his wife who is a citizen the wicked man has vice for offspring, and passion by his concubine. For the whole soul, like a citizen, is conjugal partner of reasoning power, while soul that is culpable brings forth vices. The nature of the body, on the other hand, is a concubine, by means of whom the birth of passion is beheld" (Cong. Erud. Grat., §§ 11, 12).

The word Hades originally denoted nothing more than the shadowy receptacle of souls, and was marked by a vague incompleteness. But in Philo, as for example in a quotation made above, we see the word beginning to be used in a moral sense, and marking the opposite of the heavenly state. The ancient picture of the Elysian Fields was rather of a supernal region of Hades, than of its polar opposite. The conception of Hades as a distinctly evil state became gradually degraded into the materialistic hell of the hideous Calvinistic dogma.

"There being two existences, the mind of the all, which is God, and the mind of the individual, he that escapes from the mind that is in respect of himself flees to the mind of the universe; and he who forsakes his individual mind confesses that the affairs of the human mind are nothing, and ascribes everything to God" (Legis Allegor., iii. § 9).

"The wicked man sinks down into his own scattered mind, fleeing from the real mind" (Legis Allegor., iii. § 12).

But the Father does not leave the soul altogether to its self-chosen isolation; when there awakens the desire to return, he goes out halfway to meet the wanderer.

"There are some souls which God goes forward to meet:

'I will come unto you and bless you.' You see how great the loving-kindness of the Creator, when he even forestalls our tardiness, and comes forward to meet us, to the perfect benefiting of the soul" (Legis Allegor., iii. § 76).

"Who is so destitute of reason or soul, as never, either voluntarily or involuntarily, to conceive a notion of the most good? Verily, even over the most abominable there doth hover oftentimes a sudden visionary presence of the good, but they are unable to take firm hold of it, and to keep it beside them" (De Gigant., § 5).

"That which breathes in is God; that which receives is the mind; that which is breathed in is the Spirit. . . . The human mind would not have dared to shoot up to such a height as to lay claim to God-nature, had not God himself drawn it up to himself, so far as it is possible for the mind of man to be updrawn, and moulded it according to those powers which are within reach of inward apprehension" (Legis Allegor., i. § 13).

God is the true banquet-master from beginning to end. If the swine's pods are chosen in preference to the heavenly feast, he will wait until the exile longs once again for the comforts of home.

"Just as those who give a banquet do not call any one to supper before they have completed all the preparations for festivity, ... so, in like manner, did the Ruler of the Universe, like a banquet-giver, ... provide beforehand for every kind of entertainment, in order that man on his entry into the world might at once find a most sacred feast and stage,—Nature all but crying aloud that men should imitate the Supreme Author of their being, and pass their lives without trouble and without hardship in most ungrudging livelihood and abundance of needful things. And, thus it would come about, were it not for the irrational pleasures of the soul gaining the mastery and building up a stronghold of gluttony and lewdness, or for the lusts of glory, or power, or riches, clutching at the dominion of life, or for distresses contracting and warping the mental faculty, or for the evil counsellor, fear, restraining the impulses towards zeal in work, or for folly and cowardice and injustice, and the inconceivable multitude of other evils making their assault" (De Mund. Opif., § 26).

Our quotations from Philo do not form part of the parable, but illustrate it by metaphoric parallels. The "Best Robe" of the parable of the Prodigal, the "Wedding Garment" of another, come to the mind in reading the following passage :—

"Whenever it [the inward part of the soul] has withdrawn from human pursuits, and serves the Existent only, it puts on the unvariegated robe of truth, which nothing mortal will ever touch. . . . But when it passes over to mix in political affairs, it puts off the robe of the heart and assumes another one most variegated and amazing to look upon. . . . For at the manifest altar of life it will appear to exercise much prudence with respect to the skin and flesh and blood, and everything relating to the body, so as not to offend the multitude which gives the palm to the things of the body, after the things of the soul, which are honoured by the second place. At the inner altar, on the other hand, it will use nothing but what is bloodless, fleshless, incorporeal, things appertaining to reason alone" (De Ebriet., § 21).

The following passages are akin :—

"Never enter into a contest for superiority in evil, or strive strenuously for the first place in such practices, but rather exert yourself with all your might to escape from them" (De Agric., § 25).

"Resist not [set not up a match with] evil" (Matt. v. 39).

In the passages next quoted we find the symbol of a stone conveying possibly the same or a kindred signification :—

"Ignorance . . . . maims the soul in its faculties of seeing and hearing, and allows neither light nor reason to enter into it, lest the one should instruct it, and the other show it things as they are. Shedding upon it dense darkness and plentiful folly, ignorance will have rendered the soul of most beautiful form a senseless stone" (De Ebriet., § 38).

"God is able out of these stones* to raise up children unto Abraham" (Matt. iii. 9).

It may be interesting to compare Philo's allegorizing with the gospel trope of the shepherd and the sheepfold (John x. 1-16). In Philo's view the shepherd is the dominant part, the sheep the subordinate faculties. Might there not have been some allusive sense of this kind in the original words which we only possess in the Fourth Gospel shape and mannerism. Read in this way there is a parallelism between the apposition of the Father and the Shepherd, and that of Heaven and the Soul in Philo's comparison: "I imagine Heaven is in the world, as the soul in man" (Quis Rer. Div. Her., § 48). But the connection, if any, is slight. It is easy to be misled by an apparent similarity between parabolic forms. We have to bear in mind that the signification of symbols varies with their position. "We have to look at the occasions on which and the manner in which each expression is used; for it often happens that the same expressions are applied to different things at different times; and on the contrary, opposite expressions are at different times applied to the same thing with perfect consistency" (Philo, Fragm. Quæst. in Exod.).

Philo's allegory is as follows: "He prays that the flock may not be left wholly without shepherd—meaning, by the flock, the entire multitude of the lovely things of the soul—but that they may meet with a good shepherd, one to lead them away from the nets of folly and wrong and every vice, and toward the principles of instruction and of other virtue. . . .

---

* There is a punning connection, it has been suggested, in the Hebraic original of this saying, between "stones" and "sons." Josephus alleges that when the Jews were engaged in warfare with Titus, the son of the Roman Emperor Vespasian, they were much harassed by a catapult. Soldiers were set to watch the preparations for its discharge and give timely notice, which they did by shouting, in their own language, "The son is coming," with supposed allusion to Titus, the equivalents of "son" and "stone" being very similar in sound.

Is it not indeed a thing worth praying for, that the flock which is akin and naturally suited to each individual of us may not be let go without any superintendent and sovereign, so that we may not, by being filled full of that vilest of bad governments, ochlocracy, which is the base counterfeit of that noblest form democracy, dwell continually in a condition of tumult and disorder and intestine discord? . . . It behoves that our mind, like a goatherd, or cowherd, or shepherd, or, in brief, any herdsman, should have rule, and choose, in preference to what is pleasant, that which is advantageous both to itself and the flock. Now the watchfulness of God is the first, and almost the only, cause that the divisions of the soul are not left without guardian, but that they rather find a blameless and absolutely good shepherd, one whose appointment renders it impossible for the company of the mind-faculty to become scattered. For it will of necessity appear under one and the same ordination, looking away from all others to the superintending care of one, since to be compelled to be in submission to many authorities is a most oppressive burden. . . . If a soul be shepherded by God, it has the one and only thing whence all things depend, and is naturally in need of none other things, and regards not blind riches, but in respect of what it has, is endowed with clearness of vision and with reverence. For this, all disciples have come to have an intense and unalterable love ; and so, with a laugh at the mere keeping of sheep, they strain after the true shepherd's craft " (De Agric., § 10, 11, 12, 13).

The following shows a familiar metaphorical use of the epithet blind : " The blind generation of the human herd, though it seems to see, is disabled. For how is it otherwise than disabled, when it sees evil instead of good, what is unrighteous instead of what is righteous, the passions instead of the happy condition, things mortal instead of things immortal ; and when it runs away from monitors and moderators, from conviction and instruction, while accepting flatterers and the reasonings which make for pleasure, of idleness, and ignorance, and luxury? The good man, then, alone sees; wherefore the ancients (1 Kings [Samuel] ix. 9) named the prophets seers" (Quis Rer. Div. Her., § 15).

The same figurative use of the epithet blind is found both in the Hebrew scripture and in the Gospels: "I speak to them in parables, because seeing they see not" (Matt. xiii. 13).

"The Word of God is not apparent in every place, but wherever there is a space vacant of passions and vices; and it is subtle to understand and to be understood, and very translucent and pure to the sight, and it is like coriander seed. For agriculturists say that the seed of the coriander is capable of being divided and cut without end, and if sown in each separate part and cutting, it shoots up just as the whole seed would. Such also is the Word of God, which is profitable both in its entirety, and in every part whatsoever" (Legis Allegor., iii. § 59).

There is a partial likeness between this symbolism of a minute seed as the Word of God, and that of the mustard seed as the kingdom of Heaven:—

"The kingdom of Heaven is like to a grain of mustard seed, which a man took and sowed in his field; which indeed is less than all the seeds; but, when it is grown, it is greater than the herbs, and becomes a tree, so that the birds of the air come and lodge in the branches thereof" (Matt. xiii. 31, 32).

The following also shows a correspondence: "There is no single existing thing which is brought to perfection by seed alone without its appropriate nourishment. For seed resembles the beginning, and the beginning by itself does not make perfect; for beware of imagining that the ear of corn blossoms and ripens solely from the seed, which is cast by the husbandman on the ploughed field; for in truth dryness and moisture, the twofold moisture which is derived from the earth, co-operate superlatively towards its growth. . . . All things that derive their origin from seed are of a greater magnitude than the seed which gives them their existence, and are seen to fill a more extended space. For often trees that reach to very heaven do shoot up from an infinitesimally small grain of seed" (Philo, De Incor. Mund., xix.).

"The Veda calls God the void space of the heart, and declares him to be smaller than the grain of paddy or barley" (Rammohun Roy).

"A husbandman, as some tell, whilst digging a hole for the purpose of planting some gently-nurtured tree, fell in with a treasure, meeting with unhoped-for good fortune. . . . When God bestows the contemplative treasures of his own wisdom, without toil or labour, then we who looked not for these things suddenly discover a treasure of perfect blessedness" (Quod Deus sit immut. § 20).

This is a conception not unlike that of "the kingdom of heaven," which "is like unto treasure concealed in the field, which when a man found, he concealed, and for his joy goes and sells all that he has, and buys that field." The treasure, in the natural sense, might be either a buried crock of gold, or a yet unrevealed potentiality of abundant harvest.

"Many persons have recovered their balance and sanity through removal from their surroundings, having arrived at cure of their mad and frenzied lusts by reason of the sight being no longer able to pander to the passion with images of pleasure. For in consequence of the sundrance it is through a void that the passion must needs travel, since there is no longer any object at hand wherein it can find provocation. And if any one has so removed himself, let him assuredly keep aloof from the revel gatherings of the multitude, and embrace solitude. . . . For as the bodies of those beginning to recover from a long illness are very subject to be caught by it again, so too the soul which is just regaining health has a falter and tremor in its mental sinews, whence there is reason to fear lest the passion, which was wont to be excited by familiar intercourse with inconsiderate people, should run back again" (Præm. et Pœn., § 3).

"As the implacable and inexorable mistresses of the body, thirst and hunger, do ofttimes strain it more or not less than persons are strained when racked to death by the torturer . . . in like manner covetous desire, first rendering the soul empty through forgetfulness of things present and recollection of what is far removed, sets it up with frenzy and madness ungovernable, and will finish off by procuring masters more afflictive than the former tyrants, while having the same names as those, to wit thirst and hunger, not of what has to do with the belly's enjoyment, but of money, glory, authority, beauty of form, and innumerable other things such as appear to be objects of desire and contention in human life" (De Concup., § 1).

"The outgoing of evil works the incoming of virtue, just as contrariwise if good stand out of the way, the lurking evil doth enter in" (Philonea, Tischendorf).

With these may be compared, and very closely, the notable gospel parable:—

"When the unclean spirit has gone forth from the man, it goes abroad through dry places seeking rest, and discovers it not. Then saith it, I will turn back to my abode whence I came forth. And when come, it finds it to be vacant, and swept, and adorned. Then goeth it and taketh along with itself seven other spirits more vicious than itself, and they enter in and take up their abode there, and the last of that man comes to be worse than the first" (Matt. xii. 43-45).*

Philo writes: "God has not thought fit to be taken hold of by bodily eyes: . . . perhaps by reason of the weakness of our sight. For it would not have been competent to bear the brightness which pours forth from the living God, when it is

* Cf. also: "He who having got rid of desire, hankers again for desire" (Dhammapada, 344).

not even able to gaze directly on the rays that proceed from the sun" (De Abrah., § 16).

"Who would venture to affirm about the First-cause either that he is a body, or that he is incorporeal, or that he is of such or such a kind or quality, or that he is without quality or attribute; or positively to declare anything in general concerning his essence or quality or constitution or movement? . . . We must be content if we are able to have knowledge of his name, to wit of his Word, which is his interpreter. For this must be God to us who are so imperfect, but the first, to those who are wise and perfect" (Legis Allegor., iii. § 73).

"No man hath ever seen God; the only begotten Son, who is in the bosom of the Father, he declared him" (John i. 18).

The mediate office of "the only begotten Son," as represented in the Fourth Gospel, singularly resembles the position ascribed by Philo to the Word, the first-born of God.

"Setting at the head his own Word (Logos), his firstborn Son, who is to receive the charge of this sacred company, as a lieutenant of a great king" (De Agric., § 12).

The expression "only and well-beloved Son" is also applied by Philo to the Kosmos, as the child of the Creator's power and knowledge. It will be remembered that Plato bestows the same epithet upon the heaven or universe.

The following are mutually illustrative :—

"What the eye is in the body, such is the mind and wisdom in the soul" (Ques. and Sol. in Gen. i. § 11).

"What the mind is in the soul, that the eye is in the body. For each has sight, the one of things that exist perceptible by the intellect, the other of things perceptible by the senses. The mind is in need of knowledge for the cognition of the incorporeal, and the eyes of light for the apprehension of the corporeal" (De Mund. Opif., § 17).

"Almost all the acuteness of perception of the eye is an attribute of the mind, which is in no need of borrowed light, being a star itself, and almost a representation and copy of the heavenly spheres. Assuredly diseases of the body effect a minimum of injury when the soul is in a sound state" (De Fortitud., § 3).

"The lamp of the body is the eye; if thine eye be sound thy whole body will be full of light" (Matt. vi. 22).

Philo's inferiority to Jesus in point of style is so marked, that it is sometimes difficult to detect a similarity of thought, even where it really exists. The following is a translation of Philo's words:—

"There are, so to speak, two heads of supreme import as compared with the countless particular propositions and doctrines; the one consisting of reverence and piety towards God, the other of brotherly love and righteousness towards men" (De Septen., § 6).

The corresponding words of Jesus are as follows:—

"Teacher, which commandment is great in the law? And he said unto him, *Thou shalt love the Lord thy God with all thy heart, and with all thy soul, and with all thy mind.* This is the great and first commandment. A second is like unto it, *Thou shalt love thy neighbour as thyself.* On these, the two commandments, hang the whole law and the prophets" (Matt. xxii. 36–40).

In the following we find concurrence of thought, in the one case smoothly, in the other incisively expressed:—

"If a man would become noble and good, let him show himself well pleasing unto God, to the universe, to nature, to the laws, to wise men, and let him repudiate self-love" (De Concup., § 11).

"He that found his soul will lose it; and he that lost his soul for my sake will find it" (Matt. x. 39).

"If any one desires to come after me, let him discard himself, and take up his cross, and follow me. For whosoever shall desire to save his soul will lose it, and whosoever will lose his soul for my sake will find it" (Matt. xvi. 24–25).

The only true gift, according to this high ideal, that man can make, is himself. By the nature of the case it must be a free gift; it cannot be otherwise.*

The following will compare with the criticisms in the gospel of the showy pretences of the scribes, and the gifts made by the rich only of their superfluity:—

"If one builds a temple with brilliant adornments at great expense, or offers up hecatombs, and incessantly sacrifices oxen, or adorns the shrine with costly offerings, bringing woods without stint, or works of art more precious than silver or gold, still let him not be reckoned with the pious. For he has gone astray out of the path of piety, taking ceremonial observance in place of holiness, and giving gifts to him that is unswayed by bribe, . . . and flattering the One that is not subject to flattery; who loves those that worship unfeignedly; and worship unfeigned is that of the soul that carries truth as its naked and only offering" ("Worse against Better," § 7).

"These were the morals, this the immovable school of rigid Cato; to keep bounds, and hold fast to purposes, to follow nature, to spend one's life on one's country, to deem one's self born, not for one's self, but for the whole world. It was a banquet to him to have conquered hunger" (Lucan, ii. 380).

"If any persons, accounting as nothing the wealth of nature, pursue that of vain opinions, supporting themselves on what is blind in preference to what has sight, and taking one that is crippled for guide of the way, to fall is their due of very necessity" (De Fortitud., § 2).

"Leave them; they are blind leaders of blind men. And if a blind man lead a blind man, both shall fall into a ditch" (Matt. xv. 14).

In his article on the Talmud, Deutsch wrote, "Were not

---

* "Self is the lord of self; what other lord could there be? The wise man who has become master of himself finds the law.

"Self is the lord of self; what other lord could there be? The wise man who has become master of himself finds what is glorious" (Udânavarga, xxiii. 11, 12).

the whole of our general views on the difference between Judaism and Christianity greatly confused, people would certainly not be so very much surprised at the striking parallels of dogma and parable, of allegory and proverb, exhibited by the Gospel and the Talmudical writings."

Philo, though he wrote in Greek, and at Alexandria, was almost a Talmudist. He describes himself as an Expositor rather than a Doctor, or Rabbi; but though his works are mainly those of the commentator, some of his interpretations are so broad and suggestive that they reach the level of original work. His philosophy so far interested his countrymen that several of his books were translated into Hebraic; and references may be found to him in Rabbinical literature, where he is designated Jedidiah—the darling of Jehovah.

Philo, then, being as deeply involved in Talmudical Judaism as in Greek philosophy, we may reasonably expect to find in his writing the same parallelism with the Christian metaphysics as Deutsch points out as subsisting between the Gospel and the Talmud.

Among such resemblances may be counted the fact that there is to be found in Philo a Trinitarian conception of Deity. It is to be remembered that what is advanced by Philo is fluid and suggestive rather than hardened into dogma. This fact distinguishes him more from the Christian metaphysics than any profound divergence of his theory, The doctrine of the Trinity, though it has been subject to variation according to the different schools within the Church that have wrangled over it, has been put forward as an authoritative formula of belief. Philo would have been shocked at such creed-making, and would never have claimed more for his conception of a Trinity than its own reasonableness, and the aid it might afford towards realizing Deity in relation to Humanity—Deity that by any doctrine whatever is conceivable only in part.

" The creative power is God, for by this he stablished and

ordained the universe. The royal power is the Lord; for it is seemly that the creator should have rule and dominion over the creature. The centre, being attended as by bodyguards by each of his powers, presents to the sight-endowed mind a vision at one time of one, at another of three. Of one when the soul is consummately purified . . . and hastens onward to the unmoved and uncombined idea, by itself in need of nothing else whatever; and of three when . . . it can attain to a comprehension of God, only through his acts, as creator or governor.

"There are three different classes of human dispositions, each of which has received as its portion one of the aforesaid images. The best has received that which is the centre, the vision of the truly living God. The next after that has received that which is on the right hand, the vision of the beneficent power which has the name of God. The third has the vision of that which is, on the other hand, the governing power, which is called Lord" (De Abrah., §§ 24, 25).

The attributes of God, active and essential, are regarded as forming a Pleroma, or divine fulness: "As that sweetest and clearest of thinkers, Plato, says: Envy is set outside the Divine Company; whereas Wisdom, that most divine and communicative of all things, never closes her meditative school [Phrontistery, Thinking-shop], but always opens wide her doors to take in those that thirst after fresh drinkable words, and upon them pours a grudgeless fountain of undiluted instruction, wooing them to the intoxication of the drunkenness that is indeed most sober" (Quod Omn. Prob. Liber § 2).

The following presents a different triple conception, that of Father, Mediator, Man: "One [logos] is an archetypal pattern above us, the other is the copy that abides with us. . . . The mind which is in each of us, which is strictly and in truth the man, is a third image of the Creator. The intermediate one is a model of our mind, an impression of God's" (Quis Rer. Div. Her., § 48).

Philo describes the sacred vestments of the high priest as constituting a symbol of the universe, the hyacinthine robe reaching to his feet being a representation of air, the pomegranate fringe of water, the flowery hem of earth, the scarlet of the over-robe an emblem of fire, the mantle over the shoulders a symbol of heaven, and the twelve stones of the breastplate denoting the signs of the zodiac, which is the type of the ratio and regulation of the universe, and so a symbol of the Divine Word. Josephus reads some of the symbols in a different sense, but both he and Philo concur in understanding the dress to symbolize the universe. The universe, according to Philo, is the Son of God, Nature being "the most ancient and well-established law."

Of the high priest so robed, Philo says: "It were indispensable that the man who is consecrated to the Father of the Universe should find for a paraclete, his son, in virtue most perfect, to procure an amnesty for misdeeds, and an abundance of grudgeless blessings" (De Vit. Mos., iii. § 14).

The world which God has made, the power and life of nature with which man is surrounded, is thus presented as a paraclete, or advocate for him, with the Father, which reminds us of the divine pity expressed in the Psalms as due to us for this very cause: "Like as a father compassioneth his children, so the Eternal compassioneth them that fear him; for he knoweth our frame; he remembereth that we are dust."

This is one idea of propitiation; another mediator, according to Philo, is the high priest himself: "The man who has been assigned to God, and has become the leader of the sacred order, ought to be withdrawn to another country, as it were, than the things of creation, ought not to be liable to give way to partiality for parents, or children, or brothers, so far as to pretermit or put off any one of those holy things which on every account it were better should be performed forthwith. For the law designs that the arch-priest should be endowed with a nature superior to that according to man, inasmuch as he approaches nearer the divine; being, if one must say the truth, on the borders of both, in order that by some one's mediation men may propitiate God, while God may use some subordinate minister, and so stretch out and abundantly supply his gracious things to men" (De Monarch., ii. § 12).

We may see in this passage the germ of the doctrine of the canonization of Jesus, which no doubt was an early step towards his ultimate deification.

More than the only son, the Universe, or the divine-natured high priest, the Paraclete upon whose office as Mediator or Propitiation Philo loves to dwell, is " the Divine Word."

Ever with the Jewish race a peculiar reverence was paid to the supreme attributes and even to the name of Deity. Being felt to be incommunicable, his essence was shrouded in mystery, and his name was ineffable, and only to be pronounced by the high priest on certain solemn occasions. Through this sense of awe, combined with a fear of materializing the conception of Deity, it came to pass that certain functions of divine providence were defined as powers intermediate between man and the eternal secrecy of God's essence. By personification, this power or these powers came to be regarded as the Deity that could enter into relation with human affairs, and though still recognized as God and not gods (in the polytheistic sense), they left the central idea of Deity at its unapproachable distance, and undwarfed by attempts to realize it approximately to the standard of man. To the mind of Philo there is present ever "God who is before the Word," but the providential influence which he feels to be in relation to himself is that of the Word: "The head and sum of propitiation resides in the sacred Word, in which when one dwells one does not directly reach God as he is in essence, but sees him as from afar. . . . The intermediate Divine Word. . . . God, not deeming fit to come unto the region of external sense, makes apostles of his own Words. . . . When one has arrived at the external senses, it is no longer God that one meets, but the Word of God. . . . God no longer bringing near the visions that proceed from himself, but only those that proceed from his subordinate powers. . . . The Divine Word manifesting itself on a sudden, brings an unexpected hope-transcending joy, as being about to become way-companion to the desolate soul" (De Somn., i. §§ 11, 12).

As the Christian doctors added to the Gospel according to Jesus a new and dogmatic enlargement of these mediatory doctrines, it may be of interest to trace their origin in the Hebrew canonical and apocryphal scriptures, as well as their development by Philo.

A series of passages will show how an attribute of Deity was personified and regarded as a separate and individual entity, and conversely how a messenger was regarded as one with him that commissioned him.

In the following, for instance, the powers of Deity are represented by the Angel of the Presence: "He was their saviour. In all their affliction he was afflicted, [or, in another reading, In all their adversity he was no adversary] and the angel of his presence saved them, . . . but they rebelled and vexed his holy spirit" (Isai. lxiii. 9, 10). Deity here is saviour, messenger, holy spirit, and never an adversary, or satan.

In the passage that follows, the Word fulfils a similar function: "As the rain cometh down, and the snow from heaven, and returneth not thither, but watereth the earth, and maketh it bring forth and bud, that it may give seed to the sower, and bread to the eater: So shall my Word be that goeth forth out of my mouth; it shall not return to me void, but it shall accomplish that which I please, and it shall prosper in the thing whereto I sent it" (Isai. lv. 10, 11).

In the following, we find Wisdom occupying a like office:—

"Wisdom shall praise her own soul,
And shall exult in the midst of her people:

* * * * *

"I came forth from the mouth of the Most High,
And as a mist overshrouded the Earth.
From the beginning, before the sweep of time, he established me,
And the æon through I shall nowise fail."

(*Wisdom of Jesus, son of Sirach*, xxiv. 1, 3, 9.)

In the following majestic passage, Wisdom, a personification, not a person, is represented as feminine (the Holy Spirit is similarly accounted feminine in an apocryphal book):—

"I prayed, and understanding was given me,
I made invocation, and there came to me the spirit of Wisdom.
I preferred her before sceptres and thrones,
And esteemed riches nothing in comparison of her.

* * * * * *

"I loved her above health and beauty of form,
And chose to have her instead of light,
For the radiance that cometh from her never goeth out.

* * * * * *

"Wisdom, which is the artificer of all things, taught me;
For in her is a spirit of perception, holy,
Only-begotten, manifold, subtle, mobile,
Piercing, undefiled, sure, and harmless,
Loving the good, quick, unfettered, well-disposed,
Kindly to man, steadfast, safe, unfretted,
All-powerful, all-surveying, spreading through
Spirits perceptive, pure, and subtlest.
For Wisdom is more moving than any excitement,
She extends and spreads through all things by reason of her pureness;
For she is the breath of the power of God,
A palpable emanation from the Almighty's glory:
Therefore can nought defiled creep into her;
For she is the flashing beam of the everlasting light,
The spotless mirror of the workfulness of God,
And the imaged form of his goodness.
Being as she is but one, she compasses all things,
And, abiding in herself, she makes all things new,
And generation by generation she passes over unto holy souls,
And ordains them friends of God and prophets."

(*Wisdom* vii. 7, 10, 22–27).

In the following the Word is represented as the Demiurge, or framer of the lower creation, and Wisdom as seated on the throne of God :—

" O God of my fathers and Lord of compassion,
Who madest the universe by thy Word,
And through thy Wisdom didst ordain man,
That he should have dominion over the creations that came from thee,
And should order the world in equity and righteousness,
And execute judgment with straightforwardness of soul:
Give me Wisdom, whose office is to be seated by thy throne !
And reject me not from among thy children " (*Wisdom* ix. 1-4).

" With thee is Wisdom, which knoweth thy works,
And was by when thou wroughtest the world,
And understandeth what is pleasing in thy sight,
And what is direct in thy commandments.
Send her forth out of the holy heavens,
And from the throne of thy glory speed her,
That with helping presence she may labour with me,
And I may learn what is well-pleasing unto thee " (*Wisdom* ix. 9, 10).

The Holy Spirit, like the Word and Wisdom, is a name for the powers that proceed from God :—

" Thy counsel who hath known, unless thou gavest Wisdom,
And didst send thy Holy Spirit from the highest " (*Wisdom* ix. 17).

" It was neither herb, nor emollient, that wrought them healing,
But thy Word, O Lord, that healeth all things " (*Wisdom* xvi. 12).

In the following, the personification is most vivid, but the Oriental mind is poetic and not scientific. No distinct person is signified, but only a distinct energy :—

" Whilst all things were wrapped in stilly silence,
And night was in the midst of her own fleet course,
Thine almighty Word from heaven leaped forth,
Out of the royal throne, an absolute man of war,
Into the midst of the pestilent earth,
Bearing the sharp sword of thy unfeigned commandment,
And stood up and filled all things with death :
And while it had hold of heaven, it stepped upon earth."
(*Wisdom* xviii. 14-16.)

" By his Word all things consist."
(*Wisdom of Jesus, son of Sirach*, xliii. 26.)

In the following is another expression, the Messenger of the Covenant, reminding us of the Angel of the Presence :—

> "Lo, I will send my messenger,
> And he shall prepare the way before me :
> And suddenly he shall come to his temple,
> The Lord whom ye seek ;
> Even the angel of the covenant, in whom ye delight,
> Lo, he shall come, saith Jehovah of Hosts.
> But who may abide the day of his coming,
> And who shall stand when he appeareth ?
> For he is like a refiner's fire,
> And like the washer's soap :
> And he shall sit as a refiner and purifier of silver,
> And shall purify the sons of Levi" (*Mal.* iii. 1–3).

In the following it will be observed that "Jehovah" and the "angel of Jehovah" are expressions used indiscriminately :—

"And the angel of Jehovah found her [Hagar] by a fountain of water in the desert, . . . and said unto her, Behold thou art with child, and shalt bear a son, and shalt call his name Ishmael [God heareth] ; because Jehovah hath hearkened to thine affliction. . . . And she called the name of Jehovah that spake unto her, Thou God of seeing" (Gen. xvi. 7–13).

"And the angel of God said unto me in the dream, Jacob . . . I am the God of Beth-el, where thou anointedst a pillar, and where thou vowedst a vow unto me" (Gen. xxxi. 11, 13). In the Septuagint we read, "I am the God that was visioned to thee in the place of God."

"And the angel of Jehovah appeared to Moses in a flame of fire out of the midst of a bush. . . . God called unto him out of the midst of the bush. . . . Moreover, he said, I am the God of thy fathers, the God of Abraham, the God of Isaac, and the God of Jacob. . . . I will be with thee. . . . 'I am that I am.' . . . Thus shalt thou say unto the children of Israel, I AM hath sent me unto you" (Exod. iii. 2–14). In the Septuagint, "I am the Being."

"The angel of God, who went before the camp of Israel,

removed and went behind them ; and the pillar of cloud removed from before their face, and stood behind them. . . . And it came to pass that in the morning watch Jehovah looked forth upon the host of the Egyptians through the pillar of fire and of cloud " (Exod. xiv. 19, 24).

The most vivid personifications, it will be observed, come from the poetic books :—

" By the Word of Jehovah were the heavens made ;
And all the host of them by the Breath* of his mouth."
(*Ps.* xxxiii. 6).

" They cry unto Jehovah in their trouble,
And he saves them out of their distresses.
He sends his Word, and heals them,
And delivers them from their destructions " (*Ps.* cvii. 19, 20).

" He sendeth forth his commandment on the earth ;
His Word runneth very swiftly " (*Ps.* cxlvii. 15).

"Jehovah possessed [or, formed] me [Wisdom] in [or, as] the beginning of his way,
Before [or, the first of] his works of old.
From eternity I was formed,
From the beginning before the earth was.
  * * * * * *
" When he appointed the foundations of the earth ;
Then I was by him, a master workman [making harmony, LXX.]"
(*Prov.* viii. 22, 23, 30).

" All wisdom cometh from the Lord,
And is with him for ever.
  * * * * * *
" There is one wise and greatly to be feared seated upon his throne :
The Lord himself created her and saw and reckoned her through,
And poured her out upon all his works.
She is with all flesh according to his gift,
And he bestowed her upon them that love him."
(*Wisdom of Jesus, son of Sirach*, i. 1, 8-10).

As in the instances cited from the Hebrew scriptures, the minister, messenger, or angel of God is not sharply differentiated

---

* The holy breath, holy gust, holy spirit,—the word is the same.

from God himself, so also we find a somewhat double use of the word Logos in Philo. In translating "Logos" by "Word," it has to be said that "Word" is a very inadequate rendering of a term of which no perfect representative in our language has yet been found. Logos is thought, or the expression of thought; it is wisdom's energy; if we look upon intelligence as secret, remote, and wonderful, the Logos, as found in Philo, is the manifestation of that intelligence. It is God's power brought near and palpable to us, whether we call that power that we feel so near us the mighty virgin Wisdom, or the secondary god, Logos; or it represents God's dutiful ministers in any shape, who, bearing his mission and speaking or doing nothing of their own, are to those to whom they appeal true manifestations of Divinity.

"The man who follows God does of necessity enjoy, as the companions of his way, the Words (Logoi) which are his attendants, whom we are wont to call angels" (Migr. Abr. § 31).

"The angels—the Words (Logoi) of God" (Somn., § 23).

"It was impossible that aught mortal should be made in the close likeness of the Most High and Father of the Universe, but like the second God who is the Word (Logos) of the Father)" (Fragm., Euseb., viii. 13).

"Those who are unable to bear the sight of God regard his image, his messenger Word (Logos), as himself" (Somn., § 41).

"The images of the creative power and of the kingly power are the winged cherubim which are placed upon the ark. But the Divine Word (Logos) which is above these, comes not into visible appearance, for it is not like any of the things that come under the external perception, but is itself an image of God, the eldest of all the objects of internal perception, and the nearest, without any partition of severance, to the only truly existing God.... The Word is, as it were, the charioteer of the powers, and he who utters it is the rider who directs the charioteer how to proceed, looking toward the proper guidance of the universe" (De Prof., § 19).

An architect "first of all sketches in his own mind nearly all the parts of the city which is about to be completed—temples, gymnasia, town halls, markets, harbours, docks, lanes, constitution of the walls, foundations of houses, and of public and other edifices. Then having received in his own soul, as on a waxen tablet, the typical forms of each, he carries in mind the image of an intellectually apprehensible city, the shapes of which he stirs to and fro in his natural memory, and still further impressing within himself the seal of their character, like a good artificer, with his eyes fixed on the pattern, he begins to produce the city of wood and stone, making the corporeal substances a copy of each of the incorporeal ideas.

"Now, we must form an opinion something of the same kind respecting God, who when he purposed to create the mighty city, first conceived its typical forms, wherefrom he composed a universe intellectually apprehensible, and then completed the one visible to the external senses, using the first as a pattern.

"As therefore the city when first shadowed forth in the architect's art had no external place, but was impressed upon the soul of the craftsman, so in the same manner can the universe subsisting from ideas have no other local position than the Divine Word (Logos) which gave to these things their order" (De Mund. Opif., §§ 4, 5).

"Were any one to desire to use terms more undisguised, he would not describe the universe that is perceptible by the internal sense, as aught else but the Word (Logos) of God who is now producing universal order. . . . It is also plain that the archetypal seal itself, which we affirm to be the universe perceptible by the internal sense, must verily be the archetypal pattern, the ideal form of forms, the Word (Logos) of God" (De Mund. Opif., § 6).

"The invisible and inly apprehensible Divine Word, he calls the image of God. And the image of this image is that inly appreciable light, which has become the image of the Divine Word. . . . Verily it is a star above the heavens, the source of the stars that are externally apprehensible, and were one to call it the universal fount of light he would not very greatly err" (De Mund. Opif., § 8).

As the poetic halo gathers round the conception of the Word, epithets are employed which to any but the Oriental mind would apply only to a distinct individual :—

"After the manner of a flock of sheep, the earth and the water, the air and the fire, and all things therein, whether plants or animals, divine and mortal alike, the nature of heaven too, and the periods of the sun and moon, and the phases and harmonious courses of the other stars, are led by God as a shepherd and king, according to justice and law, for he sets immediately over them his own straightforward Word, his first-born son, whose it is to receive the charge of the sacred company, as the lieutenant of the great king. For it is somewhere [Exod. xxiii. 20] said : ' Behold, I am He, I will send my messenger before thy face, to keep thee in the road '" (De Agricult., § 12).

"The father who generated the universe gave to the archangelic and eldest Word a pre-eminent gift, to stand in the borders and separate that which came into being from the Creator. This very Word is not only a suppliant before the Incorruptible on behalf of the mortal, ever wasting under its doom, but an ambassador from the sovereign to the subject. And the Word rejoices in the gift, and pluming itself thereon tells the tale of it thus, 'And I stood in the midst between the Lord and you' (Num. xvi. 48), neither being uncreate as God, nor created like you, but midway between the poles, serving as a hostage to both sides: with him that planted, a pledge that the whole race would never disappear and revolt entirely, choosing disorder instead of order; by the side of that which was planted, as a good hope that the God of Mercy would not ever be unregardful of his own work" (Quis Rer. Div. Her., § 42).

"The image of God is the Word, by which all the world was fabricated" (De Monarch., § 5).

[The verb here is that which gave rise to the term Demiurge.]

"The shadow of God is his Word, which he employed like an instrument in making the Kosmos. And this shadow and, as it were, copy, is the archetype of the rest" (Legis Allegor., iii. § 31).

The allegory of manna: "You see the food of the soul of what nature it is; the continuing Word of the Lord, like unto dew, encompassing the whole soul in a circle, and suffering no single portion of it to be without its share" (Legis Allegor., iii. 59).

"God sharpened his own Word, the divider of all things, and distributes the formless and unqualified essence of the universe" (Quis Rer. Div. Her., § 27).

"If there is anything anywhere that is consolidated, by the Divine Word is it bound together. For this is glue and a chain, and it has filled up the universe with its essence" (Quis Rer. Div. Her., § 38).

The following gives Philo's own explanation of the relation between Deity and that emanation or energy which, though spoken of as a son, is not begotten but proceeding:—

"He who anchors on the hope of divine alliance ought not to crouch or cover, when moreover he hears the voice, 'I am the God that was seen by thee in the place of God' [Gen. xxxi. 13, Septuagint]. It is at least an all-beautiful glory to the soul, for God to deem it worthy to manifest himself and hold converse with it. Do not slur over what is said, but carefully examine, whether in reality there are two Gods, for it is said, 'I am the God that was seen by thee' not in my place, but 'in the place of God,' as if of a different being. What, then, must one say? God in very truth is One; while there are many so-called by misapplication of the term. Wherefore the sacred word [that of Moses] in the present instance has indicated by the article the very God, the expression being, 'I am the God,' whilst there is indicated by the absence of the article the God so called by misuse of the term, where it says 'that was seen by thee in the place' not of the God, but merely 'of God.' What Moses here calls God is His eldest Word, for he is not superstitious about the position of the names, but sets before him one end only, that of making progress with his discourse. For in other things, when he examines whether there be any name of the One that Is, he manifestly knew that whatever any one may call him, he will employ in such application no adequate phrase; for the Living God is not of a nature to be described, but only to Be.

* * * * * *

"To the souls incorporeal, his ministers, there is a likelihood for him to manifest himself as he is, conversing with them as a friend with friends: but to those still in the body he must appear in the likeness of angels, not by change of his own nature, but by implanting in the recipients the presentment or idea of his having a separate form, so that they assume that the image is not an imitation, but the very archetypal form itself.

"The scripture has spoken of God under the likeness of a man.... For the writers knew that some men are so utterly dull by nature, as to be unable to form any conception whatever of a God apart from a body.

* * * * * *

"In like manner as those who are unable to gaze upon the Sun himself, look upon his reflected radiance as a sun ... so likewise the image of God, his angel Word, is considered to be God himself" (De Somn., i. §§ 40, 41).

The following is an instance of the converse notion, to

which we have previously referred, that of a delegate rising by his office into a kind of godship :—

"We say that the arch-priest is not a man, but is a divine Word, being one that has no participation, not only in all intentional, but also in all involuntary misdeeds. For Moses says [Lev. xxi. 11] that he cannot be defiled either 'in respect of his father,' that is to say, the mind, or 'of his mother,' that is, the external sense ; because, I opine, he received incorruptible and wholly pure parents, God being his father, who also is the father of all, and Wisdom his mother, through whom the whole universe came into birth ; because, moreover, 'his head is anointed with oil' [Lev. xxi. 10, *seq.*], by which I mean that his ruling part is illumined with radiant light.

"Now the most ancient Word of the Living God is clothed with the Kosmos for raiment ; for it enshrouds itself in earth and water, and air and fire, and what proceeds therefrom. But the soul, viewed particularly, is clothed with the body, and the mind of the sage is clothed with virtues" (De Profug., § 20).

"God himself is called a place, from the fact of his encompassing the universe, but being encompassed himself by absolutely nothing, and from his being the refuge of all ; and moreover, since he is himself his own district, reaching to himself and being environed by himself alone. . . . Perhaps 'place' [Gen. xxviii. 11] is the equivocal expression for two things, one of which is the Divine Word, and the other the God that is before the Word" (De Somn., i. § 11).

"Wherefore, as if some other God were alluded to, it is said [Gen. i. 27], 'In the image of God I made man,' but not in the image of himself? Of perfect beauty and wisdom is the rendering of this oracle. For it was impossible that anything mortal could be brought into the likeness of the Most High and Father of the Universe, but it could only be made in the likeness of the second God, who is his Word. For it was fitting that the type of reason within the soul of man should receive its graving and stamp from the Divine Word, since the God before the Word is high above all of mere rational nature; and to him above the Word, since he subsists in the most excellent and as it were specially ordained semblance, there were no manner of right for a created being to be exactly likened" (Euseb. Fragm., Præp. Ev., vii. 13; Quæst. in Gen. ii., § 62, Armenian version).

"Even though there prove to be no one as yet sufficiently deserving to be called by the name of Son of God, let him nevertheless strive earnestly to be ascribed to his first-born Word, the eldest angel; nay, an archangel of many a name; for he is addressed as Archè [origin, beginning], as Name of God, as Word, as the Man according to the Image, as He that sees Israel. . . . For although we may not yet have become worthy of being reckoned the children of God, yet no doubt we may be sons of his eternal image, the most Sacred Word, for the eldest Word is the image of God" (De Confus. Ling., § 28).

The expression, "the Man according to the Image," is explained in the following; it means the archetypal, incorporeal man:—

"There is a vast difference between man as at present moulded, and man as originally brought into being after the image of God. For man as now formed is perceptible to external sense, partaking of qualities, subsisting of body and soul, man or woman, by nature mortal. But man made after the divine image is, as it were, an idea, or an element, or a seal, perceptible by mind, bodiless, neither male nor female, incorruptible by nature. . . . By the expression, 'God breathed into man's face the breath of life,' is meant nothing else than the Divine Spirit proceeding from that blessed and happy nature, being sent to take up its remote habitation here, for the benefit of our race, in order that, although man is mortal as regards his visible part, he may be immortal at least as regards that which is unseen" (De Mund. Opif., § 46).

"We shall at least be simply within right in affirming that the Artificer [Demiurge] who wrought the Universe is like for like with the Father of the thing produced ; while the Mother is the knowledge appertaining to the Creator, with whom God united, not as a man unites, and sowed the seed of genesis.

"And she received unto herself the seed of God, and when her throes came to accomplishment, she brought forth her only and well-beloved son, perceptible to the external senses, namely this very Kosmos.

"Wisdom, at all events, is introduced alongside of any one of those that form the divine company, speaking of herself after this manner:

"'Me did God get to himself as the first of the first among his own works,
And before the cycle of time my foundations he laid' [Prov. viii. 22]."
(De Ebriet., § 8.)

The expressions of endearment—"only son," "first-born," "well-beloved," used in reference to the Word or to the Kosmos, show how ready was the Oriental mind to affectionately personify an attribute of Deity, and to enshrine it in the language of fancy rather than the language of metaphysics. Concurrent with this tendency was the disposition to regard an angel or a mortal engaged unselfishly upon some divine work as a vicegerent of God, and within the limits of that office, as very God in manifestation. Even the generosity of a superior in rank is accounted as a subordinate godhood.

In the address of Joseph to his brethren, after their father's decease, Philo makes him say, "If all things which I did were done well and kindly for my father's sake, I will adhere to the same course now that he is dead. But in my judgment no good man is dead, but will indeed live for ever without waxing old, in an immortal nature which is no longer bound up in the body's necessities. And why should I remember only the father who was born ? We have the uncreate, the incorruptible, the eternal, who oversees all things and gives ear to all people even when they are silent, who always beholds the things which lie in the recesses of the mind, upon whom I call as a witness of my conscience that my reconciliation is sincere. For I (and marvel not at my words) am in the place of God (Gen. l. 19), who has changed your evil designs into an abundance of good things" (De Josepho, § 43).

In another chapter of the same book we find: "Be not cast down; I give you a complete amnesty for all the things which you have done to me. Do not deem that you need any one else as a paraclete" (De Josepho, § 40).

The higher the mission, the more distinct becomes this conception of intermediate Deity: "Angels are the servants of God, and are considered actual gods by those who are in toils and slaveries" (De Profugis., § 38).

We may call to mind in relation to this subject the reply to an allegation of blasphemy, ascribed to Jesus: "Is it not written in your law, *I said, Ye are gods?* If he called them gods, unto whom the Word of God came (and the scripture cannot be annulled), say ye of him whom the Father consecrated and sent into the world, Thou blasphemest; because I said, I am God's son" (John x. 34–36).

The paraclete, or advocate, is a familiar Hebrew conception. In the following we are reminded of the Zoroastrian idea of a man after death being met by his personified qualities:*—

"R. Liezer ben Jacob said, He who performs one precept has gotten to himself one paraclete, and he who commits one transgression has gotten to himself one accuser" (P. Aboth, iv. 15).

"If a man performs one precept, the Holy One, blessed is He, gives him one angel to guard him" (Shemoth Rabba, xxxii.).

---

* Cf. also, "Giving no pain to any creature, let him collect virtue by degrees, for the sake of acquiring a companion to the next world, as the white ant by degrees builds his nest. For, in his passage to the next world, neither his father, nor his mother, nor his wife, nor his son, nor his kinsman, will remain in his company: his virtues alone will adhere to him" (Inst. Menu, iv. 238).

Two conceptions, it is evident from the quotations we have made, were familiar to the Jewish mind in Philo's time. They are these:—

That the Divine power is unsearchable in its essence, but may be visible to man in the action of its energies, which are subordinate powers—a manifestation of Deity which is yet one with him: the Word, or Wisdom in activity, is the eldest son of God, and yet is God.

That an angel or a man who is so far removed from self that he can be inspired with the mission and work of God, is to the extent of that delegation to be regarded as God himself. The Word of God has filled him, and he is therefore one with the Word, as the Word is one with God.

These conceptions probably at first went no further than the philosophic mind, and there remained fluid, a fleeting mirror of the mystery of truth.

It is the ignorant and plebeian mind, the mind without background, the vision without intuition, which demands the solidification of suggestive thought into hard, concrete, and contracted dogma. For fear the ethereal vision should be blown away, it must be pegged down. To the inspired soul, on the contrary, such a course is worse than unnecessary; it is to drag down into contact with the soil a wing which would otherwise help the soul to rise toward heaven. So to act is to be confessedly without the belief that if supernal visions should become dimmed, the source from which they spring remains; it is to be outside the instinctive faith of the truly spiritual mind, that any clouds that hide the light are but for a moment, and from below, and that the light shines on for ever from above. A person who really believes in the fact of heaven does not fret himself over doctrines of heaven.

Is there any evidence, it may be asked, beyond an inference sought to be drawn from the gospel writings, that these two philosophical conceptions, that of the subordinate manifestation of Deity, and that of the divinized status of a missionary man, ever converged into one?

In the writings of Clement of Alexandria, we find the Philonic conception of the Word in actual combination with the apotheosis of a man who foremost among men reached to a knowledge of God. The old phraseology is found adapted to either conception, and both become one. In the following passages we may see the actual step being taken from philosophy to doctrine, through the medium of an essentially poetical faculty of sight, and the introduction of the notion of a special providence:—

"A beautiful breathing instrument of music the Lord made man, after his own image. And he himself also, surely, who is the supramundane Wisdom, the celestial Word, is the all-harmonious, melodious, holy instrument of God" (Clem. Alex., Exhort. i.).

"The Word of God became man, to educe from man the lesson how man may become God" (Clem. Alex., Exhort. i.).

"Our Instructor is like his Father God, whose son he is. ... God in the form of man, stainless, the minister of his Father's will, the Word who is God, who is in the Father, who is at the Father's right hand" (Paid., i. 2).

"Formerly ... the Word was an angel; but to the fresh and new people has been given a new covenant, and the Word has appeared, and that mystic angel is born—Jesus" (Paid., i. 7).

"We, too, are first-born sons, who are reared by God, who are the genuine friends of the First-born, who first of all other men attained to the knowledge of God" (Exhort. ix.).

The novel notion of a special providence, as distinguished from the constant and universal beneficence of God, is very marked in the *apologia* for the doctrine of the Word made flesh, to which are devoted the first chapters of the Epistle to the Hebrews, beginning, "God, having in many portions and many ways spoken of old unto the fathers in the prophets, at the end of these days spoke to us in a Son, whom he appointed inheritor of all things, through whom also he made the aeons; who being an effulgence of his glory, and an impress of his substance, and bearing all things by the expression of his power, having made a purification of sins, sat down on the right hand of the Majesty on high."

The very term here translated "impress," the stamp from a seal, is one by which Philo defines the relation of the Eternal Word to the great Cause.

We may now turn again to the philosophic conception of the Word, as we have seen it in Philo, and to its adoption, extension, and application in a new and personal sense in the Fourth Gospel:—

"In the beginning (Archè, firstness) was the Word, and the Word was with (close to) God, and the Word was God" (John i. 1).

In Philo we find: "The Divine Word . . . the closest to God without any distance interposed" (De Prof., § 19).

There is a curious bit of the subtlety which is so marked a Rabbinical quality, to be noted in this connection of the Word and the Archè. Every jot and tittle of their ancient scripture was wont to be overfilled by the Rabbis with a meaning often not its own. The World is described as created by Sayings, because in Genesis the preface to each creative act is the expression "God said," as in "God said, Let there be light." One act of creation, however, is described as "*In the Beginning* God created the heavens and the earth." In another place (Ps. xxxiii. 6) is to be found the verse, "*By the Word* of the Eternal were heavens made." To the Rabbinical mind, therefore, the Beginning and the Word appeared to be necessarily very closely connected, and to be as two aspects of one personification. We find Wisdom introduced (Prov. viii. 22) as saying, "The Eternal possessed me in the beginning of his way, before his works of old. I was anointed from everlasting, from the beginning, before ever the earth was;" and in a

Talmudic commentary upon Genesis this speech is put in the mouth of wisdom, "By me, who am Archè, God created heavens and the earth" (Jalqut, 2). The composer of the Fourth Gospel, in associating the Archè and the Word, is thus at one with the Talmudists as well as influenced by Philo.

The notion of a more or less concrete personification of the Word may be said to pervade the early Hebrew scriptures —"There came unto me the Word of the Lord, saying," is the common preface of the prophet's utterance. "The spirit of Jehovah" is a corresponding expression, and yet carries with it the notion of some individuality of character in the messenger. For instance, where (1 Kings xxii. 24) a false influence has corrupted the speech of certain prophets, one of these taunts another who has spoken differently, "Which way went the spirit of Jehovah from me to speak unto thee?" Or, according to the Septuagint, "What sort of a spirit of the Lord is that which has spoken in thee?" The spirit or Word here is represented as an individual, and, like the Satan of Job, or adversary-angel, a servant of God.

But that the powers of God, when viewed as separate, were yet not always regarded as persons, may be judged from such phrases as, in the later writings, "Thy Almighty Hand, which made the universe of formless matter," when compared with "Thy Almighty Word leaped out of thy royal throne," and, "O God, who madest the all by thy Word, and ordainedest man by thy Wisdom," which are to be found in the same book (Wisdom ix. 1; xi. 17; xviii. 15).

Through the Word, according to Philo, the entire universe was fashioned. "You will find that God is the cause of the universe, from whom it sprang; . . . the Word of God is the instrument, through which it was fashioned" (De Cherub., § 35).

According to John, "all things came into being through him [the Word], and no single thing that has come into being came into being without him."

Philo writes: "The unseen and spiritually apprehensible [or ideal] Divine Word Moses speaks of as the Image of God. And he speaks of the ideal Light as being itself the image of this image, inasmuch as it has come into being as the image of the Divine Word which gave the utterance to its genesis [spoke it into birth: 'Let there be Light, and there was Light']. The pure and unmingled Light is, however, dimmed in its transmission from the ideal world to that which is discerned by our senses, for no object of sense is ever wholly pure" (De Creat. Mund., § 8).

John says that in the Word is "Life, and the Life was the Light of men;" it "shines in the darkness, and the darkness took no hold on it."

The spiritual Light, according to Philo, is the efflux of the Divine Word which gives it its being. But these different relations are not to be too literally regarded; it would be mere confusion to attempt to define minutely either the Word, which is Wisdom, or the Light which is "not the phenomenal sun, but the most brilliant and glorious Light of the unseen and mighty God. When this light irradiates the mind, the secondary rays of words [or angels] set" (De Somn., i. § 13). The Light, or the Word, according to John, confers a childship of God, a divine birth derived neither from blood, as ordinary relationship, nor from any will originating in the flesh, or in what is merely human. According to Philo (Quæst. in Gen., i. 4) the spiritual part of man is what becomes the image of the Word which gives the Light.

So far there is a very close accord between Philo the expositor and John the theologian. The latter then diverges. The philosophic conception of the Word, the irradiating Light which shines in many a way from God to the spirit of man, he converts to a special purpose. The change is very slight, but has had a momentous result. Jesus embodies the Word;—Jesus is the Word embodied. Jesus is all unself, is all God;—Jesus is God. The flesh is the nidus of the

Divine outpouring;—the Word is made flesh. The Word is made flesh in man; the Word is made flesh in one man. The difference is scarcely perceptible, yet immense. On the one hand, general philosophy; on the other, special doctrine.

This mighty bridge, of a hair's-breadth, being once regarded as spanned over, the philosophic attributes of the Word are reverted to. Philo says of the Word, the first-born son, "No mortal thing could have been formed after the similitude of the supreme Father of the Universe, but only after the pattern of the second Deity, who is the Word of the supreme Being (Quæst. and Sol. in Gen., ii. § 62, and Frag. Euseb., P. E., vii. 13). "Who would stand to a positive affirmation about the essence of God? ... We must be content if we can be able to have knowledge of his name, to wit, of the interpreter, the Word. For this is what must be God to us, imperfect as we are" (Legis Allegor., iii. § 73). John says, "God none hath ever seen; the only-born son that is in the bosom of the Father, he made him plain." With Philo, the son of God acting as paraclete for man with the Father of the universe, and for an amnesty for sins, is the very universe itself (Vit. Mos., iii. § 14); or a high priest, or the Word, may equally be regarded as a paraclete: with John, "If any man sin, we have a paraclete with the Father, righteous Jesus Christ" (1 John ii. 1).

The noblest use ever made of this term "paraclete," which was so evidently a familiar word with Hebrew scholars, is to be found in the Fourth Gospel:—

"I will ask the Father, and he will give you another advocate (paraclete) to be with you for evermore,—the spirit of truth, which the world is unable to receive, for it neither sees nor knows it, but ye know it: for with you it remains, and in you it exists" (John xiv. 16–17; text of Westcott and Hort).

The helper here is one that goes far beyond the bounds of any sectarian religion. A man simply bent on truth—

scientific, naturalistic, or mystic—is both fearless and free. "Ye shall know the truth, and the truth shall make you free. . . . If the son [and not licence, which is no son but a slave] shall make you free, ye will be free indeed" (John viii. 32, 36). Compare the Talmud: "You shall go with man—you, mine own Seal, Truth; but you shall also remain a denizen of heaven—between heaven and earth an everlasting link."

This may be described as an imperfectly explored region of Christianity; and it may be commended to the attention of those who wish to see the old Church brought into harmony once more with the religious spirit. There yet remains in the words of Jesus life enough to explode the idol that has taken his place.

As, with Philo, the Word is the nourishment of souls, the God of the imperfect; so, with Clement of Alexandria, Jesus is the "perennial Word," the "eternal Light," and similarly acts as the divine helper of the lowly, represented under a poetic metaphor as the "wing of unwandering birds."

The main injury done by this convergence of the two grand conceptions, is that when the result of the combination had been made a doctrine, it contracted the noble images of the infinite divine activity in its relation to man, by excluding all but one express manifestation. The defined special providence tends to obscure the constant, which if truly infinite is then indeed infinitely special. The figurative representation of an eternal process of divine energy, when converted into the dogmatic statement of a single occurrence, may have gained by concentration, in its power to appeal to the unthinking; but the acceptance of such a creed as a finality has been a stumbling-block in the way of the exploring mind bent on the "divine philosophy," which is—

> "Not harsh and crabbèd, as dull fools suppose,
> But musical as is Apollo's lute."

If the doctrines which sprang into prominence after the death of Jesus were conversions of older philosophical images, it may naturally be expected that the field of comparison through which we have passed will afford further likenesses.

The following is an allegorized reminiscence of a Mosaic story, and contains a symbol which was afterwards turned to a Christian use:—

"God sends forth upon it the stream from his own sheer Rock of Wisdom, and gives the converted soul to drink of unchangeable health . . . the souls that love God, when they have drunk, are filled also with the most universal manna" (Legis Allegor., ii. § 21).

The same Mosaic story, in the same allegoric manner of Philo, is made available as the type of another conception than that of the Word or Wisdom—the Christ; a heightened and spiritualized modification of the older notion of Christs or Messiahs, the anointed ones who were the supreme officials of the early Jewish theocracy, the king and the priest.

The two conceptions, that of the personified Word, and that arising from the spiritualization of the office of the Christ, or anointed one, were both adopted by degrees and blended into one, as a poetic, a reverential, and afterwards a doctrinal aureole for the head of Jesus.

"Our fathers . . . did all eat the same spiritual food, and did all drink the same spiritual drink; for they continued to drink out of a spiritual attendant Rock, and the Rock was Christ" (1 Cor. x. 1–4).

A further comparison may be made of the imagery of spiritual food. In Philo we find:—

The Divine Word, from which flow all teachings and wisdoms that never fail. This is the heavenly food . . . "*Behold, I rain upon you bread from heaven*" (Exod. xvi. 4). In very truth it is God who showers down from above ethereal wisdom upon well-disposed and exploring minds" (De Prof., § 25).

"The most high Divine Word, which is Wisdom's fount

... if one draw from the stream he finds instead of death life eternal (De Prof., § 18).

The corresponding symbolism of bread of immortal wisdom and water of eternal life is to be found in the passages that follow:—

"Labour not to earn the food which perishes, but rather the food which abides unto life eternal, which food the Son of Man gives unto you, for on him the Father God did seal approval. . . . They said . . . Our fathers did eat the manna in the wilderness, even as it is written, *He gave them bread from heaven to eat.* Jesus therefore said unto them, Verily verily, I say unto you, it is not Moses that has given you the bread out of the heaven, but the true bread out of the heaven it is my Father that gives you. For the bread of God is the bread that descends out of the heaven and gives life to the world. . . . Your fathers ate manna in the wilderness and did die; the bread which descends out of the heaven is this, that one may eat of it and not die" (John vi. 27–33, 49, 50).

"I know that his [God's] commandment is life eternal" (John xii. 50).

"Every one that drinks of this water [of the well] will thirst again: but whosoever drinks of the water that I will give him will never thirst; but the water that I will give him will become in him a well of water springing up into life eternal" (John iv. 13, 14).

There is some obscurity in early Christian compositions owing to a peculiar use of the expression *aeon*, which is variously translated "age," "time," "world," "ever."

"The ages (aeons) which are to come" (Eph. ii. 7).

"In this time (season) . . . in the time (aeon) that is to come" (Mark x. 30).

"Worthy to obtain that world (aeon), and the upstanding from the dead" (Luke xx. 35).

"For ever (for the aeons)" (Matt. vi. 13).

"For ever (for the aeon)" (John xii. 34).

The clue to what the Pharisaic Rabbi understood by the word, which in Greek is represented by *aiōn*, and in Hebrew has the root-signification " to hide," we may find in Philo :—

Aeon is an expression descriptive of life of the universe of spiritual perception, as Time of the life of the universe of external sensation " (De Mut. Nom., § 47).

A quotation from the Talmud will exemplify this use of the term : " Morning sleep and mid-day wine, and the babbling of youths, and frequenting the meeting-houses of the vulgar, put a man out of the aeon " (Pirq. Aboth, iii. 16). On the other hand, " He that increases Thora [the Divine Law as identified with Wisdom] increases life. . . . He who has gotten to himself words of Thorah, has gotten to himself the life of the world to come " (Pirq. Aboth, ii. 8). A corroboration of this teaching, and of the meaning of the aeon, is to be obtained from the following : " Search the scriptures, for ye deem that in them ye have aeonian life " (John v. 39).

The aeon thus has nothing to do with the measures of the movements of our terrestrial spheres ; it is a part of the endless flow of eternity, and therefore comes to be understood as representing the state described as " the world to come." The epithet " aeonian," so commonly rendered "everlasting," should never be understood as in relation to duration ; when applied to life it means life of the aeon, spiritual, or eternal life.

By an extension of the spiritual sense of the term " aeon," it became used by the gnostics to signify celestial beings.

Another similar expression used in the same expansive way in reference to the spiritual condition, is " the day of the Lord," " the great day," " the day of judgment." With a similar meaning the Talmudic Rabbis spoke of " the aeon of selection."

It is possible that such an entrance into the interior state —a fleeting vision to the incarnate—is signified by the expression of the Apocalypse (i. 10). " In spirit I came to be in the sovereign day." This rendering is only suggested as a possible one. That such expressions as "aeon" or "day" are inadequate to represent, and only dimly denote, the kind of life that is beyond the limits of terrestrial time, is confessed in the words, "One day with the Lord is as a thousand years, and a thousand years as one day" (2 Pet. iii. 8).

Before continuing the study of Philo's attitude towards the universal problems of philosophy, we may ask the question, What is he—gnostic, mystic, ascetic, or transcendentalist? He is not an extreme ascetic, he is conscious of the beauty of the body, as a part of nature; but he sees in it a dead and soulless thing, if viewed by itself, but assured of a high destiny if ruled and governed by the sovereign principle. There is in the soul, or vital part, an irrational element, the faculties which appeal and do not reason. So far, then, the soulic part ought not to be called dead if taken by itself, but this very life is a kind of life that is but temporary, and may almost be called death. Philo is a mystic, but sane, and not given to superstition. He is a gnostic, but a spiritual gnostic, that is, he keeps close to such realities as are made known to the spiritual instinct or inspiration; he is not a gnostic whose theories have become over-intellectualized, and who has spun out the plain and wholesome spiritual food into the gossamer threads of excited fancy. At first study he may be thought to be as deeply lost in fancy's maze as any theosophical speculator, but this effect upon the practical mind is due, not to gnostic extravagance, but to the Rabbinical methods which he follows. He says, "Great things are often made known by an outline of smaller things" (De Abrah., § 15); a fact which is true enough. But the Rabbinical snare into which he falls is the attempt to make great things reveal themselves by an outline of smaller things which have no original connection with them, but with something else. His peculiarity is that his thoughts are sane, even though apparently evolved by an insane method. This method, at once supersubtle and puerile, he owes to the fashion of his race, and to the fact of the very letter of the Jewish scriptures being held in such reverence that all philosophy had to be drawn through it, and none could meet with attention that professed independence of the canonical law.

Philo is thus not an absolutely independent thinker, his thought being necessarily coloured to some extent by the medium in which he works. His endeavour is to "combine the philosophy of Plato with the sanctions of Hebrew religion;" * but the philosophic expansion with which in that process he can endow the narrowest and most apparently matter-of-fact sentence of the ancient Hebrew record is something to wonder at.

The personification of the various properties that make up the complex nature of man forms a not uninstructive parabolic study. And Philo is not alone in the cultivation of such a poetico-philosophical pursuit. If we turn to Buddhism, we stumble upon the injunction (absurd unless it be a symbolic paradox) to the devout disciple to murder his father and mother, and destroy a kingdom with all its subjects. In the gospel parables we find much that is unedifying, unless understood of the constituents of human nature, when it at once becomes full of suggestiveness. These, however, it is easy to accept as made for fable, not told for fact. In Philo, on the other hand, the almost ludicrous peculiarity is that the mysterious symbols are found so parasitically entwined with the records of time-honoured historical characters, that sober chronicle and occult myth seem to have become one.

We are accustomed to regard Abraham as a patriarchal sheikh who more than held his own in a rude age against the petty chieftains of his neighbourhood. The accounts of such exploits it is much easier to regard as legendary and semi-historical than as a deliberate weft of symbol. But in Abraham Philo sees a type of spiritual conquest only:—

"Abraham, after the destruction of the nine kings, that is

---

* Charles Gipps Prowett, "Philo the Jew," *Fraser's Magazine*, Aug., 1874.

of the four passions and the five powers of the outward senses" (De Ebriet., § 27).

In a similar manner, Pharaoh himself ceases to be an earthly sovereign, and becomes a quality of soul :—

"The king of Egypt, the arrogant mind 'with the six hundred chariots,' that is to say, with the six harmonically arranged movements of the organic body, and 'with the chief men set upon them.'. . . 'The horse and his rider he had thrown into the sea, because after he had done away with the particular mind which rides away upon the irrational impulses of that four-footed and restive animal, passion, he was becoming an ally and champion of the sight-endowed soul'" (De Ebriet., § 29).

The significations here brought out in so singular a manner are strangely akin to the Buddhist doctrines as to "the five aggregates" of sensual feeling, "the three poisons" of covetousness, anger, delusion, "the five obscurities" of envy, passion, sloth, vacillation, unbelief; and the like numerical modes of classifying qualities.

In Philo's view, the manifestation of man is in harmony with that of the divine powers, the epiphanies of the unsearchable God; the ideal existence comes first, thence follows the more external : " After producing the type of the generic man, in whom they say the male and female sex are contained, God at length works out the species, the Adam" (Legis Allegor., ii. § 4).

This may remind us of the traditionary saying of Jesus, in answer to the question when the Kingdom of Heaven should come, that it would be "when the two had become one, and when the male and the female were neither male nor female," that is, when the angelic state, the ideal type and perfection, had been attained or regained.

But while he regards the corporeal faculties as occupying a comparatively lowly place, Philo is sufficiently rational not to despise them, seeing that they belong to a divine scheme of use. Man is placed by God in Nature in order to learn from it; a sense of Art, Music, Taste, forms part of his endowment :—

"Having settled his reasoning faculty as king in the sovereign part of him, he bestowed upon him as a suite of body-guards the capacities for the apprehension of colours and sounds, flavours and odours, and the like, which in the absence of external sense man would have been unable to get hold of by his own unaided power" (De Mund. Opif., § 48).

As we all know, these sturdy body-guards, the senses, are not seldom found so assuming that the king himself is almost obliterated. Many a cry has gone up from the struggling inner heart of man, that its birthright and supremacy are being done away; the world presses too closely upon it. The following expressions of the soul's cry, both of dismay and of triumph, may be compared :—

"The corruptible body makes the soul heavy laden, and the earthly tabernacle weigheth down the much-musing mind" (Wisdom ix. 15).

"Come unto me, all ye that are labouring wearily and burdened, and I will give you rest. . . . My yoke is easy and my burden is light" (Matt. xi. 28, 30).

"In this [earthly] tabernacle we groan, being burdened" (2 Cor. v. 4).

Philo speaks explicitly, as is his wont, on this subject :—

"They toil to earn and make a system of the things dear to the flesh, with all speed making their own that composite earthy mass, that statue of plasm, that quasi-house of the soul, which—from birth until death so great a burden—it lays not down, but carries like a corpse" (De Agric., § 5).

"The little housings in the nether world are what bring bondage and disaster and fell humiliation upon the soul. For in very truth the passions of the body are spurious and foreign to the mind, being produced of the flesh, wherein they have firm root" (Quis Rer. Div. Her., § 54).

We are strongly reminded here of the Buddhist view, and of the apostrophe to the lust of the flesh and the pride of life as the responsible authors of corporeal existence: "O maker, thou hast been discerned; thou shalt not build up this tabernacle again."

Perhaps Philo goes too far in saying that bodily passions have their absolute origin in the flesh, which rather may be said to give desires their expression. We may correct the thought by the deeper truth that although in external life they take their form, it is "from within, out of the heart of man" that they take their rise.

The following, from Philo, is in close accord with the myth of creation as given in Genesis, but it falls short of giving the whole secret of incarnation. The irrational part is but too truly an integral part of us:—

"It is owing to bodily pleasure that men exchange the immortal and fortunate existence for that which is mortal and ill-starred" (De Mund. Opif. § 53).

"The part of our soul as distinct from the sovereign principle is divided sevenfold, into five senses and the vocal organ, and besides all, the productive faculty" (De Mund. Opif., § 40).

We are reminded, by the allusion to Genesis, how orthodox an adherent, according to the Pharisaic interpretation, was Philo to the Mosaic scriptures:—

"In five ways at first the serpent winds itself round insinuatingly. For truly there are pleasures that consist in sight, and in hearing, and in taste, and in smell, and in touch. But the most vehement and intense are those of intercourse with women" (Legis Allegor., ii. § 18).

In the following passage it is doubtful whether Philo does or does not take a broader view and show a belief that body is not the culprit upon whom alone all responsibility must be thrown:—

"Death is of two kinds, the one being the death of a man,

the other the peculiar death of a soul. The death of a man is soul's severance from body, but the death of soul consists in the destruction of virtue, combined with adoption of vice. When Moses speaks not merely of dying, but of dying the death, he is not denoting common death, but that peculiar and especial death which appertains to a soul entombed in passions and all kinds of vice. . . . Well did Herakleitos in this respect follow the doctrine of Moses, when he says, ' We live their death, we have died their life.' For now, when we are alive, it is with the soul dead and entombed in the body as it were in a grave-mound ; but were we to die, it would be with the soul living its own life, and released from the evil and dead body wherewith it is bound" (Legis Allegor., i. § 33).

If the soul going downwards finds death, striving upwards it finds life :—

"The mind is vivified by God, and the irrational part of the soul by the mind ; for the mind is as it were a God to the irrational part of the soul" (Legis Allegor., i. § 13). This is a corresponding procession of life to that which is affirmed of the universe of nature as uttered into life by the Word, and the Word by God. These are abstract thoughts, and to most minds it is more congenial to think only of the concrete and the personal. The irrational mass of humanity is vivified by the catholic and apostolic few. These few, or the one who is pre-eminent, are regarded in fear or in love as the Light that proceeds from God. In course of time the apostle becomes canonized, and humanity, instead of looking upwards to the radiant source from which all scattered lights proceed, worships at the feet of an image, the original of which perchance was treated with despite.

Plato never uses the word angel to convey his notion of daimonic existences ; the Hebrew prophets of the olden time do not speak of souls as disembodied individuals ; Philo is a connecting line between Greek and Hebrew. As he expresses it, "If you regard Souls and Daimons and Angels as differing indeed in name, but as one and the same thing in reality, you will remove from yourself that most oppressive burden, superstition. For as men in general speak of good and evil daimons, and in like manner of good and evil souls, so also it is with regard to angels, as being some of them worthy of a good appellation, as ambassadors from men to God, and from God to men, inviolable and holy on account of this blameless and all-comely ministry; while as to others, again, you will not err if you take them to be unholy and unworthy of the appellation" (De Gigant., § 4).

The following commentary upon Jacob's dream conveys these ideas of Philo's more fully, and also evidences a considerable indebtedness to Plato :—

"'And he dreamed a dream; and behold a ladder was planted solidly upon the earth, the head whereof reached unto the heaven, and the angels of God ascended and descended upon it' (Gen. xxviii. 12). Admirably does Moses by the figure of a ladder planted solidly on the earth present an image of the air.... The air is the abode of incorporeal souls, inasmuch as it seemed good to the Creator to fill all parts of the world with living creatures.... Were it not absurd that that element whereby others have been endowed with soul should itself be destitute of souls?

"Of these souls, some descend to be bound up in mortal bodies, such, namely, as are most near the earth and most fond of body. Others soar upwards, being again distinguished according to definitions and times which have been marked out by nature. Of these souls, some yearn for the association and habits of mortal life, and go back again to it; others charge it with much trifling folly, and pronounce the body to be a prison house and grave-mound; and flying from it as from a gaol or a tomb, have raised themselves up aloft on light wings to the ether, and for their aeon engage themselves on sublime things.

"There are others, again, the most pure and excellent, who have succeeded to greater and diviner minds, not ever reaching out at all for any of the things of earth, but being viceroys of the All-sovereign, as it were eyes and ears of a great king, having all things in their view and hearing. Philosophers in general call these daimons, but the sacred word is wont to call them angels, using a name more naturally suitable. For indeed they are angels who convey the injunctions of the father to the children, and the needs of the children to the father. . . . It is the lot of us, subjects of fate, to use words as mediators and intercessors. . . . The ladder was something of this sort; but if we examine the soul which is in men, we shall find that its foundation (the corporeal nature), corresponding to the earth part, is external sensation, while its head, corresponding to the heavenly part, is the purest mind" (De Somn., i. §§ 22, 23).

The following fine and picturesque passage is essentially Platonic: "Those beings whom other philosophers call daimons Moses usually calls angels; they are souls that take flight by air. . . . However incapable our sight may be of receiving the images of the impression made by souls, it does not follow that souls do not exist in air: but in order that like should be contemplated by like, it is essential that they should be apprehended by mind.

"Some among souls descended into bodies, while others have not deigned ever to adapt themselves to any of the quarters of the earth. These, once hallowed and compassed by the Father's care, the Demiurge is wont to employ as helpers and ministrants for the charge of mortals. But the others, descending into body as into a river, at one time are carried away and swallowed up by the sweep of a most violent whirlpool, while at another they strive with all their power to resist the current, and at first manage to float up, and afterwards thither to fly off again, whence they started.

"These are souls of those that somehow drew from above

a love of wisdom, and from the beginning to the end took diligent care to die to the corporeal life, in order that they might get in exchange the incorporeal and incorruptible life, in the presence of the Uncreate and Incorruptible. But those which are swallowed up are the souls of such other men as disregarded wisdom, giving themselves up to unstable and chancy affairs, not one of which bears reference to the mightiest part of what is in us, soul or mind, but all to our corpse yoke-fellow, the body, or to things even more soulless than that, I mean popularity and money, and offices and rewards, and all such other things as by those who have not fixed their eyes on what is beautiful in real truth, are plastered up and painted into life by the cheat of false opinion" (De Gigant., § 3).

Platonic though this may be, it is quite in accord with the spirit which dictated the utter subjection of the body, and even a reluctance to escape the supreme trial of martyrdom, with a view of so obtaining "a better resurrection." A truth, enthusiastically extended, was and is the spring of all fanatical readiness for martyrdom,—the truth that, in spite of appearances which make for the contrary, the soul is really the important part, the only part worth saving. Philo gives a complete code of ethics in the following pregnant passage: "The body in the absence of the soul, the soul in the absence of reason, reason in lack of virtue, is by nature bound to perish" (Quod Det. Potiori Insid., § 39).

The body, in other words, is secondary to the soul, soul-saving is a delusion without reason, and reason is only kept wholesome and true by conduct.

The following passage continues the subject, and is one of Philo's wonderful extractions of a metaphysical meaning out of the letter of his national scripture :—

"'Who slays Cain shall suffer sevenfold.' ... The irrational part of the soul is divided into seven parts—sight, smell, hearing, taste, touch, speech, generation. If, therefore, one were to do away with the eighth, which is mind, that is to say, Cain the ruler of them, he would paralyze the seven also; for while by the stout strength of the mind, all are made strong, by its weakness they are made to suffer in sympathy, and by its decay, if brought on wholly by vice, they become slackened and dissolved altogether" (Quod Det. Potiori Insid., § 46).

Whether, or not, there be in the letter of the ancient Hebrew scriptures any hidden original root of parable, Philo finds no difficulty in planting one there. Again and again we find him, in reference to a passage that seems to contain nothing beyond its *primâ facie* meaning, urging that for the explanation, "We must have recourse to allegory, which is dear to visionary men [men of sight or of insight], for truly the sacred oracles do most manifestly offer us inducements to the pursuit of it" (De Plantat., § 9.).

Or again: "The literal statement here is plainly fabulous" (Legis Allegor., ii. § 7).

In a number of passages Philo endeavours to do away with imperfect anthropomorphic conceptions of Deity, which no doubt to some extent were due to expressions in the older sacred books of his race. The following, for instance, very considerably enlarges the idea of creation, which is so often represented as a series of disjointed or intermittent acts :—

"God never ceases at all from creation, but just as it is the property of fire to burn, and of snow to chill, so it is of God to be creating. . . . He makes things to rest which appear to be creative, but are not really endowed with energy; but he himself never ceases from creative action" (Legis Allegor., i. § 3).

"Thou shalt take away, O soul, everything created, mortal, changeable, profane, from thy conception respecting God the uncreate and incorruptible, and immovable, and holy, and only blessed" (De Sacrif. Ab. et Caini, § 30).

The following is a splendid passage from first to last, and

will help to show why men are to be found who will painfully thread their way through the uneven paths of error and turmoil, in the consciousness that there is indeed a promised land, one brief glimpse of which through the mountain mists will be unspeakable reward :—

"Neither is God a being of the form of man, nor is the human body of the form of God; but the resemblance is spoken of with reference to the mind which is the sovereign of the soul. For the mind, which is in each of those who are in part, was made after the likeness and in relation to that one mind of the universe, its archetype, being in some sort the god of that body which bears it and holds its image. Whatever rank the great Sovereign holds in the whole universe, such, it seems, holds the human mind in man. . . . Led on by love, which is the guide of wisdom, it surmounts all the existence that is perceptible by the senses, and then longs after that which is perceptible by the inner mind. And beholding therein, and of surpassing beauty, the patterns and the ideas of the things perceptible by the senses which it saw here, it becomes possessed with a sober intoxication, like those in the Corybantian fervour are seized with ecstasy, and becomes filled with a desire of a different order, a more excellent longing, by which it is conducted to the topmost arch of things inly apprehensible, and appears to be reaching the great King himself. And while it strives with eager desire to behold him, pure and unmingled rays of divine light are poured forth like a torrent, so as to bring a dizzy bewilderment upon the eye of the mind by the radiant splendour" (De Mund. Opif., § 23).

The road upon which the pilgrim soul so often stumbles, and from which it is so often enticed into the by-paths of vice, whence it emerges lame, and able to proceed but slowly, —this road, in a beautiful expression of Philo's, "ends at the Father of the universe." Such an ending is indeed a beginning. Another similarly inspired thought is thus expressed :

"After the world, there is not place, but God" (Quæst. in Exod., ii. § 40).

The assured manner in which Philo enunciates his views leads to the conclusion that he was not the first to affiliate himself to a religious philosophy drawn from Platonic and Hebrew sources indiscriminately, but that a school possessed of a large traditional learning with liberal tendencies of thought, must have been in existence for some time.

The accounts of the Essenes, the relics of the Talmudical Rabbis, and the so-called apocryphal books written by Hellenized Jews, all tend to prove the existence at the beginning of our era of a very considerable religious philosophy, stretching beyond what we call Judaism.

The following is quite from a teacher's point of view, and singularly parallels the Parable of the Sower, as regards the varied reception of the seeds :—

"Those that seek after philosophy, breathlessly, as it were, go through with one prolonged discourse about virtue. What advantage is derived from what is said? For instead of giving heed, men turn their mind upon other errands, some to shipping and market, others to rents and agriculture, others to honours and politics, others to the gains accruing from each craft and avocation, others to revenge upon their enemies, others to the indulgences of the amorous appetites, and in fine every one is under the influence of some distracting idea or other. So that, as far as the subjects under illustration are concerned, such persons are become wholly deaf, and are present with their bodies only, but are far removed with their minds, differing not a whit from images or statues.

"And if some do attend, they sit for the length of time listening, and when they have got a little distance away, they do not remember a single word of what was said; in fact, they came rather to be pleased through the sense of hearing than to be advantaged. So their soul has not availed to comprehend anything or to become pregnant with an idea;

meanwhile that which was the moving cause of pleasure becomes inoperative, and their attention is extinguished.

"There is a third class of persons in whose minds the things said find some answer while still fresh in their ears, but they turn out to be sophists rather than wisdom lovers; their speech is praiseworthy, but their life is blamable; they are mighty to speak, but powerless to do that which is the best.

"It is then hardly possible to find a man both attentive and remembering, giving honour to deeds before words" (Cong. Erud. Grat., § 13).

We have spoken of the light which Philo's philosophic expositions may throw upon the subject-matter of the parabolic literature of his time. We cannot here enter at length into the analysis of the parables, but a comparison of the following passages (taken in conjunction with others that illustrate the division of man's nature into subordinate functions which at times get the better hand, and a higher part which ought to be regnant within him) may afford a key to the meaning of the parable of the Husbandmen who slay the heir sent to redeem the vineyard.

First we may glance at some expressions of revolt against the higher law: "Kings of the earth range themselves, and men of mark band themselves against the eternal, and against his anointed, saying, Let us break their bands asunder, and cast away their cords from us" (Ps. ii. 2). "Touch not my christs, and deal not wrongfully with my prophets" (1 Chron. xvi. 22). This conception of despite to the messengers of God, Philo carries away from the political plane to the field of combat within the soul :—

"If any one cleaves asunder and destroys that upright and sound and stedfast Word, which testifies to God alone that in his power are all things, if any one be found in the act of breaking in upon it, that is to say, in the act of wounding and destroying it, because he acknowledges his own mind as the source of energy, to the exclusion of God, he is a thief, taking away what belongs to other. For all possessions are of God" (Legis Allegor., iii. § 10).

The lower qualities, which as the event proves are but for a time, seize upon the divine messenger of conscience that makes its appeal, and cry, "This is the heir, let us seize him, that the inheritance may be ours."

The vineyard in this parable has been understood in a semi-political or sectarian sense. Possibly a parable was composed so as to have a show of exoteric or ostensible meaning, which on a deeper plane of thought conveyed an inner sense and purport. Philo takes such an ostensible meaning in the passage that follows, but immediately proceeds to convert it into a more esoteric one: "'The vineyard of the Lord Almighty is the house of Israel' (Isa. v. 7). Now Israel is the mind devoted to contemplation of God and of the universe; for the name Israel is interpreted 'seeing God,' and the abode of the mind is the whole soul" (De Somn., ii. § 26).

It does not follow that in a given parable containing the term vineyard, that symbol would signify the mind regarded in its faculty of contemplation. Another spiritual aspect might be the motive of the parable, which would have to be interpreted according to the reciprocal relation of all its parts. As Philo says, "Those who apply themselves to the study of the sacred Scriptures ought not to fight over syllables, but ought first to look at the spirit and meaning of the nouns and verbs employed, and the occasions on which, and the manners in which each expression is used; for it often happens that the same expressions are adjusted to different things at different times, and on the contrary, opposite expressions are at different times applied to the same thing without any lack of poetical consistency" (Fragm. Damasc.).

The symbol of a husbandman Philo himself uses to signify "a mental disposition unchastised and unsound," bringing forward "nothing useful for its fruit," but rather vices.

The husbandmen, or faculties which usurped a proprietorship beyond their proper function, it will be remembered, were to be replaced by others. In the following, the imagery is different, but the principle is the same:—

"That which is announced as the husbandry of the soul makes this profession. The trees of folly and intemperance, of unrighteousness and cowardice, I will altogether cut down. I will also cut away the shoots of pleasure and of lust, of anger and of passion, and of like affections, yea, though they should reach as high as heaven. And I will burn down their very roots, launching the blast of flame to the very bowels of the earth, so that no portion, no trace or shadow whatever, be left behind. These things I will assuredly destroy, and I will plant in the souls of such as are of a teachable age, young shoots whose fruit shall nourish them. They are these: the practice of writing and reading with facility; the diligent study of things to be found among wise poets; geometry, and the study of rhetorical arguments, and the complete scholarship acquired by encyclical education. And in those souls which are now arrived at the period of youth and manhood, I will implant that which is better and more perfect, the shoot of wisdom, of courage, of temperance, and righteousness, and of every virtue" (De Agric., § 4).

In the following, again, a different set of images represents the soul as not refusing the divine messages, but seeking the presence of God within itself:—

"Seeing that he doth enter invisibly into this [the inner and intellectual] region of the soul, let us prepare that place in the finest way possible, so as to be worthy of becoming a dwelling-place of God. For if we do not, he will imperceptibly remove to another abode which shall appear to him to be of more excellent workmanship.

"For if when we are about to receive kings we prepare our houses in the most splendid way . . . what sort of abode ought we to prepare for the King of kings, the sovereign God of the universe? . . . shall we prepare him a house of stone or of wooden material? Avaunt! such an idea it is not guiltless even to utter. For not even, were the whole earth to change its nature and on a sudden be turned to gold or something more precious than gold, and were it then to be used up by the arts of cunning workmen who should prepare porticoes and vestibules and apartments, and precincts, and temples—not even then would it become a footstool for his feet. And yet a well-inclined soul is a house worthy of him" (De Cherub., § 29).

The following shows a special aspect of this divine possession, accompanied by some noble images :—

"The best kind of trance (ecstasis) of all is a divinized and most possessive madness, which the prophetical race has to do with. . . . A prophet utters nothing of his own, but all things that he utters are strange and foreign and prompted by some one else . . . 'About the setting of the sun a trance fell upon Abraham' (Gen. xv. 12). . . . As long as our mind still shines around and revolves, pouring as it were a noontide light into the whole soul, we are masters of ourselves and not possessed; but when it comes toward setting, then in all likelihood there falls upon us a trance, or divinized and most possessive madness. For indeed when the divine light shines, the human light sets, and when the divine light sets, the human rises and dawns. This process is wont to come about with the prophetical race. For indeed the mind that is in us is removed from its place at the arrival of the divine Spirit, but is again restored at the departure of the Spirit. . . . In very truth the prophet, even when he appears to be speaking, 'is silent,' and another is using his vocal organs, his mouth and tongue, to make known what things he will" (Quis. Rer. Div. Her., § 51, 52, 53).

"Intellect," says Philo in another place (Quæst. in Gen., i. § 50) "is a divine inspiration." The humblest man who is without the pride of self, may hope for the entrance of the spirit :—

"To speak succinctly, as for all things whatsoever that are good, whether of soul or body or circumstances, the man who is not a self-lover shows forth the only true first-cause God as the first-cause of them. Let no one therefore of those that seem to be somewhat obscure and humble, from a despair of any better hope, shrink back from becoming a suppliant to God. Even if he no longer looks forward to greater blessings, let him give thanks according to his power for such things as he has already. Countless are the gifts which he has received—birth, life, nurture, soul, senses, fancy, inclination, reason. Reason is a very short word, but a most perfect miniature thing, a fragment of the soul of the universe, or . . . according to those who follow the philosophy according to Moses, a faithful impression of the divine image" (De Mut. Nom., § 39).

Merely human pride Philo holds in much contempt, as indeed might any one who considers what pretensions it makes and for how small and uncertain a time it can maintain itself.

"If thou, being a man, shouldst be cast out from the land, whither wilt thou turn? Wilt thou dive under water, imitating the aquatic nature? Why then thou wilt die forthwith that thou art submerged in the water. Or wilt thou take wings and float in mid-air, and so yearn to traverse the welkin, changing the character of a terrestrial for that of a flying animal? Well, if thou canst, change and remodel the divine sanctions. Nay, but thou canst not. For in proportion as thou dost raise thyself more soaringly; so much the more rapidly wilt thou be borne from that loftier region, and with the greater impetuosity to the earth, the place of thine affinity" (Qu. Det. Pot. Insid., § 41).

"It is shown to be most natural that elevation of the soul through conceit is its real descent, while its true ascent and height is its subsidence from arrogance" (Fragm. Monac. MS.).

From Philo's manner of reference to the name Yeschua

or Jesus, we have noted the probability of the conclusion that he never met the prophet of Nazareth. Or if, on his pilgrimage to Jerusalem, he ever encountered the then obscure Master on one of his journeys, the inference may fairly be drawn either that he knew him under some other designation than that of Jesus, or that he thought so much more of the man than of his name that interest in the latter was never markedly aroused. For example, Philo gives a minute account of the manner of life of the Essenes and Therapeuts, with whose unworldliness he is evidently much in sympathy; but he does not give the name of a single one of their leaders. It is to be remembered that the name Jesus was so common as to be scarcely a distinctive mark by itself, as is evidenced by the balance alleged to have been made of the claims of "Jesus, called a Messiah," as compared with those of the outlaw whose name according to some readings was "Jesus, the son of Abba" (Jesus Barabbas). No doubt it was not until long afterwards that the name Jesus came to be regarded as appropriate, significant, or important in itself. Still, as Philo had pressed a recondite meaning into the name in honour of the memory of a great Israelite commander who bore it; if his memory of having done so served him, he might have been the first to see a sacred suggestiveness in the name of the Galilean Rabbi. Being a man of many words, as he devoted none to Jesus or his name, the inference is, on the whole, a fair one, that he knew of neither.

Notwithstanding this, the title, the Christ, is once brought in with a doctrinal significance in a work bearing the name of Philo.

To one who had imbibed the Christian dogma, the slightest of touches seemed necessary to complete and render edifying a Jewish thinker's writings. In the apocryphal book of Baruch, for example, attributed to a writer of about the middle of the second century before our era, we find a strictly Jewish thought thus manifestly added to by a pious commentator, probably where the end of a chapter left a convenient gap in his manuscript: "God invented every way of assured knowledge, and gave it unto Jacob his child, and Israel his beloved. After this he was seen upon the earth, and lived along with men" (iii. 37). This is a little too like "The Word was made flesh, and dwelt among us." A still more manifest corruption is to be found in the "Wisdom of Ben-Sirach," where the sentence, "By his counsel he calmed the deep, and planted in it islands (nesous)," is found in some MSS. to terminate thus: "And Jesus (Iesous) planted it" (xliii. 23).

There are certain works of Philo which are lost in the original Greek, and only known in an Armenian version. The fact that fragments are existent in the Greek verifies the general authenticity of the Armenian version, which shows nevertheless trifling interpolations. There is, however, a continuation of one of the books of comment upon Genesis, evidently by another hand than Philo's. Therefore, when in one of these books (Quæst. in Exod. ii., § 117), we find an argument upon "Christ the Lord," as having the world under his feet, and being enthroned close to his Father, there is little difficulty in regarding it as an after addition. A writer like Philo, even if, according to the story told by Eusebius and Jerome, he had encountered Peter at Rome, and if he had accepted the Christian extension of his own doctrines, would scarcely have contented himself with so slight an indication of his conversion as a single bare enunciation of Christian metaphysics.

Another passage is perhaps open to suspicion of a gloss, owing to its having come down only as a fragment attributed to Philo in a monkish manuscript:—

"The things of creation are remote from the Uncreate, even though they should be brought exceedingly near, following upon the attractive love-influences of the Saviour."

In Philo, however, may be found passages in which the expression Saviour is a title ascribed to Deity. If, however, in the passage just quoted, Philo is designating an intermediate divine personification, akin to that of the Word, or manifest activity of God's wisdom, by the name Saviour, he comes here singularly close to the Christian use of the term which is so familiar.

The following will serve for example of his use of the title of Saviour: "The kind Saviour allows a space for the repentance of sinners.... The divine nature remembers not the evil, and is a lover of virtue; when therefore it beholds faithful virtue in the soul, it bestows upon it wondrous largesse of honour, to wipe out from the first all ills that are impending over it from sin (Quæst. in Gen. ii., § 13). The term Saviour, as a title belonging to God, is found in the older Hebrew scriptures, but there is a gentleness and benignance in Philo's use of the phrase that brings it nearer to the Christian conception. In the older writings the conception is somewhat more austere: "I, even I, am Jehovah; and beside me there is no Saviour" (Isai. xliii. 11).

In the same way generals or other protectors are spoken of: "According to thy manifold mercies thou gavest them Saviours, who saved them out of the hand of their enemies" (Nehem. ix. 27). "Saviours shall come up on Mount Zion to judge the mountains of Esau; and the Kingdom shall be Jehovah's" (Obad. 21).

How it came that Philo wrote in Greek, yet made his main appeal to persons of the Jewish persuasion, a few words will show, and show also how his writings could come to be circulated among the early Christian divines in different parts of the world.

In the travels of Paul, we may remember as one instance of his contact with Greek-speaking Jews, that he visited a part of Macedonia where there was a Jewish synagogue, and strongly impressed a large number of persons described as "observance-keeping Greeks." His "discourse from the Scriptures" would have had small relevancy to such auditors as these, had they been of pure Greek race. They were doubtless of Hebrew origin, expatriated in an early dispersion.

The immense colony living about Alexandria spoke Greek, read the Septuagint, and would be hardly distinguishable from Gentiles except from their hold upon tradition.

The passage which follows is one evidence out of many that these Hellenized Jews did not wholly lose their connection with the mother country, but that such as could made, at least once in their lives, a pilgrimage to the temple at Jerusalem.

"There were certain Greeks among those that were coming up to worship at the feast: these came to Philip who was of Bethsaida of Galilee, and asked him, saying, Lord [or, rather, Sir], we desire to see Jesus" (John xii. 20).

If we were writing in the romantic style in which it is the modern fashion to recompose the legends of the founders of our Churches, we might draw a fanciful picture of the possibility of Philo having formed one of these polite inquirers. We might show how Philo did come to worship at the Feast in this very way, and imagine how the courtly philosopher and diplomatist in his kindly condescending manner might have inquired curiously about the new light that had shone out from the north—from Galilee beyond the pale. We might portray how the young prophet was found interesting, but "impossible;" so simple and spiritual as to have the appearance of dogmatism to the cultured Alexandrian, and too pronounced to be worked into any philosophic series, with any comfort to the critical mind. We might add how the princely Greek and his friends kept silence thereafter upon the subject; and how, nevertheless, when the genial gnostic came to his writing-table once more, the recollection of that new prophet's face, the effect of the gentle flame of his eyes, the unconscious divinity of his mien, stole in to inspire full many a rhetorical period with a new and moving emotion. There is that elevation now and again in the interminable commentaries of Philo, and he did visit Jerusalem after the manner of his devout countrymen, and would have been fitly styled a Greek, though not—as one of the most popular of English bishops described the inquirers after Jesus *—a heathen Greek. This, however, is all we know; the rest is mere romance.

Philo had before him as the one great object of his life "the promulgation of a catholic system of religious belief, of which Judaism should be the basis." In all sincerity he loved the teachings of Plato; and, finding with his thirsty openness of mind that he could drink in spiritual thoughts equally well from these as from the inner heart of his own scriptures, read as he was taught to read them, he unconsciously blended and made one the Hebrew and Greek philosophical tradition, until Plato could be regarded as a sort of "Attic Moses," Moses as at heart a Plato; while scholars smiled and said, "Either Plato Philonizes, or Philo Platonizes." With this broad and grand work in hand, how little he knew that his own fate was neglect and oblivion; that a new spiritual impetus was being given to the world through the work of a man whom if he had seen he might have dearly loved; and that the followers of this great apostle of a revived faith, acceptable alike to Jew and to Gentile (as many a Rabbi now allows, so far as regards the unchristianized teachings of Jesus),

---

* The Bishop of Manchester, at the opening of St. Andrew's Church, Dearnley, May 8, 1880: "There were some heathen Greeks there, intellectually speaking highly educated men, but what their motive had been in coming to see Jesus did not transpire: possibly it was mere curiosity, but sometimes even this is productive of a large amount of good." The Authorized Version is not quite clear, and may be responsible for the slip. It reads, "And there were certain Greeks among them that came up to worship at the feast." This might be understood, "Among the crowd of Jews that flocked to Jerusalem for the celebration, there chanced to be (for their own purposes) certain Greeks." The true sense of the original is, "Among the arrivals for the purpose of worship at the feast, were certain Grecized Jews." On the subject of such Hellenized Jews we may call to mind the taunting query of the Pharisaic officers in reference to Jesus Himself (John vii. 35): "Is he about to go unto the dispersed among the Greeks, and teach the Greeks?" Since this work was in the printer's hands, the good Bishop has departed (Oct. 22, 1885). Requiescat in novis laboribus!

would actually borrow secretly from his (Philo's) commentaries the very lines of reasoning by which he had formulated his catholic system. And this to build up into a formal and dogmatic creed a doctrine which Philo would have found no difficulty in accepting in its simple unspoiled form. He was ready to accept the leader of the sacred order as one endowed with divine mediatorial functions: he would in all likelihood have been ready to accept from the depositaries of the relics of Jesus, in his own genial and philosophic way, the doctrine of their master's divinity.

THE SACRED AND THE PROFANE.

THE Olympian religion, which had reached its height in the worship of a spiritual Zeus, and the elevated cult of Apollo, eventually reduced itself to the absurd, and so died. The poetical symbolizations of the forces of life became at length so florid, that the legends only drew smiles from men of reason. Perhaps it is due to this fact that in Greece we first find secular studies differentiating themselves from sacred.

Aristarchus was proclaiming the motion of our globe in space, while, by his friend Moschus, deity of the Olympian order was being celebrated in the person of a Venus, who went about shouting that if any one had seen her straying child Eros, and would tell her, he should have a kiss from her; while if the youngster were brought to her, the boon should be a kiss—and more.

About the time of what is called the Alexandrian age, physical science was developing itself. The seed of learning may have come from Egypt, but wherever derived, it fell on good ground in Magna Græcia, as Aristotle, Euclid, Archimedes and others attest.

But a great arrest of progress soon afterwards occurred, and going back little more than two hundred and fifty years from the present day we find, at the head quarters of the Christian faith, a philosopher forced by imminence of torture to disavow the recovered truth which had been known to Aristarchus nineteen centuries before. The heresy was that the earth moves, and is not the one stationary and central point round which a subsidiary universe revolves. Such a heresy as this was dangerous, because it suggested difficult questions, if not obvious doubts, with regard to the universality of the scheme of the atonement. At about the same time, we in England not only had an inspired Bible, which it was death to criticize, but were informed—and very much misinformed—in the headings of the chapters, what we were to understand by it. This reproach has only a few months ago been removed by the issue of a Revised Version, in which we are told that these headings "it was thought advisable to abandon, as involving questions which belong rather to the province of the commentator than to that of the translator." At last we may study a mystical love-song, about a fair girl with dove's eyes and a green bed, without being told that the meaning of it all is—" the church and Christ congratulate one another!"

What wonder that once again science separated itself from religion; and that, "faith in the thing grown faith in the report" having been followed by loss of faith altogether, the mind of many should bear the same attitude of patronizing tolerance to the symbols of the dead faith, as the verse of Moschus manifests towards the last pretty denizen of Olympus.

As it is not the object of this work to give a history of science, we shall not follow the thread of Greek discovery.

Since, however, there is a mass of matter, belonging to a considerable period of time, which shows certain points of correspondence with the gospel relics, and therefore may serve to illustrate their true and original meaning, and so to contribute to their universal and unsectarian value, we shall make at random a few extracts, Greek, Roman, or otherwise, which ought to be of interest to Christian students.

It will, perhaps, however be necessary for them to advance a little further than one who has posed successfully as a Hellenist and heretic, who wrote so recently as 1860, declaring that "the interpretation of Scripture requires . . . at least a moral and religious interest which is not needed in the study of a Greek poet or philosopher."

It would be interesting if this well-known personage would so far substantiate his doctrine as to illustrate the moral and religious difference, for instance, between such passages as the following :—

"Euripides says : 'Who now can tell whether to live may not be properly to die, and whether that which men do call to die, may not in truth be but the entrance into real life?" (Diog. Laert., IX. viii.).

"Whosoever would save his life will lose it : and whosoever shall lose his life . . . shall find it" (Matt. xvi. 25).

Here the Greek writer, for the study of whose solemn and serious thought "a moral and religious interest" is not needed, is only a poetic playwright. The differentiation, therefore, one might presume, should be very easy.

In the following, the pagan Greek has some claim to be regarded as a philosopher, so probably the exposition of the distinction between study requiring and not requiring moral and religious interest may be somewhat more difficult :—

"Socrates did well in correcting the maxim held in favour by the generality, that one ought to deal kindly by one's friends, but ill by one's enemies, by this one, that while one ought to deal kindly by one's friends, one ought to do no ill to one's enemies, but to translate them into friends" (Themist., vii. 95).

"Ye have heard that it was said, Thou shalt love thy neighbour, and hate thine enemy : but I say unto you, Love your enemies, and pray for them that persecute you" (Matt. v. 43).

It is true that there are questions which have agitated the minds of learned Christian divines, on subjects more difficult than any presented in heathen authors, but in the present day, so characterized by absence of superstitious reverence, they are not likely to count in any serious comparison of sacred and profane literature. How did the serpent get into Eden? Had Adam and Eve the usual *omphalos*? Did Jesus ascend into heaven with or without clothes?—from the consideration of such questions as these, which occupied mediæval Christian divines, we may turn away with a smile.

The passages which follow, in which sacred authors compare with profane, we shall not attempt to group. More or less, they are mutually illustrative.

There is a Greek proverb, "One ignorant of learning sees not when he sees." There are similar plays upon words expressive of sight and vision in classical and philosophic writings :—

"When they looked, they looked in vain; giving ear they heard not" (Æschylus, Prom. Vinct., 446).

"Some men, indeed, give off light. . . . The mystic secret, however, and that in which are the sacred things in their fulness, he so contrived, that those uninitiated even when holding it held it not" (Themist. de Aristot., xxvi. 719).

"The Proverb of the seers that see not and hearers that hear not" (Demosth. Or., i. c. Aristog.).

Pythagoras concealed the meaning of much that was said by him, in order that those who were genuinely instructed might clearly be partakers of it ; but that others, as Homer says of Tantalus, might be pained in the midst of what they heard, in consequence of receiving no delight therefrom" (Iamblich. Vit. Pyth., ch. xxv.).

"Thou wilt know, too, men suffering under self-incurred woes, hapless ones, who being near to good things neither see them nor hear them ; for few know how to find redemption from evils" (Pythagoras, Aur. Carm., 54–56).

"Is not perception by the senses often deprived of its own powers ? It is when we see and see not, and hear and hear not, since the mind ever so little has clung to and is brooding over some other object" (Philo. Leg. Alleg., ii. 17).

"The holy spirit departed from Jacob, and seeing he saw not, and hearing he heard not" (Bereschith R., xci. 6).

"The Lord hath not given you an heart to know, and eyes to see, and ears to hear, unto this day" (Deut. xxix. 4).

"I fear that I may be speaking before one dull of hearing, and in some way be dancing the sacred things into view by showing them to one uninitiated. After all, however, like as in a myth, there is some recondite esoteric word which will be spoken for those that are able to hear" (Aristides, T. 2, p. 391).

"Why speakest thou unto them in parables? ... Unto you it is given to know the mysteries of the kingdom of heaven, but to them it is not given. ... Therefore speak I to them in parables; because seeing they see not, and hearing they hear not, neither do they understand" (Matt. xiii. 10–13).

"Pythagoras said that it is much better to be injured than to kill a man; for that judgment is deposited in Hades, where the soul, and its essence, and the first nature of beings, are properly estimated" (Iamblich. Vit. Pyth., xxx.).

"It is not death, but a bad life, that destroys the soul" (Pythagorean:—Sexti Sentent.).

"O race astounded by the fear of gelid death! why dread ye Styx, why darkness, why empty names? Whether the funeral pyre with its flame, or long lapse of time with its decay, have carried off your bodies, deem not that any ill is suffered; the souls are free from death, and always when the old abode is left behind, live in new homes" (Ovid, Metam., xv. 151).

"When thou walkest through the fire, thou shall not be burned; neither shall the flame kindle upon thee" (Isai. xliii. 2).

"Let us not fear him that seemeth to slay. Great is the strain of soul, and danger laid up in eternal [aeonian] torture-test for those that transgress the commandment of God" (4 Macc. xiii. 14).

" Be not afraid of them that kill the body : . . . but rather fear what is able to destroy both soul and body in Gehenna " (Matt. x. 28).

" In my father's house are many homes " (John xiv. 2).

"When going abroad from thy house, turn not back, for the Erinyes go after thee " (Pythagoras, Frag. Phil. Gr., i. 506).

"In the precept that a man when beginning a journey abroad should not turn his eyes back, he recommends those that are departing from life not to cling eagerly to living, and not to be attracted by the pleasures here " (Diog. Laert.).

" The symbolic saying of the Pythagoreans. . . . When going toward the temple, turn not back ; signifying that one who has set off toward God must not be of divided opinion, nor cling to human matters " (Simplic. in Epictet., p. 332).

" Leave the dead to bury their own dead ; but go thou and publish abroad the kingdom of God. . . . No man, having put his hand to the plough, and looking back, is fit for the kingdom of God " (Luke ix. 60).

In the following passages we meet with a fragment from the ethical wisdom that seems to have descended from a common source to many peoples, and to have grown proverbial :—Easy is the descent of Avernus ; the way of effort lies uphill ; or, in other metaphor, the one is wide and facile, the other narrow and difficult to push through :—

" The way of evil may be easily chosen even by crowds, for the road is smooth, and she dwells close at hand ; but as for virtue, deathless gods set sweaty toil right ahead ; the track that leads to her, moreover, is tedious and steep and rough at first, but when thou hast won the peak, it is thenceforward one of ease, however harsh before " (Hesiod, " Works and Days," 285).

"It was a saying of Pittakos : It is a hard thing to be really a good man " (Simonides, cit. by Diog. Laert.).

" A city is builded, and set upon a broad field, and is full of all good things. The entrance thereof is narrow, and set on a sheer cliff, with as it were fire on the right hand and water on the left. And one only path between them both, even between the fire and the water, so that there could but one man go there at once. If this city now were given unto a man for an inheritance, if he shall never pass the danger set before it, how shall he receive this inheritance?" (2 Esdras, vii. 6–9).

"The earliest oracles are in every respect manifestations of the divine virtues—the compassion and kindness whereby he makes men supple for noble conduct; and pre-eminently his service-devoted band, for whom he opens up the way that leads to happiness" (Philo, Vit. Mos., iii. § 23).

"Dost thou not see a certain small door, and a path before the door, a path which is not much frequented, but very few proceed thereon, as if it appeared a difficult path, both rough and rocky? This is the road which leads to the True Discipline" (Tablet of Kebés, the Theban; "one who investigated well the reasons of argument" [Phæd., vii. 63 a]).

"The way of sinners is made level with stones, but at its uttermost part is the abyss of Hades" (Ben-Sirach, xxi. 10).

"What Heaven has conferred is called The Nature: an accordance with this nature is called the Path; the regulation of this path is called Instruction.

"The path may not be left for an instant. If it could be left, it would not be the path" (Confucius, "Doctrine of the Mean").

"Enter ye in by the narrow gate: for wide is the gate, and broad is the way, that leadeth to destruction, and many be they that enter in thereby. How narrow is the gate and straitened the way, that leadeth unto life, and few be they that find it" (Matt. vii. 13).

The following evidence a like use of a proverb expressing contrariety:—

"Fabius used to call a benefit harshly bestowed by a hard man, bread of stone" (Seneca de Benef., 117).

"He bears in the one hand a stone, in the other he shows bread" (Plautus).

"What man is there of you, who, if his son shall ask him for a loaf, will give him a stone?" (Matt. vii. 9).

The following passages show an affinity:—

"Not one of them [sparrows] shall fall on the ground without your Father" (Matt. x. 29).

"Never without God flew the good-boding bird" (Odyssey, O., 530).

"This befalls not without the presiding genius of the gods" (Æneid, ii. 777).

"There comes never a work upon earth without thee, Daimon" (Cleanthes ap. Stob. Ecl. Phys.).

A common measure is manifest in the following:—

"We ought to scatter after the manner of seed, which however small it be, when it finds itself occupying a suitable place, unfolds its forces, and from being minute, expands into mighty growths. The same is seen in the case of speech; it does not cover a large area, if you look at it; but in its action it enlarges itself. The things spoken are few, but if they are well caught up in a mind, they grow strong and spring upwards. There is, I say, the same condition in precepts as in seeds" (Seneca, Ep. 38).

"The kingdom of heaven is like unto a grain of mustard seed," etc. (Matt. xiii. 31).

A single thought furnishes the motive of the passages that follow:—

"Without unity of purpose neither can a city be well administered, nor a house rightly managed" (Xenophon, De F. and D. Socrat., iv.).

"Evil there is none greater than anarchy; it alike brings states to destruction, and makes houses all in upheaval" (Sophocles, Antig., 687).

"What house so stable, what State so firm, that it cannot be overthrown from its foundations by hatreds and dissensions?" (Cicero, Lælius, 7).

"Neither can a State be happy in sedition, nor a house in the discord of its masters" (Cicero de fin. bon. and mal., i. 18).

"Every kingdom divided against itself is brought to desolation; and every city or house divided against itself will not stand" (Matt. xii. 25).

The parable of the Pearls and the Swine in the gospel will occur to the mind in relation to the following:—

"When Empedocles said to him, that the wise man was undiscoverable, he replied, Very likely, for it takes a wise man to discover a wise man" (Diog. Laert., Xenophanes, iii.).

"Speak not in the ears of a fool, for whatever the wisdom of thy sayings, he will despise it" (Prov. xxiii. 9).

"When Bias was asked by an impious man the question, What is piety? he made no reply. And when asked the reason of his silence he said: I am silent because thou art asking questions of things wherewith thou hast no concern" (Diog. Laert., Bias).

"The sophists infuse divine doctrines into confused and turbid manners. He who pours pure clear water into a muddy well does but disturb the mud, and destroy the clear water" (Iamb. de Vit. Pythag., ch. xvii.).

"The statuaries, when ordered to make a statue of Hermes, search for wood adapted to the reception of the proper form; but those who teach for reward pretend that they can readily produce the works of virtue from every nature" (Iamb. de Vit. Pythag., ch. xxxiv.).

The uselessness of indiscriminately pressing for acceptance upon those unfit to receive it, that which is only got by seeking after it, until it is undervalued and trampled, or the sacred offering is bolted untasted in ungrateful doglike fashion, is implied in the Pythagorean symbol, "Sing not your song before a fourfooted thing!" and also in the hint of the Persian proverb, "Hold not up a mirror in the assembly of the blind."

We are reminded in the following, of the fable of the Mote and the Beam : "We are all wise in giving good advice, but when we sin ourselves, we know it not. ... No one sees clearly as a whole his own vices, but when another brings himself to disgrace, he wishes to see it" (Menander Incert., 85).

The teaching of the story of the woman taken in adultery belongs to Pagan as well as to Christian charity :—

"He that brings accusations against others, and passes judgment on all, ought himself to be beyond all question blameless" (Demosth. Aristogit., i.).

"How beseems it for one who is wicked himself to chastise others on account of wickedness or laxity ?" (Xenophon).

"How might we men live most virtuously and righteously? If we never do ourselves, what we blame in others" (Diog. Laert.—Thales).

The motive of the following passages will be familiar to any student of the Gospels :—

"If to have care availeth aught, be anxious and let thyself have care ; but if the Daimon careth for thee, why be a source of care unto thyself?" (Anthol., i. 89. 2).

"O noblest of men, seeing that you are an Athenian, of a city the greatest and most renowned for wisdom and valour, are you not ashamed to be caring for moneys, how you may obtain them in the greatest abundance, and for glory and honour ; whilst you are not caring a whit nor taking any thought for wisdom and truth, and for your soul, how it shall be in the best condition ?

"I go abroad doing nothing else than persuading the young and old among you to take no care for the body or for riches, in preference to or more assiduously than the care of the mind, telling you that virtue does not spring from money, but that from virtue proceeds wealth unto men, and all other good things both private and public" (Plato, Apol. Socr., 30 a).

The following may be compared with the aphorism that " No man can serve two masters : "—

" It is impossible for a man to be at once a pleasure lover, a body lover, a money lover, and a God lover. For the pleasure lover is also a body lover, and the body lover is without doubt a money lover, and the money lover is of necessity unjust, and the unjust man is both profane towards God and lawless towards men, so that even should he sacrifice a hecatomb, he is all the more profane, and impious, and atheistic, and deliberately sacrilegious " (Demophili Simil. Fragm. Phil. Mullach., i. 499).

" Nay, what are you doing? you are being torn different ways by a double hook. Are you following this one or that ? You must needs alternately approach your masters with doubtful obsequiousness, alternately blunder " (Persius, v. 154).

" Without doubt he is not possessed of riches, but possessed by riches : in title King of the island, in disposition a miserable bought slave " (Valerius Max., ix. 4).

" This then is now quite clear in a state, that to give honour to riches and at the same time adequately practise temperance is an impossibility with the citizens; but either one or the other must of necessity be neglected " (Plato, Rep. viii. 555 c.).

With the following compare Matt. v. 28 :—

" Xenocrates, the companion of Plato, said that it differed nothing whether our feet or our eyes were set on another person's house " (Ælian V. H., xiv. 42).

" Pericles said that a magistrate not only ought to keep his hands restrained from gain of money, but also his eyes free from any longing look " (Valer. M., iv. 3).

" Goodness does not consist in the refraining from wrong doing, but in the absence of inclination to do wrong " (Democrates, Golden Sent.).

" If thou hast thy mind clean, thou art clean in all thy body " (Epicharmos ap. Clem. Al., Str. vii.).

"If thine eye be single, thy whole body will be full of light" (Matt. vi. 22).

"Apollo becomes not manifest unto all, but only unto him that is good" (Callimachus, In Apoll., 9).

"Blessed are the pure in heart; for they shall see God" (Matt. v. 8).

"Sacrifice to God by a state of perfect righteousness, not shining as to thy garments, but as to thine heart" (Menander, as cited by Clem. Alex., Str. v., xiv.).

"First be reconciled to thy brother, and then come and offer thy gift" (Matt. v. 24).

"Avoid an oath, even though you should be swearing righteously" (Menander).

"Take no oath at all" (Matt. v. 34).

"Thou seest, O Crœsus, that I have treasures also, but whereas thou biddest me gather them together into mine own hands, and for sake of them envy and hate, setting also hireling custodians over them, in whom to trust; I, on the other hand, enrich my friends, and reckon them my treasures, and custodians of our goods—more trustworthy guardians to boot, than if I had appointed hireling watchmen. . . . Moreover, I serve the gods, and stretch out ever for more abundance; and whensoever I acquire, what things I see to be over and above mine own sufficiency, therewith I satisfy the deficiency of my friends, and by enriching and benefiting mankind, I obtain goodwill and friendship, and reap therefrom security and good report, which neither rot away by corruption, nor spoil by over-fulness" (Xenoph. de Cyri instit., I. viii.).

"Treasures upon the earth, where moth and rust consume, and where thieves dig through and steal, . . . treasures in heaven, where neither moth nor rust doth consume, and where thieves do not dig through nor steal" (Matt. vi. 19, 20).

"If God is spirit, as our hymns declare, the chief worship he ought to have of thee is a pure mind" (Catonis Distich).

"Everything is sacred to the good word, for it is the mind that will have speech with God" (Menander).

"We reasonably worship God, if we render the mind that is in us free from all depravity as from a spot" (Pythagorean: Frag. Phil. Gr., i. p. 493).

"Oblations and sacrifices convey to God no honour; votive offerings are no adornment to him; but the god-inspired mind continually is conjoined to God, for like must needs continually advance toward like" (Pythagorean. *Ibid.*, p. 497).

"God is spirit; and they that worship him must worship by spirit and truth" (John iv. 24).

"They that eat me (Wisdom) shall have further hunger, and they that drink me shall thirst for more" (Sir. xxiv. 21).

"With the bread of understanding shall she feed him, and give him the water of wisdom to drink" (*Ibid.*, xv. 3).

"I have intoxicated every thirsting soul, and filled every soul that hungers" (Jer. xxxviii. 25, LXX.).

"Moses . . . sat down upon a well, waiting to see what good that could be imbibed, God would rain down upon his thirsting and eager soul" (Philo, Allegor., iii. § iv.).

"Whosoever drinketh of the water that I shall give him will never thirst, but the water that I shall give him will become in him a well of water springing up unto eternal life" (John iv. 14).

"Out of the abundance of the heart the mouth speaketh" (Matt. xii. 34).

"A man's character is discerned by his words" (Menander).

"As is the disposition, so is the word" (Aristides).

The following are versions of the Golden Rule, the immortal maxim of our planet, never lost, never realized. What angel brought the truth first? what people received it? It is the gospel of humanity, yet man cannot reach up to it. Meanwhile all other sermons are vain, until this one is followed.

"What you do not wish done to yourself, do not to others" (Khoung-fou-tseu, Confuc. Analects).

"Solon, when asked how men could be most effectually debarred from committing injustice, said, If those who are not injured feel as much indignation as those who are" (Diog. Laert., i. § 11).

"Thales, when asked how men might live most virtuously and justly, said, If we never do ourselves what we blame in others" (Diog. Laert., i. § 9).

"Do unto no man that which thou hatest" (Tobit).

"What a man hates incurring, let him not do himself" (Philo ap. Euseb. P., viii. 7).

If it requires a sixth wit to distinguish between the sacred and the profane in the ethical and mystic utterances of human thought, it is at least as difficult to discover the essential difference of quality between canonized legends and stories rejected as fable.

Generation after generation has looked with an eye of wonder upon the rich colouring of a painted window. The central design is of a rude stable, or cave,* in the midst of which is a manger, wherein a new-born babe in swaddling clothes is lying upon a bed of straw. An ox and an ass † stand by in meek attitude as of adoration. An old man, in the habit of a carpenter, stands by the virgin mother of the child. Through one opening is seen a group of shepherds keeping night watch, and listening to a chorus of angelic apparitions. Through another opening are seen in the distance mages gazing upon a star. Subordinate designs are—a lamb with a flag upon its shoulder, and the motto "Agnus Dei;" a dove, a triangle, an annunciation to a virgin by an angel, a fish. Upon scrolls are inscriptions in glowing hues: "And kings to the brightness of thy rising." "The city hath

---

* Protev. Jac., xviii.; Evang. Inf. Arab., ii., iii.; Pseudo-Matth. Ev., xiii., xiv.; Hist. Josephi Fab. Lign., vii.; Hist. de Nat. Mar. et de Inf. Salv., xiv.

† Suggested to the artist by tradition from the gospel of Pseudo-Matthew.

no need of the sun, neither of the moon . . . the Lamb is the light thereof."

From the window pictures, so glorified by art, so sanctified by a vanished devotion, we turn to the books, some of which have outlived a century of generations of men :—

"To Agni. The young mother bears the royal child mysteriously hidden in her bosom. . . . The queen has given it birth; for it is the germ of an ancient fertilization that has developed; I saw it at its birth, when its mother brought it into the world. Yes, I have seen this god of the shining colours, . . . and I have spread over him the immortal unction . . . I have seen him rise from his place all resplendent. . . . Enemies had relegated to the rank of mortals him who is the King of beings and the desired of nations" (Veda).

"Of the three persons of the Aryan Trinity, there is one that has played in religion a rôle more important than the two others, it is Agni. His action in physical nature commences with the sun, in which he resides eternally, and of which he is the glory, . . . he is the king of the heavens, the head of the ether ; . . . from the lofty regions where he is placed, he sees all things, knows all, the depths of the sky, the races of the gods, and of men, and all their secrets ; for all beings are contained in him. In a lower region, Agni burns in the bosom of clouds, amidst the lightning and the thunder ; . . . but it is principally in the sacred enclosure that the rôle and theory of Agni develope themselves. . . . The sacred fire has for father Twastri, and for mother the divine Mâyâ. Twastri is the divine carpenter who prepares the pyres and the two pieces of wood named aranî, the friction of which is to engender the divine child. . . . The birth of Agni is signalled to the astronomic priest by the apparition of a star : . . . so soon as he has seen it, the priest announces to the people the good news ; soon the sun commences to whiten the horizon above the hills ; the people of the country rush forward to adore the new born. Scarcely has the feeble sparkle sprung from the maternal bosom, that is to say, from that of the two sticks which is called the mother, ... before it takes the name of babe: we find in the Veda hymns of a ravishing poetry upon this frail and divine creature, which has just come forth. The parents place the little babe on straw: by its side is the mystic cow, that is to say milk and butter, and with other Aryans, the ass which has carried upon its back the fruit, the juice of which has afforded the sacred liquor; before it, is a devout ministrant; ... he holds in his hand the little oriental fan in form of a flag, and waves it to stimulate the life which threatens to become extinct." [In ecclesiastical symbolism what is it that the "Lamb" carries upon its shoulder?] "Thenceforward the little babe is born upon the altar: it has acquired a marvellous force, which overpasses the comprehension of its adorers; all is illuminated around it; its inapprehensible light destroys the darkness and reveals the world; angels (dêvas) and men rejoice. ... How is this transfiguration of Agni effected? At the moment when one priest placed the young god on the altar, another poured over his head the sacred liquor, the spirituous *soma*, and soon has given him unction in spreading over him the butter of the holy sacrifice. ... These inflammable materials have made him expand; his flame leaps forth environed with glory; he is splendent in the bosom of a cloud of smoke which mounts in a column towards the sky, and its light goes to join itself to that of the luminaries on high. The 'god of beauteous brightness unveils to men that which was hidden:' from the midst of the enclosure where he is throned he instructs the doctors, he is the master of masters" (Émile Burnouf).

"Embryos were conveyed to the mother by the nurse of the universe enjoined by the God of gods." She bore "the lotus-eyed deity, the protector of the world. ... On the day of his birth, the quarters of the horizon were irradiate with joy, as if moonlight were diffused over the whole earth. The virtuous experienced new delight, the strong winds were hushed, and the rivers glided tranquilly. . . . The seas with their own melodious murmurings made the music, whilst the spirits and the nymphs of heaven danced and sang: the gods walking the sky, showered down flowers upon the earth, and the sacred fires glowed with a mild and gentle flame. At midnight, when the supporter of all was about to be born, the clouds emitted low pleasing sounds, and poured down rain of flowers" ("Vishńu Puŕána," H. H. Wilson, p. 502).

"The glory of the Lord shone round about them. . . . I bring you good tidings of great joy which shall be to all the people, for there is born to you this day in the city of David a Saviour, which is the anointed lord" (Luke ii. 9).

"So soon as he was born, he was in possession of his power" (Justin, Dial., 88).

"Let us contemplate how the Blessed Virgin Mary, when the time of her delivery was come, brought forth our Redeemer, Jesus Christ, at *midnight*, and laid him in a manger" (Third Rosary).

Salome, who according to an ancient tradition was the sister of the Virgin, enters the cave and stretches out her hand to examine, for she will not believe that a virgin has brought forth. Straightway she draws back and shrieks, "Woe to my wickedness and unbelief, for I have tempted the living God; and lo, my hand is on fire, and falls away from me" (Protev. Jac.).

Is the babe in this case Agni (ignis) or Agnus?

At the birth "the cave was filled with lights, exceeding the brightness of lamps and candles, and greater than the light of the sun" (Ev. Inf. ed. Syke, 1697, cf. Pseudo-Matth. and Protev. Jac.).

"Our sages tell us that about the hour of the nativity of Moses, the whole house was filled with light" (Talmud, Sota, i. 48).

"At the hour when our father Abraham was born, upon whom be peace, a certain constellation stood in the east, and swallowed four stars, which were in the four quarters of the heaven" (Jalqut Rubeni, f. 32. 3).

"Hail, woman privileged to be the mother of noble offspring, . . . an object of adoration shalt thou be to Argive women, . . . son of a marriage of immortals shall he be called" (Theocritus Id., xix. 72).

"Hail, thou that art highly favoured, the Lord is with thee. [Blessed art thou among women.] . . . He shall be great, and shall be called the son of the Most High" (Luke i. 28, 32).

It is interesting to trace how the emblem-work of one tradition can be inlaid upon the devices of another, like embroidery of lace. For instance: "Fear not, Mary, for thou hast found favour before the Lord, and thou shalt conceive of his Word" (Protev. Jac., xi. ; Tischendorf, Evang. Apocr., p. 21 f). This would appear to be derived from the Alexandrian-Hebraic doctrine of the Logos. A conception of triune deity comes from India, and the Word as the fructifying element is replaced by Holy Spirit, while the Word becomes identified with the third deific person, the Son. Then comes the ceremonial of sun-worship from the East, and adds its glowing imagery to the narrative. The nativity of the divine child is indeed attended by the mages from other lands, with gifts of gold, frankincense and myrrh, to enrich the legend's shrine.

The Memphis Stele at Berlin bears the inscription, "God making himself God, existing by himself, the double being, the begotten from the beginning." The Harris Papyrus from Thebes contains the legend, "Double being, begotten from the beginning, God making himself God, himself engendering himself."

"The only begotten Son of God, Begotten of his Father before all worlds ; God of God, Light of Light, Very God of very God, Begotten, not made, Being of one substance with the Father." This is from the creed drawn up at Nicæa,

A.D. 325, but afterwards added to or modified at Constantinople and Toledo. It is a neat piece of metaphysics, if not wholly original in conception. It may be compared with the Egyptian form without prejudice, as Protestants do not claim that the creeds are inspired.

"I am the beginning, the middle, and the end" (Bhagavat-Gita, x.). "I am the Alpha and the Omega, the first and the last, the beginning and the end" (Apoc. xxii. 13).

"I am all that is, that has been, that will be" (Inscription from the Temple of Sais: Plutarch, Isis and Osiris; Procl. In Tim., i. p. 30).

"Which is and which was and which is to come" (Apoc. i. 4, 8).

"Who has made all that is, and nothing has been made without him ever" (Walls of Temple of Philæ and Gate of Temple of Medinet-About: Mariette, "Mém. sur la mère d'Apis").

Why may not these ancient temples win our reverence as fully as a modern conventicle? they all equally owe their construction to the birth-struggle of the soul of man.

"All things were made by him, and without him was not anything made that hath been made" (John i. 3).

"Taò is before all things, and nothing precedes him; all things are through him, and nothing is without him. He alone is the foundation and first cause of all being" (Laò-tsè, Taò-tĕ King, ch. 25).

The Chinese version of the New Testament reads in John i. 1, "In the beginning was Taò," etc. The idea of duality which gives rise to the conception of a Logos or Demiurge, is thus formulated by the Chinese sage: "Taò, if he can be expressed, is not the eternal Taò."

This theosophic doctrine may be paralleled in the "Key" of Hermes Trismegistos, as addressed to his son Tàt: "The god and father and the good is neither spoken nor heard" (Kleis, 9). "Intelligence, being the male-female god, life and light subsisting, gave birth by word to another and a demiurgic intelligence" (Poimandres, i. 8).

As ideas appear to be nomadic, we may speculate upon the question of the possibility of the Chinese Taò, or Tau, owning a common origin with the Tàt of Alexandrian gnosticism, in the ancient Egyptian deity Tahuti, or Thoth.

"He shines in heaven, and is on the right and left hand of the Highest Lord" (Shi-King, trans. Von Strauss and Tornay).

"The luminous Word that proceeds from Intelligence [the deity] is Son of God" (Hermes Trism. Poimandres, i. 6).

"From henceforth shall the Son of man be seated at the right hand of the power of God" (Luke xxii. 69).

"All beings come forth together, and we see them come back: after they have been developed, each being returns to its origin. To return to our home means to rest: to rest means to have fulfilled our task: to have fulfilled our task means to exist for ever" (Laò-tsè, Taò-tĕ King, ch. 16).

"I came out from the Father, and am come into the world: again I leave the world, and go unto the Father." "I ascend unto my Father and your Father, and my God and your God." "My meat is to do the will of him that sent me, and to accomplish his work." "I know that his commandment is life eternal" (John xvi. 28; xx. 17; iv. 34; xii. 50).

"He who knows the eternal is Taò's, therefore everlasting, he loses his body, without any harm" (Laò-tsè, Taò-tĕ King, ch. 16).

"Be not afraid of them which kill the body, but are not able to kill the soul" (Matt. x. 28).

"Heaven is long and earth is lasting. That by which heaven and earth are long and lasting, is their not aiming at life. This is the reason why they live long. Therefore the sage puts himself last and yet is first; abandons himself, and yet is preserved. Is this not through his having no selfishness?" (Laò-tsè, Taò-tĕ King, ch. 7). "He that grasps, loses" (*Ib.*, ch. 29).

"Whosoever shall seek to gain his soul [life] shall lose it; but whosoever shall lose shall make it alive" (Luke xvii. 33).

"Him who is identified with Virtue, Virtue also rejoices to receive. Him who is identified with default, the defaulters also rejoice to visit with default" (Laò-tsè, Taò-tĕ Kīng, ch. 23).

"With what judgment ye judge, ye shall be judged: and with what measure ye mete, it shall be measured unto you." "Give and it shall be given unto you; good measure, pressed down, shaken together, running over, shall they give into your bosom." "All they that take the sword shall perish with the sword" (Matt. vii. 2; Luke vi. 38; Matt. xxvi. 52).

"He who is self-displaying does not shine. He who is self-approving is not held in esteem. He who is self-praising has no merit. He who is self-exalting does not stand high" (Laò-tsè, Taò-tĕ Kīng, ch. 24).

"Whosoever shall exalt himself shall be humbled" (Matt. xxiii. 12).

On the theory of the verbal inspiration of the biblical chronicles we have to face a curious dilemma: an error is sacred; to point it out profane. In the present day, however, we need not fear that the deluge will follow, if we show any imperfection in the Christian evidences. It is not Christianity that holds together the English people, so much as common sense. In everyday life, Christianity is followed by professing Christians about as much as the naked principles of evolution are followed by the men of science who profess them.

From such difficulties as analysis suggests, there is a way out for clerics in a quandary; that is to revert to Bishop Butler's view of Christianity as a republication of natural religion. On this holding, if the good tidings was fairly given, nothing of natural religion can be discordant with it, whereas, if anything in it is at variance with natural religion, it is due to error which has crept into the publication, and can be rectified or removed, provided prejudice, cowardice, and habit are not allowed to stand in the way of truth. There is visible on the horizon an inclination to revert to this sound and sensible view. For instance, in a discourse delivered at St. Paul's Cathedral, August 30, 1885, Dean Church proclaimed the oft-forgotten truth, that, great as was the change wrought by the presence of Jesus on earth, he emphatically disclaimed any break with truths received before. A layman is more likely to put this statement, so to speak, the other side up, as a poet to the writer, "Your notes ought to make people who think a little understand that the story of Jesus is the crystallization of an immense Oriental mass of traditions."

For those who, like Mr. Froude, have found a great and new interest in the New Testament since reading it *humanly*,* it does not lessen, but rather enhances the value of its primitive currency of thought, to discover that it is in a great measure a re-issue of old coins. It so forms a part of a universal mint, rather than the whole of a limited, partial and exclusive one. No religion can claim to stand alone, or to hold a position absolutely unique and separate. But evolution and tradition do not preclude inspiration: plants and animals, however descended, cannot be kept alive without daily sunshine and fresh air.

Virgo is a constellation whose assumption into the sun's brightness corresponds with the feast of the assumption of the blessed Mary ever-virgin, on August the 15th. Isaac Newton pointed out that the Christian festivals are determined upon an astronomical basis. Pious moderns accept the fact. A reverent traveller writes, in the poetic spirit of the Third Gospel, "It is at Rome that the coincidence between the phenomena of the seasons and the festivals of the Church is most perfect. There the summer flowers perish towards the Assumption, while the sky is lighted up by magnificent clouds, as if they glowed with purple for the reception of the

* "The Nemesis of Faith," 1849, Pref.

Virgin" (Forster, "Annales d'un Physicien Voyageur"). In the East this festival is called Mary's Easter.

The serpent, the bull, the lamb, the fish, are all signs of the heaven, and find their place in religious myths.

If the Christian collections have not the sole copyright of their ethical part, would they pretend to a more absolute proprietorship of the legendary accretions?

Keeping in view the exclusive claims of the custodians of the Christian traditions, we may well ask by what faculty in man he is expected to discover, amid legends of different dates, and varied birth-place, which is fact, which poetry; where material truth ends, where the truth of fable begins.

Who shall decide which relics belong to sun and star emblems, and zodiacal myths; which form an organic part of an integral and consistent scheme—the great body of Catholic doctrine, the true corpus of divinity, all within which is sacred, all without common and unclean? Can Protestantism furbish its faculties and champion the unique claims of its Bible, re-establishing the supremacy of a book over mind that gave it birth? Or is there no support to be found but the dogma of an infallible Church, which defines this to be gospel, that spurious, not because of accordance or conflict with reason, but because the Church has so pronounced?

It was once possible for the Defender of the Faith to tighten "subscription," to frighten latitudinarians, "requiring our loving Subjects to continue in the uniform Profession" of certain incredible dogmas, and "prohibiting the least difference from the said Articles." That day is over, and any Parliament that should attempt to enforce its own laws, in order to stifle wholesome "Diversities of Opinions," would perish by its own weapon. If "all further curious search be laid aside," as enjoined three centuries ago, religion and science are doomed once again to be obscured under a pall such as covered the human mind in the Middle Ages, from which there is at least a good hope that we have emerged.

The heavier the shackles, the more slowly they rust away. There is enough uncorroded iron remaining in our chains, to require a blow to break them. It is not to be forgotten that at the present moment the national Church of England is still bound by a tissue of doctrinal immorality, which was ratified by Parliament in 1571.

The lust of the Christian has the nature of sin (Art. ix.).

The good works of the Pagan also have the nature of sin (Art. xiii.).

There is therefore condemnation for him, for his good works, but as to the concupiscence of the Christian, "there is no condemnation for them that believe and are baptized."

There is surely enough vitality remaining in the teachings of Jesus to destroy the monstrous growths that have taken shelter under his name.

It is pitiful to see great powers obscured by temporizing and self-delusion; valuable energies wasted upon the attempt to find a *via media* between the two alternatives,—the way of ignorance, obscurantism, and fear; the way of freedom, of hope, of effort and of helpfulness. Are we to esteem the native human faculties as profane, and to lay them, bound, upon the sacred altar of submission, placing our trust in the salve of ecclesiastical infallibility to dull the crippling pains; or dare we accept the simple and sufficient doctrine that the truth—any kind of truth—makes man free; and so follow in the tracks of that wise young Master whose influence is visible in the saying that, "Love is the fulfilment of the Law," and who, walking on as difficult a road as any one, found "his yoke easy and his burden light," because he was not weighed down by worldly prides, the passions of selfishness, or the dead traditions of a Pharisaic Church?

The piercing words of S. T. Coleridge occur to the mind: "He who begins by loving Christianity better than truth will proceed by loving his own sect or Church better than Christianity, and end in loving himself better than all."

The immorality of the prevalent doctrine lies in its inculcation of the belief that by a magical formula of salvation, we can escape the consequences of our actions, and find a royal road which has no existence in the universe.

The untruth of the same teaching is that the doctrine rests upon the sacred authority of the misunderstood "disciple of the light," who would have repudiated it, and ground it to powder.

The most fearful fact that weak evangelists need confront, is that the gospel which they are empowered to preach is larger than they supposed,—that is all. And it may be reduced to very simple dimensions,—that no one can do, or can be expected to do, more than his best. The great teacher whom teachers claim to follow, had something of the divine patience, and knew that it was not "given" to all to penetrate the mysteries. The book of life is man's own nature, and forced growth is not healthy growth, but dies down before its time.

There are Pharisees professing reverence for the Supreme Being, even to the point of pronouncing the name of God with a drawl in a subdued voice, who regard human nature either with horror or with an affectation of well-bred indifference, and stigmatize the main functions of the organization with which we are endowed by the God of nature as common and unclean. With them it is sacred to think of being an angel, it is profane to learn how big a thing it is to be a man.*

As we must all begin here, and know our alphabet well before we go any further, it would be a happy thing if we could revise our conventional notions of the sacred and the profane. Can any one discover any other possible gate of

* "How easy it is to be a priest; how hard to be a man!" (Roebuck, "Oriental Proverbs").

Paradise, than that which is entered through the faculties of his own nature? If these are dwarfed by unnatural religion, or brought into decrepitude by vice, the way is blocked; but when functions and faculties are in their best and highest harmony and discipline, heaven opens to their lord. As in the parable, man's own soul is the kingdom of heaven. He who has planted beauty there, finds his reward in the beauty which he sees. Honour is honour's meed. And he who has the large talent of love, finds it increases by being given away.

THE GENIUS OF PARABLE.

To define Parable in the general sense of the word, especially now that the parabolic accomplishment has become a lost art, is as difficult as to define Poetry. Parable appeals to us in some subtle way, and varies its face in harmony with our mood, as the sun, when earth looks upon him, varies according to the thickness of the cloudy veil in which she wraps herself.

If we may say of words, which after all are arbitrary themselves, and only approximate vehicles of thought—

"Words have a province large, a wide range here and there"
(Il. xx. 249)

we may say the same with greater force of parables. They reflect like a mirror, and that mirror a magical one, for it receives pictures from far and from near, from the heaven as well as from the earth. What it reflects it also retains, and its power of continuing to give out its rays depends both on the quality of the crystal and the clearness of the eyes that look into it.

Parable is the highest term of all that represent in any way oblique, indirect, or extraordinary speech. Parable is a mode of thought; the minor terms that cluster round it represent chiefly methods of expression. Parable, says Dr. Johnson, is "a relation under which something else is figured." "Something else" is a piece of language containing a grand and most appropriate vagueness. Metaphor is not parable, but only one of its elements; metaphor belongs to the imaginative plane, and its lively suggestions should be self-evident to any person of poetic apprehensiveness. The gist of a parable is not so readily appreciable, for it is more complex, and sometimes appertains to deeper things. The dictionary definition of metaphor, however, is almost large enough to include parable, even in its Johnsonian sense. Metaphor is, according to Richardson, "a transference, or translation, as of the application of a word from its literal meaning—denominating some sensible object, or action, or operation—to supposed similar or corresponding objects, or actions, or operations of the human mind; also, from one object or class of objects to another, founded upon some similarity or resemblance." More briefly, it is the transference to one word or expression, of the sense of another by way of some fancied or real similitude. This more limited definition would not include parable. Metaphor is the most beautiful and suggestive of earthly forms; parable at its orbit's farthest projection is like music that claims to reach beyond the range of sense to the sphere of soul. Figurism, indeed, represents the blossom of the power of language, and embodies something of the creative faculty. "What a pliant and flexible instrument it is in the hand of one who can employ it skilfully; prepared to take every form which he chooses to give it! Not content with a simple communication of ideas and thoughts, it paints those ideas to the eye; it gives colouring and *rilievo* even to the most abstract conceptions." Without metaphor, language would indeed be flat and tame; its magic takes us amidst the exhilarating scenery of hills, and brings colours down from the poetic sky. Parable carries us farther, even into the avenues of the inaccessible mounts, which as the uplooking traveller reaches with his eyes, he feels in a vague and confused way that it is somehow "good to be here." Metaphor, if not leading always into such holy ground, draws us into a dainty and exquisite region whither heavy feet cannot find their way. "Every metaphor," says Cicero (De Oratore, iii. 53), "ought to be modest, so that it may bear the appearance of having been gently led down, not of having forced its way into an alien resting-place, but of having come of its own accord and not by constraint."

Shakespeare is the great metaphorist; with him metaphor is so facile as to have become his strong and natural language. His heroic prince, confused by his own over-intense thought and the baffle of things that are, asks of himself—

> "The question,
> Whether 'tis nobler in the mind to suffer
> The slings and arrows of outrageous fortune,
> Or to take arms against a sea of troubles,
> And, by opposing, end them."

This is an instance of what a power of concentrated thought and feeling metaphor will contain, and with what an impressive gesture it bears its burden to us. Critically speaking, the metaphorical element here is most compound and peculiar. First we have the vigorous personification of fortune, remorselessly assailing us with slings and arrows, the most difficult to evade of ancient war weapons. Then we dream of buckling on our own panoply to meet these missiles, and, looking a little further, find that we are brandishing our arms, not against individual slinger or bowman, but against a vast vague sea of troubles rushing in upon us. Objection has been raised here to a mixing and confusion of distinct metaphors; but we should be sorry to lose the momentary picture of helplessness, as the attempt to wield ordinary weapons as against an adversary is met by a manifold wave, a very sea of adversity. Even before this mighty sea the mind will not be frighted, but, recovering from its feeling of helplessness, shows a bold front, and, let troubles come what way they will, claims to disperse them and to end their power.

A brief reference to the terms expressive of figurative representation will enable a clearer position to be given to parable. Allegory is a description of one thing, or certain things, under the image of others. Says Quinctilian, it exhibits one thing in words, another in meaning. Tyndale, the martyred biblical translator of the early part of the sixteenth century, describes it as "an example or similitude borrowed of strange matters, and of an other thing than that thou entreatest of." An allegory can be made, "by another understanding," of a description not originally given with allegorical intent. To make Mount Sinai, or Egypt, or "Jerusalem that now is" into expressions containing a new and occult meaning is to allegorize.

An allegory deals with some lesson or intelligence about which there is no doubt or obscurity, but which it is not intended to deliver or convey in plain terms. In giving instruction in this manner there is no intention of concealment; the analogy is intended to be obvious, or at least communicable, and the student is expected to make the application for his own use, the figurative garb luring his imagination into interest. Personifications of ideal virtues may be the *dramatis personæ* of allegory. A well-known object, as a growing vine in its different seasons or conditions, may be the allegorical representation of a people. The "Sacred Vineyard," where the disciples sat in blooming rows, "arranged as vine-plants in a vineyard," * was a poetic mode of representing a Hebrew college.

By the Haggadists of the Talmud, says Deutsch, "the persons of the Bible—the kings and the patriarchs, the heroes and the prophets, the women and the children, what they did and suffered, their happiness and their doom, their words and their lives—became, apart from their presupposed historical reality, a symbol and an allegory." These innocent and poetic devices, may, if overlaboured, become most wearisome and trifling; and, depending largely upon temporary and local conditions, they may readily lose force and appreciability, and become dull and tedious, requiring antiquarian dictionaries for their elucidation.

* Talmud of Jerusalem, Berachoth, iv. 2, Gemara.

A modern critic has said, "The service of philosophy, and of religion and culture as well, to the human spirit is to startle it into a sharp and eager observation. . . . Theories, religious or philosophical ideas, as points of view, instruments of criticism, may help us to gather up what might otherwise pass unregarded by us." This is especially the case with philosophy put in enigmatic form.

An instance where to startle is the first object, is to be found in the following: "A certain sage went as an itinerant trader in spices into the neighbourhood of Ziporah, and called aloud, 'Who will buy the balm of life?' A crowd gathered round him to buy the elixir, to whom he said, 'If you want to possess this life-prolonging balm, here it is. And taking the Book of Psalms from his pocket, he read aloud—'Where is the man that desireth life? who loveth many days to enjoy good: Guard thy tongue from evil, and thy lips from uttering guile'" (Parasha).

A similar story, told by Deutsch in reference to the legal and allegorical divisions of the Talmud, will aid us to realize why the most serious subjects are so often treated in the most apparently inappropriate manner: "We had long pondered over the best way of illustrating to our readers the extraordinary manner in which the 'Haggadah,' that second current of the Talmud, suddenly interrupts the course of the 'Halacha,'—when we bethought ourselves of the device of an old master. It was a hot Eastern afternoon, and while he was expounding some intricate subtlety of the law, his hearers quietly fell away in drowsy slumbers. All of a sudden he burst out: 'There was once a woman in Egypt who brought forth at one birth six hundred thousand men.' And our readers may fancy how his audience started up at this remarkable tale of the prolific Egyptian woman. 'Her name,' the master calmly proceeded, 'was Jochebed, and she was the mother of Moses, who was worth as much as all those six hundred thousand armed men together who went up from

Egypt.' The professor then, after a brief legendary digression, proceeded with his legal intricacies, and his hearers slept no more that afternoon. An Eastern mind seems peculiarly constituted. Its passionate love for things wise and witty, for stories and tales, for parables and apologues, does not leave it even in its most severe studies. They are constantly needed, it would appear, to keep the current of its thoughts in motion" (Deutsch, " Remains," p. 44).

Symbol, in the original use of the term, signifies something divided, of which the two portions may be separately valueless, but when they are brought together and tally, they form a complete and perfect whole. In this sense two halves of a broken ring are the symbols of parting and meeting again. But the word "symbol" has come to be used in a less restricted and more metaphorical sense, as the token, distinctive mark, or sign, of a latent conception or idea, the outward expression of a hidden meaning associated with it by some simple or subtle correspondence. Thus, for instance, by both Hebrew and classical writers, arrows were used as symbols of sudden and inevitable danger, as of calamity or disease. They also are taken to denote anything at once abstract and injurious, as a cruel lie, a harsh word. Again, they represent energy only, as of eloquent or indignant words. Salt was used as the symbol of a covenant, in consequence of a custom of eating salt by the contracting parties in ratification of their engagement. Probably the preservative quality of salt was at the bottom of the custom, and this attribute therefore shows the way to the real and permanent use of the word "salt" as a symbol. It was applicable in the most suggestive ways. There was a saying in Jerusalem, when money had been lost, "the salt was wanting to the money." And if the question were asked, "What salt is it that keeps money good?" the answer is "Charity." Colours have through history retained symbolic meaning : *white* is everywhere the emblem of purity and innocence, and also of triumph and festivity; *blue* is the celestial colour, both with Hindoo and Hebrew; *purple* the royal; *crimson* the emblem of life. The Egyptian Tau cross is also a sign of life; but the origin of the symbol is now doubtful. Sex, Sun, and Spirit represent the mysterious sources of life, and symbols of them have been worshipped on the altars of millions of beings like ourselves. The *cup* with the Hebrews became the symbol of a condition which one had to face, or image of what bitter or difficult draught of life man had to drink; it even typified the last dread draught of all—death. Symbolism of this kind may be found in all literature of any value, and forms the grammar of parable

The word *type* has been used by theologians in a sense removed from its original one, which was that of a stamp or impress, to which the antitype corresponded, as pattern and copy, blow and resistance or rebound, hammer and anvil. The *shadow* formerly expressed that adumbration of what was indicated, which is now represented by *type*. The ancient hierophant, or revealer of holy things, was regarded as the shadow—which we should term a *type*—of the Deity.

A great difficulty has stood in the way of the doctrinal exponents of typology; when the prefiguration to which an act has been referred has every appearance of being an ordinary historic event. But the difficulty is mostly due to inability to appreciate the strength of the tendency to symbolism which characterizes the Oriental mind. Frequently in such difficulties it may be found that the ostensibly historic or actual event was really itself but a figurism; while, where that which is referred to did really occur, its aspect as a fact was readily merged by the poetic mind of the East into its newer aspect as an accepted symbolic suggestion.

The term "trope," which merely means a turning of language, a changed or figurative expression, is not so commonly used now as formerly. The word "enigma" has now become specialized in signification, though "enigmatic" retains something of the earlier meaning, that of a dark or riddling saying. The root of the word is nothing more than story or tale, coming to mean fable, common saying, proverb. Parable itself has a rival expression (*paroimia*, used in the Fourth Gospel), which has its root in the notion of the currency gained by any striking utterance, which thus became a by-word, proverb, or saw.

Fable is something spoken, into which enters the idea of the lofty or the marvellous, and the word comes to mean a feigned story or tale, a fiction. A stricter sense has supervened of fable as a fictitious tale, intended to enforce some useful truth or moral precept. It was thus defined by Johnson in his "Lives of the Poets:" "A fable or apologue . . . seems to be, in its genuine state, a narrative in which beings irrational and sometimes inanimate are, for the purpose of moral instruction, feigned to act and speak with human interests and passions." We hear of the "Scaldic fablers," the "classic fablers," the romantic or poetic fabling of early peoples; but the word has never lost the suspicion of deceit or illusion, and has been often used in a bad sense, as, for instance, in the sixteenth century we hear of "the fond dreams of doting monks and *fabling* friars." Waterland, in the eighteenth century, spoke of the distinction of "the true and proper allegorists from the fablemongers or mythics." On the other hand, an equal contempt has not seldom been poured upon dream-spinning allegorists.

The word "myth," which in its root represents, like fable, something delivered by word of mouth, has now come to take its place when a more dignified term is required. It means fiction of a kind that is not untruthful, legend of the religious order, narrative that, although not historic, covers some meaning drawn from fact, and heightened by images or personifications of phenomena, whether spiritual or natural. Theogonies, mystical renderings of natural facts, metaphysical speculations, find their embodiment in myths.

In our ordinary speech the profusion of simple metaphor that we employ is very significant of its value to us. For the most abstract ideas we evidently prefer to resort to modes of expression that would be hyperbolical were they not familiarized by custom. The growth of slang or unconstrained speech is constantly enriching language with rude metaphorical forms. Amongst such metaphorical expressions as "killing" time, the "march" of intellect, etc., etc., the best are being continually draughted off into accepted language. Poetry, the unconstrained expression of crystalline minds, produces a large and fine harvest of metaphor.

"Solidity" of intellect, mental "grasp," "sound" doctrine, "sparkling" style, a "flash" of thought, "scattered" wits, "shattered" hopes, "breaking" the peace, "overthrowing" a political opponent, the "narrow circle" of a sect, speaking with "point" or "weight," the "infancy" of a schism, an "unquiet" fancy, a "load" of guilt, "seeds" of dissension, a "rooted" belief, "borrowing" light, "echoing" a thought, a "standing" admonition, a "sacrifice" of honour, monetary "entanglement," "cementing" of friendship, "falling" into a dispute, a "pillar" of commerce, "rigid" rules, "stooping" to flattery, "awakened" instinct, "fiery" temper—such metaphors as these are become so customary by use that we forget that they are metaphors at all. In "discussing" a "subject" we forget altogether that the words mean radically the shaking asunder of something cast under or brought beneath us.

Perhaps sometimes we are conscious of the original vertebra of the phrase we employ: "Man cannot narrate without metaphors, so much more does he see in every transaction than the bare circumstances" (Helps, Comp. of my Solitude).

This may be a reason for our continued use of metaphor, but in a thousand instances we use metaphorical expressions quite unconsciously, and in the gravest language. If, then, to the most ordinary mind the best expression of an abstract or ideal conception is found in a physical symbol, we see at once the great necessity of parable to express the deepest thoughts, and with special and favouring conditions can imagine its power to be almost to express the ineffable.

The oracles, which in their prime were important and not ignoble factors in the history of Greece, cannot be overlooked in an essay on parable.

"I have come," says Hermes, in the prologue to the *Ion* of Euripides—"I have come to this land of Delphi, where, taking his seat in the very navel of the earth, Phœbus utters his chants to mortals, ever soothsaying to them both *that which is* and *that which shall be.*" Whether it was upon the present or the future that light was thrown, the lamp was hidden in a cloud; the truth was only darkly hinted at, and its revelation to some extent depended upon the faculty of the receiver.

"It may be incidentally observed," writes Mr. A. W. Ward, "that much of this obscurity, as it seems to us, was not really such to the recipients. This is a point which has been copiously illustrated by Lobeck in his *Aglaophamus*. Unlike those profound critics who start with the in itself absurd notion that the object of the Pythia was not to enlighten but to mystify inquirers—as if men would have resorted to Delphi for centuries to hear curious riddles—he endeavours to *account for* the form in which the oracular responses were usually couched. He recalls the fact—which the history of literature so abundantly exemplifies—that allegorical speech is more moving, more pleasing, more esteemed than direct; and this, not because it conceals the truth, but because it conveys the truth more impressively. He further shows that there was a poetic language, dealing largely in metaphor and paraphrase, which was certainly not used in the ordinary conversation of men, but which was partly derived from ancient and popular speech, and perfectly intelligible when used in its proper place—the surviving language of gods and of antiquity—might I venture to call it the biblical speech, which, like that of the oracles, serves to illuminate and not to obscure the oratory or conversation of periods remote from it in date."

That parable and oracle were regarded as on the same plane, may be learned from the expressions of very primitive Christians. Papias, of the second century, wrote five books, which are lost, entitled "An Explication of the Oracles of the Master," in which, says Eusebius, he set down some things "as having come to him from unwritten tradition,—both certain novel parables of the saviour's, and teachings of his, and some other things more of the nature of myth." Which leads Eusebius to observe that Papias "did not see through things that were spoken mystically by way of similitude."

An element fitly represented in the highest parable is that of inspired utterance. When ordinary eloquence rises into emotion, and some truth transcending the speaker's ordinary range finds its moment of evolution, that heightened thought cannot baldly express itself, but finds in metaphor its only fit exponent. So it is with parable. When the seer is rapt by some supernal vision, and has truly something to reveal; instead of telling it in the language that intellectually would seem the most appropriate, the cultured and refined phraseology of the metaphysician and the philosopher, he seems compelled by some invisible power to pass by all abstractions and idealisms and abstrusities. These he waves aside with scorn as a cloudy vapour generated only by laborious logicians and critics, and resorts to some supreme fountain-head for an essence potent to draw and gather rude strong physical facts into a cluster, so composed as to symbolize his meaning. Such a cluster is apparently formed after a like law to that which leads the invisible magnetic attraction to draw into relation with itself no impalpable gases, nebulous fluids, or vagrant masses of air, which, by their fluttering instability, would seem the most easy to be drawn hither or thither; but, on the contrary, particles of solid metal, which, if they come within its range of power, are found to leap to it and form an orderly and interrelated congeries at its pole. Let us picture a seer's glowing vision as being a piece of glorious, vital, and sympathetic substance, ready to be brought down from its high place to a lower and grosser one. It is reluctant, it can find no adequate expression in a sphere devoted to thoughts quite alien to itself, thoughts on a different level from its own. The seer endeavours more and more ardently to realize it, to draw down its unwilling beauty. In its clear simplicity, as it seems to him, it undoes and brings to nought the involved abstractions, the laborious intellectual approximations, of subtle minds, the roundabout logical processes, the ponderous arguments; it flies to hide itself in simple concrete things that, taken one by one, seem to contain some distant reminiscence of, or correspondence to, each facet of the luminous shape he sees.

Improvised in the clear avenues of emotion, these symbols come into view with surprising readiness and spontaneity; they seem to obey some law in their mode of flocking together, and a crystal of parable is the result—a tangible form on its own plane, but conveying in some remote, dim, but definite manner the form of the seer's waking dream.

If, as many a mystic has believed, every single terrestrial object is in absolute correspondence to some one of the higher forms of expression of the celestial spheres, through which down to each lower type a divine thought has mediately outflowed, then the most perfect parable is the bosom of Nature herself—Nature, whose face is so full of suggestion and enigma, and her voice "a dark saying" of bright things. And herein is indeed our parable, the great alphabet of man.

But man is inquisitive, the alphabet contents him not; he hastens to have vision—even if premature, even if it be only glimmer—of words and sentences. So he peers upwards into those hidden regions from which they come. If he were pure and strong in his mastery of the world that seems all fluid and gossamer-like to the ruder sense; if he were a magician able to hold fast the lovely spiritual forms that poise and float free in clear ether; if he were so free from intellectual prejudices and dulnesses, and bare or worn places of mind, that he could lead down these seeming dreams by a smooth and uninterrupted road; if his poetic image-forming faculties were large and full, a treasury of every symbol earth contains;—then he might produce a parable indeed, that would be a standing marvel to appreciative men, and the despair of the critic who dwells in the straitest circle of matter of fact. But a mist swims about his ether visions; the road of his mind is broken and rough, and cumbered with obstructions; and he has to cast about for lost words from his vocabulary of symbol. While this process of struggle is going on, the mood passes, the visions slip from his hold and flit away, the clouded and uneven mirror reflects but broken scintillations of the ray, and we get a parable as we mostly find it—beautiful, suggestive, picturesque, but blurred in its design, deficient in its composition—a dark saying from out of dreams, a strange opalescent gem with a sort of undershine of unearthly lambency.

These are not the only difficulties which lie in the field of parable. Perhaps the manner of stating the one that follows is somewhat too transcendental. A glowing particle from one province of the infinite thought-substance, though shining differently upon different reflective and absorbent surfaces of mind, must retain an essential unity. A parable might be differently interpreted, and yet a fundamental harmony subsist between each theory which it suggests. According to its recipiency, within a *nidus* more full of love or one of more relative predominance of intellect, not only must the appreciation vary of a spiritual thought, but even its outward form. This produces an element of critical uncertainty. "To the mean person, the myth always meant little, to the noble much" (Ruskin, "Queen of the Air "). Correspondingly, to the very matter-of-fact person, a parable may mean nothing at all.

Two different parables may contain the same thought, while a pair externally almost alike may convey very dissimilar meanings. As an instance illustrative of such latent unity, may be cited two separate embodiments of a well-known boding dream. A Pharaoh of Egypt is related to have seen himself in vision standing upon the bank of the Nile. "And, behold, there came up out of the river seven kine, fat-fleshed and beautiful of form; and they fed in the reed-grass. And, behold, seven other kine came up after them, poor and very ugly in form, and lean-fleshed, such as I never saw in all the land of Egypt for badness. And the lean and ugly kine did eat up the first seven fat kine. And when they were in their insides, it could not be known that they were in their insides; but they were still ugly, as at the beginning. So I awoke. And I saw in my dream, and, behold, seven ears came up upon one stalk, full and good. And, behold, seven ears, withered, thin, and blighted with the east wind, sprung up after them. And the thin ears devoured the seven good ears" (Gen. xli. 17–24). The official sacred scribes must have fallen into too drowsy a life, for they could form no clear conjecture upon the meaning of the fable. The young slave, called Joseph-the-Phœnician, was brought out of a dungeon-pit, where his interior perceptions had perhaps had an opportunity of becoming more active, in the absence of more external and sensuous attractions. He sees at once: "The dream is one;" and straightway interprets it. These two visions have a relation one to the other of an entirely opposite kind to that of two companion pictures. The latter are similar, but separate; the former are dissimilar, but the same.

Where an enigmatic utterance has been persistently misunderstood by those who have aided in its preservation, it is an argument for its authenticity, for it is unlikely that its originator should be found among them. A parable is a kind of magic casket; a crystal vase that holds drops of distilled thought, which bestow themselves upon the lips that touch it aright. To the unseeking mind, to the prejudice of the dogmatist, to the fanatic's frantic endeavour, the secret is undisclosed; and even if the casket be broken, no sparkling ichor is found within, and all that remains in the hands of those who, to use a well-known metaphor, would seize the kingdom of heaven by violence, is a heap of fragments of an ordinary jar.

There can be no study in which there is no difficulty. The philosophic Joubert will help us to a truth as to where such difficulties reside; they are in our clogged perceptions and ignorance :—

"There are some things that man can only know vaguely. About these, men of great intellect are content to entertain but vague notions. But this does not satisfy vulgar minds. Naturally and necessarily overwhelmed with ignorance, they, in their childish vexation, will bear with it in no form. The only way of quieting them is to offer them, or allow them to forge for themselves, fixed and definite ideas upon matters in which all precision is erroneous. These commonplace intellects have no wings; they cannot support themselves where there is nothing but space; they must have resting-places, fables, falsehoods, idols." These are the people who must have the foreground of a picture, which the eye truly focussed upon the main composition does not note, made up of prominent realities like market gardeners' bunches.

A parable does not absolutely fix thought; it contains it in a more or less fluid state. In a parable there is a crystal on the surface, and beneath a fluid that, according to the hand that grasps the crystal, can become as rare and vague as gas, or as concentrated as an electric spark.

The first compositions in order of time that we know of which bear upon them the label of parable (possibly 700 B.C.), are of vivid but not of universal interest. They emanate from an ancient prophet of the Euphrates, who was sent for by a Moabite ruler seeking a divination adverse to the tribe of Israel, which, on its migration from Egypt, was threatening danger to Moab. Balaam's parable was evidently understood as "a message of enchantment" or result of seership. Such compositions would seem to have been prefaced by such an introduction as—

> "The man whose eyes have been opened hath uttered it;
> He hath uttered it who heard the words of God,
> And knew the knowledge of the Most High;
> Who saw the vision of the Almighty,
> Falling into a trance, and having the veil withdrawn from his eyes."

Where the term parable is used in Job, it subserves no trivial office, being more than once used to express parts of Job's own speech and declaration, his utterance of supreme convictions upon the profoundest subjects. One of the most pregnant with recondite thought of the Psalms gathered under the name of David (the 49th) is prefaced by the words:

> "My mouth shall speak wisdom,
> And the thought of my heart shall be of understanding.
> I will incline mine ear to a parable;
> I will open my dark [or, subtle] saying upon the harp."

In the Septuagint the expression "dark saying" is represented by the Greek term which we have adopted in our word "problem." This word and "parable" are etymologically very closely akin.

In Proverbs (xxvi. 7, 9), the quality of a parable is well indicated:—

> "The legs of the lame hang useless;
> So is a parable in the mouth of fools."

It may carry an earnest man into heavenly regions; it is

as useless as lame legs, to a fool; it will not carry him anywhere, nor can he direct it for any one else.

> "As a thorn that goeth up into the hand of a drunkard,
> So is a parable in the mouth of fools."

In blundering hands it may become annoying and even dangerous.

In Ezekiel, national vicissitudes, political injuries of which it might have been dangerous to speak outright, are summarized in a riddle of figurative expressions. And as the history of his unhappy country constituted a burning question to the captive priest, the clear view of its future in the dawn-light of hope seems so grand that he calls his parable Jehovah's utterance and message. To "utter a parable" and to "prophesy" are evidently regarded as synonymous phrases. To prophesy is to forthtell present happenings in the light of their significance when viewed in a large spiritual atmosphere in which they become radiant with many a flash of suggestiveness, and even—for the field of vision stretches out so wide—disclose something of the coming future. After one of his prophecies, he exclaims: "Then said I, Ah Lord God! they say of me, Is he not a speaker of parables?" (xx. 49). In the remains of other prophets, we find the term parable applied only to such messages as are of deep inner significance, as representing the dealings of God with Man.

"By the hand of the prophets I have used similitudes" ["I was likened," Septuagint] (Hosea xii. 10).

The word parable is also used to denote a hostile engine, a figure of denunciation, a "taunting proverb."

The special office of parable is not to act as the vehicle of physical truths: they tell their own story, or are represented by myths. If it touches upon actual history, it is to tell it in ethical light—to give it, as it were, in its essential form and relative spiritual contour.

If Nature is, as she seems, a parable for herself, there is nothing left for the literary parable but either to paraphrase her, or to endeavour to draw down and provide with a body the truths relating to that part of man which transcends obvious Nature. The government of divine law, the spiritual status of man, the relation of his visible to his hidden self, the relation of time to that different quality of existence which we call eternity, the meaning of birth and death, the direction of the soul's journey—these profundities form the motive life that we find flowing into the crystal matrix of parable, whenever it goes beyond the naturalistic myth.

Descriptions of the matter of fact, of the routine of the world on which we stand, of things of daily and servile use, tend to prosaic expression.

When romance enters, and we shake off the shackles of the everyday and commonplace, description tends to poetry.

When a higher sphere is touched, of which love and passion make us dimly conscious, the sphere from which inspiration comes, and those glimpses that make us stir in our sleep, and move to a rhythm we do not understand, then there is no description, but only a kind of depiction by parable, symbol, and poetic metaphor. As Browning tells it :—

> " Emancipate through passion
> And thought, with sea for sky,
> We substitute, in a fashion,
> For heaven—Poetry :

> " Which sea, to all intent,
> Gives flesh such noon-disport,
> As a finer element
> Affords the spirit-sort."

The life that penetrates us is not the life of our ordinary plane, and can only be represented, as it were, obliquely, in a dark but musical whisper.

The following humorous passage from Browning is not without its truth :—

> " Give country clowns the dirt they comprehend—
> The piece of gold : our reasons, which suffice

> Ourselves, be ours alone ; our piece of gold
> Be, to the rustic, reason and to spare !
> We must translate our motives, like our speech,
> Into the lower phrase that suits the sense
> Of the limitedly apprehensive. Let
> Each level have its language. Heaven speaks first
> To the angel, then the angel tames the word
> Down to the ear of Tobit ; he in turn
> Diminishes the message to his dog."

In Homer we find the expression παραβλήδην ἀγορεύων (Il. iv. 6), where it signifies speaking with a side-meaning—with a covert allusion,—parallelwise ; also παραίβολα κερτομέειν (Hymn. Hom. Merc., 56), expressive of a sidelong sneer of treacherous meanings.

The following instances a more developed conception of parable : "There is many an arrow in my quiver, full of speech to the wise, but for the many they need interpreters" (Pindar).

In the Talmud, where great things are so inextricably mingled with small, alternating according as Rabbi of whim or Rabbi of wisdom succeeded to the leadership of the schools, we have to search for many a ray of light both upon the theory and actual substance of parable. We have to look both for parabolic forms, and for evidence of the quality of thought which these forms were understood to enshrine. Fortunately we can find many specimens of parable, and also, both from the interpretations now and again attached to them, and from the manifest bent of the thoughts that cluster round them, are able to discover the key to the secret which they enclose.

As parables are implicit not explicit, there was a doubt whether books containing them could belong to the Scripture Canon. "At first it was said that Proverbs, Song of Songs, Qoheleth [Ecclesiastes] were apocryphal, because they spoke παραβολας, and that they were not of the Kethubim, until the men of the Great Synagogue arose and interpreted them" (C. Taylor, Excursus ii., "Sayings of the Jewish Fathers").

An example or two will help us to appreciate the peculiar quality of spiritual thought for the conveyance of which parable would appear to be the normal vehicle.

"A man of great wealth and of a kindly disposition desired to make his slave happy. He gave him, therefore, his freedom, and presented him with as much as he could carry away in a single ship of articles of merchandise.

"'Go,' said he, 'sail to different countries, and dispose of these goods, and that which thou mayest receive for them shall be thine own.'

"The slave sailed away with his gifts, but before he had been long upon his ocean voyage he was overtaken by a storm. His ship was driven upon a rock and split in sunder; all on board was lost, all save the slave alone, who swam to an island shore near by. Sad, despondent, with nought in the world, he left the shore, and walked deeper and deeper into the island, until he drew nigh a large and beautiful city. There many people approached him with joyous shouts of welcome, and cries of 'Long live the king!' They brought a sumptuous carriage, and, placing him therein, escorted him to a magnificent palace, where many servants gathered about him, clothing him in royal robes, addressing him as their sovereign, and expressing their obedience to his will.

"The slave was filled with amazement; he believed that he must be dreaming, and that what he saw, heard, and experienced was mere passing fantasy. But as by degrees he became convinced of the reality of his condition, he said to some that were about him, toward whom he felt drawn by a friendly feeling—

"'How is this? I cannot comprehend it. That you should thus elevate and honour a man whom you know not, a poor, naked wanderer whom you have never seen before, making him your lord, causes me a wonder that I cannot readily express.'

"'Sire,' replied they, 'this island is inhabited not by men but by spirits. Long since they prayed God to send them year by year a son of man to reign over them, and He has answered their prayers. Yearly He sends them a son of man, whom they receive with honour, and elevate to the throne; but his dignity and power end with the year. At its close his royal garments are taken from him, he is placed on board a ship, and carried to a vast and desolate island, where, unless he has previously been wise and prepared for this day beforehand, he will find neither friend nor subject, and be obliged to pass a weary, lonely, hapless life. Here is chosen a new sovereign, and so year follows year. The monarchs who preceded thee were careless and indifferent, enjoying their power to the full, and recking not of the day when it should end. Do thou, then, be wiser; let our words find rest within thine heart.'

"The new-made king listened attentively to all this, and felt grieved that he should have lost even the time he had already missed for making preparations for his loss of power.

"He addressed the wise one who had spoken, saying, 'Counsel me, O spirit of wisdom, how that I may prepare for the days which are to come.'

"'Naked thou camest to us, and naked wilt thou be sent to the desolate island whereof I have told thee,' replied the other. 'At present thou art king, and may do as pleaseth thee; send therefore to this island, workmen, that they may build houses, till the soil, and give beauty to the surroundings. The barren soil will be changed into fruitful fields, people will journey thither to live, and thou wilt have established a new kingdom for thyself, with subjects to welcome thee in gladness, so soon as thou shalt have lost thy power here. The year is short, the work is long; wherefore be earnest and diligent.'

"This counsel the king followed. He sent workmen and materials to the desolate island, and before the close of his temporary power it had become a pleasant and attractive spot, and full of bloom.

"The rulers who had gone before had anticipated with dread the day when their power should come to an end; or had smothered all thought of it in revelry. But he looked forward to that day as a day of joy, when he should enter upon a career of peace that should not pass away, and happiness that should have no end.

"The day arrived; the freed slave, who had been made king, was deprived of his authority. With his power were lost his royal robes. Naked he was placed upon a ship, and its sails were set for the desolate isle.

"When he approached its shores, however, the people whom he had sent there came to meet him with music, song, and great joy. They made him a prince among them, and he lived with them for ever in pleasantness and peace."

Parables have been grammatically divided into their *protasis*, the first or defining proposition, and their *apodosis*, the consequent or answering proposition; the first part consisting of the literal and apparent sense, and the second of the mystical or figurative sense. Sometimes this *apodosis*, or interpretation, is found expressed or partially expressed, and appended to the symbolic part; and it is a strong argument for the virtue inherent in the parabolic form of speech, that while the interpreting clause is most generally found damaged in the course of its tradition, the parable proper is more often found integral and intact. Parable indeed seems to be a kind of organic form, impregnable save to a loving and cunning finger, staunchly silent or broken into atoms before a misappreciator. The interpretation, on the other hand, is no closed casket, responsive to the touch only upon the discovery of its secret spring; but is open, and so subject to the destructive handling of prejudice and sectarianism, the blundering dislocations of ignorance, or the sly interpolations of craft or caprice.

In the case of the parable quoted above, the accompanying

interpretation is merely imperfect. It gives, however, a consistent clue to the significations of the principal symbols.

As in many parabolic instances, the House-master represents the Supreme Power. The slave is the soul as disparted from its pre-existent home and endowed with freedom or individuality. The island is the portion of the corporeal world appertaining to that soul.* The friends who give good counsel are good inclinations. The year of his reign is his span of terrestrial life; the desolate island is the future world; the workmen and material are the good deeds by which alone it can be made a pleasant and peaceful dwelling.

From these deciphered symbols it is easy to construct the whole interpretation. It should be premised, however, that formal interpretation is foreign to the idea of a parable, which is nothing if not suggestive. Its suggestions are itself, its true interpretation should live fluidic in the mind, where its significance can be lit up with greater or lesser light according to the stretch of the mind's own horizon, and the variously illuminative power of its experience.

The wealthy House-master representing Deity, how can we speak in other than parabolic form of his intentions towards his offspring, of the mode of differentiation of finite from infinite, or of the process of spiritual entity becoming mortal creature? We can but say that the slave, first intimately bound up in embryonic life, is made a free soul, and endowed for merchant's functions, with a power of exchanging sympathies and buying experience. The different countries represent a span, or successive spans, of different kinds of life. The interpreter must judge by such analogies as he may. Mortal memory, as a rule, cannot go back far, before it comes to the waters of oblivion. What is gained in this commerce

---

* " Yes: in the sea of life *enisled*,
   With echoing straits between us thrown,
   Dotting the shoreless watery wild,
   We mortal millions live *alone* " (MATTHEW ARNOLD).

of life is truly one's own. The thought comes into relation here with the Parable of the Ten Talents.

The soul glides away from the infinite into the variety of finite existence. Either finite spiritual existence is impossible without character being first acquired by difficulty, the sweet gifts of the spirit's love-infancy being soon broken up (symbolized by the storm which wrecks the vessel and loses its cargo and passengers; the sundering of the ship perhaps also typifying that cracking of the bi-une spiritual sphere which it has been said disparts into division of sex before it can reach a corporeal plane); or the shipwreck is an image of the relinquishment of the bright celestial world with its loves and friendships, and of the inexplicable state that must be the concomitant of the process of birth.

With regard to the water, we may call to mind the stream, whether Nile or Jordan, which has been taken by so many in humanity as the type of what the soul passes through on its journey from earth life. Here it is swum through on the same passage, but the journey is made the reverse way, not out of, but into the corporeal world. This world, with its separation from other spheres, the comparative independence and isolation of its inhabitants, its ingress and egress alike by water which must be swum through, unless special pity or special circumstances provide a boat, is the island of the parable. Approaching this abode, the naked soul is appalled by the "solid unrealities" it meets with.

What means this apparatus of senses and qualities, inclinations and functions, faculties and powers, to a soul that has yet only known the pure slavery of love, as the mollusc may know the sunshine, or the floating sea-weed the water that enwraps it? Here are a very formidable troop of powers—hearing and seeing, and smelling and tasting, and feeling; and in the palace in the city, to which the soul is led by the carriage of nerves and message bearers, are there not emotions that shout for joy, passions that are grand but rebellious, and thinking functions that—lightsome Ariels as they are—are glad to be exercised, but require a master to bring them to rule and order? This supremacy and kingliness must be established before the rich robes, representing all the qualities and subordinate faculties which come together to endow and clothe their lord, can be worn in fitting harmony. The spark of wandering and lost and naked spirit may feel itself abashed in presence of so lordly an appanage and retinue. The range of rule must seem so vast, the position so responsible. In a dream we might deem ourselves monarchs of a world, and see obsequious ministers and bowing lacqueys before us, and all manner of pride and power within our grasp. The awakening, with its sharp reproof, would show us that we had been indulging in fantasy, and had been made its prey. This is a fine metaphor to convey the idea of a fresh-come soul endeavouring to comprehend its domain of personal and sensual existence.

The men about the slave who is made king, to whom he resorts for advice, might seem to represent spiritual existences with whom he is still in communion, were it not for the fact that these men, for whom he experiences a friendly feeling, are inhabitants of the island over which he rules; that is to say, what they typify must belong to the domain of his own embodiment with all its functions, capacities, and attributes, into which by his rule he pours that quality of his own which he brought from the kindly master's house. These men must, therefore, symbolize those natural instincts of his which seem really at one with inspiration; and his questioning commune with them resembles that perplexity caused by external things, which is not uncommonly found in imaginative and spiritually sensitive persons, even in these latter days.

In what exact phraseology a Rabbi would have interpreted the expression, "Sire, this island is inhabited by spirits," it would be difficult to determine. But we may instead submit a meaning familiar to modern study. This corporeal frame is supported by many inhabitants. The physiologist speaks of germ-cells, of " separateness of nervous pieces," " involuntary actions," " deflection of nerve." As a poetic physiologist once said, " The whole system is a *quasi* thing; a mental theatre or drama. The spinal cord moves as though it felt; the medulla oblongata breathes and eats, as if it were instinct with appetites; the senses feel as if they were conscious; and the brain understands as though it were a spirit. The cheek, too, blushes, as though it were ashamed; and so forth. But all is *quasi*, and depends upon a reality somewhere which is in none of the actors; and which reality proximately lies in a spiritual organism or in the human mind. Take this away, and the mimicry is soon at an end." The heart, the lungs, the brain, the skin, the nerves, each have their own proper motions and life. But this comes into activity only when they can find service with a living creature, and the highest of such creatures for whom can be done most abundant lordly service is the son of man, the spiritual being that inherits the essence of all this composite man-life. With every soul that comes into the world these earth spirits gain their opportunity of activity and service. In all dignity they enthrone him, but at the end of his term of office he must go, the robes of state then fall off from him, the throne is shaken, he is cast out; and the earth spirits are ready for the entrance of another soul to make a kingdom in which they can live.

As to the immortal spirit, again there is that water of truth to pass, before there can be any new extension of life. According to the parable, there is indeed a kingdom prepared for the indifferent and careless king, but it is vast and desolate. He is alone, he has neither friend nor subject, he is neither in the bosom of ante-natal existence nor in the activity of physical life; he is a spirit, and face to face with his own dreary and isolated state. A terrible picture, which cannot be made much clearer than it is, or translated altogether out of metaphor!

The hero of the parable applies his heart unto wisdom,

and instead of looking forward with dread to the close of his earthly career, or smothering the thought of it with revelry, he tries to make up for lost time, and turns his attention to what he has to do.

To understand the meaning of the symbols of what he does now, we must realize that the spirit of man has lordship at once over the two islands of the parable. He is in earth life, and has command over its faculties. Hidden though the spiritual part of him may be, he is no less a spirit, and as such has his island of individual existence in the world of spirit. We can thus understand the transfer of "workmen and material" from island to island during the soul's corporeal reign. The workmen are the spiritual inclinations, the material is the good they carry forward into actual work.

A striking difference will be observed between the conditions of entry to the two islands. In coming to the first, the naked slave finds the city ready, the people acclaiming; he has to use them as he finds them, and rule as best he may. The spirit, that is to say, has no hand in the production of the bodily frame and conditions with which he is to be identified. He finds parents to whom is due the physical nest in which he is to live. With regard to the other island, on the contrary, he must send his own workmen, prepare his own palace, till his own fields. The spirit in the spiritual world is father of his own fate, fashioner of his own presentment. The beauty or ugliness of his life, even the character of what we call surroundings, emanates from himself alone; with this reservation, that the island is originally a divine creation, and is the material upon which the tenant can work what way he will.

While the man is passing away, the island for which he is bound is described as desolate:—during the process of physical dissolution it would be hard to expect even a spirit to be able to marshal his faculties, be master of his actions, or dispense the beauties of life.

The deposed king, exiled from earth, glides along in his mystic boat. As he draws near to his spiritual home his faculties awake, his interior energies revive, his capacities expand, his love seeks to give itself out again, and as he approaches his new anchorage all his chosen subordinates are at his beck and call, meeting him, in the words of the parable, with "music, song, and great joy." He is again lord of himself, prince of a varied retinue of living properties and powers.*

What if on arrival at the island the prince cannot attain *anastasis*, cannot stand upright, and be made the master and lord of all his latent potencies? What if, while prince of the former island, he have sent bad workmen and bad material to the unseen realm across the sea? What of the slave who, reaching the first island, cannot attain to kingship over its tribes; what is he when he comes to the second island? This parable does not say! We will now proceed to search for light upon these and other subjects, and for further evidence of the subtle virtue of parable, from the crystal legacies of the great parabolist.

In passing from Talmudic parables to those of Jesus (whom some cultured Hebrews love as a mighty Talmudist) we have to face certain marked prejudices, if we would enter

---

* Shakespeare brings the parabolic element into his most thoughtful sonnets. The following is closely akin to the Talmudic parable itself:—

> "Poor Soul, the centre of my sinful earth,
>   Fooled by those rebel powers that thee array,
> Why dost thou pine within, and suffer dearth,
>   Painting thy outward walls so costly gay?
> Why so large cost, having so short a lease,
>   Dost thou upon thy fading mansion spend?
> Shall worms, inheritors of this excess,
>   Eat up thy charge? is this thy body's end?
> Then, Soul, live thou upon thy servant's loss,
>   And let that pine to aggravate thy store;
> Buy terms divine in selling hours of dross;
>   Within be fed, without be rich no more:—
> So shalt thou feed on death that feeds on men,
> And death once dead, there's no more dying then."

upon the discussion of the parables from the side of literature and art, rather than that of doctrinal theology. We have to contravene the fixed opinion that the parables evidence a design on the part of Jesus to reveal to a sect of his own formation something which was to be arbitrarily denied to enlightened men while still remaining in orthodox Judaism. Hillel and Gamaliel were accustomed to parabolic forms themselves, and probably felt the need of some such mode of expression. Refreshing indeed must have been the sense of expansive freedom, to be found in the untrammelled suggestiveness of a parable, to those oppressed by the burden of an overwhelming respect for the minutest letter of an almost strangling obligatory law. These earnest doctors, moreover, had a very obstinate, prejudiced, and spiritually unbelieving generality to do with, a people of a kind not unknown in other history, whom anything palpably outside the orthodox tradition would have dangerously aroused. The teachings of Jesus were, like any philosophical truth, or poetical conception, for all time and for all that could appreciate them : " He that hath ears, let him hear."

Jesus had more splendid vitality and less of the conventional caution than any rabbi of his era ; indeed, he moved in the more glowing atmosphere of prophetic insight ; hence he was more of a disturber than any,—bruising the old Pharisaic puff-ball, which, like all effete establishments, was dying of petty dignity and jealous emptiness. But it by no means follows that all his parables were new made. It would have been impossible to get a word listened to if he had shown no links between accepted tradition and his own readings of life. Rabbi hung to rabbi, text to text, and commentary to commentary, as in a cluster of swarming bees the fore legs of one cling to the hinder legs of another. Hillel in an inspired mood might have made one of the gospel parables, more than one of which are introduced in a manner as of something professedly familiar already. " That man is not the discoverer of any art who first says the thing; but he who says it so long, and so loud, and so clearly, that he compels mankind to hear him" (*Edinburgh Review*, 1826). On the other hand, the spirit of every utterance of Jesus (glosses apart) is at once so elevated and so homogeneous, that, whether he fused old metal or virgin ore in his crucible, his splendid originality cannot be seriously disputed.

Another kind of prejudice that has to be met is of later growth; but it is unsupported by fact, history, and probability, equally with the older prejudices that lie in the doctrinal approaches to the parables.

The oldest prejudice we may term that of ignorance and bigotry; the newest the prejudice of blind materialism and unappreciative indifference. The great teacher saw the principles of life in its pure essence; he loved to penetrate the veil rather than to classify the strands of the web. Therefore, the argument against him is, that he had no knowledge. He was an amiable enthusiast, making pretty parables that were a tissue of charming impossibilities; he was a country-bred youth who knew nothing of the world, save in a rustic prism of his own naïve and innocent nature.*

This is the theory. As a matter of fact, this simple creature was brought up in largely populated and busy Galilee, its outskirts being the Gelil-ha-goyim, or Circle of the Gentiles. Not to speak of the Egyptian legend of his childhood, he traversed as a pedestrian parts of four very different provinces at least—Phœnicia, mother of letters to his race, and touched by Egyptian lore; his own Galilee, outside which, but within

---

* "Qu'il n'eût aucune connaissance de l'état général du monde, c'est ce qui résulte de chaque trait de ses discours les plus authentiques. Le terre lui paraît encore divisée en royaumes qui se font la guerre; il semble ignorer la 'paix romaine,' et l'état nouveau de société qu' inaugurait son siècle. . . . Les charmantes impossibilités dont fourmillent ses paraboles, quand il met en scène les rois et les puissants, prouvent qu'il ne conçut jamais la société aristocratique que comme un jeune villageois qui voit le monde à travers le prisme de sa naïveté. . . . Quoique né à une époque où le principe de la science positive était déjà proclamé, il vécut en plein surnaturel" (Renan, "Vie de Jésus").

a day's journey of his reputed native place, was the capital city of all Palestine, while within a short walk of Nazareth was a college of rabbis, and a court of justice established by Rome; Samaria, sectarian thorn in the side of Judaic nationalism, a province sown with Herodian cities and palaces, including many towns where Jewish rites were not performed; and Judæa herself, with her close Pharisaic borough of Jerusalem, which, nevertheless, even to the temple's outer precincts, was open to crowds of alien Jews— Alexandrians, Babylonians, Medians—as well as to Greek-speaking officials and Roman soldiers. Beyond these familiar districts, his wanderings extended to Peræa, a region bounded by Arabia, to Syria, Ituræa, Gaulanitis, the Decapolis, and, in the south, to Idumæa. He can scarcely have been without either experience or culture; while, as a matter of fact, he seems indeed to have been as well acquainted with his country's literature and literary methods as Plato with Greek thought and the Socratic argument. Moreover there are evidences of his not having been entirely unacquainted with Plato's own thoughts; evidences as distinct as the footmark on the shore of Defoe's island.

Those, therefore, who affect to patronize him as an imaginative villager, ought either to confess to the densest critical ignorance, or to go beyond a supercilious verdict upon his naïve and charming triflings, and, in consideration of his enormous influence, to pronounce him the most dangerous misleader in the world.

The allegation is no doubt true that he did live in a sense "in full supernatural." Great poets, prophets, and thinkers, while living usefully in the world, have from age to age penetrated more or less deeply into the unseen spheres that permeate our life. With him this faculty was pre-eminent. But he appears to have had no prophetic soul to give warning that accurate classification of observed external facts—a very wholesome and valuable study so far as it goes—was, as recently discovered, the one thing needful; and, while showing a face both bright and brave on the corporeal plane, he loved to look with other eyes into his never-abandoned spiritual home, where essential life is to be found.

Of this he discoursed, and of the light thereby thrown upon the world in which we live. The whole question of the appreciation of him and of his oracles and parables hangs on the difference between eyes that see, ears that hear; and eyes closed, and ears dull of hearing. To speak slightingly of the experience or common sense of the author of the "parables of charming impossibility," merely because of his spirituality, is the same as to impugn a painter of culture for preferring blossomy landscapes and the aspects of the skies to scenes representing dramas of court intrigue, or minute studies of the bric-a-brac of a palace. The real founder of a new era, we are told by the great French critic, was ignorant of a new state of society that began with his time, and sadly neglected solid, positive science for idle parabolic extravaganzas! The idea is so flagrantly ludicrous, that it is marvellous the author was not laughed out of his eminent position for giving it birth. The "Roman Peace"!—the world has had many such, but none the less now as then are the kingdoms of the earth warring one with the other. Diplomatic intrigue, civilized slaughter, competitive selfishness, vieings of vanities!—with these as they exist in the new era, we can well justify the battle picture of the old. Bloodthirstiness has somewhat yielded to worldthirstiness.

Unless some truth of this kind can be seen, it is useless to approach the parables. And it is worse than useless unless through some cleft of emotion may enter the earnest desire that opens to sight the vista of the way of life; for it is not to every one that it is given to transcend the physical and intellectual machinery to which we are adjusted here, and without losing sanity to direct the unveiled eyes into the realms of light. The parables can wait; to the discerning, appreciative eye, the pearl has lost neither brightness or value because it has been trampled under the feet of swine.

The method of Jesus as a teacher is very clearly given:—

"Peter said; We remember our lord and teacher, how as with a command he said to us: Guard the mysteries for me and for the sons of my house. Wherefore also he explained to his disciples privately the mysteries of the kingdom of the heavens" (Clement. Hom., xix. 20).

"It is not in the way of envy that the lord announced in a certain gospel: My mystery is for me and for the sons of my house" (Clem. Alex., Strom. v. cap. x.).

"Unto you is given the mystery of the kingdom of God: but unto them that are without, all things are done in parables. . . . Know ye not this parable? then how shall ye know all the parables? . . . How shall we liken the kingdom of God? or in what parable shall we set it forth? . . Without a parable spake he not unto them: but privately to his own disciples he expounded all things" (Mark iv. 11, 13, 30, 34).

Rabbi Meir, a great allegorist, was said to have told three hundred allegories taking their story from the fox alone. Three fragments alone survive. It is possible that hundreds of the parables of Jesus are similarly lost. What a shock it would bring to some, and an anxiety to others, if a score or two of these were yet to be found in some uninterpolated papyrus! What a flutter in the dovecote until it was seen if they were all quite orthodox!

The following parable is a simple and beautiful one:—

A certain House-master planted a vineyard; and set a fence thereabout; and dug a winepress therein; and built a tower; and let it out to husbandmen; and went abroad [for a long time].

"And when the season of the fruit drew nigh, he sent his bond-servants to the husbandmen, to receive the fruits.

"And the husbandmen took his bond-servants, and one

they flayed with stripes, and another they murdered, and another they stoned [or: beat one, shamefully handled another, and sent them away empty].

"Again he sent other bond-servants of more account than the first, and they did unto them in like manner.

"[And again he sent unto them another bond-servant; and him they wounded in the head, and handled shamefully.]

"[He had yet one, a beloved son.] Now, at last, he sent unto them his son, saying, They will reverence my son.

"But when the husbandmen beheld the son, they said within themselves, This is the heir; come, let us slay him, and possess his inheritance. And they took him, and cast him forth without the vineyard, and slew him.

"When, therefore, the lord of the vineyard shall come, what will he do unto those husbandmen?

"[They say unto him] He will put them, being evil, to an evil destruction, and will let out the vineyard unto other husbandmen, such as will render him the due fruits in their seasons.

"And when they heard it, they said, Heaven forfend!"

Before proceeding to the analysis of this parable, it may be well briefly to touch upon the system of ancient society. Whether persons or possessions, the House-father, or head of the family, had all its constituents equally "in his hand;" he had under his paternal authority and jurisdiction his immediate kin and family, including his heir; his servants and dependents of various degree, bond-servants, emancipated slaves, and inferiors in a state of semi-freedom, who cultivated his lands, of which they had the administration, not the ownership. But his was no private or personal ownership; by undisputed right of status and without need of proclamation or possibility of question, he was the representative of the clan. It was indeed embodied in him; he was the person beneath whose control all smaller individualities merged, and before whom they were but units in a corporate whole, whereof all the external functions vested in its representative. Over every member of the clan and its dependents, the House-father in archaic society held the power of life and death—an authority held with the same absoluteness over the son as over the slave, though naturally exercised in a widely different spirit. Cultivators of lands acquired by the lord—lands oftentimes at some distance from the head-quarters of the clan—were of two kinds. There were husbandmen who were held to have acquired, in the third generation of occupancy, a native right in the soil; that is to say, who were irremovable from the land so long as they performed their customary obligations. There were migratory cultivators, strangers induced by the lord to take up a temporary tenure of land, with a position determined by contract.

From historic sources we can thus give some amount of clearness and definition to the characters of the little parabolic drama, and these facts are also an evidence that the narrative is a sufficiently natural one in its exoteric sense.

We will now submit a tentative interpretation, following the same manner as was followed by the rabbis in the parable cited from the Talmud.

The House-father is, as before, the Deity. The vineyard, girt about with its fence, suggests a parallelism with the island of the other parable, surrounded by its isolating sea. The hedged vineyard is the individualized man, the field of the development of the action of Divinity. As the sea which encircled the island represented that state of truth, or absence of the fictitious and the factitious, through which a soul must come in its naked journey to birth in the material world, so the "hedge" here is the sign of that external world itself—the body as the limiting enclosure of the soul, the outward mark of man's individuality or personal separateness. The "winepress" in the vineyard is the deeper and more internal part of man, the shrine of the soul, the spiritual possibilities, the place where the essential fruit is to be found. In the "tower," the lofty outlooking faculty, or intellect, finds its fit correspondence.

The "husbandmen" are the developing circumstances of the world; the natural passions and attributes. It is these terrestrial senses (as opposed to the immortal spiritual qualities, or germs) which are to develope man, and enable him to learn good or evil.

The House-master "goes abroad." We do not know the closeness of the bond that unites the not yet incarnate spirit with the divine centre from whence it proceeded; we are more conscious in our present state of the fact of the "far country." A lifetime may be presumed to be represented by the expression, "for a long time." The man, when born, is, as it were, left wrapped in matter and sensual life, in the hope that he will turn therefrom again, bringing his fruit. If the spirit were not left in this strange land of matter, we may suppose that there would be no possibility of any freedom of choice or will, but that it would always be as powerless to act individually as a sunflower to turn away from the sun.

The "season for the fruit," who can tell? For how few even try to earn the wondrous gift of life made to them, much less strive to repay it by flower and fruit of love given forth and glorious activities exercised to the furthest reach of power! The fruit is the growth of the human being; and we may believe that that growth is the only reward expected by the divine nurse, who lives and works in us.

The "servants" are the influences from without himself that act upon man. Truth in many a form is sent out unto him. Many messengers come to look for the good fruit of the world of man. This is not the history of a special individual. Examples of one man to another, suggestions of a friend, probings of an enemy, teachings of fact, experiences drawn from life, all these in the veiled scheme of the universe may be messengers of God. And the great truth-bearers, the servants of more account, that come into the world now and again, and seem to transcend ordinary mortality, being so big with the gospel of God!—truly that House-father is never weary of sending his servants; his poets and prophets are for ever waiting on us like servants to entreat us to rise to the due stature and dignity of men.

But the husbandmen, being at that distance from the lord, have some power to rebel and to reject. The earthly qualities, strong on their own plane, are active in repelling the entrance of the higher influences. The creation of man seems to be like Penelope's web; it is ever being undone. The servants are cast out and slain. Do the great teachers always evoke gratitude and results responsive to their teachings? Does not the dark mass of humanity ever reject and spurn its prophets? The utterer of the parable was one, and he has had brothers; have they not always been crying aloud, and seemingly almost in vain, to these children clinging so proudly to their prerogative in the world of sense? By the effect of habit, incarnate man takes the vineyard to be all his own; earthly aims and ambitions push out as a vanishing dream the truth of heavenly birth, and the call of the Father for even a portion of his own is treated with scorn.

At last the House-father sends his own son; in him will surely be recognized the power and the glory of the house from whence he comes; he must meet with reverence.

The identification of a quality of divinity with what we may imperfectly term personality, was familiar to the oriental mind.* The nearest son of God is not Truth, but Love. The

---

* The following, from the Talmud, will illustrate the subject in this and other respects: "When God was about to create man, the angels gathered about him. Some of them exclaimed, 'Create, O God, a being who shall praise Thee from earth, even as we sing Thy glory in heaven.' Others said, 'O God, create no more! The glorious harmony of the heavens which Thou hast sent to earth will be by man destroyed.' Of a sudden God turned to the contesting hosts of heaven, and silence fell upon them all. Before the throne of glory appeared the Angel of Mercy on bended knees. Sweet was the voice which said entreatingly, 'O Father, create Thou man. He will be Thine own noble image on earth. With heavenly pity will I fill his heart, with sympathy towards every living thing impress his being. They will all praise Thee through him.' The Angel of

son that is sent is the pure spirit of love, specially striving to enter and soften the encrusted heart. Love yearns for the fruit of the human vineyard; life has come of love's great gift, and therefore love is natural heir to a willing tribute, but cannot be heir in reality until the response of love, the love of love, can be awakened. In this case there is recognition. "This is the heir," is the cry; the voice of conscience arises, and tells them that they have been ill-using the gifts of heaven, the sacred vessels into which spirit was poured; they see suddenly their wasted life.

But at the inner sting of conscience, arises the desire of the external nature in which the man is living, to quench, deaden, and ignore it, and so cast it out. The sense of independence arises and asserts itself; the terrestrial elements will recognize neither gentle heir nor mighty lord; they will slay this constraining love, shake off this claim of heirship, destroy this thraldom over themselves.* If we can but cast out this offensive interference, they say to themselves in effect, then we are free, we can hold to what is our own without

---

Mercy ceased, and the Angel of Peace, with tearful eyes, spoke thus: 'O God, create him not! Man will disturb Thine own peace. Blood will follow his advent. He will invent war, confusion, horror, to blot the earth, and Thou wilt no longer find a pleasant place among Thy works on earth.' Then, in stern tones, spoke the Angel of Justice: 'Thou, God, wilt judge him; he shall be subject to my law, and peace shall again find a dwelling-place on earth.' The Angel of Truth approached, and said, 'Father of Truth, cease; with man Thou sendest a lie to the earth.' Then all were silent, and out of the deep quietness came the Divine word: 'Thou shalt go with him, thou mine own Seal, Truth; but thou shalt yet remain a denizen of heaven—betwixt heaven and earth shalt thou float, an everlasting link between the two.'"

* On the plane of individual lives as opposed to the ground upon which is transacted the subtle drama of qualities, we may find the following illustrative of the kind of feeling here manifested:—

> "The kings of the earth assemble themselves,
> And the princes take counsel together,
> Against the Eternal, and against his chrisome one, saying,
> 'Let us break their bands in sunder,
> And cast away their cords from us'" (*Psa.* ii. 2, 3).

"Touch not my chrisome ones [christs] and do my prophets no wrong."— 1 Chron. xvi. 22 (LXX.).

scruple. "Self is the lord of self" for ever; and may close the door against the divinest visitant. Man has his independence if he will, notwithstanding the tenderest or the most terrible appeals of Love. Whatever he may choose to hold is in effect given over to him for the while, but though he may do what he will, Love is still the true heir. The fruit may be yet offered to him after the most stubborn seasons of refusal to admit him.

One inevitable fate awaits these husbandmen—dismissal; the destruction of the habits to which the soul has been subjected, in which it has grown content, even to finding therein its only refuge. The divine power, in his eternal love, will even take the spirit of the man from the place where he has put him, and away from the influences by which he is surrounded, and will give his vineyard new conditions of culture, a new set of husbandmen or fostering influences, another chance of bearing fruit, and of surrendering, at length, a voluntary offering of his inheritance to the true heir. "Other husbandmen"—it is not said whether or not they are to be of a different order, and represent a different life-plasm from that of earth. But the parable ends with an expression of assured faith that there will be yet a season of fruit, and that the fruit will be made a willing offertory to the vineyard's lord.

In the study of parabolic art, the following conditions have to be borne in mind as constituting the *sine quâ non* of an interpretation. Though a reading from one sphere into another can only be approximately effected, it should be seen that the separate details of the body of the esoteric sense hang together as closely as those of the external form, and constitute on their own plane as apparently consistent and reasonable a whole. There should further be some connecting link of analogy, however slight, between the external symbol and its hidden sense. This may be invisible to very dull eyes, and require as fine a faculty, in its own line, as that of a scientific analyst, for its apprehension. Collateral support should, if possible, be drawn from unparabolic thought of the date of the composition under notice, or of the school or influences likely to affect it or be in sympathy with it.

To estimate how far the first condition is fulfilled in this case, we may briefly and roughly sum up the argument of the parable. The Divine Father seeks to foster into growth Man, the spirit. He makes him individual. He sets an external fence around him, places him in matter; he gives him a brain, also a spiritual shrine for the fruit of his life to be developed in; and physical senses which work upon him with their varied promptings, temptations, influences, passions, upheavals. To prevent the real inner nature from being utterly lost in an external existence, yielding fruit only to itself, and that of worsening quality, the Spirit of Life sends into the world of nature messengers to remind, and many an influence to awaken the soul, and appeal to it for its fruit. If truths and examples, facts and everyday experience, natural life and beauty, eloquence of poet and exhortation of prophet, fail to call forth any growth and fruit and good in the man, but are rather thrust aside with violence; He pours his own love into the heart, it may be under guise of some deep sorrow, it may be felt dimly in the pulse of some great joy. This love is the true heir and lord of the children of men, but if they will not be the children of love, but rather rebels living in selfish independence and isolation and wantonness, then love is driven out from them, and cannot enter the vineyard. But the process of creation is patience; a great change comes, and in the passage through physical death the arrogant senses are all left behind, the defaulting husbandmen are dismissed and destroyed. The spirit is shown an avenue into new surroundings, new influences, and a new field of life, wherein, maybe, its diviner energies will be evoked, and it will be led to bring forth fruit in due season, and an honest recognition of, if not a loving response to, the love that is the real giver of it all.

This may perhaps be regarded in "dry light" as a fairly consistent metaphysical theory, and not quite one of those beginning in nothing and ending nowhere. Mathematical accuracy, it would, of course, be unreasonable to look for in the present state of our faculties. "There will be no scientific evidence of God's working in nature," says Agassiz, "until naturalists have shown that the whole creation is the expression of a thought, and not the product of physical agents." But the solution of the parable of nature can never be stated in mathematical terms. The question with which the student has to do is a historic one: Is the suggested *apodosis* of the parable in harmony with the modes of regarding the mystery of life familiar to the race and epoch from which the parable emanated?

It may be interesting to compare with the above rendering of the parable of the vineyard, an explication drawn from the text-books of the followers of Swedenborg. The two versions are quite separately evolved, but allowing for minor deviations, are evidently on the same broad general track. If there be a science of the peculiar Flora and Fauna, so to speak, of parabolic imagery, it is natural that mistakes should be made in the process of arriving at it.

"The spiritual sense does not relate to any one particular Church, but is of universal application, having reference neither to time nor place, but to states of spiritual life. . . . The vineyard signifies . . . the Church as formed in man by the Lord implanting in his mind the principles of goodness and truth. . . . *Neither religion nor the Church can exist among men except so far as they exist in them.* But the Church, while it exists in its principles in the mind, exists in its fruits in the life. Between the implanting of religion in the mind and the producing of its fruits in the life, the great struggle takes place; for conflict and sorrow are experienced in bringing forth into actual life that which has been implanted in the mind. . . . The wine-press and tower

are emblematic of principles of the rational mind. . . . W
the Lord, as the Creator, has formed the human being, and
endowed him with every faculty that belongs to his nature,
and provided him with every means that may be requisite
for the proper and profitable exercise of his faculties, he
leaves him to work out his own salvation. His leaving him
to himself is only an appearance, or rather, it is a mode of
expressing the fact of man's being left to act from liberty,
and under a full sense of his responsibility. . . . The servants
whom the Lord sends are the truths . . . which seasonably
remind us of our stewardship. . . . Nor is it enough to make
this acknowledgment in words; we must make it in deeds;
not with the intellect only, but with the heart. . . . The
natural mind resists with all its power, and many struggles
are required to overcome its opposition. . . . It is disposed
to pervert the truth, which is meant by beating one of the
servants; to reject it, which is meant by killing another; and
to falsify it, which is meant by stoning another. . . . As
the unregenerate man falls into deeper states of evil, and as
the regenerate man falls into deeper states of temptation, the
Lord applies to them other truths more suited to their states,
and therefore capable of enabling them to resist evil and
do good, and to render Him the fruits of their life and experience. . . . 'Last of all He sends unto them His son'— . . .
those who reject the truth of doctrine from their understandings are too liable to reject the truth of love from their
hearts" (W. Bruce, Comm. Matthew, 1867).

To complete the elucidation of the parable we have
quoted, it remains to draw from the literature of the time
of its composition collateral evidence upon the quality of
thought then prevalent. Were this not done, a would-be
interpreter of parables might be in danger of falling into
the temptation of reading them forwards, or producing a
version more in harmony with the current thought of his own
later period, than with the intention of the parabolist. The

following, from a contemporary of Jesus, will serve to illustrate the picture, which, indeed, it greatly resembles in its ethical basis, of the robber husbandmen standing over the wounded and bleeding messenger whom they have cast out :—" If any one should gash and cleave asunder that Reason [Logos] which stands upright and is wholesome and straightforward, which ascribes to God alone the might of the universe ; and should be discovered in the act of breaking in upon it—that is to say, standing over it, thus being wounded and cloven through, being filled with assurance that it is his own mind and not God that is the source of activity, he is a thief taking away what belongs to others. For all things gotten belong to God " (Philo. Leg. Alleg., 3, § 10).

In a more prosaic and less attractive manner than that of our parable, Philo also discourses of husbandry with the same symbolic under-meaning. If we look closely, we shall discover more than one point of resemblance between the course of his thought aud the interpretation given above of the parable of the husbandmen. He speaks (De Praem. et Poen., § 2) of "Seed . . . which the Creator has sown in an excellent soil, namely, the rational mind. The first is hope, the fountain of our lives. Hope of good weal incites those zealous after virtue to study philosophy, so that by this means they may be able both to discern the nature of things, and to do things that are in conformity with the perfecting of those two most excellent modes of life, the contemplative and the practical, he who attains to which is at once in true good weal. There are some now who either, like enemies, have burned the seeds of hope by kindling the blaze of vices in their soul, or, like persons careless of the art of the husbandman, have let them perish by neglect. There are others, moreover, who, while appearing to give proper heed, cling rather to self-love than to devotion, and have attributed the causes of their upright actions to themselves."

He illustrates a similar metaphoric train of thought when

he speaks of "expelling the vices, and driving them out of the boundaries of the disposition, and establishing the virtues as settlers within them" (On Seeking Instruction, x.). We find a parallel to the notion of the tower in the vineyard in the words, "He has established reason, like a scout upon a watch tower" (DeSomn., § 25).

The following is a parable that has been generally mistranslated and misunderstood :—

"When the unclean spirit is gone out of the man, it goes through waterless places, seeking rest, and finds it not. Then it says, I will return unto my house whence I came out; and having come it finds it empty, swept and garnished. Then it goes and takes with itself seven other spirits more evil than itself, and they enter in and dwell there; and the last state of that man becomes worse than the first."

We have already seen human individuals made to stand in a parable for qualities, as Philo shows was the method of the time, when he says, in reference to a Hebrew scripture name which he is using didactically in an allegorical sense, "Abandon the idea that this expression is used about a man, and rather turn your eyes upon the soul, with a kind of dissecting glance" (On Seeking Instruction, xi.). Similarly a personified evil spirit may represent parabolically a quality.

A curious question is suggested by this parable: Why it is so easy to a seer to confound or confuse qualities and persons? Why do individual beings and individual attributes so readily merge and become indistinguishable in mystic writings? Even in cultured Philo, because his mind is spiritually inclined, he seems to slide with unconscious ease into the same confusion. In fact, a condition by which a quality becomes, as it were, set forth and made substantial in the guise of a dramatic person, seems of the very essence of parable. To appreciate parable, we must, therefore, find a theory which will account for this puzzling phenomenon.

We earth-folk are, we will at least suppose or assume,

spirits underneath our terrestrial raiment; we therefore have certain spiritual attributes, however obscured; and from them we can tentatively advance by analogy to such spiritual powers as may exist in a less shackled state of being. For instance, we are sometimes led blindly by our desires; as we familiarly say, led by the nose; as if the desire, passion, or weakness were a sort of intimate person not always to be trusted, a slave, maybe, cajoling his master, or a child pertinaciously dragging along a parent. The road our will takes in any enterprise is the road of our sympathies; we make for what is kindred to ourselves. We stay as long as we can in society we like. We are under the law of necessity as well, and have to do task work to maintain the bodily life; but, apart from bodily conditions, we are inclined to stay in alliances and relations arising out of sympathies for as long as those sympathies hold. We cannot really go any whither without holding on to a clue of sympathetic connection. As a fable runs:—

"A certain pragmatical, gay, fluttering coxcomb would needs make a visit to a philosopher. He found him alone in his study, and straightway fell a marvelling how he could endure to lead so solitary a life. 'Sir,' quoth the philosopher, 'you are much mistaken; for I was in very good company until you came in.'"

The coxcomb evidently did not enter into the company of the unseen friends of the bearish philosopher, but he disturbed momentarily the thinker's relations with them, forcing him first, by the easily sundered, slight, and superficial sympathy which we call civility, to enter into relation with himself, and then being cast out rudely from that slender ground of meeting, by the antipathy which at length was generated and pushed him backwards.

Supposing the same coxcomb to have entered a room where a learned society was holding a conference. He would not thereby come any nearer to the learned society. He would indeed be in a room with the members, but it would be little more than a vacancy to him if he had no relations of interest to its contents. He would be side by side with a number of corporeal forms of more or less dignified appearance, but unless some chord could be touched in him responsive to some object of the society, he would be no nearer to it for his entrance into the room than if he were a thousand miles away. His distance from it might be approximately measured in years; if ten years' study could enable him to appreciate the objects of the society, he would be at least ten years off it, and might eventually really enter it. But he would need to abandon coxcombry for earnest study, and perhaps to be helped by some fostering friendliness of the members, and so would have to make his way in by the way of sympathy after all.

We have only to predicate for spiritual beings more directness of impulse, and much greater plasticity, elasticity, and responsiveness of substance; we have only to allow them perceptions equal to a telegraph instrument at a central office, and a power of living in interests in proportion to the attraction of such interests, and irrespective of what we call locality; and from our own faculties we may then learn something of the way in which an individual may appear to blend with a quality. The same law that makes friends here draw near to one another's minds, and be attracted by kindred tastes, would draw a spiritual being into relation with such qualities in men as might be in harmony with himself. As a man may come in contact with one set of cultivated persons on a ground of musical tastes, with another on some special plane of thought, with others on account of parallelism of moral attitude; so we may surely presume a spirit may be in rapport with a number of individuals each of whom has for ruling passion some quality towards which he himself shows proneness or sympathy.

Eliminating space, it is evident that a spirit's dwelling-place would vary according to the interests in which he would live, and the way in which they would present themselves for him to dwell in. One interest might be a sympathetic quality in a man, by fostering or exciting which he himself would live with greater fulness. Or that sympathetic bond might link, not two virtuous but two vicious intelligences, or two average intelligences, in respect of one virtuous or vicious attribute. Were the man to adopt strenuous measures to alter his own state, as, for instance, by directing moral earnestness upon any vice, into which he had fallen, and so strengthening his nature against it, the interested patron of, or sympathizer with that vice would be surely pushed back by every such effort made. He would feel that his friend was not so close to him as before. If the man's own spirit could become settled in its vanquishment of a particular evil, the old place of that evil within him would no longer afford a road for spiritual intimacy to travel by, and be no longer a beacon familiar to kindred qualities in others; some former spiritual sympathizer would feel repelled, and have to realize that in one soul the less he could now count on finding a friendly home.

The following passage may help to illustrate the subject: "Watch inwardly, viewing the ramparts of your temple with the keen eye of a sentinel of war, and visit also, as with a lighted taper, the innermost cells and dungeons, not omitting also to look even into the shrines, wherein are loves and affections, and the very sanctuary of religion itself. For enemies swarm around you, and they are those that have no shame as to where or how their trap is laid. If you admit them, they endeavour slowly to undermine the temple and build thereon another of their own devising. But be not afraid: the temple is your own; none can enter there unless you leave the door open and forget to watch it. Otherwise you may move in impenetrable armour among men and spirits. For a practical illustration:· When you suffer aught but a religious and righteous disturbance to enter your mind, be sure one who is unworthy stands at the door—shut him out and be calm. Or, when the ill-humour of another provokes in you a return, know that you have opened the door to a companion of the presiding genius that has inspired the ill-humour; and so run a risk of losing your citadel! Unless you feel your better self regnant, know that you are but a part owner of your own house. When you admit good, you are then only a part owner with God, but he is the life you have, the air you breathe. Do not imagine the action of good and evil inspirations to be at all alike. Good spirits only foster by companionship and outward encouragement the good in your soul; they have far too great a respect for individuality and force of character to attempt to enter the soul's domains as do the evil ones. If they acted thus, the power of good being much the greater, those who should be developed by struggle would be brought to a kind of infantine good. But even friends may only give a helping hand, a warning word, and keep the evil from being overstrong. Goodness must be attained by purely internal effort."

Referring now to the parable of the Unclean Spirit, which depicts the life of an individual in its depths, we may turn to the cognate thought expressed in Plato in terms of qualities: " Sometimes . . . some of the cupidities get destroyed, while others are dethroned, because of the coming into play of a certain modesty in the youth's soul, and once again he gets restored to order. . . . And, again, there are other cupidities, kindred to the dethroned ones, that gain secret nurture, and, for lack of experience of a father's charge, they grow numerous and masterful. They are wont to draw him then towards the same intimacies as before, and, through their secret connections, give interior birth to a multitude. Eventually, I think, they are wont to seize upon the citadel of the youth's soul, since they perceive it to be vacant of discipline, virtuous pursuits, and true principles—the best watchmen and guardians over the rational part of a man beloved by God. And, then, indeed, false and vagabond considerations and opinions rush up in the stead of these, and take possession of the identical region in such a man" (Rep., viii. 560 a).

Philo also comes in his discourse very near to an interpretation, even in detail, of the parable. He says: "As, unless some one tames them at their height of savagery by drinks and foods, those unappeasable and inexorable mistresses of the body, thirst and hunger, ofttimes strain it more, or, at all events, not less, than those are strained who are racked even unto death on the wheel by the torturer: so, in like manner, covetous desire, which first renders the soul empty, and then attaches within it tormenting desire and ungovernable madness, introduces into it heavier masters than the former tyrants. And yet they have the same names with them, to wit, thirst and hunger; not of those things, however, which concern the belly's enjoyment, but of money, glory, authority, and fine figure, and innumerable other things which appear to be objects of envy and contention in human life" (De Concup., § 1).

The following passage, in which we see a passion regarded as a person, and as roaming through a desert outside the soul, is also wonderfully close in its relation to the parable: "Many persons have recovered sanity by removal from their surroundings, having been cured of their mad and frenzied lusts by reason of the sight being no longer able to pander to the passion with images of pleasure. For in consequence of the sundrance, it is through a void that the passion must needs rove, since there is no longer any object at hand whereby it can be inflamed. And, if a person find such sundrance, let him assuredly keep away from the revel gatherings of the multitude, and embrace solitude, seeing that there are snares in a foreign land resembling those which are found in a man's own country. . . . For as the bodies of those beginning to recover from a long illness are very subject to being caught by it again, so likewise the soul which is just regaining health is faltering and shaky in its intellectual sinews, a fact which makes there be reason to fear lest the passion which was wont to be excited by familiar intercourse with inconsiderate people may run back again" (De Praem. et Poen., § 3). Again, Philo speaks of familiar customs as powerful charms, the phantasies of which may again arouse "the indwelling appetite for base pursuits, and restore to vitality the still-remembered memories of things which it were well to have forgotten."

We may throw light upon the symbolic expression "dry places" by comparing with it a saying of Heraclitus "the dark master," which, it is important to note, was a familiar one to Philo, Plutarch, Clement of Alexandria, and Porphyry. Bacon ("Apophthegms") thus understood the saying, "Heraclitus the obscure said, 'The dry light is the best soul, meaning, when the faculties intellectual are in vigour, not drenched, or as it were blooded, by the affections." If we are careful to note here that the word affections is employed by Bacon in a quasi-physical sense, and does not mean pure benevolence, or the yearning of unselfish charity, we shall understand the meaning of the "dry light." It is light unhindered by cloudy vapours of sensuality and the blinding mists of personal selfishness. As the saying comes down to us in another form, "That soul, according to Heraclitus, is dry and the best, which traverses the body like lightning the clouds," that is, the lower pleasures have no hold upon it ; the spirit is "ether-like and pure," as the ancient commentators have it. The "dry places" might thus represent regions removed from sensual life, regions delightsome indeed to an aspiring spirit, but very much the reverse to one such as the parable depicts, earth-bound and restless, seeking gratification, and longing for some kind of covert to dwell in.

The unclean spirit represents the ruling evil of the individual, and in his consent to that evil he gives it house and home. The context seems to show that the parable is a clinching of thought on the question of the value of a "sign" or portent. Will a startling shock be of any avail in converting a person who has no desire for improvement, who has nothing but suspicion of good faith, and scepticism towards good work, because he disbelieves in goodness itself? Should, for a moment, the spirit of self-satisfaction be shaken by the most powerful of external marvels or sensible signs, the effect must be but temporary, and the deep-rooted quality which enthrals the man will return with renewed force.

The ruling passion is expelled from the individual, and with it the unclean spirit that finds its home therein, and so has battened upon the man. Torn from its hold, it passes abroad through arid regions where there is no gratification of sense. It is restless, and yet seeking rest, and some way of drowning its feverish fire. "Seeking comfort" is the phrase according to the Peschito version. None is to be found. So it craves its old activity in the man's heart. Trying the entrance, it finds no opposition; the heart is vacant of any nobler inhabitant or angelic affection; is in a state, in fact, of well-garnished emptiness. "Garnished," perhaps, we should understand as brought into conformity with the lust that has departed, and, though not actually calling it back, yet showing the ready welcome of a swept and suitable home. An unclean spirit may be got rid of, but if its place be not filled at once with higher and nobler impulses, with inhabitants able to bar its entrance, it will speedily return, for it has no home to go to but such as this one, and its only chance of sensual comfort is after this fashion. It is useless to drive away a vice unless its place be filled by a virtue. The ease of its welcome, or the roominess of the shrine opened for it, leads it to seek further delight in companionship of its own kind. The evil quality comes back with a rebound, and assumes its sevenfold or utmost force, and the man surrenders himself to his vices as to his natural masters. It is a "horrid image" which the parable presents, that of a belt composed of unsettled parasitic spirits, so numerous, that where one finds hiding-place he is like not to be without a host of companions worse than himself, and anxious to share in the smallest corner of a home opening out into external activity of life. But the proverbial words "from bad to worse" show that experience has marked the truth which the parable conveys, and everything in nature tells us how soon standing still becomes retrogression; slackness, decay; and vacant listlessness, entrance of evil.

We turn now to a parable of great artistic beauty, that of the Ten Virgins.

"At that time shall the kingdom of the heavens be likened unto ten virgins, who took their lamps, and went forth to meet the bridegroom. And five of them were foolish, and five were wise. For the foolish, when they took their lamps, took with them no oil; but the wise took oil in the vessels with their lamps. Now while the bridegroom tarried, they all slumbered and slept. But at midnight a cry is raised, 'Behold the bridegroom; come ye forth to meet him!' Then awakened all those virgins, and trimmed their own lamps. And the foolish said unto the wise, 'Give us of your oil, for our lamps are going out.' But the wise made answer, saying, 'Lest there suffice not for us and for you, do ye rather go unto them that sell, and buy for yourselves.' And while they went away to buy, the bridegroom came; and the ones that were ready went in with him to the wedding-feast, and the door was shut. Afterwards come also the rest of the virgins, saying, 'Sir, sir, open to us.' But he answered and said, 'Verily, I say unto you, I know you not.' Be watching, therefore, for ye know not the day nor the hour."

Is this merely the innocent story of an ignorant villager, as Renan would have it; or is there an unearthly solemnity about it, ill befitting the simple narrative of a wedding feast? A bridegroom's house is being prepared for a ceremony to take place, as was usual, after sundown. Youths and maidens who are bidden, decked with myrtle chaplets, and with palm branches in their hands, attend the bridal pair, bring music and gaiety, and make the evening bright by carrying tall lamps or torches. These are made of staves bearing at the top a little vase or dish, filled with oil and pitch, and containing a wick made of a strip of rag, or a ravelled piece of a linen dress. The picture is true to life, but so slight and imperfect; it is a selection from incidents; what does the selection mean? and why is the effect so solemn, when it seems to proceed from no more serious incident than that of the shutting out of a few careless young folk from a revel, because they are not ready to perform their part properly in the procession? How it jars upon us in the gay picture to find the bridegroom churlish who should be all love at such a time, and ready to make allowance for every one, as befits a man when he is happy! When, in reply to the knocking at the door, he says to his old friends, who really have gone to try to buy oil to make up for their want of foresight, but gone too late, to the closed bazaars, "Verily, I say unto you, I know you not," how cold and stern seems the expression, how strangely out of keeping with the hour! The legend is no lightly composed story, it is designed with purpose and intended to convey a meaning.

We must not expect to find, in the fabulous shell of a parable, an equal probability with that of a matter-of-fact story. As a narrative, it must be sufficiently consistent to hang together, but it is only a memorial vehicle of the meaning it contains. Samuel Johnson (not the Doctor), of the seventeenth century, whose works are a model of strong literary style, detected the incongruity of parabolic form with ordinary fable: "Prophetic Dreams and Visions, and the Schemes of their Language and their Descriptions, are more wide from the thing itself, and more unlike, than the harshest Metaphors that ever were in the world" ("Works," p. 49).

The interpretation which we attempt of this parable is in harmony with the mode of Oriental thought, as evidenced in the Sohar, the Talmud, and the works of Philo, but we cannot but own that it must seem unfamiliar to the practical, not to say materialistic and unphilosophical, mind of the day.

Of endo-physical matters difficult to describe with any closeness, parable affords a kind of remote depiction. It is difficult, for instance, to treat of that mysterious entity, one's soul, in everyday language, in spite of the Sunday labour that is spent upon the effort. In parable is a vehicle by which mystery can be appropriately conveyed.

The context of the Parable of the Ten Virgins refers to the passage of man; the parable itself is the legend of a mystical nativity.

At that time is a reference to the hour of the body's death and the birth in the spirit. *The kingdom of heaven* is the whole nature of man; temperament and character, soul and body. God works in his living creatures, and man is preeminently his province. The *ten virgins* are the totality of the qualities and inclinations of man, taken in their singleness, without excuse or shade; ten symbolically implying completeness or totality, as we shall afterwards illustrate by example; and virginity very appropriately marking separateness. The *lamps* are the special lights or functions of each quality as viewed separately. The *bridegroom* is the living spirit to whom these qualities appertain; he is making ready to be born as an inhabitant of a new world, and his garments are robes of light, to which, in the earth-sphere which he is preparing to quit, the bright dress of a bridegroom is the best approximation.

As to the *virgin* symbols, his attributes as manifested in the state which he is now quitting, are made up of the physical faculties of earth and of spiritual qualities, typified as *five* and *five*. Half are called *prudent*, because they are ready for the office that is devolving upon them, with which those who are symbolized as *foolish* have nothing to do ; further attendance, or continuance of energy, being none of theirs. In other words, there is, as betokened by the taking *no oil*, no spiritual life or replenishment in the senses and qualities proper to earth, which are but for a time. That time is drawing to a close, and the failure or waning of the oil is a manifestly expressive symbol of the coming extinction of their functions. *The wise took oil ;*—the sister qualities, on the contrary, are of divine or eternal birth ; theirs it is to burn with the perennial oil of God's love, which they take into the receptive faculties, and are ready to give out again in the flame of purposeful life.

While the bridegroom tarried—that is, during the mysterious process of death—in the interval, so to speak, between life and life,* the *virgins all slumber and sleep*, the various qualities are dormant. The man is dying ; the physical signs of his life are depressed and burning down. The spiritual qualities are at once existent in the spiritual life when the first throe of death comes, but they slumber at that dread moment, for they have no *animus ;* the being whom they ought to inspire has, to use a rude metaphor, not quite picked himself up or pulled himself together. The soul part of him is being slowly withdrawn from the body (according to some orderly process of birth, no doubt, which science "*in the spirit*" can watch, but we un-seers cannot observe) by the actual spirit, who is putting on his appropriate garb, the robes of light, the beauty of which we are left to convey to ourselves by the symbol of a bridegroom's gala dress.

The picture is a weird one ; in the silent hours, while the body lies a-dying, the qualities once so eager, so busy, so full of life, so fully one with the man who was their lord, are

---

* Christian fathers named the state or experience of the soul, after its summons has reached it, the *psychopannucheia, pervigilium,* or night-long vigil. The Greeks had a cognate fancy respecting this intermediate period : " The night long the spirit of hapless Patroklos stood by me " ("Iliad," xxiii. 105).

waiting in still reserve and latent strength, hybernating in the mysterious and pregnant winter time of death.

Midnight comes, sign of an ending time that is also a beginning. The physical frame has reached its final and deepest darkness; there is no longer a man, but a corpse. Its midnight passes, its new day that is beginning is chemical only; its pride of organic function is over. The *cry* of the parable is an unearthly one; it marks at once the midnight, and a different new day; friendly forms are around the unconscious being, who is not yet adjusted to his new plasm. These friends have marked the midnight, and cry gladly to each other that the hour has come for them to commence their ministrations.

Behold, the bridegroom! Go ye forth to meet him. Instantly, on the birth of a soul into its new existence, its qualities must be awakened and called into life and force. If on our own plane we could picture such a condition as that of a new-born babe ushered into life with no surroundings whatever, no circumstances to evoke its action, no soft voice of a mother, no sight or sound of earth, the only conclusion we could draw as to the effect of such a state of things (granting also that respiration and nutrition could be dispensed with, for air is the first awakener and food the supreme interest) is, that it would result in imbecility. Quality by quality, a child's faculties are evoked, its intense interest catching hold of the slightest appeal to its primitive and unspoiled senses. So we may reason analogically that in process of spiritual birth, which seems so dim a dream, the first step necessary is the awakening.

Then awakened all those virgins. The qualities are bidden to go forth to meet the summons of their head. They awaken from their trance, and reassert the temper and character of the individual. The sleepy virgins arise and *trim their own lamps;* each faculty is called into activity; each light is in trim and burning bright again, as in actual life, once more.

No, not all; all the virgins arose and trimmed their lamps, but when it came to a question of giving light, the foolish five found only smouldering, smoky, burnt-out tinder, dry for want of oil; and then, according to the symbol, whose meaning so clearly speaks for itself, *the foolish said unto the wise, give us of your oil, for our lamps are going out.* The deserted bodily functions crave the spiritual forces back again, to replenish them with life. "No good *originates* from the body," as a Pythagorean said; and if we look at a corpse the saying needs no comment.*

Now comes the strain upon the character, the actual judgment of the man's life. Is it not as great a judgment, being transacted in the individual alone, as that imaginary assize, by the verdict of which millions on millions are sent in mass in two directions only? He is in a spiritual world, wherein his physical qualities are out of their element. If his spiritual qualities are undeveloped, and his nature is made up of a large preponderance of material functions, he is left for the nonce almost characterless. The portly magnate of earth, who has lived for nothing but selfish and mundane ends, when all his outer wrappages are removed, is essentially a very poor creature, an immature bridegroom, attended by starving virgins, bearing torches whose light is wan and sickly. If he is persistently bad, or exclusively materialistic, in his inclinations, who of us shall judge him? he judges himself, and will act according to his state. Whether earth's attractions will eventually be too much for him, and he will migrate thither, or whether he will form a depraved and unlovely sphere where he is, neither does the present parable disclose, nor has any priest of the oracle declared.

* "The simple act—the thing done—is the separation of two organic forms, which before had acted together as one. That form, in which life resided, still retains it; and that which was dependent upon the other for all its power, and even for the ability to resist the common forces of nature and retain its form, has lost it, and is as powerless to love, to think, to feel and act, as the substances which compose it were when they were metals, earth and gases" (Chauncey Giles, "Nature of Spirit." New York, 1869).

The parable is a general lesson, and not the history of any special individual. The corporeal qualities beg for a supply of oil ; they are rebuffed by the spiritual qualities which are now in activity. *Lest there suffice not for us and for you, do ye rather go unto them that sell and buy for yourselves.* Nothing can be truly given which is not fairly earned : no angelic quality could feed a terrestrial one with an oil that would burn in heaven. Can we imagine a spiritual faculty being raised from a remarkable propensity for roulette, or out of a capacity for imbibing a gallon of beer in half an hour? The foolish virgins are bidden to go and buy for themselves. Aught that is spiritual says ever, when appealed to by aught that is material, degraded, or evil, " Turn to God : he alone can supply the oil of Love." And to these perishing functions he would give it, if it were needed ; but if those qualities could or would receive the gift of eternal life, they would then be no longer material.

While these confused and rapid-disappearing corporeal or mundane qualities are turned back from the spirit under the symbol *while they went away to buy* oil (the expression of their trying to be what they cannot be), *the bridegroom comes ;* —the spirit is fully freed from the body. The relative qualities are at his side at once, and rejoice within him in the delight of spiritual life. These are they *that were ready*, and that *go in with him to the marriage feast.*

The door is shut between spiritual and mortal, soul and body ; it has been more or less ajar, but now it is closed. The individual is again alive, and, if he be full grown, those qualities which have no life in the spiritual world are shut out for ever. *Afterwards come also the rest of the virgins, saying, Sir, sir, open unto us.* Returning from their bootless quest, and feeling themselves nigh annihilation, the lower qualities rush blindly praying for life. They cling to a despairing hope, appealing as it may be, by old habits and memories, by compunctions of feeling, by good fellowship, boon-companionship, by twinges from not yet forgotten escapades, by allurements of old delights. The life and atmosphere around the spiritual man cast them off, but they will arise within him and pray for life. Happy for him if his true life is so large and full that he is able to say to them with joy of emancipation, *I know you not.* He is now a spirit standing upright in a glorious *anastasis*, and what would be a temptation to a low physical man is almost meaningless to his more highly developed nature.

The parable of the Ten Virgins, read as has been suggested, fulfils the condition of being prophecy as well as parable. "Prophecy," as defined by Clement of Alexandria, "does not employ figurative forms in the expressions for the sake of beauty of diction. But from the fact that truth appertains not to all, it is veiled in manifold ways, causing the light to arise only on those who are initiated into knowledge, who *seek the truth through love.* The proverb, according to the barbarian philosophy, is called a mode of prophecy, and the parable is so called, and the dark saying" (Strom., vi. 15).

This parable is so recondite, it partakes so much of the original Hebrew term for this kind of composition, *chidvth* or *cheedah*, the root meaning of which is to tie a knot, that it requires much study before it can become familiar, and it is necessary to have every possible light thrown upon it from the philosophy current at its time.

The number ten had a symbolic significance, from being regarded as the representative of definite completeness or adequacy. A synagogue was not constituted if nine persons only assembled; but it was a congregation if ten were present. "Where ten sit and read the law, the Divinity (Shekinah) rests among them" (Pirqe Aboth., iii. 9). The seven nuptial benedictions were not to be pronounced in the presence of less than ten persons.

In the *Sepher Yezirah,* the earliest Hebrew cabalistic or philosophical book known, we find a passage, not only illustrating the use of the number ten, but also at the same time exemplifying the division of man, here represented as the decade, into spiritual and corporeal halves: "The decade out of nothing is analogous to that of the ten fingers and toes of the human body, five parallel to five, and in the centre of which is the covenant with the only One, by the word of the tongue and the rite of Abraham." This is, no doubt, somewhat obscure, but the Hebrew commentary brings the meaning into clearness: "The tongue is, as it were, the descriptive pen of all the *spiritual issues*, and the genital parts" (referred to under the sign of the Abrahamic rite of circumcision) "are the originators of the *corporeal substances*. Every one of them is an eternal covenant, in order to preserve the human race for ever, according to its twofold being, body and spirit, each working after its own way, physically and spiritually."

The association of the idea of completeness, or of a thing complete in itself with the number ten, or doubled five, in all probability has arisen from the use of the fingers of both hands in primitive arithmetic, and the fact that the gestation of man occupies ten moons has perhaps added value to the number. Some instances which offer themselves of the facility with which familiar numbers lend themselves to metaphor are interesting enough to quote.

The Pentathlon, or Contest of the Five Exercises,[*] in the Greek Games, entitled those only to the prize who were winners in all—leaping, the race, the disc-throwing, the spear-hurling, the wrestling. The athletes who had performed all were called Pentathloi. These were the heroes of the physical life, and may remind us of our Parable. Plato, then, ("Rivals," 138 d), applies the term to an all-round philosopher: "You appear to me, Socrates," said he, "to understand fairly what pertains to a philosopher, in comparing him with the Pentathlos. For he is undoubtedly such a man as is not a slave

---

[*] Appropriately summed up in the pentameter, ἅλμα, ποδωκείην, δίσκον, ἄκοντα, πάλην.

to anything, and has not spent his labour upon anything with such closeness of application that, owing to attention to that one thing, he has been distanced by all other things, like a handicraftsman, but has touched pretty well upon all."

Diogenes Laertius quotes Thrasylus to show that if the "Rivals" is really the work of Plato, then Democritus must be the interlocutor. "He," adds Diogenes, "was veritably a Pentathlos, or master of five branches, in philosophy. For he had cultivated physics, ethics, mathematics, the encyclic system, and had some experience in all the arts." In this group of five, we are reminded of the enduring qualities represented by the five wise virgins of the parable.

The idea of completeness, as here represented by the number five, became so expanded that the term "Pentathlos" was applied to one who went in for everything (Xen. Hell., 4. 7 ; 5), a champion contending for every prize, and so, in depreciation, a "jack-of-all-trades."

Not only, as already named, was the number ten required to be made up before a synagogue was constituted, but the completeness of the group of ten was politically familiar to the Hebrews in the Decapolis, or state of ten towns adjoining Galilee. The grouping of five was familiarized to the Greeks by the Pentapolis, or group of five cities, as in our incorporated Cinque Ports ; to the Carthaginians by the Pentarchy, or Magistracy of the Five. The Hebrew Scriptural Canon completes itself in the same number—the Pentateuch, or Five Books of Moses.

Because we may think these numerical correspondences trifling, and find no interest or mystery in the Pythagorean Pentagram, or the still legal quincunx, or in the fact that two Fives balance each other in the Roman numeral Ten, it by no means follows that those who made use of these signs meant little by them. Until we have discarded the counting by tens, because our fingers are ten in number, it is not for us to cast a stone at ancient numerical habits and fancies. The scientific duodecimalists of the future will probably look down on us.

At present, however, we are satisfied to do as our fathers have done in this respect. If in prehistoric ages man had not looked at his fingers and arrived at the grand discovery that he could count them, and then count by them, we should have had no such representative institution as the Tything in which our English ancestors were enrolled; no grouping of Tythings into Hundreds; we might, perhaps, even have had no Tithes; and if the fingers on the human hand had been six, the Hebrew parable of the Ten Virgins would probably have had another numerical basis than the decimal.

The same idea of completeness associates itself with the number of the fingers in the following early Christian injunction :—

"Let every one that cometh in the Master's name be received, but afterwards on applying some test ye shall know him; for ye shall have understanding of the right hand and the left" ("Teaching of the Twelve Apostles," ed. Bryennios, xii. 1). This means a sufficiently complete understanding, like the "armour of righteousness of the right hand and the left" (2 Cor. vi. 7). The conception is further enlarged by the parable of the separation of the sheep and the goats—the sheep to the right hand, or fortunate side (a superstition to which we still adhere, as in shaking hands, for instance), and the kids to the left, or ill-omened side; that of the foolish virgins, we might say, for the metaphoric sense, derived originally from the comparative clumsiness of the left hand, lives still in our epithet "sinister."

A doctrine ascribed to Pythagoras curiously illustrates the contrary fates appertaining to the representatives of the polarity of the right hand and the left :—

"He ordered that temples should be entered from places on the right hand, and that they should be departed out of from the left hand. For he asserted that the *right hand* is the principle of what is called the odd number, and is *divine;* but that the *left hand* is a symbol of the even number, and of *that which is dissolved*" (Iamblichus, Vit. Pyth., tr. T. Taylor, ch. xxviii.).

The antithesis here between the divine and the perishable, is singularly apposite to that of the wise and the foolish virgins.

This notion of a formal division in man's nature is not so unfamiliar as it would seem at first sight. There are five virgins attendant upon man that most certainly depart with the dissolution of the corporeal frame, our "five wits," the physical senses of seeing, hearing, feeling, smelling, and tasting. The Saxon language affords the word "inwyt," as well as "wit;" but it does not disclose what our five "inwyts" are. We must not, however, tie down the signification of the parable so closely as this; the symbol is sufficient to represent the totality arrived at by combination of the range of the earthly faculties and functions with that of the glorious faculties of the spirit, of which we are by no means without gleams, even though we live most distinctly in our more external powers.

The Rabbis, with their tendency to lose themselves in minor and trifling detail, and to overshoot wisdom by subtlety, were constantly harping upon this comparison of faculties. "In this world, men eat and drink, carry on business, marry wives, and beget children; but in the world to come those things do not occur" (Pirqe R. Elieser in Jalqut Simeoni, P. 1, f. 34. 4). There are, as they hold, the host below and the host above. "On high they neither eat nor drink, nor beget nor bear children, nor die, but live for ever. But among the lower host they eat and drink, beget and bear, die, and live not" (Pesikta Rabbathi; also Bereschith R., xiv. 3, v. 11). The following is more trifling and absurd in its details, but it will show how familiar was the notion of opposite and balancing qualities, as symbolized by the five wise and five foolish virgins. "Six things there are in man, of which he holds three in common with the beasts, three with the angels of ministry. The former three are, to eat and drink, to propagate his kind, and to pass excrement; the latter are, that he is endowed with reason, walks erect, and speaks in the Hebrew tongue" (Aboth R. Nathan, c. 36).

The Parsees classed precepts, elementary virtues and other qualities, in groups of five; one of these groups consists of thinking good, speaking good, doing good, hearkening, and being pure. They regarded the division of the soul as threefold, but in the later systems it is made to consist of five parts. Numbers are quite arbitrary when used for qualities that cannot be separated; no number can really describe the infinite variety of spiritual faculties.

It may be thought to be foreign to the poetic nature of a parable to analyze its construction down to such trifling, or even inordinate detail; but in face of the fact that an infallible synod professes to hold by tradition the keys that unlock all the problems of its sacred books, and that in this country alone there are thousands of eminent persons ready to furnish a glib exposition of any parable, it behoves a lay member of the Church of England * who suggests a new and unfamiliar rendering to look well to the supports on which it rests. And surely these should be best found in the philosophic views actually current at the period of the parable, and among the race from which it sprang.

In the manuscripts of the first Gospel, in which alone

* Sacerdotalists who might peradventure challenge this modest claim, are referred to the "Ecclesiastical Polity" of Richard Hooker, named "The Judicious," where it is laid down as beyond dispute that "there is not any man of the commonwealth who is not also of the Church of England." Dissent from the Articles, as declared by the sovereign and ratified by Parliament, whereof it is required of "all our loving subjects to continue in the uniform Profession," does not alter the position of the subject, and is an offence punishable only in the case of public Readers in the Universities, Heads or Masters of Colleges, or any preaching or printing Divine in the Universities; and "we will see," the Declaration adds, "that there shall be due execution upon them." "Suave mari magno, etc."

the parable of the Ten Virgins is to be found, the various readings of the text are not of great importance. After the words, "went forth to meet the bridegroom," some copies add, "and the bride."

If we accept this additional symbol, its interpretation is not difficult. The "bride-chamber" is a familiar expression to denote a temple of the mysteries, dedicated to the deities of fertility, and supposed to have originally presented a certain symbolism in its shape. In the three first Gospels Jesus applies the phrase "the sons of the bridechamber" to the disciples, or initiates, of his school. The words of the Fourth Gospel will also be remembered, which evidently have a "twist of parable:"[*] "He that hath the bride is the bridegroom."

The "bride" is a symbol with the Rabbis to denote "wisdom" or "science,"—"assiduously to be courted, not lightly to be won, and easily estranged."[†] The "bride-chamber," correspondingly, is the house of learning, the *beth-ha-midrash*.

The Greek word for "bride" is transliterated into "nymph," a term applied to goddesses of fertilizing moisture and other powers of nature. Seers and prophets in a state of rapture were designated "nymph-seized," "nymph-possessed."

The Hebrew word for "bride" is also the technical term to represent the highest college, or assembly of disciples.

Certain traditional side-meanings would seem to have been associated with this group of words, which a translation into their English equivalents does not convey. We may laboriously and with difficulty investigate these subtleties of speech, and after all only approximately reach an under-

---

[*] "In the twists of parables he will be engaged. He will seek out the secrets of dark sayings, and will be versed in riddles of parables" (Wisdom of Ben Sirach, xxxix. 2, 3).

[†] "I sought to make her [wisdom] my bride" (Wisd. viii. 2). "Love is the keeping of the laws of Wisdom" (*Ib.*, vi. 18).

"I have had my heart joined with her [wisdom]" (Ben Sirach, li. 20).

standing of phrases that were household words to those to whom the parables were addressed.*

If it were not for the minute symbolism of the parable of the Ten Virgins, and the indicative words that follow it, these figurative terms would suggest an interpretation of it as denoting the regeneration, and assumption of the yoke of the kingdom of the heavens in the technical Talmudic sense.† The disciple, so born again "as a little child," must shut the door upon his baser passions and selfishness; and his higher faculties will staunchly refuse to lend the oil with which they must maintain their own living flame. The warning words might even signify, "Assume the sacred discipline, that your faculties may be awake when the call comes and the door opens of the new æon."‡

In the "Secret Sermon on the Mountain" of the so-

---

* Etymologists have found a difficulty in tracing the root of the Hebrew *klhe*, or *kallah*, which signifies both "bride" and "college." Some have regarded the word as identical with the Greek *scholē*, "school." It is submitted that it is one of a large family having their origin in Egypt. *Kar, ker, khar, kher* signify "circle," "womb," "shrine," "prison," "cave," "cell." In Egyptian grammar there is no distinction between *l* and *r*. *Kha* signifies the *adytum* of Isis, "the birth-place of Horus," "the womb of the great mother." In Greek we have *kleis*, a key, a narrow pass, the first lock known in Greece ("Odyssey," viii. 447) being a knot, or intricate fastening. The word is associated with temple symbolism and esoteric treatises. The *kleidouchos*, or key-bearer, is a priestess, a tutelary goddess; in the Anthology, a judge of the dead, a post afterwards associated with Peter. In Latin, familiarized in a symbolic sense by Ruskin's "Fors Clavigera," is *clavis*, a "key," and *cella*, a "cell," or "shrine." The French equivalent for *clavis* is *clef*; and from the key-root come *close, clause, cloister, seclude*, and probably also *cell*; and following the older root, and the *r* instead of the *l, garth, garter, garden, girth*.

If we attempt to trace the connection between the meanings, we find ourselves in a labyrinth of ancient symbolism and nature-worship, and ready to believe that the looped cross, "the representation of divine energy in conjunction with passive matter," the "generative knot," the key of life, is the cherished secret of thousands of years of worship of the potencies of life. In Palestine these mysteries had possibly come nearly to the dregs, and were intermittently opposed by the Jews. But a glamour still clung to the old symbols.

† As instanced in "The Tradition of the Elders," p. 192-4, of the present volume.

‡ Cf. "Let us receive in season the kingdom of God in love and righteousness, for we know not the day of the appearance of God" (Clem. Rom. pseud. Ep., ii. 12).

called Hermes Trismegistos, the antitheses of human life are represented by the numbers twelve and ten. The human tabernacle is associated with the zodiacal circle, constituted of twelve signs. The qualities represented, which are styled the "senseless avengers of matter," the "revenges of darkness," are ignorance, grief, intemperance, concupiscence, injustice, avarice, error, envy, craft, rage, rashness, malice. The ten are more mysterious; by them the twelve are thrust out and driven away. "The decade is the generator of the soul." The *gnosis* of God, the *gnosis* of joy, temperance, continence, justice, communion, truth, are the preliminaries. Then comes the good, together with life and light. "Life and light are unified where the number of unity is born of the spirit. Therefore unity possesses the decade and the decade unity." "From the maturing of the decade, the ideal birth is accomplished, and the banishment of the brood of the twelve."

A link between this gnostic maze (which is probably the work of some eclectic Egyptian Jew) and the parable of the Virgins, may be fancied to exist in the halt in the development of the ultimate monad, the soul, until the decade has been built up. It ascends from morals and truth into goodness, which at once brings the gush of life and light, completes the decade, and fuses it into unity. If the bridegroom of the parable had not won the bride "wisdom," the orderly process which the symbols indicate would not have been consummated. The five wise virgins would not have found themselves in absolute unison with the bridegroom. The foolish virgins might have prevailed upon him to transfer some of the oil which appertained to the others, to them; and the nuptial feast would have been delayed, or badly illuminated.

The following is a variant of the same interior drama of the energies of the soul:—

"Temperance consists of mastery over lusts. Now of lusts, some pertain to the soul, others to the body. . . . The temperate mind is possessed of power to gain the upper hand over the passions, and to modify some, and neutralize others. ... At the time when God established man, he implanted within him his passions and dispositions, and then also he enthroned above all, the holy prince, Mind, through the medium of the æsthetic faculties. And he gave to this prince a law, by administering according to which he will maintain a temperate, and just, and good, and manly reign" (4 Macc. i. 31, 32; ii. 18, 21–23).

If the English mind objects to the kind of thought that emanates from the deep and subtle Hebrew mind, and to the tediousness of penetrating into it, one mode of relief is obvious. But so long as these sacred traditions hold their present high and special place, a place which indeed they deserve in the midst of the grand literature of the ancient world, no trouble should be deemed too great for the proper understanding of them.

The work has now been well begun at our universities, and the next generation may hope for more wisdom and less assumption.

That minute analysis is necessary, may be urged by the following passage from the representative treatise of Talmudical gnomology (Pirqe Aboth., iv. 3): "Who is rich? He that is contented with his lot; for it is said, When thou eatest the labour of thy hands, happy art thou, and it shall be well with thee (Ps. cxxviii. 2). 'Happy art thou' in this world; 'and it shall be well with thee' in the world to come." On this the Rev. Charles Taylor ("Sayings of the Jewish Fathers," Cambridge University Press, 1877) comments: "It is a characteristic of Talmudic exegesis that, as far as possible, *every expression* of Holy Scripture is regarded as having a *separate significance.* In such texts as the above, the *darshan* [teacher of the school of the mystics] allows no mere cumulation of phrases for the sake of symmetry or emphasis, but he sees distinct allusions to the present and future worlds."

A consideration of the way in which a saying from the

Psalms (xxxvii. 32) is parabolically interpreted will help us in the present study: "The wicked watcheth the righteous, and seeketh to slay him." "The 'wicked' is man's evil nature (Sukka, 52 b), which he must subdue, yet not wholly destroy and eradicate, for this would be to ruin the body by the destruction of the psychic force." While we continue here, in the long day before heaven's nuptial feast, we cannot do without the lamps of the five foolish virgins. "The evil *yeçer* rules over the animal soul, which a man is commanded to preserve: 'Take heed to thyself, and keep thy soul diligently' (Deut. iv. 9); and in order to do this, he must to a certain extent follow the promptings of the *yeçer*. Even the evil *yeçer* is good, for it is said: 'And God saw everything that he had made, and behold, it was very good.'" The word is difficult to translate; *penchant*, bent, propensity, individuality, physical idiosyncrasy, personality, *proprium*, come near it.

The tendency of the greatest Rabbi mystics was not to a flurried asceticism, but to a large acceptance of life. The lamps of the foolish virgins were giving light until that midnight of new openings of day drew nigh. Had they been starveling lamp-bearers with penurious lamps, type of a mean and shrinking animal soul—the sort of nature that escapes sin, not by victory over it, but through lack of the oil of passion—the outer court at least of the bridegroom's palace would have been but poorly lit. The parable of the prodigal son, and his brother who stays at home in assured but colourless respectability, will be recalled by the following: "The strong and great man is he in whom the evil nature is strong: 'and therefore our wise men of blessed memory have said, In the place where penitents stand, the faultlessly righteous stand not, for it is said (Isai. lvii. 19), Peace, peace to him that is far off, and to him that is near; to the far off first, and afterwards to the near' (Berachoth, 34 b)."

Aulus Gellius, who lived at Athens and Rome in the second century of our era, and was a great collector and student of philosophic writings, of which he made several books of extracts, might without any great improbability have heard some of the parables of Jesus, and such sentences as are quoted above from the Talmud. If he did, he either learned the parables in conjunction with an ancient interpretation which is now lost, or he was able to read for himself as an initiate would read. The parable of the wheat and the darnel would for him represent the diverse and opposite qualities of man's nature growing up together. He says (xix. 12, 4), "Those affections and emotions of the mind which, when too much in excess, become vices, are inwoven and intertwined with certain healthy activities and ardours, and on that account, if we ignorantly pluck them up altogether, there is a risk of our losing also the good and useful qualities of mind that adhere to them." The darnel, or mock-wheat, represents most strictly only apparent or hypocritical qualities—such counterfeits of true good as can only exist in the natural life, for in the state of truth everything is seen as it is.

However foreign to our intellectual methods may be the involutions of Hebrew thought, yet, when once we have reached the thought itself, we can embody it in what form we please. But whether we neglect the inner heart of our own accepted traditions or not, the least amount of study of them on a proper plan must lead us to more respect for the value and depth of ancient thought. Of the Essenes—those mysterious contemporaries of our era's beginning—we learn with regard to their study of their Scripture heirlooms: "Most things are philosophically treated of by them through symbols, according to the ancient mode of pursuit."

Philo, who tells us this, makes no parables; but he has learned from them. He speaks of elucidations which "I have heard from god-illumined men, who regard the generality of what is contained in the laws to be plain symbols of obscure meanings, and forms of expression of the undivulged" (De Spec. Leg., § 32). Who were these great illuminati? We can only suppose, if it is not the Pharisaic doctors that are referred to, that they were the Rabbis of the Essene communities, dwelling in scattered groups, but perhaps mostly in the regions between Palestine and Alexandria. The theory has been advanced that Jesus acquired his literary knowledge within the schools of this small but important society. Whether he did or not, his own sphere was so splendid that it cannot but outshine his school.

We may recall the curious question which the compiler of the Fourth Gospel makes the starting-point for the usual Johannine rhapsody : " For how long dost thou carry our soul [in suspense]? If thou art the anointed one, tell us in plain speech " (John x. 24).

This suggests the possibility that one of the many phrases to express one of the many Messianic conceptions that were current, may have been employed by Jesus parabolically. Such a proceeding would have been quite in accordance with Talmudic methods. The phrase " the one that is to come" (which has an obvious likeness to the exclamation with which a bridegroom was welcomed, "Blessed is he who is now come") may have been used to denote a mystic part of man in like manner with the symbol of "the bridegroom" in the parable of the ten virgins. Perhaps in the same Oriental light, we ought to read the legend of Elijah [or the mortal part] standing on the mountains of Judæa three days before the appearance of the Messiah [on this hypothesis, three days before the upstanding or *anastasis* of the immortal part].

In his picture of the religious services of the Therapeuts. Philo conveys as follows their expository method :—

" The explanations of the Sacred Scriptures are made by giving the deep meanings which lie in the allegories. For the whole range of laws seem to these men to be like a living organism, which has for body the express commandments, but for soul the invisible meaning which is stored up within the letter, in which meaning the rational soul begins distinctively to contemplate what is proper to itself, beholding as it were by means of a mirror of the mere terms the extraordinary beauties of thought introduced, and while unfolding and revealing the symbols, bringing the inner sense bare to the light, unto such as are able by the aid of slight indications to behold what is unseen through what is in appearance " (De Vitâ Contempl.).

It may very fairly be urged that it militates against the interpretation given above of the parable of the ten virgins, that while it receives support from Talmudic sources, it is not to be found in the oral tradition of the Christian Church. Alas! were not most of the early traditions lost when the Church divided into spiteful sects, and unruly Athanasius created a belief in dogma as superior to divine philosophy?

Nevertheless, it is not a little suggestive to find Clement of Alexandria apparently making casual reference to this parable (Strom. v. 14), comment so strangely upon the closing injunction, " Watch," as to observe that it is "as much as to say, 'Study how to live, and endeavour to separate the soul from the body.'" What has this to do with ten virgins, but by an interior sense of the parable being understood, a sense evidently akin to that which we have indicated?

Again he says (Strom. v. 6), " Great is the crowd that keeps to the things of sense, as if they were the only things in existence. 'Cast your eyes around,' says Plato, 'and see that none of the uninitiated listen.' Such are they who think that nothing else exists but what they can hold tight with their hands, but do not admit as in the department of existence, actions and processes of generation, and the whole of the unseen. For such are those who keep by the five senses. But the knowledge of God is a thing inaccessible to the ears and like organs of this kind of people." Clement is also in the same groove as the Talmudists as to the constitution of man. He says (Strom. vi. 16), " There is a ten in man himself; the five senses and the power of speech, and that of reproduction, and the eighth is the spiritual principle communicated at his creation; and the ninth, the ruling faculty of the soul; and tenth, there is the distinctive characteristic of the Holy Spirit, which comes to him through faith." Here he binds down to definite attributes the complex being of man; a true parable does not so specify, it suggests.

The following is an attempt to present the scene of the parable as it might be painted:—

> An ivory palace on a steep hill-side,
>   A marble stairway leading up thereto;
> From lattices, and portal opened wide,
>   The midnight's lamps flash down the avenue.
>
> From slumber on the threshold of the stair,
>   Five youths awaken with a startled mien
> And hands unready; taken unaware,
>   Their drowsy eyelids sleep yet hangs between.
>
> Their torches all, because of lack of oil,
>   Refuse their office, wane and flicker out;
> Like brooding wings that fly not, a black coil
>   Of smoke goes up and covers them about.
>
> Anon one stirs, and would by gesture guide,
>   Then sinks again. Sleep's swaddling-clothes annul
> Life in their flesh, its beauty and its pride;
>   Their souls are heavy, and their hearing dull.
>
> Where the way leads up to the door of gold,
>   Where shines the brightest through the olive-trees
> The beckoning light, another group behold!
>   Singing for joy, alert and strong, are these.
>
> The festal hour is here, the bridegroom goes
>   With eyes as flame, and step elately gay;
> The princely virgins whom he loves and knows,
>   Embrace and lead him on the luminous way.
>
> Their long-stemmed lamps burn brightly, and, held high,
>   Gleam like a cluster of auspicious stars
> Upon their eyes resplendent. Hark, the cry!—
>   Haste, haste, ye wise; his door the bridegroom bars.

This is but a pictorial impression, with a touch of local colour,* of the plain outside of the great Hebrew Rabbi's parable. In illustration of its signification, and of the mysterious upward passage of "nature's priest," who—

> " By the vision splendid
> Is on his way attended,"

it may be of interest to quote a few correspondences from the works of our own poets. It is to them that we must look for help in the understanding of the ancient symbolic lore. They can aid us by stretching out nearer and more familiar hands than those of the strongest of far-off days. In their glowing crucibles of sympathy they can make alive again symbols that were dead, and by their insight can retrieve meanings that were lost. That is, such as are poets, and have not shut themselves from the blue heaven in little boudoirs of versification.

Several poets have dared to treat of the midnight scene of the parable. We say dared, for the scene is one so remote from the orbit of the ordinary mind that it requires courage even to fling out a silver line of parabola round it. And the outstretching soul that catches a gleam from the light beyond that of "common day" is liable to a charge of cometary eccentricity or extravagance. Yet strange is the idea of remoteness, for the scene is so very near. Compare its distance with that of historic pictures—for all who can read this it is certainly not so far off as the eighteenth century is, and for a large number of us the way to it is not so long, but that it will be reached before the twentieth century begins. As for remoteness of space, that is but a mode of expressing the sense of separation. Southey wrote, in his ode to the memory of Heber:—

> "Heber, thou art not dead, thou canst not die!
> Nor can I think of thee as lost.

* This is mainly drawn from the Psalm appointed for the Feast of the Nativity, entitled a "Song of Loves," one expression being borrowed from Tate and Brady's version.

> A little portion of this little isle
> At first divided us; than half the globe:
> The same earth held us still; but when,
> O Reginald, wert thou so near as now,
> 'Tis but the falling of a withered leaf,
>   The breaking of a shell;
>   The rending of a veil?"

A pretty fancy, says the æsthetic materialist, which is not meant to be seriously believed. But the true poet and prophet does believe it in every era of the world. Even the critic, when he has refined his faculties, feels bound to give the warning: "Do not confound what is spiritual with what is abstract; and bear in mind that philosophy has a muse, and ought not to serve merely as a laboratory for argument" (Joubert).

This neglected Muse of Philosophy is the true leader of the poet or parabolist into regions that at first seem remote and unfamiliar—regions that are only affrighting because the ignorant mind has a blur in its eye and is aghast at shadows:—

> "What angel but would seem
> To sensual eyes ghost-dim?"
>   (E. B. BROWNING).

The only cure is for the reluctant intellect to be, so to speak, patted and soothed like a frightened animal, and brought to a nearer view of the terrifying object. The materialist says, "It is nothing; it is folly to be afraid; don't be superstitious." The true mystic says, "It is something, but not to be afraid of; don't be superstitious, but come a little nearer; look a little more clearly." We allow, because it is rationally necessary, the existence of an unseen ether hanging between star and star, and, though so infinitely thin and impalpable that it cannot be weighed, measured, or analyzed, yet potent to carry a vigorous wave of message sheer through what we call a solid; but it is held unscientific to regard that ether as full of life. And yet, as says a simple and wise old English divine, "Little know we how little a way a soul hath to go to heaven when it departs from the body; whether it must pass locally through moon, sun, and firmament (and, if all that must be done, it may be done in less time than I have proposed the doubt in), or whether that soul *find new light in the same room, and be not carried into any other, but that the glory of heaven be diffused over all*, I know not, I dispute not, I inquire not."

We are allowing ourselves to dwell upon this theme, because some gentle consideration of it is necessary to the study of parable, which, like poetry, will not confine itself to the terrestrial condition of man. As an old dictum runs, containing a fine appreciation of the parabolic quality of all representation here, we may find " Umbra in lege, imago in evangelio, veritas in cœlo." The law gives a shadow, the gospel a phantom image, heaven has the utter truth ; we see through a glass darkly here.

To return to the poetic expressions that parallel the parable of the ten virgins read in the manner suggested, we may cite Elizabeth Barrett Browning's eloquent words, which form a vivid picture of the scene :—

> " No type of earth could image that awaking,
> Wherein he scarcely heard the chant of seraphs round him breaking
> Or felt the new immortal throb of soul from body parted."

This picture too, by the same lady of insight, is a brave one. To George Sand she writes :—

> " Whose soul, amid the lions
> Of thy tumultuous senses, moans defiance,
> And answers roar for roar, as spirits can."

This is expressive metaphor for the lifelong conflict prior to the final one, which is represented in the parable by the words, " Sir, sir, open to us. . . . Verily, I say unto you, I know you not ;" when the virgins that have been refused oil for their lamps, vanish at last in what Augustine would surely call *mitissima damnatio*, the least and gentlest damnation possible, like that of the cast-off slipper we fling after the wedding party. But oft the dismissed servants are young and strong, and will not give up their disestablished office; the virgins (not necessarily girls, by the way) shouting outside the Master's now shut door in the parable, as also the unclean spirit with his seven friends, had made themselves known to Browning when he drew the similitude of—

> "Sin
> Which steals back softly on a soul half-saved" (*Pauline*).

How bright even the lamps of the foolish virgins may be, if those of the wise ones are not obscured, many a poet has seen :—

> "Before I taught my tongue to wound
> My conscience with a sinful sound,
> Or had the black art to dispense
> A several sin to every sense,
> But felt through all this fleshly dress
> Bright shoots of everlastingness."
> (H. VAUGHAN, 17th Cent.)

The drama of the parable, we must remember, is the experience of a well-balanced nature, ready for the call. It is possible to imagine a case in which the wiser virgins, even if supplied with oil, should have mismanaged their lamps, and afforded but little light to herald the bridegroom. In which case his state is a poor one, and he has to turn to looking after his servants. But it is not necessary to stigmatize even the foolish virgins as representing sin; they represent earth life, and creation is a slow process :—

> "Earth fills her lap with pleasures of her own;
> Yearnings she hath in her own natural kind,
> And, even with something of a Mother's mind
> And no unworthy aim,
> The homely Nurse doth all she can
> To make her Foster-child, her Inmate Man,
> Forget the glories he hath known,
> And that imperial palace whence he came."
> (WORDSWORTH.)

The finest poem we have from Mrs. Lydia Sigourney is

a suggestive picture which we may draw into subsidiary relations to our parable, by describing it as representing the "good-byes" which pass at length between the bridegroom and the old companions, whose engagement to bear the lamp terminates itself. The soul thus addresses the body :—

> "Companion dear! the hour draws nigh,
> The sentence speeds—*to die, to die.*
> So long in mystic union held,
> So long with strong embrace compelled,
> How canst thou bear the dread decree,
> That strikes thy clasping nerves from me?
>
> * * * *
>
> If I have ever caused thee pain,
> The throbbing breast, the burning brain,
> With cares and vigils turned thee pale,
> And scorned thee when thy strength did fail,
> Forgive! forgive!—thy task doth cease,
> Friend! lover!—let us part in peace.
> If thou didst sometimes check my force,
> Or, trifling, stay mine upward course,
> Or lure from Heaven my wavering trust,
> Or bow my drooping wing to dust,
> I blame thee not, the strife is done;
> I knew thou wert the weaker one,
> The vase of earth, the trembling clod,
> Constrained to hold the breath of God.
> Well hast thou in my service wrought!
> Thy brow hath mirrored forth my thought;
> To wear my smile thy lip hath glowed;
> Thy tear, to speak my sorrows, flowed;
> Thine ear hath borne me rich supplies
> Of sweetly varied melodies;
> Thy hands my prompted deeds have done;
> Thy feet upon my errands run—
> Yes, thou hast marked my bidding well.
> Faithful and true! farewell, farewell!"

The dread turn of the night is very brightly presented in the following :—

> "Life! I know not what thou art,
> But know that thou and I must part;

> And when, or how, or where we met
> I own to me's a secret yet.
>   Life! we've been long together
>   Through pleasant and through cloudy weather;
> 'Tis hard to part when friends are dear—
> Perhaps 'twill cost a sigh, a tear;—
>   Then steal away, give little warning,
> Choose thine own time;
> Say not good night,—but in some brighter clime
>   Bid me good morning" (MRS. A. L. BARBAULD).

Proverbs, allegories, and enigmatic sayings accorded well with the acuteness of the Orientals, and with their most laudable love for brevity of speech. There were doubtless as many varieties of parables as there are now of poems. As the province of parable has been very little studied—indeed there is room for a classified collection of the parables of the world—there is a deficiency of terms by which to distinguish the different varieties.

Defoe presents us with a useful word to express speech that has a side meaning: "The old pilot laughed; 'O Seignior Inglese,' said he, 'you speak in colours.'—'In colours!' said I; 'what do you mean by that?'—'Why, you speak what looks white this way, and black that way; gay one way, and dull another way; you tell him it is a good wall to keep out Tartars; you tell me, by that, it is good for nothing but to keep out Tartars; or will keep out none but Tartars. I understand you, Seignior Inglese, I understand you.'"

Adopting this phrase, there is a kind of parabolic form, which may be styled *mestizo*, or half-coloured. As a literary form it does not appear to be familiar to criticism, and the name hemiparable may be coined to describe it. This mode of speech resembles the sphere of the new moon, half in light, half in a darkness which is relieved only by such rays as are afforded by the earth's reflections.

In these peculiar parables, the part in colour forms an antithesis to the plain-spoken part. The following are examples from Homer, the first showing how the suitors of Penelope are to sup off destruction:—

"It was with laughter they had managed to get a feast, sweet and plentiful, for they slaughtered abundantly. Whereas nothing else could be more unpleasing than a supper, such as a goddess and a mighty man were soon about to set them, for they were first contriving injurious things" (Od., xx. fin).

"Thou biddest me obey the flowing-winged birds of augury. . . . There is one bird of augury, the best,—to be a defence for one's fatherland" (Il., xii. 237).

The following, when literally translated, is another example of the same: "The wind bloweth where it listeth, and thou hearest the voice thereof, but knowest not whence it cometh, and whither it goeth: so is every one that is born of the wind" (John iii. 8). To one accustomed to this literary form, it would be obvious that the second reference to the wind was to be read allusively. The authors of the Revised Version show by their notes that they were in a quandary how to treat such passages, which they could not render so as to make the sense obvious on the surface.

Gilbert Wakefield ("Matthew," published in 1782) appears to have been the first to point out this form of composition, of which he instances the following examples:—

"Whosoever shall break one of these least commandments, and shall teach men so, shall be called least in the kingdom of heaven" (Matt. v. 19).

"When thou wast young, thou girdedst thyself, and walkedst whither thou wouldest: but when thou shalt be old, thou shalt stretch forth thy hands, and another shall gird thee, and carry thee whither thou wouldest not" (John xxi. 18).

"I suffer hardship as far as bonds, as a malefactor; but the word of God has not been put in bonds" (2 Tim. ii. 9).

"I will not drink henceforth of this fruit of the vine until that day when I drink it [this fruit of the vine, that is, wine] new with you in my Father's kingdom" (Matt. xxvi. 29). To drink must, or new wine, was the sign of commencement of a new season (See Juvenal Sat., x. 248).

Other instances may readily be found :—

"Think not to say within yourselves, We have Abraham for our father: for I say unto you, that God is able of these stones to raise up children unto Abraham. The axe lies already at the root of the trees: every tree therefore that bears not fair fruit is being cut down, and being cast into fire" (Matt. iii. 9, 10).

There are examples also which may be noted, in Matt. iv. 19; v. 15, 16; vi. 19, 20; 24; ix. 15; xi. 11; xvi. 18; John iv. 13, 14: Rom. ii. 28, 29.

The most remarkable of these parabolic forms, and the one that has baffled translators the most, is Matt. iii. 11, 12 ; which is referred to in the present volume in the section entitled "Did Jesus know Greek?" (p. 75).

Another, and a striking example of this mode of dovetailing plain speech with parable is the following: "The foxes have holes, and the birds of the heaven have roosts ; but the son of man hath not where to lay his head" (Matt. viii. 20).

The first half of this passage has an obvious meaning, but it is not possible to read the latter half as a matter-of-fact statement relating to Jesus himself. The narratives clearly show that, although often engaged on journeys to and fro, Jesus was not always a homeless wanderer, but during one period at least "came and dwelt in Capernaum" (Matt. iv. 13), that is, he inhabited a house or lodging in the ordinary way. Indeed, on the very day referred to, Jesus is represented to have cured Peter's mother-in-law at Peter's house, and could not in common gratitude have been refused a resting-place there, had he been without one. The guest, in the East, did not enter the inner parts of the house, but required only a mat, or his own cloak, in the general room, with a stone covered with a folded cloth, or a crescent-shaped block of wood, on which to lay his head.

We are thus forced to the conclusion that this is a parable of the peculiar form described; and it only remains to discover its meaning.

"My life is now at rest, . . . without any personal aim, feeding on unearthly joys, like the bright gods above," says Buddha. The converted man is "free from desire, without entanglements, released from the impediments of the world." 'The swans [supposed to be understood to mean devotees] go on the path of the sun, they go through the ether by means of their miraculous power; the wise are led out of this world, when they have conquered Mâra and his train." "A wise man should leave the dark state (of ordinary life) and follow the bright state (of the devotee). After going from his home to a homeless state, he should in his retirement look for enjoyment where there seemed to be no enjoyment." "They who, having abandoned attachment, cling to that which is free from attachment; they who have mastered their desires, and are full of light, become free even in this world."

"Khùng-tsè [Confucius] . . . said to his disciples: I know that birds can fly, and fish swim, and beasts run; the runner may be snared, the swimmer netted, the flyer shot; but there is the dragon!—I know not how he mounts on the winds and clouds, and soars to heaven. To-day I saw Laò-tsè; and can only compare him to the dragon" (Tsē-mà-thsiān).

Notwithstanding the fact that they belong to a different tradition, the passages just quoted will help us to understand what was meant by the contrast expressed in the parable of Jesus.

Swinburne, in his essay on William Blake, gives a figurative expression to one of the Articles of the mystic faith, as he sees it in a design of Blake's. This "gives a symbol of man's birth into the fleshly and mutable house of life . . . encircled by the likeness and oppressed by the mystery of material existence. The pre-existent spirit here well-nigh disappears under stifling folds of vegetable leaf and animal incrustation of overgrowing husk. It lies dumb and dull, almost as a thing itself begotten of the perishable body, conceived in bondage and brought forth with grief." The holes and roosting-places perhaps may be understood in the same sense as mere types of material existence.

To return now to the applicant for membership of the school of Jesus. The master at once presents the life in the aspect the most likely to test with severity the stability of the purpose of the would-be disciple. The old masters insured a whole-hearted following by placing a most arduous ordeal in the way of entrance into their discipline. With Pythagoras this lasted at least five years. This scribe, we may perhaps suppose—we have no certain knowledge about him—was induced to make his request for discipleship from ambitious or personal motives: he may have thought that his training would insure him a high place in a school recruited from the ranks of fisher-folk and people of low estate, especially if the movement should become a great success.

Gamaliel shut the door of admission to the house of study upon all whose interior and exterior were not in accord. Jesus brushes away by a designedly repellent hand all worldly prospects, which he may have discerned to form the attraction to the inquirer. A true man, if met by difficulties and contrarieties, would have persevered the more earnestly: of this scribe we hear no more.

Cunning animals and wandering birds have their lurking-places and home on earth. The son of man, that is, the man who is regenerate or born again in a spiritual birth, is not a denizen of any terrestrial covert. He stands homeless and free from earthly attachments, with his head lifted up to breathe the ether of another sphere and a higher life. He finds no refuge or delight in the earthward homing flight of ambition, or the shrewdness that wins sectarian success, in which, as in holes of animals and roosting-places of birds, even great Rabbis and consequential scribes have been allured to dwell. The only rest for the emancipated soul is in the love that is free from taint, in the breath of the ether that comes pure from the source of life. Straining towards the mark of this high calling, it cannot find a place to lay the head in any terrestrial compromise.

It is difficult to catch the true sense of such a parable as this, because the state to which it refers is exceedingly rare in a mixed world of imperfectly grown humanity. We may learn a lesson from the Buddhists, and say it is a state in which no disappointment is ever possible, for there is no personal or selfish aim to disappoint. The spiritual hero takes trouble, suffering, misunderstanding, danger, death, merely, so to speak, as part of his day's work. Where the spiritual nature is as yet feebly developed, such a state is quite impossible; life is unlivable without some temporary support on which to lay the head.

Since parable conveys that which cannot be adequately conveyed save by parable, it is well to forget any formal interpretations that have been suggested, and to dwell on the symbols themselves without any commentary but that which our awakened instincts may attach to them, and without any argumentative support but that which crowding analogies, drawn from our experience—link finding link through all the world—will suggest to us. The analyser, the paraphraser, the commentator, is but as the lion's provider in the forest, spurned when he has brought his tribute to the king of beasts. When once we are made to understand the poet or the prophet and are held by him, it is the poet we love, not the man who has pointed him out to us. When, by whatever lessons, we have been brought into close rapport with a poem, it is its power that we feel, and within its cordial grasp that we remain. And with the parable, dark and mystic brother of the poem, the same law must hold.

PRINTED BY WILLIAM CLOWES AND SONS, LIMITED,
LONDON AND BECCLES.

www.ingramcontent.com/pod-product-compliance
Lightning Source LLC
Chambersburg PA
CBHW030323020526
44117CB00030B/959